Peace Psychology Book Series

Series Editor
Daniel J. Christie

For further volumes:
http://www.springer.com/series/7298

Olivera Simić • Zala Volčič
Catherine R. Philpot
Editors

Peace Psychology in the Balkans

Dealing with a Violent Past while Building Peace

Springer

Editors
Olivera Simić
Griffith Law School
Griffith University
Gold Coast, QLD, Australia

Zala Volčič
School of Journalism and Communication
Centre for Critical and Cultural Studies
The University of Queensland
Brisbane, QLD, Australia

Catherine R. Philpot
School of Psychology
The University of Queensland
St. Lucia, QLD, Australia

ISBN 978-1-4614-1947-1 e-ISBN 978-1-4614-1948-8
DOI 10.1007/978-1-4614-1948-8
Springer New York Dordrecht Heidelberg London

Library of Congress Control Number: 2012931344

Printed on acid-free paper

Springer is part of Springer Science+Business Media (www.springer.com)

Acknowledgements

Throughout the process of preparing our edited volume, we have enjoyed the support of friends and colleagues who have been helpful with their generosity and hospitality, challenged us with their critical feedback in our own work, and sustained us with their intellectual energy. We want to especially thank Prof. Dan Christie, our series editor, and Springer, our publisher, for their encouragement and enthusiasm. Prof. Dan Christie has been constant support offering a number of helpful advices and feedback on our work and chapters.

Olivera Simić would like to thank to Law School at the Griffith University and its stuff who provided a supportive environment for her interdisciplinary work. I would also like to thank my parents, Simić Desimirka and Milenko for their faith and love. Many thanks to Stojan Ignjatović whose patient love enabled me to complete this work.

Zala Volčič would like to thank Graeme Turner for all his support regarding this project. The Center for Critical and Cultural studies at the University of Queensland, its stuff and administrators provided a supportive and creative environment during the development of this volume. Many thanks to Mark Andrejevic and Karmen Erjavec who remain constant source of strength.

Catherine R. Philpot wishes to thank the colleagues that have mentored and supported her throughout her career as a peace psychologist, especially: Nikola Balvin, Di Bretherton, David Mellor, Dan Christie, Matthew Hornsey and Laura Smith. None of her achievements would have been possible without the love, support, and faith of David – you are much loved. For Harrison, Samuel and Jacob, my greatest productions.

The Editors

Olivera Simić is a Lecturer with the Griffith Law School, Griffith University, Australia. She holds an LLB from Nis University's Law School (Serbia), an LLM from Essex University (UK), an MA from UN University for Peace (Costa Rica) and have recently submitted PHD at the Melbourne Law School (Australia). Her research engages with transitional justice, international law, gender and crime from an interdisciplinary perspective. Olivera has published in journals such as *Law Text Culture, Women' Studies International Forum, Journal of International Women Studies, International Peacekeeping* as well as in books and book chapters.

Zala Volčič is a Postdoctoral Fellow at the Centre for Critical and Cultural Studies, and a Senior Lecturer at the School of Journalism and Communication, University of Queensland, Australia. She has published numerous articles and book chapters on topics including nationalisms in the Balkans, the cultural consequences of globalization, and media identities in former Yugoslavia. Her work has appeared in journals such as *Discourse and Society, Popular Communication, Journal of Children and Media, Journal of Global Mass Communication, Canadian Journal of Communication, Social Semiotics, Information Communication & Society, ICMR/ Islam and Christian-Muslim Relations, Critical Studies of Media Communication, and Harvard International Journal of Press/Politics.* Her latest book, *Serbian Spaces of identity, has been published by Hampton Press in 2011.*

Catherine R. Philpot conducts research that cuts across the domains of social, clinical and peace psychology. One unifying theme is her interest in processes, both individual and group, that contribute to the development of peace after conflict. More specifically, her research has focused on the effect of apologies given between groups; the identification of factors that can predict forgiveness after intergroup conflict; and on factors that can promote psychological wellbeing for refugees and other individuals that have experienced intergroup conflict. Her work has been published in the *European Journal of Social Psychology*, *Personality and Social Psychology Bulletin* as well as in books and book chapters. She currently holds a postdoctoral fellowship at the University of Queensland in Brisbane, Australia where she also teaches applied psychology. Catherine has a BBehSc from LaTrobe University and a PhD from the University of Queensland.

Contents

Contributors

Dean Ajduković is a professor of psychology at the Department of Psychology and Head of the Chair of Social Psychology. He has extensive experience in working with refugees, post-conflict community social reconstruction and community-based mental health interventions. He has directed several major international research projects, published over 100 papers in journals, and his books were translated to English, Macedonian, Russian and Albanian languages. He lectured in a number of centers of excellence in US and Europe. Dr. Ajdukovic serves as a reviewer for several international journals. He was a consultant and trainer in countries affected by upheaval such as Albania, Russia, Georgia, Azerbaijan and Ingushetia on trauma and violence, psychosocial program development and evaluation, and community crisis interventions. He is a Council member of the International Society for Health and Human Rights and past Board member (1997–2007) and president (2003–2005) of the European Society for Traumatic Stress Studies.

Despina Angelovska is a Lecturer at the Postgraduate programs for Gender Studies and Political Studies of Southeast Europe at the "Euro-Balkan" Institute, at the University for audiovisual arts, ESRA, and at the Faculty of philology, University Sts. Cyril and Method, Skopje, Macedonia. Her fields of interest are cultural identities, gender theory and nationalism, women's and minority rights, balkanism and postcolonial theory. Her work seeks to connect literature, performing arts and cinema with gender and nationalism studies. Her publications include numerous articles and books, including "Negotiating the name, renaming the nation-state", in *Renaming machine* (2010), "Identités translationnelles et perspectives post-coloniales", *Identities: journal for politics; gender and culture*, 2007; "Transition trouble" in *Capital and gender* (2001), and "(Re)situating the self: nation, gender and multiculturals perspectives", in *Komsi-kapicik, culture and politics* (2000).

Mirjana Beara is a Lecturer at Department for Psychology, State university in Novi Pazar, Sandzak, Serbia. She graduated psychology from Belgrade University, Serbia, and finished her MSci studies at Novi Sad University in Management in

Education, with a thesis on teachers' psychology. Before employment in higher education, Ms. Beara worked for 5 years as a school psychologist in secondary school in Novi Sad, and 4 years in Ministry of Education and Sport – School authority in Novi Sad. She was also active in different NGOs from 1993 to 2002, especially oriented towards psycho-social support to victims and other people jeopardized by the Balkan conflicts war (refugees, war veterans, host families, citizens), as well NGO's aimed at civil society development after the conflicts. Her fields of interests are psycho-social support to children and youth, management in education and educational psychology, human motivation, professional development and positive psychology. She delivered trainings and had expert missions in Serbia, Bosnia and Herzegovina, Macedonia, Albania and Germany. Her work has been presented and workshops held in several international conferences and seminars: in Calgary, Maissen, Kopaonik, Novi Sad, Budapest, Bukurest, Prag. She is a co-editor and co-author of the manual "School development planning" (Ministry of education and sport, Serbia, 2003) and author of several articles and book chapters about school and teachers' development.

Sandina Begić is a doctoral candidate in Socio-Cultural Psychology at Clark University, Worcester, MA, USA. She is currently working on her dissertation related to social representation of self-in-neighborhood in the context of Bosnia and Herzegovina, a postwar society in transition. Her interests are related to exploring socio-cultural potential of ordinary people in fostering development of a civil society and positive peace. More specifically, she is interested in the role of culture in development of both personal and social identity generally, and in the context of societies in transition particularly, with a special interest in South Eastern Europe. She has spent 2 years conducting the initial phase of her dissertation field research in Bosnia and Herzegovina. During this time, she has served as a research mentor to SIT students from American universities conducting research in Bosnia and Herzegovina and has provided professional support to a local foundation fostering development of a civil society. She is presently preparing for the second phase of her field research in Bosnia and Herzegovina.

Dinka Čorkalo Biruški a professor of psychology at the Department of Psychology University of Zagreb. Her research interests are in the area of ethnic identity and inter-group relations, with emphasis on divided communities. She has been investigating issues of ethnic/national identity and nationalism, the role of social context in trauma recovery and reconciliation, and post-war social reconstruction processes in divided communities. In 2003/2004 Dr. Corkalo Biruski was a Fulbright Visiting Scholar at the University of Massachusetts at Amherst, where she was doing a research comparing the nature of patriotic and nationalistic identifications among American and Croatian students. In 2005 she, together with Dean Ajduković, received the annual National Scientific Award for the contribution to the understanding of social reconstruction processes in communities affected by war trauma. Dr. Corkalo Biruski is a head of the Postgraduate Program in Psychology at the Department of Psychology, University of Zagreb.

Boris Bizumić is currently lecturing social and personality psychology at the Australian National University, Australia. He received his B.A., M.A, and Ph.D. from the University of Auckland, New Zealand, and has previously held a research fellowship position at the Australian National University. His research interests are in social, personality, cross-cultural, and political psychology. The overarching theme of his research is ethnocentrism and attempts to understand its conceptualization, causes, and outcomes. He has also conducted research into authoritarianism, personality traits, social identity, and attitudes towards peace and war. He has investigated these subjects across diverse populations around the world, including the Balkans (Serbia and Romania) as well as Australia, the United States of America, France, New Zealand, Denmark, and Israel. His work has been published in international psychology journals, including the *European Journal of Social Psychology, Political Psychology,* and *Applied Psychology: An International Review,* and has been presented at numerous international psychology conferences.

Sabina Čehajić-Clancy (B.A. 2003, University of Sarajevo; M.Sc. 2005, Ph.D. 2008, University of Sussex) is an assistant professor of political psychology at the Sarajevo School of Science and Technology, Department of Political Science and International Relations. She has received the SPSSI Dissertation Award and her research has been supported by the Guggenheim and Soros foundations. She works in the field of intergroup relations, more specifically on reconciliation in post-conflict societies, collective emotions of guilt and shame, collective (moral) responsibility, dehumanization, and other moral (dis)engagement strategies. She has published articles and chapters in several major journals and books and has presented her work at numerous national and international conferences. Contact: sabina.cehajic@ssst.edu.ba

Vasile Cernat is an associate professor at the Petru Maior University of Târgu Mureş, Rumania. He is interested in the psychology of intergroup conflict, stereotyping, prejudice and discrimination. He was a Fulbright visiting researcher at New York University and his Ph.D. dissertation on the Romanian ethnic conflict from March 1990 received a Harry Frank Guggenheim Dissertation Award. He published a book on stereotypes in 2005 (*Psihologia stereotipurilor*, Iaşi: Polirom) and now is about to finish a book on intergroup conflicts.

Karmen Erjavec received her Ph.D. in communication science at the University of Salzburg (Austria) and is now associate professor of communication studies at the University of Ljubljana (Slovenia), Faculty of Social Sciences, where she lectures in Media/Journalism History; Media, Culture and Society; Journalistic Discourse, and Media Education. She has published a number of articles and books, including articles in *Discourse & Society*; *European Journal of Communication; Communications; Journalism Practice*; *Journalism Studies* and *Journalism.*

Namik Kirlić earned his B.A. in Psychology from Middlebury College, VT, USA. He is currently working as the Project Coordinator/Lab Technician at the Phenotype Genotype Project at the Massachusetts General Hospital in Boston, which uses multimodal approaches (neuroimaging, behavioral experiments, and genetics) to study reward, addiction, mood disorders, and movement disorders. As a high school student in Bosnia, Mr. Kirlic attended numerous seminars and conferences on conflict resolution and peacebuilding. His interests include psychological trauma, PTSD, substance abuse disorders, and peacebuilding and conflict resolution. In 2003, Mr. Kirlic spoke at the United States Institute for Peace and KROC Institute for International Peace Studies conference at Notre Dame, which resulted in the following publication: Helsing, J., Kirlic, N., McMaster, N., Sonnenshein, N. Young People's Activism and the Transition to Peace: Bosnia, Northern Ireland, and Israel. In *Troublemakers or Peacemakers? Youth and Post-Accord Peacebuilding*, edited by Siobhán McEvoy-LevY. University of Notre Dame Press, 2006.

Melita Poler Kovačič received her Ph.D. in communication science at the University of Ljubljana (Slovenia) and is now associate professor of journalism studies at the same university, in the Faculty of Social Sciences, where she lectures in Introduction to Journalism and Journalism/Media Ethics. She has published articles in numerous Slovenian and international journals including *Journalism Studies, Journalism Practice*; *Journalism; Journal of Mass Media Ethics*; *Javnost/The Public; European Journal of Communication*; *Communications* and *China Media Research.*

Adela Langrock is a member of the Department of Psychology at Middlebury College in Vermont. She is interested in examining the effects of how exposure to stressful situations and environments effects short- and long- term emotional and behavioral adjustment. Two active lines of research include children coping with parental depression and coping with the stress of college life.

Ivana Milojević is a researcher and an educator in sociology, gender, peace and futures studies. Originally from former-Yugoslavia she now resides at the Sunshine Coast, Australia, where she is an Adjunct Professor (University of the Sunshine Coast, Faculty of Arts and Social Sciences). Since 2008 Dr Milojević has also been Visiting Professor at the Association of Centres for Interdisciplinary and Multidisciplinary Studies and Research, Center for Gender Studies, University of Novi Sad, Serbia. She has taught a range of undergraduate and postgraduate subjects/courses at universities in Australia and Yugoslavia/Serbia since 1992 including: *Gender and Society; Peace Education; and Introduction to Peace and Conflict Studies.* Dr Milojević is the author, co-author and/or co-editor of several books and the author of some 40 book chapters and refereed journal articles. She has published peace and conflict subject related articles in *Journal of Peace Education, Journal of the Australian Women Educators, Journal of Futures Studies, Social Alternatives, Development,* and has contributed to the *Routledge International Encyclopedia of Peace.* Some of those articles as well as her full bio are available at www.metafuture.org.

Tijana Mirović is a doctoral candidate in Clinical Psychology at University of Belgrade, Serbia, and a psychotherapist working in private practice. Before enrolling in the PhD program Ms. Mirovic obtained a Master of Science degree in clinical psychology, and completed trainings in Systemic Family therapy and Rational-Emotive Behavioral Therapy. Prior to this, she completed a Peace studies program, and worked as project manager for the humanitarian organization "The first children's embassy" and as an associate in several NGOs in Serbia (Center for Antiwar Action, Jefferson Institute) and USA (World Vision, Harbor House). In 2001 her poster presentation "Adolescents in exile" presented at International Congress on Adolescence, held in 2001 Salvador de Bahia, Brazil, received an award from International Association for Adolescent Health. Her publications in English include: chapter "Adolescents in Serbia and Montenegro" in Jeffrey Arnett (ed.) "International Encyclopedia of Adolescence", Rutledge, New York (2007) and "The crusaders of non-violence: Gandhi and Martin Luther King", published in "The introduction to the peace studies", Belgrade (2000).

Iva Pauker is a doctoral candidate in the Department of Political Science, The University of Melbourne. She is currently completing a thesis on post-conflict inter-ethnic relations in Former Yugoslavia. She has previously published "Reconciliation and Popular Culture: A Promising Development in Former Yugoslavia?" in *Local–global Journal*, Vol. 2, 2006. Iva has a Bachelor of Arts (Honours) from Monash University where she wrote a thesis on Yugoslav identity on the internet after the breakup of Yugoslavia.

Scott Nicholas Romaniuk is affiliated with the University of Aberdeen, Department of Politics and International Relations, and the University of St. Andrews, Centre for the Study of Terrorism and Political Violence. His research interests traverse the fields of extremism and political violence, war and genocide, and military and strategic studies. His work has been published in Peace, Conflict and Development, Journal of Politics and Law, and Genocide Studies and Prevention. Recipient of the Geoff Weller Prize from the Canadian Association for Security and Intelligence Studies (CASIS), his books include The Second Front, 1943–1944 (2010), and Competing Powers: Security in the Wider Black Sea Region (2011).

W. Duffie VanBalkom is a professor of education at the University of Calgary, where he teaches graduate courses in organizational development, leadership and internationalization. He holds a Ph.D. in Comparative and International Education from McGill University and a Certificate in Educational Management Development from Harvard, where he subsequently was an invited Visiting Scholar. Dr. VanBalkom has 24 years experience in Higher Education, including senior administrative posts as Dean of Education and Associate Vice President- International. His international activities include teaching, research, program design and consulting in over three dozen countries, with a particular interest in the role of education in post-conflict reconciliation. Recent post-conflict experience includes Kosovo, Serbia, South Africa and Afghanistan. He is a senior fellow with UNITAR and is currently engaged in leadership development for Afghan civil servants. Duffie's latest publications include edited books on public policy and professional development in education (published in three languages) and chapters on cross-cultural learning, leadership, and sustainable development in a 2007 book, entitled *Facilitating Change: Reflections on 6 Years of Education Development Programming in Challenging Environments*. He is currently the guest editor of a special issue of *International Education* devoted to education and international development and the principal investigator of a multi-case study of schools and inter-ethnic peace making.

Igor Vobič is a teaching assistant at the Department for Journalism and young researcher at the Social Communication Research Centre at the Faculty of Social Sciences of University of Ljubljana, Slovenia. His research interests are centered around normative transformations of journalism in contemporary media environment, articulations between journalism and technology, and transformations of newswork in late modern society. From 2004 to 2006 Vobič worked as an international news reporter for the news programme 24 h at the Slovenian television station POP TV.

Chapter 1
Peace Psychology in the Balkans: In Times Past, Present, and Future

Olivera Simić, Zala Volčič, and Catherine R. Philpot

Abstract This chapter provides an overview of the contributions that Peace Psychologists have made to the understanding of conflict and peace in the Balkan region. The recent history of physical violence in Balkan nations, such as Bosnia-Herzegovina, Croatia, Serbia, Macedonia and Romania, make this an important area of analysis given its potential to broaden our understanding of peace and conflict processes world-wide. The analysis provided in this chapter is multi-directional in its consideration of past, present and future realities. Explanations for the history of conflict in the region are identified, the present realities of peace and conflict explored and pathways to a more peaceful future proposed. The analysis is also multi-faceted considering both micro-level and macro-level factors relevant to the history and future of peace in the region. Micro-level factors, such as social norms, individual attitudes and relations to other ethnic groups, are shown to have complex interactions with macro-level factors, such as politics and economics, in predicting both peace and violence in the Balkan region. The analysis is relevant to academic disciplines as diverse as peace studies, politics and sociology, but remains firmly embedded within a peace psychological framework.

Keywords Peace psychology • Peace building • Structural violence • Physical violence • The Balkans • Negative peace • Positive peace • Ethnic prejudice • Discrimination

---

O. Simić (✉)
Griffith Law School, Griffith University, Gold Coast, QLD, Australia
e-mail: o.simic@griffith.edu.au

Z. Volčič
School of Journalism and Communication, Centre for Critical and Cultural Studies,
The University of Queensland, Brisbane, QLD, Australia
e-mail: z.volcic@uq.edu.au

C.R. Philpot
School of Psychology, The University of Queensland, McElwain Building,
4072 St Lucia, QLD, Australia
e-mail: c.philpot@uq.edu.au

O. Simić et al. (eds.), *Peace Psychology in the Balkans: Dealing with a Violent Past while Building Peace*, Peace Psychology Book Series, DOI 10.1007/978-1-4614-1948-8_1,

The Balkan region is marked by post-communist and post-war transitions. It is a region that roughly corresponds to South East Europe and although the number of countries that comprise the Balkans is contested, for our purposes, we include the former Yugoslavia as well as Albania, Greece, Romania and Bulgaria. The collapse of communism and the Yugoslav wars left the Balkan countries in an ambivalent state economically, politically, culturally and psychologically. Economically, they are going through the process of transition from centralized, socialist, state-run economies to privatized, market-driven economies. Politically, these states are involved in building a specific type of (ethno) national identity, while at the same time, addressing dilemmas of migration and multiculturalism. Culturally and psychologically the Balkans are going through the painful process of reconciling with the traumatic past. They are faced with the challenge of remembering communist times, working on reconciliation between ethnic groups and attempting to building a durable form of peaceful co-existence.

As Ugresic (1996) argues, the Balkans are undergoing a process of dealing with the past while building new nation states. In order for the present to be released from the shackles of the past, both of these processes, one looking back and the other looking forward, need to be carried out simultaneously. On the one side, Balkan communities need to look to the past so that injustices can be dealt with. But on the other side, communities need to look to the future, to changes that can and should be made to establish equitable relations and prevent further violence. These processes are dependent on one another: initiatives to prevent violence in the future can be informed in part by analyses of predictors of violence in the past. But in order for these reflections on history or visions of the future to maintain their relevance it is also necessary to keep a firm grasp on the present reality of life in the Balkan region.

The importance of each of these processes for the Balkan region: explaining the past, examining the present and envisioning the future, has influenced the construction and organization of the chapters that appear in the present volume on peace psychology in the Balkan region. While many of our authors' analyses have touched on various processes, for each chapter, we have sought to extract the dominant theme and place the chapter within the framework of past, present, or future.

Thus, after this introductory chapter the book is divided into three main sections. In the first section, chapters focus on explaining the history of conflict (Cernat) and potential contributing factors, such as ethnocentrism (Bizumić), violent masculinities (Milojević), and education (VanBalkom & Beara). The second section focuses primarily on present realities of peace and conflict within the Balkan region. This section consists of analyses at the macro-level of the media (Erjaveč, Volčič, Kovačič, & Vobič) and symbols (Pauker), as well as micro-level analyses of individuals (Begić), refugees (Mirović) and young people (Kirlic & Langrock). The final section of this volume is hopeful, as various authors outline strategies for the promotion of peace within the region. These analyses encompass both macro and micro-level factors (Romaniuk) and call for changes in culture (Čehajic-Clancy), the arts (Angelovska) and education (Čorkalo Biruški & Ajduković). In this introductory chapter, we briefly underscore some of the contributions of each author to the understanding of peace in the Balkan region. In so doing, we draw three key conclusions that have relevance to the study of peace and conflict more broadly:

(1) the explanation of past violence requires a nuanced understanding of the multiplicity of causes at various levels which interact to promote violence; (2) the examination of present peace needs to consider not only the presence (or absence) of physical violence but also the existence of structural inequalities that cause harm; and (3) the envisioning of a peaceful future needs multi-faceted solutions operating at multiple levels, commensurate with the violent forces that would otherwise dominate relationships within and across levels.

However, before we attend to these tasks we will first situate peace psychology within the Balkan context and identify research and practice in the Balkan region that contributes to peace psychology.

Contributions of Research and Practice in the Balkans to Peace Psychology

Peace psychology emerged as a area of psychology in the 1980s in the shadow of the Cold War (Christie, Wagner, & Winter, 2001). Yet peace has been a focus of psychological research from the beginning of the discipline (Christie, 2006). William James, spoke at length about the need to find a "moral equivalent for war" as early as 1906 and, more recently, Deutsch (1995) has referred to James as the first peace psychologist.

The "peace" that peace psychologists aim to promote has shifted emphasis over the years (Christie et al., 2001). Peace psychologists initially focused their efforts on establishing negative peace defined by an absence of direct or physical forms of violence. However, the discipline's focus now also includes efforts to promote positive peace – the absence of structural inequalities that systematically disadvantage and harm peoples (Christie, Tint, Wagner, & Winter, 2008). This more inclusive emphasis is derived in part from Johan Galtung, an influential scholar in the multidisciplinary field of Peace and Conflict Studies. Galtung maintains that violence is "present when human beings are being influenced so that their actual somatic and mental realizations are below their potential realizations" (1969, p. 168). Growing recognition of the inter-related and systemic nature of negative and positive peace processes has also contributed to the broadening conceptualisation of the "peace" in peace psychology (Christie, 2006). For example, Staub (1999) notes that many forms of direct violence, like genocide, have their origin in systematic structural inequalities. These inequalities unfairly disadvantage groups within a society and in turn promote destructive intergroup ideologies.

Relevant concepts in the promotion of negative peace include: "peacekeeping", which is typically the enforced separation of would-be combatants and "peacemaking", which is the development of settlements in conflict situations (Galtung, 1975). In contrast, the promotion of positive (and consequently negative) peace typically relies on "peacebuilding" strategies, defined by Galtung as interventions that aim to reduce social injustice and create equitable social conditions for all members of society.

Thus, the conceptual domain of peace psychology includes "the prevention of structural violence and intergroup conflict as well as the promotion of positive intergroup relations" (Vollhardt & Bilali, 2008, pp. 15 & 16). Within the field of psychology, peace psychology overlaps most closely with political and social psychology (Christie, 2006). However, there are points of intersection between peace psychology and specialties as diverse as clinical, educational, and community psychology – where research and practice are aimed at the prevention of violence and the promotion of positive intergroup relations. This volume includes several examples of peace psychological research arising from clinical (Kirlić & Langrock; Mirović), educational (Van Balkom & Beara), community (Angelovska; Begić), political (Cernat; Romaniuk) and social psychology (Bizumić; Čehajić-Clancy; Čorkalo-Biruški & Ajduković).

The importance of developing a psychology of peace that is sensitive to geohistorical context is frequently emphasized by scholars in the discipline (Christie, 2006). This ideological commitment has demonstrable effects on the nature of publications within the discipline. Publications within peace psychology are more likely to focus on non-Western contexts and emanate from non-Western academic authors and institutions than are publication in the related field of social psychology (Vollhardt & Bilali, 2008). The commitment to geohistorical sensitivity also applies to efforts within peace psychology to remove structural inequalities in the academy that privilege American and Western paradigms (cf. Hwang, 2005). Importantly, sensitivity to geohistorical context leads to an enhanced indigenous voice and a more nuanced understanding of psychology within different cultural contexts.

The expertise of scholars from the Balkan region in understanding and dealing with the effects and after-effects of war is hard to overstate. Psychology has been active as a discipline in the Balkan region since the early twentieth century (Čorkalo-Biruški, Jerkovič, Zotovič, & Krnetič, 2007; Rus & Pečjak, 2004). Historically its strengths have been in other sub-disciplines; particularly psychophysiology, vocational, educational and clinical psychology. As a result of the Yugoslav wars however, many Balkan psychologists were thrust into the world of peace psychologists. Čorkalo-Biruški et al., note that many Croatian and Bosnian psychologists became involved in developing and administering interventions for dealing with war trauma, while in Serbia many psychologists became active in anti-war protest movements. In Romania too, Cernat (this volume) reflects upon the way in which witnessing ethnic violence led him to reconsider issues of power, ethnicity and peace.

The unique contribution of this volume then is not only that it covers a part of the world that is not represented in the Peace Psychology Book Series, but also that the volume is the first book-length project based on the research and writing of local Balkan experts. The volume includes contributions from authors originating from Bosnia and Herzegovina (BiH), Croatia, Macedonia, Romania, Serbia, and Slovenia. The majority of the authors belong to new generations of post-war and post-communist scholars who appreciate the value of developing and applying peace psychology scholarship to matters that are vital to human well being and survival. Local scholars and activists are the ones who live the realities on the ground and because of the uniqueness and originality of their personal, academic and lived experiences we deliberately invited them to contribute to the volume.

In this volume, we intend to bring forward voices from the Balkan context that challenge oversimplified notions of the origins of war (e.g., ancient hatreds) and historical accounts that have treated the people who settled in the region as the "Other" and inferior to Western Europeans. Moreover, peace building and possibilities for reconciliation have both emerged as master narratives at the beginning of the twenty-first century when individuals and entire nations struggle to overcome the legacies of suffering ranging from rape and domestic violence to collective atrocities of state-sponsored terrorism, dirty wars, genocides, and ethnic conflicts (Scheper-Hughes & Bourgois, 2004). In light of the worldwide interest in peace building and reconciliation, the Balkan geohistorical context is particularly relevant and scholars steeped in this context are well positioned to contribute to our growing understanding the nature and scope of peace psychology.

The Balkan Region

The term "Balkan" has contested meanings. Todorova (1997) argues that the Balkans were and are seen as the dark side of Europe – an identity that the people's of the Balkans are eager to eschew. Bakic-Hayden and Hayden (1992) also argue that the Balkans are identified with violence, incivility and barbarism. Historically, from a Western European viewpoint, the Balkans represented the cultural and religious "other". Furthermore, Bakic-Hayden and Hayden argue that during the Cold War the ideological "other", communism, temporarily replaced the geographical, or cultural "other" – the Balkans. However, at some level, the symbolic image of Balkan inferiority was preserved and reinforced throughout. Hammond (2005) similarly argues that during and after the 1990s wars in the region, the Balkans again became a symbol of intolerance and barbarity. Sandwiched between the end of the Cold War and 9/11 it was the Balkans that served as the uncivilised "other" in Western discourse.

The historical and present construction of the Balkan identity is discussed in depth by Todorova (1997). She argues that the negative connotations derived from the term primarily have to do with Balkan wars (1912–1913) in total disregard of the actual historical and cultural contexts, or the level of violence elsewhere within the "civilized world". Todorova investigates how the Western image of the Balkans came into being and what its functions were. She argues, while reading diaries and reports, that at the beginning of the twentieth century "Balkanisation" came to denote the parcelisation of large political units into small ones, synonymous with reversal to the tribal, the backward, the barbarian. In the same manner as the Orient, the Balkans became "the other" of Europe. Even further, while the Orient has been constructed by the West as "the other", as an anti-world, the Balkans are a dark side of Europe itself. It is the darkness within. The argument goes that the stigmatization of the Balkans was an attempt to control the dark side within Europe (Wolff, 1994).

This discourse about a negative Balkan identity is not merely academic, but reflects social constructions present within Europe and the region itself. As Zizek (1993) writes, every participant in the bloody disintegration of Yugoslavia tried to legitimize their place "inside" of Europe by presenting themselves as the last bastion of European civilization in the face of Balkan barbarism.

> For *the Slovenes* the frontier is the river Kolpa, separating Slovenia from Croatia; we are Mitteleuropa, while Croats are already Balkan, involved in the irrational ethnic feuds which really do not concern us – we are on their side, we sympathize, but in the same way one sympathizes with "a third world victim" of aggression (Zizek, 1993, p. 234).

Similarly, Bakic-Hayden and Hayden (1992) write that when Slovenia started its process of declaring independence from former Yugoslavia, Slovene public discourse stressed positive identifications of Slovenia with Western European history, civilization and cultural values. In contrast Serbia was portrayed in the Slovene media basically as a Balkan state, where the Stalinist spirit was reincarnated. One example from Slovene media is an article published by famous Slovene writer, Taras Kermauner:

> We Slovenes have difficulty identifying ourselves with the pro-Asian or pro-African Yugoslavia. We cannot identify with such a Yugoslavia so long as we have the character that we have acquired in a thousand years of history… it is important to stress that we embodied the way of life that was created in Central-Western Europe (quoted in Bakic-Hayden & Hayden, p. 8).

As editors we are aware that our focus on "the Balkans" might implicitly reinforce a simplified and stereotypical image of the region. This is not our intention. Our goal in publishing a work on peace psychology in the Balkans is to enable the development of a nuanced understanding of the causes of conflict within the region. We want to encourage insight that goes beyond simplistic stereotypes of poverty, crime, passion and ethnic hatreds as ultimate causal factors. The chapter by Bizumić (this volume) is particularly relevant in eschewing an oversimplified explanation of war in the region as a result of ethnocentrism. In this way we aim to contest depictions of the Balkans as the "other".

We also aim to link the processes that contributed to war in the Balkan region to processes at play universally. We recognize that there is a tension that exists between developing an indigenous psychology and importing Western paradigms (Hwang, 2005). Indigenous movements need to be careful to avoid over emphasizing minor intercultural differences or of becoming unduly particularized and irrelevant to the research and practice agenda of the global community. At the same time, the danger inherent in Western paradigms is that they are insensitive and irrelevant to diverse cultural contexts. It is our hope that by allowing local scholars the freedom to use diverse methodologies arising from within peace psychology and related disciplines that a picture of the Balkans will develop that is both reflective of the local geohistorical context and relevant to the international community.

Finally, our choice of local scholars has strategic importance in confronting stereotypes of a "backward" Balkan region. At a very basic level, this volume aims to showcase the quality of Balkan scholarship, highlighting the very real way in which the Balkan community can contribute to the development of peace not only in its own backyard, but internationally.

We now turn to an overview of the contributions of Balkan peace psychologists to the current volume.

Explaining the Past

Authors in this section of the book have considered the history of conflict in the Balkan region, particularly in the former Yugoslavia and Romania in an attempt to account for the factors that brought about and maintained violence. We have already noted that discourse about the Balkan region has tended to traffic in stereotypes which blame characteristics of the Balkan people for the onset of violence: whether it is irrationality, poverty, passion or ethnic hatred (cf. Bakic-Hayden & Hayden, 1992; Todorova, 1997; Zizek, 1993). Such discourse not only obscures attempts to develop a nuanced understanding of the problem of violence but also contributes to violence by implying that violent actions are inevitable because of immutable characteristics of Balkan people rather than taking into account the impact of geohistorical factors. In this section we will first consider the history of conflict in the Balkan region and then turn to consider some of the contributing factors identified by our authors.

The Balkan region has experienced a long history of colonization, wars and dictatorships. Throughout its evolution, it has been a focus of power rivalry because of its unique geographical position. Situated between east and west, most of the Balkans were occupied for 500 years by the Ottoman Empire and then from 1867 till 1918 by the Austro-Hungarian Empire. After the collapse of Empires, we see the rise of nation-states and kingdoms in which Slovenes, Croats, and Serbs lived together in the common states of the Kingdom of Serbs, Croats, and Slovenes (1918–1941).

Balkan societies have never experienced political democracy in its full meaning. These countries represented for centuries ethnicities without their own states, although with varying degrees of ethnic autonomy: Bulgarians, Romanians, Serbs and Montenegrins until the fall of the Ottoman Empire after the Russian-Turkish War; Slovenes and Croats until the end of the World War I and the downfall of Austria-Hungary. In some of these states the process of democratization started after World War I, but it ended with World War II and Soviet occupation (except Yugoslavia).

After WWII, the Balkan region went through an extensive period of rule by communist dictators. Enver Hoxha ruled Albania from 1945 to 1985, Khristov Zhivkov ruled Bulgaria from 1954 to 1989, Josep Broz Tito ruled Yugoslavia from 1963 to 1980, and Nicolae Ceauşescu ruled Romania from 1974 to 1989. Ramet (1992) argues that these authoritarian regimes imposed a specific kind of "collective amnesia" on the region. Reflecting on the actual history of violence, trauma and victimization was generally forbidden in favour of the development of official histories (see vanBalkom & Beara, this volume). In Yugoslavia, Tito wished to build an empire while encouraging the development of a super-ordinate Yugoslavian identity that minimised the inter-ethnic differences of previous eras (Ramet, 1992; Woodward, 1995).

The absence of a more developed democratic tradition prevented these states from creating an original political democracy suiting the nature of their own cultures. The absence of other, mainly economic and technological, resources increased the probability that Balkan states would take on a dependent posture in relation to the Western Europe. The first democratic elections in the region were the result of a long process in which the essential element was the autonomy of civil society. The elections were an important achievement in the political development of these countries and represented the victory of democracy over political monism.

Thus, with the collapse of Soviet-led communism in the late 1980s and early 1990s people in the Balkans started to speak about what happened to them and deal with the past. The same period witnessed several outbreaks of violence across the region. Violence in Romania began after the death of Ceauşescu in 1989. Initially Romanians engaged in violence against ethnic Hungarians as well as Roma. However, violence against Hungarians resolved much more quickly than anti-Roma violence which continues to erupt periodically. In Serbia violent conflicts began with Slovenia in 1991, and with Croatia from 1991 to 1995. Later Serbia became embroiled in war in Bosnia-Herzegovina (1992–1995) and Kosovo (1999) as well. Macedonia came close to civil war in 2001, when Macedonian Albanian rebels violently demanded greater rights for the ethnic Albanian minority. Even in Albania there was serious internal violence and Albanians witnessed in 1997 the deployment of internal peacekeepers to the country.

Several proposals have been put forward to explain the onset of violence in the Balkan region. Vasile Cernat (this volume) considers explanations that have been put forward in the context of anti-Hungarian violence in Romania. His work demonstrates the importance of considering macro and micro level changes and their interaction in understanding predictors of violence. Cernat shows that macro-level changes in demography and economy are insufficient explanations for the onset and waning of violence against ethnic Hungarians. Rather, Cernat argues that micro-level changes in the way Romanian people construct their national identity were instrumental in fuelling the violence and in contributing to its de-escalation. But there is an obvious interaction between macro-level factors such as politics and economics and the onset of violence in Cernat's narrative. Cernat argues that the communist dictatorship pursued a nationalist ideology which used the supposed Hungarian desire to wrest control of the disputed territory of Transylvania to distract Romanians from worsening economic conditions. This strongly nationalist identity with its anti-Hungarian emphasis lapsed quickly into violence with the worsening economic conditions at communism's end. However, macro-level changes in the political arena, namely the desire to join the EU, encouraged further micro-level changes in Romanian identity to ameliorate tensions with Hungarians (see also Romaniuk this volume). This shift emphasised Romania's shared European history and culture which, Cernat argues, encouraged more tolerant values and identification with a superordinate identity (as European) that was inclusive of Hungarians.

If Cernat's chapter is valuable for highlighting the importance of considering the array of macro and micro level factors that interact to predict violence, then the chapter by Bizimic is equally valuable for making a related conceptual point: namely, that oversimplified explanations of the origins of violence are insufficient. Bizumic explores theories of ethnocentrism and their implications for intergroup relationships and effective peacebuilding in the former Yugoslavia. He reviews evidence indicating there was nothing unusually volatile about the ethnocentrism in this country and that contrary to stereotypes about the Balkan region (cf. Bakic-Hayden & Hayden, 1992; Todorova, 1997; Zizek, 1993), the direct cause of hostilities was not interethnic hatred alone. Rather, the analysis presented suggests many macro-level (politicians, media) and micro-level factors (social norms) reinforced ethnocentrism and led to its expression in violence.

The final two chapters in this section explore the role of specific predictors of violence in the former Yugoslavia that have been underemphasised in the literature. These chapters demonstrate the complexity of predicting violence in the Balkan context. The chapter by Milojevic examines the gendered nature of physical acts of violence. She presents qualitative evidence that the social construction of masculinity in Serbia (and beyond) is intimately linked with physical violence. Macro-level processes are not absent in this analysis of a micro-level predictors of violence. Rather, macro-level processes, like the compulsory military service in the former Yugoslavia between 1945 and 1991, contributed to the strength and pervasiveness of violent constructions of manhood.

Finally, VanBalkom and Beara (this volume) look at the role played by a macro-level factor: the education system, in the conflicts in the former Yugoslavia. This chapter again links the macro with the micro: for in the former Yugoslavia the state-determined curriculum made a significant contribution to the development of ethnic identification and ethnocentric norms in young people. Moreover, VanBalkom and Beara's analysis highlights the reciprocal nature of tensions between members of different ethnic groups (micro-processes) and educational policy (macro-processes). The example of Kosovo is given in which inter-ethnic tension increased as a result of the state's decision to make the Albanian mother tongue illegal as the medium of instruction. In response, the Albanian majority created a parallel system of education which effectively marked the beginning of a violent separation from Serbia and was one of the key triggers to the 1999 war. VanBalkom and Beara remain concerned in regard to whether the segregation in many Bosnian schools is a much needed interim phase that avoids conflict and supports healing, or prevents meaningful inter-ethnic integration and reconciliation – a point taken up by Čorkalo-Biruški and Ajduković (this volume).

Examining the Present

Although the gaze of the international community may have moved on from the intense scrutiny that characterized the periods of violent conflicts in the mid 1990s it does not necessarily follow that the region has now "achieved" peace. The absence of direct violence is a necessary but not sufficient condition for peace. Structural forms of peace (positive peace) are present when people have a sense of fairness, along with the means to address grievances, and voice in matters that affect their well being. Some authors warn against the premature celebration of the rule of democracy and capitalism in the region, pointing to the fact that the end of communism and war has been followed by collective anxiety, fear, helplessness, disorientation and disenchantment, leaving these societies particularly vulnerable to the rise of authoritarianism (Moranjak-Bamburac, Jusic, & Isanovic, 2006; Milisevic, 2006). Thus, the chapters in this volume demonstrate the distance that still needs to be traversed if positive peace is to be reached. A unifying theme is that negative peace cannot be considered in isolation. The lack of positive peace can be a barrier to negative peace and can act as a catalyst for further violence.

The media present a particular macro-level layer that has the potential to influence peace within the Balkans as the chapter by Erjavec et al., points out. The qualitative evidence they present demonstrates the way in which the media in BiH today contributes to ethnic segregation. Newspapers are strongly divided along ethnic lines and history is interpreted through the lens of ethnicity which results in divergent views of history. The disparity in media coverage highlights the absence of positive peace in the region and, as Erjavec et al. note, is a threat to the ongoing maintenance of negative peace.

The recent history of BiH also demonstrates the close relationship between negative peace and cultural violence, the latter of which refers to the symbolic sphere of human existence (Galtung, 1990). Pauker writes that in the Yugoslav wars, ethnic symbols were often a target of violence as part of the attempt to cleanse all traces of ethnicity from a region. Although a fragile negative peace has now been established, violence in the symbolic realm is still continuing as ethnic groups fight over the right to restore and create new symbols. The close link between this culturally-based conflict and direct violence is also evident in the case studies Pauker presents, for disputes over ethnic symbols seem to easily spill over into mob violence. New unifying symbols are needed to promote peace and reduce the conflict over symbols in public spaces. However, symbols are not isolated phenomena but reflections of inter-ethnic attitudes and realities. Peace in the symbolic realm would thus seem to be, in part, dependent upon peace at the micro-level; the level of individual and intergroup attitudes and relations.

The nature of relationships between individuals and groups is taken up in the chapters by Begić as well as Kirlić and Langrock. Through a single case study, Begić (this volume) ethnographically examines how a woman who has spent her entire life in the same neighbourhood in BiH experiences the macro-level changes that are taking place in her country, city, and neighbourhood. The sense of community which formerly existed despite ethnic diversity has not been replaced for this participant despite the greater ethnic homogeneity in her region. In Begić's interview we find both an obstacle and a potential for peace. Greater geographic ethnic segregation reduces the opportunity for intergroup contact and increases the likelihood of ongoing prejudice and hostility on ethnic lines (cf. Čorkalo Biruški & Ajduković, this volume; also Brown & Hewstone, 2005; Pettigrew & Tropp, 2006). But, if the longing for contact and for reconnection to the "old days" leads people to restore, maintain or create inter-ethnic friendships then perhaps a basis for peace can be slowly rebuilt.

Using a different methodological approach, a qualitative study, Kirlić and Langrock's research (this volume) also touches upon the role of relationships for people living in BiH. A survey of 134 young adults in BiH assessed both the presence of current stressors and symptoms of mental illness 10 years after the war ended. The data suggest some resiliency; participants were able to endure high levels of stress across a number of domains (political, educational and future outlook) without demonstrating symptoms of mental illness. Yet, stress in the areas of relationships, leisure time, and economic security were significant predictors of mental well-being with relationship stress the strongest overall predictor. These results testify to the ongoing structural violence of difficult life conditions that is present in BiH for many young people in BiH. Another link between the structural violence of difficult life conditions and direct violence emerges from this dataset, in that there is a relationship between specific forms of stress and aggression. As the authors note, steps to ameliorate mental health problems, particularly through the creation of positive and supportive relationships offer much hope for the wellbeing of its young people and the future of peace in BiH.

BiH is not the only country in the Balkan region that is experiencing ongoing structural violence. Mirović's chapter reminds readers that at the end of the Yugoslav wars, Serbia was the European country with the most refugees and internally displaced persons (IDPs) along with the highest rate of inflation in Europe. Major pre-displacement stressors such as trauma and loss as well as post-displacement stressors such as poor and overcrowded living conditions, lack of integration, unemployment and poverty still affect large numbers of refugees and IDPs. Despite the fact that these refugees and IDPs are largely Serbian they remain much worse off than the local Serb population. This is a form of structural violence and a potential catalyst for episodes of violence. Through the increased risk of crime and violence that is associated with poverty (i.e. Hsieh & Pugh, 2005), collective trauma, and resentment towards the ethnic groups that forced displacement.

However, Mirović's analysis closes on a hopeful note with a discussion of how family systems therapies can be used in the treatment of refugees and IDPs. This approach is recommended as it encourages familial connections and community reintegration as family units. In doing this, Mirović's paper not only examines the present situation in Serbia but envisions a way forward to a more peaceful future. This is a theme that is taken up in more depth by authors in the next section of this book.

Envisioning the Future

The development of a stable peace that encompasses both positive and negative dimensions requires the engagement of multiple forces operating on multiple levels. This is not to imply that people are inherently aggressive and peace is somehow an unnatural state (cf. Christie et al., 2008). Instead, our view is that the episodes of violence that took place in the geohistorical context of the Balkans were a result of multiple conflicts across multiple regions and encompassed multiple ethnic groups; accordingly, a powerful and multifaceted approach to the building of peace at micro and macro levels is necessary. Čorkalo Biruški and Ajduković present a cross-sectional survey of children and adolescents assessed 6 years apart in the post-conflict city of Vukovar, Croatia. The investigators were interested in the effects of time on attitudes and make a strong argument about the way forward. The data presented show very little difference in young people's attitudes towards the "other" over time. The investigators argue that the segregated schooling which exists in Vukovar is a major barrier to bringing interethnic relations closer. Their research indicates that there is very little interethnic contact; however, amongst minority group members (who by default have more opportunity for intergroup contact) intergroup attitudes are somewhat more positive. In addition, attitudes are more positive amongst those who support a change to desegregated schooling. The way forward to a more peaceful future for Čorkalo Biruški and Ajduković is clear and encompasses a number of levels. First, schooling needs to become integrated so that friendships can develop in which children once again experience interethnic contact without threat or anxiety (see also Van Balkom & Beara, this volume). Second, adults need to take the responsibility to model intergroup behaviors that are conducive to amicable interethnic norms. The message from Čorkalo Biruški and Ajduković is clear: time alone is not a healer, more is needed.

This is a conclusion that receives unanimous support in this section. Although each author brings different ideas about the ways in which peace can be promoted, these ideas complement rather than contradict one another. For example, in the very different context of the ongoing marginalisation of the Roma community in Macedonia, Angelovska focuses on the use of co-operative efforts in the arts. Tracing the development of the theatre project *Open option* Angelovska shows that its honoring of the Roma traditional wisdoms regarding peace and anti-militarism both promote peace and contribute to the development of more equal status relations between Roma and Macedonians. As a theatrical project *Open Option* offers Roma an opportunity to have their voices heard and increases the opportunity for Macedonians to have positive intergroup contact. All of these processes can be seen to be important means of reducing structural inequality, prejudice and discrimination (cf. Paluck & Green, 2009).

Romaniuk analyzes the history of episodic ethno-national intolerance and violence that Romanians have enacted against ethnic Hungarians and Roma. Learning from the successful efforts to build peace between Romanians and ethnic Hungarians (see also Cernat this volume) Romaniuk offers a number of suggestions for improving inter-group relations. In particular, Romaniuk argues that a range of instruments are necessary for cementing ethnic cooperation and regional stability including increased communication, willingness to collaborate and commitment to change by governments, institutions and people. These conditions will make it more likely to achieve a just and sustainable peace, that is, a negative peace (absence of violence) that is undergirded by positive peace (i.e., the pursuit of social justice).

The final chapter in this volume gives much needed direction as to how some of these attributes can be encouraged by looking at underlying psychological processes. Sabina Čehajić-Clancy cogently argues that ultimately for peace to be promoted, people need to be able to take on collective moral responsibility for their group's actions. Without this, there is no platform from which existing social inequalities can be challenged and changed and no effective hindsight through which past actions can be acknowledged and addressed. Certainly it is difficult to see how commitment to change can be engendered without first acknowledging one's groups own responsibility for the circumstances which require change. But how is collective moral responsibility to be aroused?

Čehajić-Clancy's research points to a number of possible avenues. Findings from quantitative and qualitative papers demonstrate that intergroup contact increases an individual's willingness to acknowledge their group's moral responsibilities for having committed atrocities. In addition, feeling self-affirmation (e.g., by writing a story about a personal success) can reduce defensiveness and increase one's willingness to acknowledge ingroup responsibility for wrongdoings against others. Completing the puzzle, Čehajić-Clancy shows that collective responsibility is linked to peaceful intentions; in the study reviewed, the acceptance of moral responsibility aroused an increased willingness to express group-based guilt, and support reparation.

Through this volume we see that positive and negative peace in the Balkans has multiple causes interacting across multiple levels and over time. Though negative peace has been achieved in many areas, there is still ethnic prejudice and discrimination, both of which can serve as causes and consequences of structural violence. The chapters in the current volume offer a partial roadmap that can be travelled to bring the peoples of the Balkans closer together in the interest of a more durable kind of peace that addresses structural violence. The roadmap is most complete in its identification of some of the ways in which the forces of peace can mitigate countervailing forces that create separation, inequality, hostility, and war.

References

Bakic-Hayden, M., & Hayden, R. M. (1992). Orientalist variations on the theme "Balkans": Symbolic geography in Yugoslav cultural politics since 1987. *Slavic Review, 51*(1), 1–15.

Brown, R., & Hewstone, M. (2005). An integrative theory of intergroup contact. In M. P. Zanna (Ed.), *Advances in experimental social psychology* (pp. 255–343). London: Elsevier.

Christie, D. J. (2006). Post-cold war peace psychology: More differentiated, contextualized, and systemic. *Journal of Social Issues, 62*(1), 1–17.

Christie, D. J., Tint, B., Wagner, R. V., & Winter, D. D. (2008). Peace psychology for a peaceful world. *American Psychologist, 63*, 540–552.

Christie, D. J., Wagner, R. V., & Winter, D. A. (Eds.). (2001). *Peace, conflict, and violence: Peace psychology for the 21st century*. Englewood Cliffs, NJ: Prentice-Hall.

Čorkalo-Biruški, D., Jerkovič, I., Zotovič, M., & Krnetič, I. (2007). Psychology in Bosnia and Herzegovina, Croatia and Serbia. *The Psychologist, 20*, 220–223.

Deutsch, M. (1995). William James: The first peace psychologist. Peace and conflict. *Journal of Peace Psychology, 1*, 27–36.

Galtung, J. (1969). Violence, peace and peace research. *Journal of Peace Research, 3*, 176–191.

Galtung, J. (1975). Three approaches to peace: Peacekeeping, peacemaking and peacebuilding. In J. Galtung (Ed.), *Peace, war and defence – Essays in peace research* (Vol. 2, pp. 282–304). Copenhagen, Denmark: Christian Ejlers.

Galtung, J. (1990). Cultural violence. *Journal of Peace Research, 3*, 291–305.

Hammond, A. (2005). The danger zone of Europe: Balkanism between the cold war and 9/11. *European Journal of Cultural Studies, 8*, 135–154.

Hsieh, C. C., & Pugh, M. D. (2005). Poverty, income inequality and violent crime: A meta-analysis of recent aggregate data studies. *Criminal Justice Review, 18*, 182–202.

Hwang, K.-K. (2005). The third wave of cultural psychology: The indigenous movement. *The Psychologist, 18*, 80–83.

Milisevic, A. S. (2006). Joining the war: Masculinity, nationalism and war participation in the Balkans war of secession. *Nationalities Papers, 3*(2), 265–287.

Moranjak-Bamburac, N., Jusic, T., & Isanovic, A. (Eds.). (2006). *Stereotyping: Representation of women in print media in South East Europe*. Sarajevo: Mediacentar Sarajevo.
Paluck, E. L., & Green, D. P. (2009). Prejudice reduction: What works? A review and assessment of research and practice. *Annual Review of Psychology, 60*, 339–367.
Pettigrew, T. F., & Tropp, L. R. (2006). A meta-analytic test of intergroup contact theory. *Journal of Personality and Social Psychology, 90*, 751–783.
Ramet, S. (1992). *Nationalism and federalism in Yugoslavia, 1962–1991*. Bloomington, IN: Indiana University Press.
Rus, V. S., & Pečjak, V. (2004). Psychology in Slovenia. *The Psychologist, 17*, 266–269.
Scheper-Hughes, N., & Bourgois, P. (Eds.). (2004). *Violence in war and peace: An anthology*. Oxford: Blackwell Publishing.
Staub, E. (1999). The origins and prevention of genocide, mass killing, and other collective violence. Peace and conflict. *Journal of Peace Psychology, 5*, 303–336.
Todorova, M. (1997). *Imagining the Balkans*. Oxford: Oxford University Press.
Ugresic, D. (1996). The confiscation of memory. *New Left Review, 218*, 26–39.
Vollhardt, J. K., & Bilali, R. (2008). Social psychology's contribution to the psychological study of peace. *Social Psychology, 39*, 12–25.
Wolff, L. (1994). *Inventing Eastern Europe: The map of civilization on the mind of the enlightenment*. Stanford, CA: Stanford University Press.
Woodward, S. L. (1995). *Balkan tragedy. Chaos and dissolution after the cold war*. Washington, DC: The Brookings Institution.
Zizek, S. (1993). Caught in another's dream in Bosnia. In R. Ali & L. Lifschultz (Eds.), *Why Bosnia?* (pp. 233–240). Stony Creek, CT: Pamphleteers Press Inc.

Part I
Explaining the Past

Chapter 2
Ethnic Conflict and Reconciliation in Post-Communist Romania

Vasile Cernat

Abstract The present chapter focuses on the first ethnic conflict in post-communist East-Europe, which took place in the Transylvanian region of Romania. Violence between Romanian and Hungarian ethnics sparked shortly after the general enthusiasm generated by the removal of Ceauşescu's dictatorship, whereas ethnic reconciliation progressed while the Romanian economy was severely deteriorating. What factors have made possible the March 1990 ethnic conflict? And how can we explain the positive evolution of the Romanian-Hungarian ethnic relationships afterward? The chapter maintains that the interaction between demographic (i.e., a relatively large youth cohort) and economic factors (i.e., severe and prolonged economic hardships) led to Ceauşescu's overthrow. This event, together with the national ideologies that conditioned Romanians and Hungarians to fear and hate each other created a volatile psychological atmosphere that was tragically manipulated by local elites and lead to the outbreak of conflict. On the other hand, the difficult socio-economic conditions of the transition period created the grounds for essential social identity changes from mainly autarchic to strongly pro-Western. The development of a pro-European orientation during the transition period had positive effects on Romanian-Hungarian interethnic relations through several social psychological processes and raised a significant barrier against intolerance and extremism.

Keywords Romania • Ethnic violence • Social identity • Nationalism • Communism

---

V. Cernat (✉)
Department of Teacher Education, Petru Maior University,
N. Iorga St. No1, 540088 Târgu-Mureş, Romania
e-mail: cernat.vasile@science.upm.ro

O. Simić et al. (eds.), *Peace Psychology in the Balkans: Dealing with a Violent Past while Building Peace*, Peace Psychology Book Series, DOI 10.1007/978-1-4614-1948-8_2,

The first ethnic clashes in post-communist South East Europe took place in the Transylvanian region of Romania, in which most of the country's 1.4 million large Hungarian minority is concentrated. Shortly after December 1989, when Romanians and Hungarians joined their forces to overthrow Ceauşescu's regime, tensions between the two ethnic groups began to escalate. Three months later, they erupted most violently and visibly in the town of Târgu Mureş, where bloody street confrontations resulted in several dead and hundreds injured. Although the post-communist economic and political situation in Romania turned for worse, the conflict did not spread and the two ethnic groups moved toward reconciliation.

Two key questions arise: Why did the conflict happen immediately after the general enthusiasm generated by the fall of the communist dictator? Why did the conflict remain limited in spite of deteriorating socio-economic conditions? What processes made the conflict and the subsequent reconciliation possible? Peace psychology approaches such questions by focusing on both macro and micro level processes, and by taking into account the interaction of several social, cultural, and historical factors (Christie, 2006). The present chapter embraces the inherent complexity of this field of inquiry and uses models from several social disciplines to study the Romanian-Hungarian ethnic conflict. The chapter will first focus on the larger picture of intergroup violence in post-communist Romania and analyze if and how a series of macro level factors can account for the general wave of social violence that engulfed Romania in the first 2 years after the fall of Ceauşescu. In the second part, the chapter will zoom in on psychological changes in terms of fundamental ideology and national identity changes to help us better understand the waxing and waning of ethnic violence in post-communist Romania.

Zoom Out: The Demographic-Economic Account

In order to properly understand the Romanian-Hungarian ethnic conflict we have to place it into the larger picture of the situation in post-communist Romania. Two observations are crucial in this respect.

First, after Ceauşescu's fall, Romania was shaken not by one but by many violent episodes of collective violence. The most important was in December 1989. Of the 1,104 victims of the Romanian revolution, only 14% died during the riots that led to the overthrow of the dictator. The vast majority died after the political power was seized by the National Salvation Front (Siani-Davies, 2007). In the next years there were also six "mineriads" or violent incursions of miners in Bucharest. The new political structure used miners as a shock force to repress political opposition and to disperse anti-communist protesters. The number of victims is highly disputed. According to the official count the number is smaller than ten while according to some newspapers and NGOs the number is higher than 100 (Ilieşiu & Rus, 2010). Moreover, the post-communist period was also marred by many collective aggressions against the marginalized Gypsy/Roma minority that resulted in a dozen dead and hundreds of houses burned or destroyed (Haller, 2009).

Second, these conflicts followed the same dynamics: violence was most intense in the first 2 years after regime change and then it gradually dissipated (with a notable exception in 1999). For example, four out of the six mineriads happened between 1990 and 1991. Similarly, of the 17 significant mob attacks against Roma recorded during the transition period, 13 happened between 1990 and 1991 and the rest until 1995. The first 2 years also accounted for 88% of the almost 300 houses burned or destroyed during these attacks (Haller, 2009).

The synchronous evolution of social violence in post-communist Romania implies that, behind their particularities, these conflicts probably could have been shaped by the same forces. If so, of what kind of processes do we talk about? The most relevant conflict risks revealed by recent research do not apply to this case. For example, according to an accurate model of civil or ethnic violence onset, the most important predictor is, by far, the regime type, followed by infant mortality rates, bad neighborhood, and state led discrimination (Goldstone et al., 2010). However, 2 years before the onset of civil and ethnic violence Romania was a full autocracy (i.e., the least risky regime type), had an infant mortality rate that placed it at the safe 36th percentile, and had no neighbors with ongoing conflicts (troubles in Yugoslavia and Transnistria had begun afterwards). The only risk factor that cannot be entirely ruled out, that of state led discrimination, was not significantly associated with adverse regime changes in the analyses of Goldstone and his colleagues.

While such facts give more weight to the assertion that Romania is one of the most idiosyncratic former communist countries (Linz & Stepan, 1996), a closer examination of Romanian society indicates, nevertheless, two potential sources of the onset of intergroup violence and one potential cause of violence waning. These factors are: (1) a relatively large youth cohort (an anti-abortion decree from 1966 increased Romania's birth rates twofold in just 1 year), (2) a severe economic crisis (the economic deprivations endured by the Romanian citizens during the last decade of the communist regime), and (3) massive migration (millions of Romanians left their countries after Ceauşescu's fall in search of a better living abroad).

Demography

Social scientists have often suggested that youth bulges (i.e., very large proportions of youths relative to the adult population) increase the likelihood of violent social conflicts (Goldstone, 2001). While most researchers have explained this relationship by focusing on macro-level variables like economic and political structures and processes (Urdal, 2006), some have underlined the importance of socially or evolutionary shaped psychological processes that are activated by large youth cohorts (Hart, Atkins, Markey, & Youniss, 2004; Mesquida & Wiener, 1996). For example, according to dominant economic approaches youth bulges could increase the likelihood of violent conflicts by lowering recruitment costs for rebellions (Collier, 2000). On the other hand, from a behavioral ecology perspective youth bulges lead to social violence because young men become more likely to form aggressive coalitions to gain access to reproductive resources (Mesquida & Wiener, 1999).

On October 1st 1966, desperate to increase Romania's population at all cost, Nicolae Ceauşescu signed a decree that banned abortion and contraceptives and punished with higher taxes those who did not have any children. As a result of this decree, natality increased rapidly. Actually, it doubled in just 1 year (Pop-Elecheş, 2006). Is it possible that by signing that infamous decree Ceauşescu generated a demographic tsunami that would lead, two and a half decades later, to violent social conflicts?

While the decree clearly had a significant demographical effect, it only worked on the short run and, eventually, could not stop the ageing of an increasingly urbanized Romanian population. If we do the math for the year 1990 we can see that Romania's youth cohorts do not reach the critical thresholds advanced by various authors. If we operationalize the youth bulge as the proportion of 15–29 young males relative to the total population of 30+ male adults, we get a value of only 45% which is below the danger threshold of 60% advanced by Mesquida and Wiener (1996). When defining the youth bulge as the proportion of 15–24 years olds relative to the total population and use the 20% threshold (Huntington, 1996), we get 17.14%. Finally, if we compute the youth bulge as the proportion of 15–29 years olds to the total adult population and use the 40% threshold, we get a value of 29.79% which actually places Romania at the border between the low and medium demographic stress categories (Cincotta, Engelman, & Anastasion, 2003). To conclude, if interpreted strictly from the point of view of a threshold value, the youth bulge approach cannot account for the collective violence that swept Romania two decades ago. There were simply not enough "children of the decree".

According to Mesquida and Wiener (1996), when a society experiences significant episodes of collective violence in spite of a small or medium proportion of young men, it most probably means that the general statistics hide an important youth bulge among one or more of its subgroups. Nevertheless, in Romania the only ethnic group that stands out from this point of view is the Roma minority, where, for example, the proportion of youth is twice as large as that of the Romanian or Hungarian ethnic groups (R dulescu, 2001). Although members of the Roma minority were involved in major episodes of collective violence, including the Romanian-Hungarian ethnic conflict, they were, by far, marginal actors. Most often, Roma were victims of collective attacks. It seems extremely unrealistic to attribute large scale events to the youth bulge of this small, marginalized, and highly discriminated ethnic group.

Nevertheless, youth bulges may not need to reach a specific threshold in order to elevate the risk of social violence. On the contrary, their effects could be continuous and moderated by other variables (Urdal, 2006). For example, the violence risks associated with large youth bulges can be reduced by education (Barakat & Urdal, 2009) or kept under control by harsh totalitarian regimes (Mesquida & Wiener, 1996). On the other hand, the effects of medium youth bulges could be potentiated by aggravating variables. One such variable present in Romania could have been the economy.

Economy

Periods of economic hardships are usually associated with collective violence. In one of the earliest tests of the frustration-aggression hypothesis, Hovland and Sears (1940) used a dataset covering almost 50 years to analyze the relationship between the status of the economy and intergroup violence in 14 U.S. southern states. According to the frustration-aggression hypothesis the frustration generated by blocked goals can lead to aggressive behaviors. During economic recession more people are likely to experience economic frustrations, and the aggression generated by these frustrations could be directed against convenient scapegoats. Consistent with these assumptions, they found that when the economy went down (e.g., lower cotton prices) the lynching of African-Americans went up (see also Hepworth & West, 1988). Similarly, based on the analysis of the relationship between weather, economic growth, and witchcraft trials in 11 regions of Europe during 1520–1770, Oster (2004) found that witch persecution was highest during the coldest years. Bad weather led to repeated crop failures and food shortages and people's aggression was channeled by the prevalent cultural beliefs toward those who, allegedly, had both the power and the motivation to change weather in a deadly manner (see also Behringer, 1995, 1999, for an historical account).

During the last decade of the communist regime, Romanians had to endure severe economic hardships. Although the national economy grew constantly during the first years of communist regime, at the end of the 1970s and the beginning of the 1980s a series of unfavorable international evolutions (e.g., the Iranian crisis), natural catastrophes (e.g., the devastating earthquake from 1977), and especially bad economic strategies and decisions (e.g., the politics of economic self-sufficiency) reversed this trend and shattered to pieces the dictator's dreams of "multilateral development".

The life quality of the average Romanian citizen was most decisively affected by Ceauşescu's determination to repay the entire external debt in a short period of time based on a strategy of export maximization and import minimization. His regime pursued this economic goal at the cost of rationing most of the basic commodities and of enforcing other severe austerity measures. In the last years of the dictatorship the personal monthly ration of many Romanian citizens came to consist of quantities like five eggs, one kilo of flour, one kilo of sugar, and some margarine. They also had to cope with drastically restricted access to electricity, heat and gasoline (Deletant, 2003; Longworth, 1997). If we link these dire conditions to the existing literature on the relationship between economic deprivations and social violence it seems easy to understand why the first ethnic conflict in post-communist East Europe happened in one of its poorest countries. Nevertheless, if economic hardships alone or in combination with the medium youth bulge can explain some of the social violence that engulfed Romania in the first 2 years of post-communism then how is it that violence calmed down while the economic crisis deepen?

Migration

The main macro-level factor responsible for the unexpected pacification could be migration. After the fall of the communist regime the borders opened and, in the following years, many Romanians were able to leave the country in search for a better living elsewhere. According to the International Organization for Migration, Romanian emigrants represent 10–15% of Romania's adult population. The typical emigrant is male, aged between 15 and 44, from urban areas, with a medium level of education (IOM, 2008). Similarly, according to Sandu (2006) one third of the Romanian families have at least one member who has emigrated for work. This translates to a total number of 2–3 millions of Romanians who left the country in three main waves: 1990–1995 (with an average migration rate of 2.8‰), 1996–2001 (with an average migration rate of 5.1‰), and from 2002 onwards, when the Schengen visa was lifted (the average migration rate between 2002 and 2006 was 19.76‰).

An account based on the interaction between economy and demography seems able to elucidate the onset of violence in Romania and the gradual pacification of this country in the '90s. The scenario would be the following: the decree signed by the dictator in 1966 determines the formation of a relatively large youth cohort that in combination with severe and prolonged economic hardships activates social violence. Most of the violence is concentrated in a short period of time because after the fall of Ceauşescu the borders opened and millions of young and middle aged Romanian citizens left the country in search of a better living elsewhere, thus easing the pressure at home.

The Demographic-Economic Account and Romanian-Hungarian Ethnic Conflict

While this all encompassing scenario seems quite plausible, can it adequately explain the Romanian-Hungarian ethnic conflict? According to Green, Glaser, and Rich (1998) because the aggressive impulses caused by frustrations have a rapid rate of decay, it is highly unlikely to document significant relationships between economic crises and collective violence unless political leaders or organizations systematically blame minorities for economic misfortunes, thus reactivating frustrations and directing attributions for responsibility against specific targets.

Whereas in Romania we cannot talk about any kind of beliefs that attribute economic misfortunes to Hungarians or any other minority, Schöpflin (1988, 1993) has argued that Hungarians were used as scapegoats by Ceauşescu's regime. The problem seems mainly semantic, however, because he does not claim that Hungarians were held liable for Romania's economic misfortunes, but rather that Hungarians were used to divert attention from such problems. Actually, it would be more appropriate to maintain that Ceauşescu used Hungarians as scarecrows, presenting them as a serious danger to the territorial integrity of the country when this danger was, in fact, not significant (Boia, 2001).

Ceauşescu needed as many diversions as possible because the political system he built encouraged citizens to view the state and its ruler as the main factors controlling their economic well-being. Even today, public opinion surveys show that most Romanians perceive the state as the main factor that shapes their personal economic well-being and that their economic discontents are translated into weaker political support (Cernat, 2010a). Under these circumstances, the only plausible direct victim of Romanians' economic frustrations seems the dictator himself.

There is another reason why the economic crisis does not seem well suited to explain the wave of social violence that engulfed Romania in the first 2 years after the fall of the communist dictatorship. Although those years were socio-politically agitated, economically they represented the eye of a hurricane, that is, a short period of apparent plenitude that was preceded by the mad economic policies of Ceauşescu and followed by the very painful effects of poorly planned reforms. Objectively speaking, the national economy was breaking apart, but subjectively life seemed better because the new political structures took measures to provide Romanians with adequate consumer goods and save appearances, at least for a short while (Demekas & Khan, 1991).

Thus, while the economic-demographic account adequately explains the onset of social violence in Romania (i.e., the anti-Ceauşescu riots), it seems less useful when trying to understand the Romanian-Hungarian ethnic conflict and the other conflicts that engulfed the country after the overthrow of the dictator. However, while this approach cannot explain why the post-communist conflicts involved specific social groups, the very events that led to Ceauşescu's fall created a highly volatile atmosphere (de Rivera, 1992) that could help us understand why the likelihood of social conflicts was elevated immediately after December 1989.

Two psychological effects seem most relevant in this respect. First, after decades of helplessness, the overthrow of Ceauşescu by mass demonstrations represented for Romanians an unexpected but strong expression of power. They rose up against an apparently inexpugnable tyrant and succeeded in bringing him down. From a psychological point of view, power is associated with action, those who possess power or are primed with power, increase their goal pursuit (Guinote, 2007) and action orientation (Galinsky, Gruenfeld, & Magee, 2003). In such situations not only is the distance between thoughts and actions considerably reduced but people are more likely to engage in risky behaviors (Anderson & Galinsky, 2006) and to treat social targets instrumentally (Gruenfeld, Inesi, Magee, & Galinsky, 2008).

Indeed, the beginning of the transition period was the scene of all sorts of public demonstrations, when crowds were pouring in the streets even for problems that are normally solved through other methods. To illustrate using my own personal history, during that period I was in high school in Târgu Mureş and I remember vividly that we did not do much in school for a couple of months after the overthrow of Ceauşescu. On the contrary, we spent most of our time demonstrating for various causes, ranging from changing the head of school to expressing solidarity with the Romanian students from the Bolyai high school. It took very little to get people into the streets and there was an obvious pleasure associated with this newfound exercise of collective power.

Second, it seems plausible to assume that the removal of Ceauşescu's dictatorship not only activated the concept of power, but also intensified the perception that things previously considered as unlikely were actually possible and quite probable. The literature suggests that people are more susceptible to persuasion during stressful periods (Baron, 2000). If the unshakable regime of Ceauşescu went down, then why wouldn't be possible for Hungarians to take over Transylvania, for foreigners to buy the country and so on? That is, it is likely that the temperature of the main fears cultivated by the communist regime rose considerably immediately after its fall.

These observations can help us understand why the psychological aftermath of December 1989 was explosive. However, in order to understand why there was violence between Romanians and Hungarians we need to identify the rifts that dominated the social psyche during that time. More specifically, we need to zoom in and focus on the beliefs and theories cultivated by the national communist ideology.

Zoom in: History, Ideology, and Identity

Psychologists interested in ethno-political conflicts have acknowledged that the nature and history of intergroup relations fundamentally shapes ethnic and national stereotype content (Bar-Tal, 1997). The relationships between Romanians and Hungarians are characterized by a long history of conflict that can be traced back as far as the early Middle Ages and has at its center Transylvania, a territory long disputed between the two groups and essential for their national identities.

Nevertheless, instead of describing a series of historical events and linking them to interethnic attitudes, I will focus on national ideological shifts. There are two main reasons for adopting this approach. First, objective events often do not correlate with subjective attitudes. For example, at the end of World War II, elements of the retreating Hungarian army in northern Transylvania committed a series of atrocities against the Romanian population. The official dead count is estimated at around 900 victims. These events are strongly active in the social memory of Romanians and have been used to justify negative attitudes toward Hungarians (Mungiu-Pippidi, 1999). Comparatively, the Allied forces bombardment of Romania or the forced instauration of the communist regime by the Soviets killed many more Romanians. However, both historical episodes are generally absent from the collective memory of Romanians, who endorse positive attitudes toward US and Britain and are nostalgic about communism. Second – and this can explain the previous point – history is often rewritten to serve the interests of socio-political elites. Next, I will shortly describe two major versions of Romanian identity and history, and how the national communist ideology laid down the psychological bases of the Romanian-Hungarian conflict.

Changing Foundational Myths and National Enemies

The construction of Romanian national identity relied heavily on historical myths (Kolarz, 2003[1946]). The myths were changed to serve pro-Western or autochthonist views, depending on the political ideologies and interests of those who controlled the country (Boia, 2001; Verdery, 1991).

When modern Romania was born at the end of the nineteenth century, its elites had a powerful pro-Western orientation and they defined national identity in terms of historical beliefs that were congruent with this ideological direction. The much emphasized origins myth that Romans and only Romans were the ancestors of Romanian people served to highlight the similarity between Romania and Western nations, to justify pro-Western political decisions and protect help from Western powers in the struggle for independence (Boia, 2001; Verdery, 1991). This myth also implied specific attitudes toward neighboring countries. For example, the central belief that Romanians are "a Latin island in a Slavic sea" (that is, a bastion of civilization in the midst of barbarity) was associated with political decisions characterized by feelings of superiority and hostility toward neighboring Slavic countries (Kolarz, 2003[1946]).

On the other hand, in order to compensate for severe economic failures and to legitimate the communist rule, Ceauşescu's regime used a nationalist ideology that took the form of protochronism, that is, the belief that Romania had been a source rather than a recipient of foreign cultural values (Niessen, 2002; Verdery, 1991). This ideology brought to the forefront myths that could stress Romania's distinctiveness, originality, and preeminence. Romanian identity was no longer linked to the West. On the contrary, Romans were rather depicted as imperialistic aggressors and were eclipsed by the Dacians as ancestors of the Romanian people. In spite of the scarce historical data, the kingdom of Dacia was depicted in glorious terms and placed at the center of the world, an image that closely corresponded to the role Ceauşescu envisioned for communist Romania (Boia, 2001).

Most importantly, Hungarians were now depicted as the main national enemy, constantly and efficiently conspiring to take over Transylvania. Such accusations represented an active attempt to divert Romanians' attention from the serious internal problems faced by their country (Boia, 2001). Consistent with this view, the most intense political tensions between Romania and Hungary developed in the eighties, when Romania's economic crisis reached its peak. During this period there were important social events (e.g., diplomatic expulsions) and both sides published many "historical" books that focused on outgroup atrocities against the ingroup.

Traditionally, these kinds of events have been politicized by the Romanian-Hungarian dispute over the legitimate "owner" of Transylvania, a territory that during the last century alone belonged to each side several times. The conflict led to the development of opposite theories, each serving the interests of the side that has elaborated or embraced it and being central for its national identity. In order to justify the idea that Hungarians were the first inhabitants of Transylvania and this territory rightfully belongs to them, Hungarian historians have adhered to a migrationist theory, according to which Romanians arrived in Transylvania after the Hungarians settled in and started to build a Western like civilization. On the other hand, Romanian historians have stressed the idea of continuity, according to which Romanians have inhabited Transylvania long before the arrival of Hungarians, who conquered the land by military force, subduing and oppressing Romanians for centuries. Each theory justifies why the disputed territory belongs to the positively portrayed ingroup, promotes negative outgroup stereotypes, and emphasizes ingroup victimization.

The politic conflict of the eighties made these theories highly salient for the general public and they became widespread among both groups. Many Hungarians think that Romanians came in Transylvania as shepherds and they found here a civilization built by Hungarians. Later, the Romanians spread like "rabbits", took over the control and are now discriminating and trying to assimilate the rightful "landlords". At the same time, consistent with the view supported by Ceauşescu's ideology, many Romanians believe that Hungarians conquered Transylvania centuries ago and oppressed their peaceful ancestors, and now, after Transylvania has been reunited with the rest of Romania, are conspiring to bring it back to Hungary (Mungiu-Pippidi, 1999).

There are two main reasons why we should expect such significant effects of the national communist ideology on Romanians' beliefs and attitudes. First, the annihilation of the small urban anti-Bolshevik Romanian elite after the installation of the communist regime in Romania, coupled with the powerful migration of the largely illiterate rural population toward urban areas (the proportion of Romanians living in rural areas fell from over 80% in the 1940s to under 50% in the 1980s) created the grounds for easy ideological indoctrination. Second, under communist rule Romania had state controlled television, state controlled radio, state controlled newspapers, and state controlled textbooks. Even interpersonal communication was controlled to a large extent by the state, because people were constantly afraid that their conversations would be reported to the Securitate and that they would suffer negative repercussions if they expressed something undesirable for the regime.

Reciprocal Fear, Manipulation, and Mobilization

If we take into account the highly volatile atmosphere created by the fall of the dictatorship and the national ideologies that conditioned Romanians and Hungarians to fear and hate each other it is easy to understand why violent conflict between the two ethnic groups was imminent (Kelman, 1999).

The significance of ambiguous social events could have been easily colored and inflated by the strong reciprocal negative stereotypes built into the two conflicting ethnic identities and thereby escalated hostility. This is exactly what happened. For example, during the anti-communist demonstrations from December 1989, in some towns the crowds behaved with extreme violence against the regime's officials, killing them and horribly mutilating their bodies. Nevertheless, whereas the events that involved Romanians against Romanians were ignored (e.g., the killing of two policemen in Cugir), the events in which Hungarian demonstrators lynched Romanian policemen were interpreted not as actions directed against exponents of the repressive regime but rather as actions directed against Romanians (e.g., the killings from Târgu Secuiesc).

Nevertheless, whereas intuitively the interaction between the psychological aftermath of December 1989 and the strong negative interethnic attitudes seems sufficient to explain the onset of violence, in fact, the situation was complicated by an idiosyncratic feature of Romanian Hungarian interethnic relationships. Specifically, although most of the Hungarian minority is located in Transylvania, in the urban areas of Transylvania Romanians and Hungarians have good opportunities for contact. In contrasts, in the rural areas the population is ethnically homogeneous and opportunities for contact are lacking. As a consequence of the extensive and good quality interethnic contact, the Romanians with the most positive attitudes toward Hungarians can be found in the Transylvanian towns. On the other hand, Romanians from rural Transylvania have more negative perceptions of Hungarians (Cernat, 2010b). Given these circumstances, it follows that the escalation of conflict in the ethnically mixed town of Târgu Mureş from a small dispute over the ethnic composition of the Bolyai high school to deadly street fights needed more than an explosive psychological atmosphere and strong interethnic prejudice. Since the two groups were not segregated residentially or in other way, the escalation also needed significant mobilization.

After the fall of Ceauşescu, Romanian and Hungarian local elites struggled for the control of Târgu Mureş, a town that is almost evenly divided demographically between the two ethnic groups. Initially, the two sides were involved in an apparently harmless conflict: Hungarians negotiated with the central authorities to transform the ethnically mix Bolyai high school into a Hungarian lyceum. Locally, Romanians opposed this plan that involved the transfer of many Romanian students to other educational institutions. The demonstrations were largely peaceful at first (when involved local pupils and students) but turned deadly when inhabitants of neighboring rural villages were brought into the town to "save" the situation.

One essential tool used by local elites to attract the masses on their side was the appeal to historical symbols and events. Relevant in this respect is that a content analysis of the two local Romanian and Hungarian language newspapers published prior to and during the March 1990 ethnic conflict revealed a high frequency of articles on national history. Both newspapers provided a biased presentation of the historical information by focusing on outgroup oppressions in the past (Bodó, Cosmeanu, Mátéffy, & Mărginean, 1995). A subsequent experiment showed that even a highly sanitized version of the information published in those days was enough to activate dangerous ethnic stereotypes (Cernat, 2001).

However, before the conflict, the social communication channels focused not only on historical oppressions but also attributed current negative intentions to the outgroup. For example, the local Romanian newspaper published articles that depicted Hungary as a threat to the territorial integrity of Romania. The slogans chanted back then by the groups of demonstrators (e.g., "We die, we fight, we defend Transylvania!") suggest that for those people, the conflict came to involve high stakes, namely an essential component of their national identity. From the point of view of the social identity theory of collective behavior (Drury & Reicher, 2000) during social events like the March 1990 demonstrations, people define themselves in terms of a common social identity, judging and acting based on its specific contents. The identities involved in this particular conflict were attributing very negative intentions to the other ethnic group and glorifying the historical characters that confronted it. Thus, once strongly prejudiced groups were brought into the town, violent confrontations were highly probable. The only thing that could have saved the situation – the determined intervention of authorities – happened only after the worst had been done.

Even though authorities eventually intervened to stop the fighting, few people were optimistic about the future evolution of ethnic relations in this region. Such attitudes were justified both by Romania's unfortunate socio-economic trajectory and by the dramatic events that took place in other East-European countries. Nevertheless, the Romanian-Hungarian ethnic conflict was among the few that did not spread in this region of the world. On the contrary, shortly after the violent clashes from March 1990, the Romanian-Hungarian relations entered a definite positive path. What factors led to such a fortunate development?

Ethnic Reconciliation: The Post-Communist Identity Shift

While the post-communist migration phenomenon and the idiosyncratic interethnic contact opportunities can help us understand why the conflict did not spread, the picture would be incomplete without also taking into account the important ideological and identity shifts that marked the Romanian transition period.

Obviously, the beliefs and mentalities of the communist era did not vanish once the regime that promoted them collapsed. Actually, their influence can be identified even today (Cernat, 2010a; Krauss, 2002). Nevertheless, in the meantime, new orientations and ideas have emerged and they are shaping Romanian society. Most importantly, if at the beginning of the transition Romanians had strong isolationist and xenophobic attitudes, in a couple of years they came to be very proud of their European identity and among the strongest supporters of the European Union (Neculau, 2002).

What has prompted Romanians to rediscover their pro-Western orientation? And, more importantly, what effects has this development had on ethnic relationships in Romania? To answer the first question, I will focus on the serious economic, political and social difficulties experienced by Romanian society during the transition period. To respond to the second question, I will analyze several psychological processes through which the pro-Western orientation could have positively altered interethnic relations.

Socio-Economic Collapse and the Resurrection of the Pro-Western Orientation

Romania was the only communist country that took very seriously the Soviet idea of war industry, investing massively in huge industrial compounds that were not viable economically (Longworth, 1997). As a consequence of this and other strategic economic mistakes that I have already mentioned, Romania started the transition with a poor economic basis that offered few chances of rapid recovery. To make things worse, other negative external (e.g., the dissolution of traditional export markets) and internal (e.g., the slow pace of reforms) factors also took their toll. Consequently, it should not be surprising that Romania's post-communist economic course was far more troublesome than other post-communist countries. These difficulties had severe repercussions on the quality of life of most Romanians, which has deteriorated almost continually. One of the most relevant statistics in this respect is that only in 2004 the Romanian GDP per capita reached the 1989 level, which itself was far from being adequate.

Social identity theory has been an essential tool for peace psychologists, helping them to understand various conflicts (Christie, Wagner, & Winter, 2001). This also applies to the present case. According to social identity theory, people are motivated to preserve a positive self-esteem and one important source of positive self-regard is membership in social groups (Tajfel & Turner, 1986). However, a situation like that experienced by Romanians during the post-communist period is likely to threaten the positivity of their national identity. When ingroup status is low we defend ourselves by running away, performing cognitive evasive maneuvers, or fighting. That is, inadequate social identity can activate three major strategies: (1) individual mobility (i.e., distancing ourselves from the ingroup); (2) social creativity (i.e., redefining the situation by focusing on dimensions on which the ingroup is superior, on inferiors outgroups etc.), or (3) social competition (i.e., acting to change ingroup position) (Tajfel & Turner, 1986).

Moreover, our responses are also affected by the status of the other groups to which we belong. Roccas (2003) demonstrated that low ingroup status leads to stronger identification with an alternative positive identity and more positive attitudes toward it. This social identity management response could explain why many Romanians have come to identify strongly with Europe and to endorse very positive attitudes toward this supranational category. Consistent with this hypothesis, Romanian students primed with negative features of the national economy reported greater identification with Europe and identification with this supranational category correlated positively with national identification (Cernat, 2003). Although no empirical studies have addressed this issue further, it seem reasonable to assume that other negative features of the national ingroup (e.g., political, cultural etc.) could also have led to stronger identification with Europe. To put it shortly, as the fruits of the autochthonist orientation grew more and more bitter, integration into a powerful and well governed supranational entity seemed brighter and brighter. This transformation was possible at a societal level in just a few years because the pro-Western orientation was, historically speaking, an important force in the Romanian society and only had to be reactivated in the collective mythology rather than built from nothing.

Though the resurrection of the pro-Western orientation has clearly served important social identity motives it is important to stress that it also involves a utilitarian dimension. Cernat (2003) also found that Romanian participants primed with economic gains from EU membership showed more positive attitudes toward EU. Thus, the accentuation of similarities between Europe and Romania is not only about feeling better about the national ingroup. It is also about legitimizing integration claims and achieving important socio-economic goals.

Pro-Western Orientation and Interethnic Tolerance

The pro-Western orientation had a positive impact on Romanian Hungarian interethnic relationships through several basic mechanisms. First, researchers interested in the improvement of intergroup relations have often emphasized the importance of superordinate identities. According to self-categorization theory, superordinate categories, which include both ingroup and outgroup members, can have positive effects on intergroup bias. This is because the perception and evaluation of individuals depends on their group membership, and people tend to be more favorable toward those who belong to self-categories (Turner, Hogg, Oakes, Reicher, & Wetherell, 1987). When people frame the situation in terms of "we" rather than "us" and "them" outgroup members are brought closer to the self and this leads to less bias (Gaertner, Mann, Murrell, & Dovidio, 1989) and more positive intergroup behaviors (Dovidio, Gaertner, Validzic, Matoka, & Johnson, 1997). The integration of Romania and Hungary in the same supranational entity could have had such effects.

Second, when peoples' group membership is salient, their thinking, feeling, and behavior will follow the ingroup prototype (Hogg, 2001). Therefore, social identities can also affect bias to the extent that their psychological correlates constrain outgroup perception and evaluation. Since the European identity is generally associated with norms and values encouraging tolerance and understanding between ethnic groups (Klein, Licata, Azzi, & Durala, 2003), it follows that it would positively affect intergroup relations through this correlates. Consistent with this view, an empirical study found that Romanians' strength of European identification is positively related to attitudes toward Hungarians and that this relationship is mediated by pro-social values (Cernat, 2006).

Third, we also have to take into account that outgroup views are shaped by major social events (Bar-Tal & Labin, 2001). In Romania, the process of European integration explicitly required concrete political and legal steps toward the better treatment of various minorities. A series of significant events, like the inclusion of the

Hungarian minority in the Romanian government or the signing of an important Romanian-Hungarian treaty, could have had positive effects on intergroup relations through a mechanism of dissonance reduction (i.e., people's motivation to minimize the psychological discomfort generated by conflicting thoughts). That is, even though many people were not enthusiastic about such measures, as long as they were not voicing revolt, the conflict between intolerance and conformation to the new norms could have led to a reduction of prejudice (Pettigrew, 1998).

Finally, the temporary migration of millions of Romanians in Western Europe in the last two decades could have also led to the importation of more tolerant values and norms. However, whereas existing analyses confirmed that migration does significantly affect a range of personal values and priorities they failed to reveal important effects on general ethnic tolerance (Sandu, 2006). On the contrary, Sandu's research only detected such beneficial effects for attitudes toward Hungarians. This particular result could be explained by the fact that the other groups included into the analyses (i.e., Gypsies, Arabs, and Jews) were more likely to be perceived as non-European.

The description of these processes does not imply that all ethnic tensions have been solved. Negative beliefs are still present. After all, the pro-European orientation is just one of the forces that drive Romanian society. However, it seems safe to conclude that its presence raised a significant barrier against ethnic violence and has encouraged the diffusion of more tolerant attitudes, at least toward the Hungarian minority.

Conclusion

The present chapter analyzed the waxing and waning of Romanian-Hungarian interethnic violence in post-communist Romania by focusing on both macro and micro level processes, and by highlighting both the commonalities and idiosyncrasies of the conflict as compared to other major episodes of social violence in Romania.

On the one hand, it maintained that the interaction between demographic (i.e., a relatively large youth cohort) and economic factors (i.e., severe and prolonged economic hardships) led to Ceau escu's overthrow. This event, together with the national ideologies that conditioned Romanians and Hungarians to fear and hate each other created a volatile psychological atmosphere that was tragically manipulated by local elites. On the other hand, the chapter argued that the difficult socio-economic conditions of the transition period created the grounds for essential social identity changes from mainly autarchic to strongly pro-Western. The resurrection of the pro-Western orientation had positive effects on Romanian-Hungarian interethnic relations through several social psychological processes and raised a significant barrier against intolerance and extremism.

References

Anderson, C., & Galinsky, A. D. (2006). Power, optimism, and risk-taking. *European Journal of Social Psychology, 36*, 511–536.

Barakat, B. & Urdal, H. (2009). Breaking the waves? Does education mediate the relationship between youth bulges and political violence?' *World Bank Policy Research Working Paper*. Washington, DC: World Bank.

Baron, R. S. (2000). Arousal, capacity, and intense indoctrination. *Personality and Social Psychology Review, 4*, 38–254.

Bar-Tal, D. (1997). Formation and change of ethnic and national stereotypes: An integrative model. *International Journal of Intercultural Relations, 21*, 491–523.

Bar-Tal, D., & Labin, D. (2001). The effect of a major event on stereotyping: Terrorist attacks in Israel and Israeli adolescents perceptions of Palestinians, Jordanians, and Arabs. *European Journal of Social Psychology, 31*, 265–280.

Behringer, W. (1995). Weather, hunger, and fear. *German History, 13*, 1–27.

Behringer, W. (1999). Climatic change and witch-hunting: The impact of the little ice age on mentalities. *Climatic Change, 43*, 335–351.

Bodó, Z., Cosmeanu, M., Mátéffy, C., & Mărginean, P. (1995). Alter/Ego tîrgumureşean. *Altera, 1*, 77–95.

Boia, L. (2001). *History and myth in the Romanian consciousness*. Budapest, Hungary: Central European University Press.

Cernat, V. (2001). I know what you did last millennium: Ethnic stereotype and attitude change after reminding people of historical events. *Current Research in Social Psychology, 7*, 11–29. Available at: http://www.uiowa.edu/~grpproc/crisp/crisp.7.2.htm.

Cernat, V. (2003). Romanians' perception of economic factors and its effects on their European identity. *Psihologia Socială, 12*, 65–76.

Cernat, V. (2006). Identificarea europeană şi reducerea părtinirii intergrupale: rolul mediator al valorilor. *Psihologia Socială, 16*, 93–105.

Cernat, V. (2010a). Socio-economic status and political support in post-communist Romania. *Communist and Post-Communist Studies, 43*, 43–50.

Cernat, V. (2010b). Intergroup contact in Romania: When minority size is positively related to intergroup conflict. *Journal of Community & Applied Social Psychology, 20*, 15–29.

Christie, D. J. (2006). What is peace psychology the psychology of? *Journal of Social Issues, 62*, 1–17.

Christie, D. J., Wagner, R. V., & Winter, D. D. (Eds.). (2001). *Peace, conflict, and violence: Peace psychology for the 21st century*. Upper Saddle River, NJ: Prentice-Hall.

Cincotta, R. P., Engelman, R., & Anastasion, D. (2003). *The security demographic: Population and civil conflict after the cold war*. Washington, DC: Population Action International.

Collier, P. (2000). Doing well out of war: An economic perspective. In M. Berdal & D. Malone (Eds.), *Greed and grievance: Economic agendas in civil wars* (pp. 91–111). Boulder, CO: Lynne Rienner.

de Rivera, J. H. (1992). Emotional climate: Social structure and emotional dynamics. In K. T. Strongman (Ed.), *International review of studies on emotion* (pp. 197–218). New York: Wiley.

Deletant, D. (2003). Romania sub regimul communist. Decembrie 1947–Decembrie 1989. In M. Bărbulescu, D. Deletant, K. Hitchins, Ş. Papacostea, & P. Teodor (Eds.), *Istoria României* (pp. 407–481). Bucureşti: Corint.

Demekas, D. G., & Khan, M. S. (1991). *The Romanian economic reform program*. Occasional Paper (Vol. 89). Washington, DC: International Monetary Fund.

Dovidio, J. F., Gaertner, S. L., Validzic, A., Matoka, K., & Johnson, B. (1997). Extending the benefits of recategorization: Evaluations, self-disclosure, and helping. *Journal of Experimental Social Psychology, 33*, 410–420.

Drury, J., & Reicher, S. (2000). Collective action and psychological change: The emergence of new social identities. *The British Journal of Social Psychology, 39*, 579–604.

Gaertner, S. L., Mann, J., Murrell, A., & Dovidio, J. F. (1989). Reducing intergroup bias: The benefits of recategorization. *Journal of Personality and Social Psychology, 57*, 239–249.
Galinsky, A. D., Gruenfeld, D. H., & Magee, J. C. (2003). From power to action. *Journal of Personality and Social Psychology, 85*, 453–466.
Goldstone, J. A. (2001). Demography, environment, and security. In P. F. Diehl & N. P. Gleditsch (Eds.), *Environmental conflict* (pp. 84–108). Boulder, CO: Westview.
Goldstone, J. A., Bates, R. H., Gurr, T. R., Lustik, M., Marshall, M. G., Ulfelder, J., & Woodward, M. (2010). A global model for forecasting political instability. *American Journal of Political Science, 54*, 190–208.
Green, D. P., Glaser, J., & Rich, A. (1998). From lynching to gay bashing: The elusive connection between economic conditions and hate crime. *Journal of Personality and Social Psychology, 75*, 82–92.
Gruenfeld, D. H., Inesi, M. E., Magee, J. C., & Galinsky, A. D. (2008). Power and the objectification of social targets. *Journal of Personality and Social Psychology, 95*, 111–127.
Guinote, A. (2007). Power and goal pursuit. *Personality and Social Psychology Bulletin, 33*, 1076–1087.
Haller, I. (2009). Conflicte nesoluționate de aproape 20 de ani. *Sfera Politicii, 138*, 34–37.
Hart, D., Atkins, R., Markey, P., & Youniss, J. (2004). Youth bulges in communities: The effects of age structure on adolescent civic knowledge and civic participation. *Psychological Science, 15*, 591–597.
Hepworth, J. T., & West, S. G. (1988). Lynchings and the economy: A time-series reanalysis of Hovland and Sears (1940). *Journal of Personality and Social Psychology, 55*, 239–247.
Hogg, M. A. (2001). Social identity and the sovereignty of the group. A psychology of belonging. In C. Sedikides & M. B. Brewer (Eds.), *Individual self, relational self, collective self* (pp. 125–146). Philadelphia: Psychological Press.
Hovland, C. J., & Sears, R. R. (1940). Minor studies in aggression: VI. Correlation of lynchings with economic indices. *Journal of Psychology, 9*, 301–310.
Huntington, S. (1996). *The clash of civilizations and the remaking of world order*. New York: Simon and Shuster.
Ilieșiu, S., & Rus, A. (2010). *Raport-rechizitoriu asupra fratricidului din 13–15 iunie 1990*. Retrieved November 12, 2010, from http://luju.ro/attachments/article/303/Raport%20-%20Rechizitoriu%20despre%20Dec%201989.pdf.
International Organization for Migration. (2008). *Migration in Romania. A country profile 2008*. Retrieved November 12, 2010, from IOM website: http://publications.iom.int/bookstore/free/Romania_Profile2008.pdf.
Kelman, K. C. (1999). The interdependence of Israeli and Palestinian national identities: The role of the other in existential conflicts. *Journal of Social Issues, 55*, 581–600.
Klein, O., Licata, L., Azzi, A. E., & Durala, I. (2003). "How European am I?" Prejudice expression and the presentation of social identity. *Self & Identity, 2*, 251–264.
Kolarz, W. (2003). *Mituri și realități în Europa de Est*. Iaşi: Polirom.
Krauss, S. W. (2002). Romanian authoritarianism 10 years after the communism. *Personality and Social Psychology Bulletin, 28*, 1255–1264.
Linz, J. J., & Stepan, A. (1996). *Problems of democratic transition and consolidation: Southern Europe, South America and post-communist Europe*. Baltimore: The Johns Hopkins University Press.
Longworth, P. (1997). *The making of Eastern Europe. From prehistory to postcommunism* (2nd ed.). New York: St. Martin's Press.
Mesquida, C. G., & Wiener, N. I. (1996). Human collective aggression: A behavioral ecology perspective. *Ethology and Sociobiology, 17*, 247–262.
Mesquida, C. G., & Wiener, N. I. (1999). Male age composition and severity of conflicts. *Politics and the Life Sciences, 18*, 181–189.
Mungiu-Pippidi, A. (1999). *Tranilvania subiectivă*. București: Humanitas.
Neculau, A. (Ed.). (2002). *Noi și Europa*. Iaşi: Polirom.

Niessen, J. P. (2002). Naționalismul românesc: o ideologie a integrării și mobilizării. In P. F. Sugar (Ed.), *Naționalismul est-european în secolul al XX-lea* (pp. 226–250). București: Curtea Veche.
Oster, E. (2004). Witchcraft, weather and economic growth in Renaissance Europe. *The Journal of Economic Perspectives, 18*, 215–228.
Pettigrew, T. F. (1998). Intergroup contact theory. *Annual Review of Psychology, 49*, 65–85.
Pop-Eleches, C. (2006). The impact of an abortion ban on socioeconomic outcomes of children: Evidence from Romania. *Journal of Political Economy, 114*, 744–773.
Rădulescu, D. C. (2001). Aspecte istorice privind indicatorii demografici specifici comunităților etnice din România. *Calitatea Vieții, 12*, 117–135.
Roccas, S. (2003). The effects of status on identification with multiple groups. *European Journal of Social Psychology, 33*, 351–366.
Sandu, D. (2006). Explorarea Europei prin migrații pentru muncă: 1990–2006. In D. Sandu (Ed.), *Locuirea temporară în străinătate, Migrația economică a românilor: 1990–2006* (pp. 17–39). București: Fundația pentru o Societate Deschisă.
Schöpflin, G. (1988). Transylvania: Hungarians under Romanian rule. In S. Borsody (Ed.), *The Hungarians: A divided nation*. New Haven: Slavica. Retrieved November 12, 2010, from http://www.hungarian-history.hu/lib/bors/bors13.htm.
Schöpflin, G. (1993). Hungary and its neighbours. EU-ISS Chaillot Paper.
Siani-Davies, P. (2007). *The Romanian revolution of December 1989*. Ithaca, NY: Cornell University Press.
Tajfel, H., & Turner, J. C. (1986). The social identity theory of intergroup conflict. In S. Worchel & W. G. Austin (Eds.), *Psychology of intergroup relations* (pp. 7–24). Chicago: Nelson-Hall.
Turner, J. C., Hogg, M. A., Oakes, P. J., Reicher, S. D., & Wetherell, M. S. (1987). *Rediscovering the social group: A self-categorization theory*. Oxford: Blackwell.
Urdal, H. (2006). A clash of generations? Youth bulges and political violence. *International Studies Quarterly, 50*, 607–630.
Verdery, K. (1991). *National ideology under socialism: Identity and cultural politics in Ceausescu's Romania*. Berkeley, CA: University of California Press.

Chapter 3
Theories of Ethnocentrism and Their Implications for Peacebuilding*

Boris Bizumić

Abstract It is impossible to understand the causes of ethnic conflicts, such as those in ex-Yugoslavia, without understanding the causes of ethnocentrism. This is one of the reasons why ethnocentrism has been studied widely by social scientists and is considered to be a fundamental concept. Nevertheless, a significant problem in the study of ethnocentrism has been a lack of conceptual clarity. Recent work in psychology has attempted to clarify ethnocentrism. It reconceptualized ethnocentrism as a complex multidimensional construct that consists of intergroup expressions of preference, superiority, purity, and exploitativeness, and intragroup expressions of group cohesion and devotion. This chapter applies major theories of ethnocentrism to the proposed reconceptualization. Theories of ethnocentrism can be broadly categorized according to what they perceive to be the main cause of ethnocentrism. These are threat perceptions, the need for self-aggrandizement, preference for those who are similar over those who are different, proneness to cognitive simplicity, broad social factors, such as social norms and representations, and evolutionary factors. This chapter shows how understanding ethnocentrism and its causes may help peace psychologists further understand ethnocentrism and ethnic conflict in ex-Yugoslavia and also help them build a long-lasting peace in the region.

Keywords Ethnocentrism • War • Peace • Ethnic identity • Conflict

In an essay titled "War," Sumner (1911) offers one of the earliest definitions of ethnocentrism: "The sentiment of cohesion, internal comradeship, and devotion to the in-group, which carries with it a sense of superiority to any out-group and readiness to defend the interests of the in-group against the out-group, is technically

*I would like to thank John Duckitt for his very useful comments.

B. Bizumić (✉)
Department of Psychology, The Australian National University, ACT 0200 Canberra, Australia
e-mail: Boris.Bizumic@anu.edu.au

O. Simić et al. (eds.), *Peace Psychology in the Balkans: Dealing with a Violent Past while Building Peace*, Peace Psychology Book Series, DOI 10.1007/978-1-4614-1948-8_3,

known as ethnocentrism" (p. 11). Although Sumner argued that ethnocentrism does not necessary result in wars, he, like many later scholars, posited that it is conducive to intergroup conflict and could lead to actual hostilities and wars. This negative impact of ethnocentrism on intergroup relations made it one of the fundamental concepts in psychology and social sciences.

The concept of ethnocentrism should be important to peace psychologists given that it could contribute to direct (i.e., overt, brief, episodic, sporadic) kinds of violence among ethnic groups, such as ethnic wars, but also to structural (i.e., slow, covert, societally arranged) kinds of violence (Galtung, 1964, 1985; see also Christie, 1997; Christie, Tint, Wagner, & Winter, 2008) because it gives more social value to certain groups over others. Accordingly, understanding the causes of ethnocentrism are highly relevant to effective promotion of both positive and negative peace (Galtung, 1985), and is central to implementing successful peacebuilding, especially in the societies affected by ethnic conflict. Given the nature of conflicts in ex-Yugoslavia, ethnocentrism, with its emphasis on the importance of ethnic identity to individual self-definition and relations with others, should be of interest to peace scholars concerned with the region. The Serbian peace activist Vesna Pesic (1993) directly implicated ethnocentrism in the regional politics: "Manipulating this kind of ethnocentric nationalism has been seen as the quickest and most effective method of gaining political power and maintaining control of the population." (p. 101).

However, what exactly is ethnocentrism? Although widely studied, it has been defined in many different ways, and an increasing number of researchers have questioned how useful the concept is. The main aims of this chapter are to define ethnocentrism, to apply different theories of ethnocentrism to account for its causes, and to discuss their implications for understanding ethnocentrism, ethnic conflict and effective peacebuilding in ex-Yugoslavia.

This chapter will not attempt to explain in detail the actual emergence of hostilities in ex-Yugoslavia in the 1990s. This is more likely to be a topic of interest for a political scientist, historian, sociologist, or anthropologist. The chapter is built on the assumption that there is nothing very unusual about ethnic conflict or ethnocentrism in ex-Yugoslavia. It also assumes that the direct cause of actual hostilities was not in interethnic hatreds that have in reality existed since ancient times or in societies with highly prejudiced and ethnocentric norms. Most scholars who study the region also tend to reject such simplistic interpretations (e.g., Bennet, 1995; Gagnon, 2004; Glenny, 2001; Mueller, 2000; Oberschall, 2000), and rather focus on a multiplicity of contemporary causes. Ethnocentrism (both "natural" and reinforced by elites) probably contributed to and facilitated the hostilities in the region, and may hinder effective peacebuilding in ex-Yugoslavia. (In fact, if the ethnic groups had non-ethnocentric attitudes of interethnic equality, consideration for ethnic outgroups, tolerance of ethnic diversity, and low group cohesion and devotion, they probably would not fight for their group against others). Accordingly, after discussing each of the broad causes of ethnocentrism, the chapter will indicate whether addressing them may help us understand ex-Yugoslav ethnic conflict and help us build peace.

Ethnocentrism

Although the origin of the concept of ethnocentrism is usually attributed to Sumner (1906), its first printed use was in a paper by McGee (1900). Both Sumner and McGee saw ethnocentrism as a group level analogue to egocentrism, that is, as ethnic group self-centeredness. This is evident in Sumner's widely-cited definition, "this view of things in which one's own group is the center of everything" (Sumner, p. 13). Although he used the term group in his definition, the context of his work suggests that he was primarily writing about ethno-cultural groups, and this is implied by the term ethno in ethnocentrism.

There has been much conceptual confusion in the study of ethnocentrism and the concept has been used in many different ways. This, no doubt, stems from Sumner's writings (Sumner, 1906, 1911; Sumner, Keller, & Davie, 1928), which appeared wide-ranging and open to interpretation (cf. LeVine & Campbell, 1972). Accordingly, ethnocentrism has been subsequently defined and conceptualized in many different and contradictory ways (Bizumic & Duckitt, 2011). LeVine and Campbell (1972) identified as many as 23 distinct facets of ethnocentrism in Sumner's writings. Most researchers have generally and uncritically followed Sumner (1906) and assumed that ethnic group self-centeredness is inevitably expressed in outgroup negativity and accordingly included it in their conceptualization of ethnocentrism. This has, however, become untenable because modern empirical research clearly shows that ingroup positivity and outgroup negativity are often independent and unrelated (Brewer, 1999).

A research program by Bizumic, Duckitt, and colleagues (Bizumic & Duckitt, 2007, 2008, in press; Bizumic, Duckitt, Popadic, Dru, & Krauss, 2009; Bizumic, Smithson, & Van Rooy, 2010) has attempted to clarify this concept and study its causes and outcomes. They argued that we should return to the original concept of ethnic group self-centeredness, and exclude from the conceptualization any facets that appeared inconsistent with the findings of modern research, such as outgroup negativity (or prejudice), mere ingroup positivity, and the association between ingroup positivity and outgroup negativity (see Bizumic et al., 2009; Bizumic & Duckitt, in press). They reconceptualized ethnocentrism as a strong sense of ethnic group self-importance and self-centeredness, which has four intergroup and two intragroup expressions. Intergroup expressions are concerned with the view that the ingroup is more important than outgroups and involve preference for one's own ethnic ingroup over outgroups, belief in ingroup superiority, wish for ethnic purity, and approval of exploiting outgroups for ingroup needs. Intragroup expressions are concerned with the view that one's own group is more important than its individual members and involve need for group cohesion and ingroup devotion.

Bizumic and colleagues tested the reconceptualization using a newly developed culture-general and balanced measure of ethnocentrism in New Zealand, the United States of America, Serbia, France, and Australia. The scale included the items emphasising ethnic group self-centeredness (e.g., "The world would be a much better place if all other cultures and ethnic groups modelled themselves on my culture," "It is better for people from different ethnic and cultural groups not to marry," "I cannot imagine myself ever developing an intense, passionate total devotion and commitment to my ethnic or cultural group" – Reversed, and "In dealing with other cultures we should always be honest with them and respect their rights and feelings" – Reversed). The findings supported the reliability and validity of the scale and indicated that ethnocentrism consisted of the six proposed dimensions that were organized as two second-order factors: intergroup ethnocentrism, consisting of preference, superiority, purity, and exploitativeness, and intragroup ethnocentrism, consisting of group cohesion and devotion. The two second-order factors were subsequently shown to form a third-order factor. This indicated a general concept of ethnocentrism at the broadest level of generalization. Furthermore, their research showed that ethnocentrism tends to predict different variables, including behaviours, over and above ethnic prejudice and mere ingroup positivity.

The data did not indicate big differences between ethnocentrism in ex-Yugoslavia, that is, Serbia (at least among university students), and other countries under investigation. For example, a re-analysis of the data from Bizumic et al. (2009) showed that ethnocentrism in Serbia was not any more warlike (and peace preventing) than in the other countries. Attitudes towards war correlated moderately with intergroup ethnocentrism (Serbia: $r=.33$, $p<.001$; US: $r=.35$, $p<.001$; NZ: $r=.23$, $p<.001$; France: $r=.22$, $p<.001$), and much more weakly or not significantly with intragroup ethnocentrism (Serbia: $r=.16$, $p<.05$; US: $r=.05$, ns; NZ: $r=-02$, ns; France $r=.13$, $p<.05$). The strength of the relationships between intergroup ethnocentrism and attitudes towards war did not appear to vary a lot across countries, suggesting that intergroup ethnocentrism appeared moderately conducive to warlikeness across all countries under investigation.

Similarly, the data from Study 2 from Bizumic et al. (2009) show that participants in Serbia, the US, and France all tended to reject intergroup expressions of ethnocentrism (see Table 3.1). The French tended also to reject intragroup expressions, while Americans endorsed them, with Serbs being on average neutral. Furthermore, a latent means analysis (see Table 3.2) compared participants' scores on the first-order and second-order factors of ethnocentrism (this analysis fully controls for the measurement error in the instrument). It showed that US participants were significantly higher than Serbian participants on intergroup ethnocentrism, and on the expressions of ethnic preference and group cohesion. Participants in France, however, tended to be lower on almost all variables than those in the US and Serbia (apart from the lack of differences on group cohesion between participants from Serbia and France). Although the data are not from representative samples, they are from relatively comparable samples of university students, and they suggest that Serbian participants tended to reject intergroup expressions of ethnocentrism, and not to be very likely to accept intragroup expressions. Although not as tolerant as French participants, participants in Serbia appeared somewhat more tolerant than those in the US.

Table 3.1 Means and standard deviations of intergroup, intragroup and six expressions of ethnocentrism in Serbia, France, and the United States

	Serbia		US		France	
Variable	M	SD	M	SD	M	SD
Intergroup ethnocentrism	−39.87	51.73	−30.99	44.81	−78.41	42.56
Preference	−1.25	14.21	3.05	11.81	−9.99	12.35
Superiority	−14.59	18.96	−11.26	14.80	−27.04	15.87
Purity	−16.35	17.73	−13.58	15.88	−26.83	12.16
Exploitativeness	−7.69	13.76	−9.19	11.36	−14.56	10.57
Intragroup ethnocentrism	−.72	31.71	4.53	20.46	−11.95	21.23
Group cohesion	−.91	16.60	2.53	10.88	−3.75	13.26
Devotion	.19	18.19	2.00	12.64	−8.20	12.24

Note. US: $N=212$; Serbia: $N=208$; France: $N=279$. The variables were measured using nine-point Likert scales, with response categories ranging from −4 (*very strongly disagree*) to 0 (*neutral*) to +4 (*very strongly agree*). There were 38 items for intergroup ethnocentrism (scale range: −152 to 152), with 8 items for preference (−32 to 32), 12 items for superiority (−48 to 48), 10 items for purity (−40 to 40), 8 items for exploitativeness (−32 to 32), and 20 items for intragroup ethnocentrism (−80 to 80), with 10 items for group cohesion (−40 to 40), and 10 items for devotion (−40 to 40)

Table 3.2 Estimated standardized latent means differences for six first-order and two second-order factors of ethnocentrism in Serbia, France, and the United States

Factor	Serbia[a] versus US	France[a] versus US	France[a] versus Serbia
Intergroup ethnocentrism	1.34*	6.42***	5.08***
Preference	3.34***	9.74***	6.40***
Superiority	.89	4.93***	4.03***
Purity	1.63	8.07***	6.43***
Exploitativeness	−.43	4.90***	5.33***
Intragroup ethnocentrism	1.28	4.76***	3.49***
Group cohesion	1.86*	3.33***	1.47
Devotion	1.07	5.49***	4.41***

Note. US: $N=212$; Serbia: $N=208$; France: $N=279$

$^{*}p<.05$; $^{***}p<.001$

[a]The country that acts as the reference group. Model fit: $Chi^2=3225.04$; $df=1218$; $p<.001$; $Chi^2/df=2.65$; RMSEA = .084; CFI = .95; NNFI = .95

What Causes Ethnocentrism?

Based on the proposed reconceptualization of ethnocentrism, major theories of ethnocentrism will be reviewed. Although no theory has dealt with ethnocentrism exactly as presently conceptualized, most theories have dealt with some of the six proposed facets. The focus of the review will be on the theories that have been widely investigated and have had significant influence in psychology during the last century. Theories of prejudice specifically will not be reviewed, unless they can be clearly related to ethnocentrism.

Social science theorists have proposed six broad causes of ethnocentrism: (1) threat and insecurity; (2) self-aggrandizement; (3) intragroup similarity and outgroup difference; (4) proneness to simplification and ignorance; (5) social factors or influences located outside the individual; and (6) evolutionary factors. It is important to note that many theorists have acknowledged two or more of these causes to be important for ethnocentrism. Nevertheless, the theories here were classified according to the central cause that they propose.

Ethnocentrism Is Caused by Threat and Insecurity

Many theories have assumed that ethnocentrism is caused by various kinds of threats or insecurities. Ethnocentrism, according to these views, can be seen as an individual or group reaction, often defensive, to these threats. This section will discuss realistic group conflict theory, authoritarian personality theory, and terror management theory.

Realistic Group Conflict Theory

Realistic group conflict theorists, such as LeVine and Campbell (1972) and Sherif (1966), have argued that ethnocentrism and outgroup hostility stem from competition or conflict over resources, such as territory, employment, and material benefits, or threat to the ingroup's access to or possibility of attainment of these resources. Threat can be also aimed at less tangible resources, such as group rank, prestige, or status (Tajfel, 1982). This theory is functionalist and argues that ethnocentrism is useful for reaching a group goal. If intergroup competition is essential for reaching the goal, then ethnocentrism and outgroup hostility would emerge in the groups that compete. On the other hand, if intergroup cooperation is essential for reaching the goal, then intergroup harmony would emerge.

Research generally confirms the basic tenets of this theory. Field experiments (Sherif, 1966) showed that when groups compete for a goal that can be achieved by only one group, certain aspects of ethnocentrism, such as group cohesion, preference, and overestimation of ingroup performance, increase rapidly. Reviewing experimental studies, Turner (1981) argued that intergroup competition increases both intragroup and intergroup centredness. Thus, people tend to give more importance to their groups when it is under threat.

Applying realistic group conflict theory to the present conceptualization of ethnocentrism suggests that the six facets of ethnocentrism are all functional responses to threat and competition. If a group was impartial in a zero-sum competition over scarce resources, showing full consideration for the outgroups, or allowing ingroup members complete individual freedom or disloyalty, it would be less likely to compete successfully against outgroups that were partial, inconsiderate, and cohesive.

A criticism of the theory is that it does not differentiate clearly between different kinds of group threats and is too broad. It is possible that not all threats increase ethnocentrism and that some may even lead to outgroup preference and perception of outgroup superiority. For example, Bettelheim (1947) argued that many prisoners in Nazi concentration camps, because of outgroup threats, often identified with the powerful outgroup, that is, the guards, and felt these were superior. Similarly, low status or minority groups, in response to threat from a high status or majority outgroup, may dislike the ingroup and prefer the outgroup (see Lewin, 1948). Thus, some outgroup threats may erase or reverse ethnocentrism.

Authoritarian Personality Theory

Authoritarian personality theory by Adorno, Frenkel-Brunswik, Levinson, and Sanford (1950) assumes that a particular kind of insecure personality (the authoritarian personality) is likely to be ethnocentric. This personality is characterized by nine traits, such as submissiveness to authority, rigid conventionalism, cynicism, superstition, and preoccupation with power. The theory is psychodynamic and assumes that because of punitive and rigid upbringings, authoritarian individuals feared their parents and other authority figures. Consequently, they felt ambivalence and repressed hostility to authority figures. To cope with this, authoritarians used defence mechanisms, such as "thinking in terms of dichotomies, i.e., in terms of pairs of diametrical opposites, and … an inclination toward displacement" (Adorno et al., p. 451), which caused ethnocentrism. The authoritarian personality theorists assumed that ethnocentrism involves all six components proposed here, but also outgroup negativity.

The link between authoritarianism and various measures of ethnocentrism has been empirically supported (e.g., Adorno et al., 1950; Altemeyer, 1998). (Unfortunately, many measures of ethnocentrism tended to involve outgroup negativity). On the other hand, the theory of the childhood origins of authoritarianism, ambivalence, and displacement has not been supported (Duckitt, 1992). Research findings have suggested that societal (Sales, 1973) and interpersonal threats (Altemeyer; Duckitt & Fisher, 2003) may play a more prominent role in causing authoritarianism than intrapsychic threats.

The causal effect of authoritarianism on ethnocentrism has not been clearly established, and it is likely that ethnocentrism may cause authoritarianism or that some external variable, such as threat, may cause both (cf. Duckitt, 1992). In addition, theory and research suggest that authoritarianism consists of only three aspects (i.e., authoritarian submission, conventionalism, and authoritarian aggression) and not nine and that authoritarianism may not be a personality disposition, but a social belief or attitude (see Duckitt, Bizumic, Krauss, & Heled, 2010).

Terror Management Theory

Terror management theory originated in the ideas of Becker (1962), and was popularized by Greenberg, Solomon, Pyszczynski, and their colleagues (e.g., Greenberg et al., 1990; Pyszczynski, Greenberg, Koole, & Solomon, 2010). It argues that ethnocentrism is caused by the intrapsychic threat of mortality. Because cultural value systems serve as buffers against death anxiety, whenever people are reminded of their own death, they experience intrapsychic threat, which they try to overcome by reasserting their cultural worldview and exhibiting ethnocentrism (i.e., by emphasising the importance of their ethnic ingroup and worldview). Research has been indirectly supportive of the theory, showing that people are more likely to prefer their ingroup over outgroups if they are reminded of death (e.g., Castano, Yzerbyt, Paladino, & Sacchi, 2002; Greenberg et al., 1990).

Summary and Implications

Psychologists have invented a number of theories that link threat and ethnocentrism. Of the theories described, realistic group conflict theory and terror management theory have empirical support, whereas the original authoritarian personality theory does not.

Many explanations of increased ethnocentrism and ethnic conflict in ex-Yugoslavia have also focused on different kinds of threats and insecurities (e.g., Bennet, 1995; Djilas, 2005; Gagnon, 2004; Glenny, 2001; Oberschall, 2000). Most explanations have focused primarily on realistic threats and their perceptions. Realistic threats to ethnic groups were indeed numerous. They ranged from threats of losing jobs because of one's own ethnicity to physical dislocation and individual or collective extinction (Djilas; Oberschall). The ethnic groups were also in competition over territories (Djilas) and had incompatible goals.

Accordingly, ethnocentrism appeared functional for ethnic group members to defend against the threats. If ethnic group members gave more importance to the ingroup over others and were also devoted to it and engaged in group cohesion, they could more successfully defend themselves against the threats. It is also plausible that the overwhelming presence of death during the ethnic wars could have also strongly increased ethnocentrism, which could act as a defence against the intrapsychic threat of mortality.

It is important to note that even though many threats were real, they were also, manipulated by the elites and the media, which spread various forms of fear and insecurities (Djilas, 2005; Gagnon, 2004; Oberschall, 2000). The elites tended to exaggerate and emphasize threat exactly because of its influence on ethnocentrism, but also authoritarianism, within the populations. Threatened group members were more likely to be devoted to the ethnic ingroup, which was ruled by the elites, and reject individual freedoms. This made the group members particularly submissive to the elites and their manipulations, which involved actions at the expense of other ethnic groups.

Attempts at peacebuilding should therefore create conditions in which ethnic group members would feel safe. In addition, in the same way that the elites and media may create and emphasize threat perception, they may create and emphasize the perception of security. Creating superordinate goals for the ethnic groups could also help foster positive interethnic relations and reduce both intergroup and intragroup ethnocentrism. Finally, terror management theory does not necessarily stress ethnicity as the only protective buffer against ever-present death anxiety, and emphasizes different worldviews, and therefore, even those concerned with openness, tolerance, and harmony (see Pyszczynski et al., 2010) may also protect against death anxiety and increase harmonious inter-ethnic relations.

Ethnocentrism Is Caused by Self-Aggrandizement

Another group of theories has assumed that ethnocentrism is caused by personal self-aggrandizement or group self-aggrandizement. The basic ideas are that people are motivated to see themselves or their groups as superior to others and/or may want to exploit outgroups for their own or their group's selfish needs. The major theories dealing with these ideas are the social identity perspective, elite theory, and social dominance theory. In addition, the dual process cognitive-motivational theory also incorporates this idea, but also argues that threat is equally important for understanding ethnocentrism.

Social Identity Perspective

The social identity perspective, which includes social identity theory (Tajfel & Turner, 1979) and self-categorization theory (Turner, Hogg, Oakes, Reicher, & Wetherell, 1987) postulates that people have different kinds of identities, such as personal, social, and superordinate (e.g., human). Social identity is seen as central to group processes and ethnocentrism and is defined as "that part of an individual's self-concept that derives from his knowledge of his membership of a social group (or groups) together with the value and emotional significance attached to that membership" (Tajfel, 1981, p. 255).

This theoretical approach was initially developed to explain ingroup preference in minimal groups, which are artificially constructed groups where there is no interaction between group members and group members do not even know who the other group members are. Although the proponents of this perspective have proposed different variables that could affect ingroup preference and ethnocentrism, the two central psychological variables, as stated by the founders of the perspective, Tajfel and Turner (1979), are group categorization and the need for positive group distinctiveness, which involves self-aggrandizement.

When people categorize themselves as members of a group, their social identity is made salient, they experience depersonalization, perceiving themselves as relatively interchangeable with other ingroup members (Turner et al., 1987). Thus, their personal identity and individual differences generally disappear and they act as members of the group, not separate individuals. In these circumstances, people discriminate in favour of the ingroup because they want to achieve a sense of positive group distinctiveness or relative group superiority.

This perspective, therefore, appears relevant to the present conceptualization of ethnocentrism, with social identity theory more clearly related to intergroup ethnocentrism, and self-categorization theory to intragroup ethnocentrism. Once people categorize themselves as ethnic group members, they should see their ethnic group as more important than outgroups, because they are motivated by self-aggrandizement in these situations. On the other hand, categorization alone, which leads to depersonalization, should lead to intragroup aspects of ethnocentrism. As Turner (1999) stated, depersonalization changes personal self-interest into a group interest, enhancing ingroup cohesion.

Elite Theory

Elite theory is associated with Mills (1956), Mosca (1939), Pareto (1935), and is influenced by Marx's ideas of the ruling class (e.g., Marx & Engels, 1970 [1845–1846]). It argues that societies develop influential elites that use various mechanisms to rule over the rest of the society. The writers who have applied this theory to ethnocentrism (e.g., Lanternari, 1980; Van Dijk, 1993) assumed that ethnocentrism is one such mechanism. According to Lanternari, ethnocentrism presumes, "an ideological function, i.e., the 'false consciousness' imposed from above by the ruling class" (p. 57). A belief that the ingroup is extremely important can be used by elites to preserve the intragroup status quo and to mobilize the group for the elites' projects. Although this theory appears useful for explaining influences on ethnocentrism that are often overlooked by social psychologists, it can be criticized for underemphasising the influence of non-elites, who are rarely passive recipients of ethnocentrism (cf. Smith, 2001).

Social Dominance Theory

Social dominance theory (Sidanius & Pratto, 1999) proposes an individual difference variable, social dominance orientation (SDO), to describe individual variation in endorsement of group inequalities. According to this theory, because of evolutionary influences, people have developed a "basic human predisposition to form group-based social hierarchies" (Sidanius & Pratto, p. 38). High SDO people support ideologies that promote group inequalities, and have attitudes, values, and attributions, which assign differential values to social groups. Given that ethnocentrism involves giving more value to the ethnic ingroup than outgroups, it is theoretically linked to SDO. Research generally supports the link of SDO to various measures of ethnocentrism (e.g., Duckitt, 2001; Pratto, 1999).

Social dominance theory seems relevant to the present conceptualization of ethnocentrism. The idea that one's own group is of extreme importance can be used to justify ethnic intergroup hierarchies, especially if the ingroup is high in status and power. Although all six aspects of ethnocentrism might be relevant for this, it appears that intergroup aspects are directly related to SDO, whereas intragroup aspects, with their emphasis on personal self-transcendence, may not be directly related to SDO.

Threat and Self-Aggrandizement Integration: The Dual Process Cognitive-Motivational Theory

Duckitt's (2001) dual process cognitive-motivational theory integrates threat and self-aggrandizement theories to account for individual differences in ethnocentrism. This theory proposes two processes that run in parallel, largely independently of each other, and cause ethnocentrism. One process starts with punitive socialization that produces conforming personalities. Such people tend to perceive the world as a dangerous place. This activates their need for security, which leads to authoritarian beliefs. The other process starts with unaffectionate socialization that produces tough-minded personalities. These people are likely to see the world as a competitive jungle. This activates the need for dominance and superiority, expressed in high SDO. It is hypothesized that authoritarianism and SDO then independently influence ethnocentrism. This model was tested in New Zealand, the US, and South Africa, and the data generally supported the theory (Duckitt & Sibley, 2010).

This theory is unique in the sense that it gives equal importance to the role of threat and self-aggrandizement in causing ethnocentrism, whilst most other theories discussed thus far have tended to emphasize either threat or self-aggrandizement. In addition, the theory attempts to account for a number of distal and indirect influences on ethnocentrism. As mentioned in the discussion of threat theories, it appears that all six aspects of ethnocentrism could be related to threat, while only intergroup aspects seem to be directly related to self-aggrandizement.

Summary and Implications

Although self-aggrandizement theories may be relevant to all six expressions of ethnocentrism, it seems that the intergroup expressions are most directly relevant. It is quite likely that in ex-Yugoslavia self-aggrandizement has in part created and increased ethnocentrism in the ethnic group members. Indeed, according to the social identity perspective, without self-categorization as an ethnic group member, subsequent depersonalization, and needs for relative group superiority there could not be ethnocentrism. Ethnocentrism, however, strongly increased in ethnic groups because of the wish for strong ethnic self-aggrandizement at the expense of other ethnic groups. Djilas (2005) argued that many influential politicians in Serbia, Croatia, Bosnia, and Kosovo propagated ethnic self-aggrandizement through territorial expansions at the expense of other ethnic groups. Indeed, many actions by the politicians, primarily in the late 1980s and in the 1990s, were primarily caused with the aim to increase the territories and power of one's own ethnic group. These politicians had strong support in their ethnic groups for a significant amount of time. This means that ethnic self-aggrandizement was a cause of increased ethnocentrism in a large number of people.

Nevertheless, increased ethnocentrism was in part caused by selfish personal self-aggrandizement of the elites. For example, many theorists assume that elites propagated ethnocentrism (ethnocentric superiority, devotion, purity) as well as violence for their own self-aggrandizement (e.g., Bennet, 1995; Gagnon, 2004; Glenny, 2001; Mueller, 2000; Pesic, 1993). Glenny argued that the real intentions of elites in ex-Yugoslavia (primarily in Serbia and Croatia) were their own "economic and/or political consolidation or aggrandizement" (p. 158). Gagnon even went so far to argue that the main reason why Serbian and Croatian elites manipulated ethnocentric sentiments, as well as wars and violence, was to demobilize the forces that were against them, such as the liberal political opposition. Self-aggrandizement among the elites was generally unrelated to intragroup expressions of ethnocentrism, as the elites were unlikely to sacrifice themselves for the ethnic group projects (see Djilas, 2005). Furthermore, Gagnon argued that certain elites only pretended to care about the ethnic ingroups, because in reality they were ready to sacrifice many ingroup members for selfish purposes.

Accordingly, effective peacebuilding in ex-Yugoslavia would need to minimise strong self-aggrandizement of both elites and ethnic group members. This can be achieved through institutional reforms and the rule of law, which would prevent the elites from abusing power, and which would give equal importance to the different ethnic groups. Given that a certain amount of self-aggrandizement is very closely related to group formation, self-aggrandisement might be encouraged in less destructive ways.

Ethnocentrism Is Caused by Preference for the Similar

Some theories have proposed that people are ethnocentric because they prefer similarity. The first perspective, belief congruence theory, involves preference for those who have similar beliefs to oneself. The second perspective, optimal distinctiveness theory, involves the idea that people satisfy their basic needs for differentiation and inclusion through the perception that they are different from outgroups and similar to (and included in) the ingroup.

Belief Congruence Theory

Belief congruence theory (Rokeach, 1960) argues that people prefer those who have similar values, beliefs, and attitudes to themselves. According to Rokeach, "*insofar as psychological processes are involved*, belief is more important than ethnic or racial membership as a determinant of social discrimination" (p. 135, italics in original). Research has generally confirmed the main propositions of the theory (e.g., Rokeach; Silverman, 1974). Nevertheless, a literature review by Insko, Nacoste, and Moe (1983) suggested that belief congruence may be particularly important when general liking is involved, whereas group membership may be more important in choosing marriage or dating partners. Furthermore, some studies, in which participants knew that group membership was randomly assigned (e.g., Billig & Tajfel, 1973), showed that categorization alone, without any similarity of beliefs, lead to ingroup preference.

Belief congruence theory seems to be related only to intergroup aspects of ethnocentrism, primarily preference, which deals with differential liking. Thus, people will prefer ethnic ingroup members to outgroup members because they see the former as having similar beliefs to themselves.

Optimal Distinctiveness Theory

Optimal distinctiveness theory proposed by Brewer (1991) argues that people are motivated to identify with groups in order to satisfy their needs for inclusion (and similarity with others) and differentiation. Those groups that enable their members to achieve a balance between these needs provide most satisfaction, so that people are particularly likely to identify with such ingroups and favour them over outgroups. This theory's proposition that people are particularly likely to prefer minority ingroups, because these are more likely to satisfy needs for inclusion and differentiation, was supported in a study by Leonardelli and Brewer (2001).

This theory seems relevant to the present conceptualization of ethnocentrism. On the one hand, intragroup ethnocentrism, that is, group cohesion and devotion, may stem from people's need to belong and be similar to others. On the other hand, intergroup ethnocentrism appears to primarily satisfy the need for differentiation.

Summary and Implications

In contrast to belief congruence theory, which is primarily related to the preference aspect of ethnocentrism, optimal distinctiveness theory seems to involve all six aspects of ethnocentrism. It appears that intragroup similarity may primarily influence intragroup ethnocentrism, whereas both intragroup similarity and outgroup difference may influence intergroup ethnocentrism.

Preference for the ethnic similar might have had a role in the development of ethnocentrism in ex-Yugoslavia, but it is unlikely that it had a very strong influence given that ethnicity is just one marker of similarity, and there are many others. In addition, preference for the ethnic similar is unlikely to lead to actual hostilities between the ethnic groups. Nevertheless, these theories imply that effective peacebuilding should emphasize similarities (and underemphasize differences) alongside non-ethnically based dimensions between the different ethnic groups in order to lower ethnocentrism.

Ethnocentrism Is Caused by Proneness to Simplification

Humans simplify the world because they are unable to fully process its complexity (Allport, 1954). As a result, they form categories, which involve objects, other living beings, and humans (i.e., social categories). The process of forming social categories for simplifying the world has often been related to ethnocentrism (Allport, 1954), because it involves only two easily manageable categories: us/ingroup and them/outgroup. Whereas the ingroup is perceived as important, trustworthy, or desirable, the outgroup is perceived as less important, less trustworthy, or less desirable.

Although all people are prone to simplifying their social worlds, some individuals are particularly prone to do so. This has been studied using terms such as dogmatism (Rokeach, 1960), intolerance of ambiguity (Adorno et al., 1950), personal need for simple structure (Neuberg & Newsome, 1993), and the need for closure (Kruglanski & Webster, 1996). These concepts are different, but share common variance (Stangor & Thompson, 2002), and are related to ethnocentrism. For example, Shah, Kruglanski, and Thompson (1998) showed that a higher need for closure was related to having more positive feelings towards the ethnic ingroup over outgroups. Stangor and Thompson found that various measures of proneness to simplification (e.g., personal need for structure, intolerance of ambiguity, and need for cognitive closure) formed one factor, which was related to ingroup preference.

People who are particularly prone to simplify could also be expected to accept intragroup ethnocentrism. For example, the simplicity of group cohesion can satisfy those people much more than allowing the complexity of individual beliefs, freedoms, and disagreements. In line with this, Budner (1962) found that intolerance of ambiguity correlated with increased group conventionality and acceptance of censorship.

Role of Ignorance

People may simplify the social world because they are ignorant of its complexity. Lack of knowledge about outgroups has often been related to ethnocentrism and prejudice (e.g., Allport, 1954; LeVine & Campbell, 1972; Stephan & Stephan, 1984). McGee (1900), for example, in his original description of ethnocentrism, related ignorance to ethnocentrism: "Knowing little of the external world, tribesmen erect themselves or their groups into centers about which all other things revolve" (pp. 830–831).

Although Stephan and Stephan's (1984) review of research showed that knowledge about outgroups improves intergroup attitudes and decreases prejudice, simple knowledge of and familiarity with outgroups is not enough (Allport, 1954; Duckitt, 1992). According to Allport's contact hypothesis, people need to experience optimal contact with outgroups to enhance intergroup relations. This contact is characterized by equal status of the participants, institutional support for the contact, common group interests, and intergroup cooperation. Confirming this, Pettigrew and Tropp's (2000) meta-analysis showed that samples experiencing optimal forms of contact were more likely to improve attitudes towards outgroups than other samples.

Most studies dealing with the role of knowledge and contact in influencing ethnic attitudes have dealt primarily with outgroup prejudice. Nonetheless, ignorance and lack of contact are clearly relevant to the present conceptualization of ethnocentrism. People may prefer ingroup members because of familiarity and may espouse superiority because they see outgroup differences as limitations. They may avoid mixing with outgroups because of the fear of the unknown and may approve of exploiting outgroups because the plight of unknown people is less likely to arouse sympathy. Finally, ignorance and fear of the unfamiliar may cause people to cling to the familiar (their ingroup and its ways), be devoted to it, and reject ingroup changes or innovations.

Summary and Implications

Both cognitive simplicity and ignorance have been invoked as explanations of ethnocentrism. Both have been used to explain the development of increased ethnocentrism and ethnic conflict in ex-Yugoslavia. For example, Djilas (2005) argued that dogmatic thinking (which had roots in many decades of communist indoctrination in ex-Yugoslavia) proved to be a fertile ground for ethnic nationalism. In addition, rural and poorly educated ethnic enclaves in ex-Yugoslavia were particularly likely to define themselves in ethnic terms, to be ethnocentric, and to largely support ethnic conflicts (see Kunovich & Hodson, 2002). This is why elites primarily mobilized such populations, which also tended to be more likely to be involved in the actual hostilities (Gagnon, 2004).

On the other hand, urban and educated populations were less likely than the rural and less educated to accept ethnicity as the main mode of self-definition and were more likely to identify with the multi-ethnic category, Yugoslavs (see Djilas, 2005; Sekulic, 2004). They were also more likely to be directly and actively opposed to ethnic wars in the 1990s. For example, when the war in Croatia begun, 85% of the reservists in Serbia's capital city, Belgrade, rejected to join the army, in contrast to around 50% in the whole of Serbia (see Gagnon, 2004). As mentioned before, research by Bizumic et al. (2009) showed that Serbian university students rejected all four expressions of intergroup ethnocentrism, and were generally neutral about its intragroup expressions.

It appears, therefore, that cognitive complexity and knowledge about outgroups could decrease ethnocentrism in ex-Yugoslavia. Accordingly, a task for peace psychologists is to attempt to influence the different ethnic groups to develop a more complex view of the world and to understand the characteristics and perspectives of ethnic outgroups. In the same way that individuals may transcend their personal self-centredness when they understand other individuals and their perspectives, ethnic groups can transcend their ethnic group self-centredness when they understand other ethnic groups and their perspectives.

Ethnocentrism Is Caused by Social Factors

It has been argued that people may be ethnocentric because of socialization in or conformity with ethnocentric social norms. Sherif (1973 [1936]) defined social norms as, "customs, traditions, standards, rules, values, fashions, and all other criteria of conduct which are standardized as a consequence of the contact of individuals" (p. 3). People usually internalize social norms though socialization (Sherif), but even if they do not internalize them, people are pressured, mainly subtly, to conform to them (Harding, Proshansky, Kutner, & Chein, 1969).

Research confirms that social norms do influence ethnocentrism. For example, Minard (1952) showed that US White and Black miners interacted on an equal basis at work, but behaved in accordance with norms of interracial segregation in their communities. Focusing primarily on outgroup prejudice, Pettigrew (1958) showed that in societies with prejudiced social norms, such as the south of the US and South Africa, social norms appeared more important in determining prejudice than individual differences. Finally, Singh, Choo, and Poh's (1998) study showed that the norms of fair-mindedness would prevent or weaken intergroup discrimination, while ingroup bias norms would strengthen discrimination.

The concept of social representations (Moscovici, 1973) has also been applied to ethnocentrism and related phenomena. Social representations are shared group beliefs, ideas, and practices, which enable group members to act and communicate. Van Dijk (1993) argued that in understanding ethnic attitudes, one needs to focus on the social representations that people have about their ingroup, about outgroups, and about the relations of the ingroup and the outgroups. In line with this, research has shown that the relationship between group identification and xenophobia is positive when the ingroup is represented as intolerant and negative when the ingroup is represented as tolerant (Billiet, Maddens, & Beerten, 2003; Maddens, Billiet, & Beerten, 2000).

The application of broad normative and social representation approaches to ethnocentrism is straightforward. Socialization in or conformity to groups with the normative belief that one's ethnic group is extremely important would lead to ethnocentrism in individuals.

A general criticism of normative explanations, according to Pettigrew (1991), is that they do not explain the origin of norms. In addition, the role of individual differences are usually underemphasized. Finally, it has been argued that neither children (e.g., Aboud, 1988) nor adults (e.g., Duckitt, 1992) are passive recipients of group attitudes.

Summary and Implications

It is difficult to explain the emergence of increased ethnocentrism solely through social norms and social representations in ex-Yugoslavia because the ethnic groups did live in harmony for several decades. Certain ethnocentric social influences, however, did exist before the actual hostilities and generally increased with them. During many years in ex-Yugoslavia, communist elites in the different republics tended to emphasize ethnic differentiation and discourage Yugoslavism, and therefore preclude the development of clear non-ethnocentric norms (Djilas, 2005; Sekulic, 2004). Nevertheless, ex-Yugoslavia was characterized by relatively weak ethnocentric norms and surveys had generally tended to document interethnic harmony (Gagnon, 2004). Even in 1990, for example, only a small minority of individuals in ex-Yugoslavia perceived ethnic relations as negative. For example, only 6% of respondents perceived bad or very bad ethnic relations at work, and only 12% in their neighbourhood (Yugoslav survey, 1990, cited in Oberschall, 2000).

Oberschall (2000), however, argues that social norms could shift very quickly with a change in one's cognitive frame. He points out that in ex-Yugoslavia, peaceful times were characterized by a normal frame, in which peaceful coexistence and cooperation between the ethnic groups was normal, but that elites activated a crisis frame, which was characterized by the perception of extreme threat to the ingroup and was reinforced by past negative intergroup experiences, and which created strong ethnocentric, prejudiced, and violent intergroup norms. So, even though the crisis frame may not be now extremely pronounced, any attempt at peacebuilding would need to address ethnocentric norms and social representations (e.g., through societal campaigns, institutional reforms, legislations).

Ethnocentrism Is Caused by Evolutionary Factors

Evolutionary theorists have argued that ethnocentrism enhances the survival of ethnic groups. For example, Darwin (1879) assumed that intergroup competition makes people more cooperative with ingroup members and that cooperative groups are more likely to prosper than non-cooperative groups. The social Darwinist Spencer (1892) argued:

> A life of constant external enmity generates a code in which aggression, conquest, revenge, are inculcated, while peaceful occupations are reprobated. Conversely, a life of settled internal amity generates a code inculcating the virtues conducing to harmonious cooperation – justice, honesty, veracity, regard for other's claims (p. 471).

According to Spencer, these two moral codes exist together in modern and non-industrial societies. Such ideas were also put forward by Sumner (1906). According to Keith (1949), group survival is possible only when intragroup cooperation and intergroup competition are combined and in balance. Otherwise, Keith assumed, too much cooperation or too much competition is detrimental to group survival.

More recent evolutionary explanations, based on sociobiological theory, maintain that ethnocentrism is an extension of the basic mechanism underlying kin group selection. Van den Berghe's (1978, 1995) explanation for ethnocentrism illustrates this approach. He argues that it is beneficial for animal species, including humans, to cooperate and the main genetic mechanism for cooperation is kin selection that maximizes inclusive fitness. Inclusive fitness assumes that genes can be transmitted to ancestors through direct and kin reproduction. Animals, therefore, tend to cooperate with their kin, which they favour over non-kin. Because of its evolutionary usefulness, humans have extended their kinship groups to ethnic groups. As Van den Berghe states, "ethnocentrism evolved during millions, or at least hundreds of thousands of years as an extension of kin selection" (p. 404).

Evolutionary explanations can be applied to the present conceptualization of ethnocentrism. Stressing the importance of the ethnic ingroup over others and over individual ingroup members should help ethnic group survival and enhance the transmission of the ethnic group's genetic material (i.e., extended kin group).

Evolutionary explanations of ethnocentrism have been criticized. It has never been convincingly demonstrated that ethnocentric groups are more likely to survive than other groups. Similarly, mechanisms that enable the extension of kin group selection to ethnic groups have not been clearly elucidated (A. D. Smith, 2001). In addition, it has been argued that central elements of sociobiological explanations are often not testable and that alternative explanations of the data are often equally plausible and some data (e.g., hostility, non-cooperation, and destruction within kin groups) even contradict the theory (Ross, 1991).

Summary and Implications

Evolutionary theories often paint a bleak picture of humanity suggesting that ethnocentrism is generally difficult, if not impossible, to change, and may often result in conflicts and wars. It is, however, more likely, as M.B. Smith (1992) put it, that "ethnocentrism … may well have biological roots in human evolution, although not necessarily of the sort assumed by the biodeterministic pessimists" (p. 84). The relationships between most ethnic groups in the world tend to be relatively harmonious or often neutral, and not necessarily conflictual. Nevertheless, a certain amount of ethnocentrism may exist in perhaps all ethnic groups, and this may be due to evolutionary influences. Furthermore, although ethnocentrism may be evolutionary, and perhaps inevitable, most scholars today reject the view that ethnic conflicts, such as these in ex-Yugoslavia, are directly caused by inherent evolutionary propensities of certain ethnic groups. Accordingly, although peace psychologists need to be acquainted with evolutionary explanations of ethnocentrism, it is important to note that evolutionary influences are distal and do not necessarily result in conflicts.

Summary and Conclusions

In the past century, theorists proposed a number of theories that seem pertinent for explaining ethnocentrism conceptualized as ethnic group self-centredness and self-importance. Thus, ethnocentrism could be seen as a product of threat, self-aggrandizement, preference for the similar, proneness to simplicity, social factors, and evolution. Although different, these factors are not necessarily contradictory, and could be seen as complementary. Indeed, it is quite possible that, for example, the cause of increased ethnocentrism in ex-Yugoslavia was due to the elite's self-aggrandising strategies, which invoked threat perception within the ethnic ingroup, and which in turn made one's ethnic identity highly salient and elicited a simplistic view of the world consisting of "us" (the ethnic ingroup) vs. "them" (ethnic out-groups); this in turn may have created strong ethnocentric norms, which precluded groups to learn about each others' perspectives.

Accordingly, effective peacebuilding in the areas suffering the consequences of ethnic conflicts, such as those in ex-Yugoslavia, needs to focus on the complexity of the different causal pathways that lead to and reinforce ethnocentrism. In addition to psychological causes, we also need to understand a variety of other causes, such as those that deal with societal, historical, political, economic, geographic, and other influences. This can only be achieved through an interdisciplinary work, which requires a joint approach by historians, political scientists, anthropologists, sociologists, psychologists, and other scientists.

References

Aboud, F. E. (1988). *Children and prejudice*. Oxford: Basil Blackwell.

Adorno, T. W., Frenkel-Brunswik, E., Levinson, P. J., & Sanford, R. N. (1950). *The authoritarian personality*. New York: Harper & Brothers.

Allport, G. W. (1954). *The nature of prejudice*. Reading, MA: Addison-Wesley.

Altemeyer, B. (1998). The other "authoritarian personality". In M. P. Zanna (Ed.), *Advances in experimental social psychology* (Vol. 30, pp. 47–92). San Diego, CA: Academic.

Becker, E. (1962). *The birth and death of meaning*. New York: Free Press.

Bennet, C. (1995). *Yugoslavia's bloody collapse: Cause, course and consequences*. New York: New York University Press.

Bettelheim, B. (1947). Individual and mass behavior in extreme situations. In T. M. Newcomb & E. L. Hartley (Eds.), *Readings in social psychology* (pp. 628–638). New York: Henry Holt.

Billiet, J., Maddens, B., & Beerten, R. (2003). National identity and attitude toward foreigners in a multinational state: A replication. *Political Psychology, 24*, 241–257.

Billig, M., & Tajfel, H. (1973). Social categorization and similarity in intergroup behaviour. *European Journal of Social Psychology, 3*, 27–52.

Bizumic, B., & Duckitt, J. (2007). Varieties of group self-centredness and dislike of the specific other. *Basic and Applied Social Psychology, 29*, 195–202.

Bizumic, B., & Duckitt, J. (2008). "My group is not worthy of me": Narcissism and ethnocentrism. *Political Psychology, 29*, 437–453.

Bizumic, B., & Duckitt, J. (in press). What is and is not ethnocentrism? A conceptual analysis and political implications. *Political Psychology*.

Bizumic, B., Duckitt, J., Popadic, D., Dru, V., & Krauss, S. (2009). A cross-cultural investigation into a reconceptualization of ethnocentrism. *European Journal of Social Psychology, 39*, 871–899.

Bizumic, B., Smithson, M., & Van Rooy, D. (2010, July). *Reconceptualized ethnocentrism and its consequences*. Paper presented at the thirty-third annual scientific meeting of the international society of political psychology in San Francisco, CA, USA.

Brewer, M. B. (1991). The social self: On being the same and different at the same time. *Personality and Social Psychology Bulletin, 17*, 475–482.

Brewer, M. B. (1999). The psychology of prejudice: Ingroup love or outgroup hate. *Journal of Social Issues, 55*, 429–444.

Budner, S. (1962). Intolerance of ambiguity as a personality variable. *Journal of Personality, 30*, 29–50.
Castano, E., Yzerbyt, V., Paladino, M. P., & Sacchi, S. (2002). I belong therefore I exist: Ingroup identification, ingroup entitativity, and ingroup bias. *Personality and Social Psychology Bulletin, 28*, 135–143.
Christie, D. J. (1997). Reducing direct and structural violence: The human needs theory. *Peace and Conflict: Journal of Peace Psychology, 3*, 315–332.
Christie, D. J., Tint, B. S., Wagner, R. V., & Winter, D. D. (2008). Peace psychology for a peaceful world. *American Psychologist, 63*, 540–552.
Darwin, C. (1879). *The descent of man, and selection in relation to sex* (2nd ed.). London: John Murray.
Djilas, A. (2005). *Najteze pitanje*. Beograd, Srbija: Artist.
Duckitt, J. (1992). *The social psychology of prejudice*. New York: Praeger.
Duckitt, J. (2001). A dual-process cognitive-motivational model of prejudice. In M. Zanna (Ed.), *Advances in experimental social psychology* (Vol. 33, pp. 41–113). San Diego, CA: Academic.
Duckitt, J., Bizumic, B., Krauss, S. W., & Heled, E. (2010). A tripartite approach to right-wing authoritarianism: The authoritarianism-conservatism-traditionalism model. *Political Psychology, 31*, 685–715.
Duckitt, J., & Fisher, K. (2003). The impact of social threat of worldview and ideological attitudes. *Political Psychology, 24*, 199–222.
Duckitt, J., & Sibley, C. G. (2010). Personality, ideology, prejudice, and politics: A dual-process motivational model. *Journal of Personality, 78*, 1861–1894.
Gagnon, V. J. (2004). *The myth of ethnic war: Serbia and Croatia in the 1990s*. Ithaca, NY: Cornell University Press.
Galtung, J. (1964). An editorial. *Journal of Peace Research, 1*, 1–4.
Galtung, J. (1985). Twenty-five years of peace research: Ten challenges and some responses. *Journal of Peace Research, 22*, 141–158.
Glenny, M. (2001). The Yugoslav catastrophe. In D. Chirot & M. E. P. Seligman (Eds.), *Ethnopolitical warfare: Causes, consequences, and possible solutions* (pp. 151–161). Washington, DC: American Psychological Association.
Greenberg, J., Solomon, S., Veeder, M., Pyszczynski, T., Rosenblatt, A., Kirkland, S., & Lyon, D. (1990). Evidence for terror management theory II. The effects of mortality salience on reactions to those who threaten or bolster the cultural worldview. *Journal of Personality and Social Psychology, 58*, 308–318.
Harding, J., Proshansky, H., Kutner, B., & Chein, I. (1969). Prejudice and ethnic relations. In G. Lindzey & E. Aronson (Eds.), *The handbook of social psychology* (2nd ed., Vol. 5, pp. 1–76). Reading, MA: Addison Wesley.
Insko, C. A., Nacoste, R. W., & Moe, J. L. (1983). Belief congruence and racial discrimination: Review of the evidence and critical evaluation. *European Journal of Social Psychology, 13*, 153–174.
Keith, A. (1949). *A new theory of human evolution*. New York: Philosophical Library.
Kruglanski, A. W., & Webster, D. M. (1996). Motivated closing of the mind: "Seizing" and "freezing. *Psychological Review, 103*, 263–283.
Kunovich, R. M., & Hodson, R. (2002). Ethnic diversity, segregation, and inequality: A structural model of ethnic prejudice in Bosnia and Croatia. *The Sociological Quarterly, 43*, 185–212.
Lanternari, V. (1980). Ethnocentrism and ideology. *Ethnic and Racial Studies, 3*, 52–66.
Leonardelli, G. J., & Brewer, M. B. (2001). Minority and majority discrimination: When and why. *Journal of Experimental Social Psychology, 37*, 468–485.
LeVine, R. A., & Campbell, D. T. (1972). *Ethnocentrism: Theories of conflict, ethnic attitudes, and group behavior*. New York: Wiley.
Lewin, K. (1948). *Resolving social conflicts: Selected papers on group dynamics*. New York: Harper and Brothers.
Maddens, B., Billiet, J., & Beerten, R. (2000). National identity and the attitude towards foreigners in multi-national states: The case of Belgium. *Journal of Ethnic and Migration Studies, 26*, 45–60.

Marx, K., & Engels, F. (1970). *The German ideology* (C. J. Arthur, Trans.). London: Lawrence & Wishart. (Original work published 1845–1846).

McGee, W. J. (1900). Primitive numbers. *Annual report of the Bureau of American Ethnology (1897–1898), 19,* 825–851.

Mills, C. W. (1956). *The power elite.* New York: Oxford University Press.

Minard, R. D. (1952). Race relationships in the Pocahontas coal filed. *Journal of Social Issues, 8,* 29–44.

Mosca, G. (1939). *The ruling class* (H. D. Kahn, Trans.). New York: McGraw-Hill.

Moscovici, S. (1973). Foreword. In C. Herzlich (Ed.), *Health and illness: A social psychological analysis.* London: Academic.

Mueller, J. (2000). The banality of "ethnic war". *International Security, 25,* 42–70.

Neuberg, S. L., & Newsome, J. T. (1993). Personal need for structure: Individual differences in the desire for simpler structure. *Journal of Personality and Social Psychology, 65,* 113–131.

Oberschall, A. (2000). The manipulation of ethnicity: From ethnic cooperation to violence and war in Yugoslavia. *Ethnic and Racial Studies, 23,* 982–1001.

Pareto, V. (1935). *The mind and society* (A. Bongiorno & A. Livingston, Trans.). London: Jonathan Cape.

Pesic, V. (1993). The cruel face of nationalism. *Journal of Democracy, 4,* 100–103.

Pettigrew, T. W. (1958). Personality and sociocultural factors in intergroup attitudes: A cross-national comparison. *Journal of Conflict Resolution, 2,* 29–42.

Pettigrew, T. F. (1991). Normative theory in intergroup relations: Explaining both harmony and conflict. *Psychology and Developing Societies, 3,* 3–16.

Pettigrew, T. F., & Tropp, L. R. (2000). Does intergroup contact reduce prejudice? Recent meta-analytic findings. In S. Oskamp (Ed.), *Reducing prejudice and discrimination* (pp. 93–114). Mahwah, NJ: Lawrence Erlbaum Associates.

Pratto, F. (1999). The puzzle of continuing group inequality: Placing together psychological, social, and cultural forces in social dominance theory. In M. P. Zanna (Ed.), *Advances in experimental social psychology* (Vol. 31, pp. 191–263). San Diego, CA: Academic.

Pyszczynski, T., Greenberg, J., Koole, S., & Solomon, S. (2010). Experimental existential psychology: Coping with the facts of life. In S. T. Fiske, D. T. Gilbert, & G. Lindzey (Eds.), *Handbook of social psychology* (5th ed., Vol. 1, pp. 724–757). Hoboken, NJ: Wiley.

Rokeach, M. (1960). *The open and closed mind.* New York: Basic Books.

Ross, M. H. (1991). The role of evolution in ethnocentric conflict and its management. *Journal of Social Issues, 47,* 167–185.

Sales, S. M. (1973). Threat as a factor in authoritarianism. *Journal of Personality and Social Psychology, 28,* 44–57.

Sekulic, D. (2004). Civic and ethnic identity: The case of Croatia. *Ethnic and Racial Studies, 27,* 455–483.

Sherif, M. (1966). *In common predicament: Social psychology of intergroup conflict and cooperation.* Boston: Haughton Mifflin.

Sherif, M. (1973). *The psychology of social norms.* New York: Octagon Books (Original work published 1936).

Shah, J. Y., Kruglanski, A. W., & Thompson, E. P. (1998). Membership has its (epistemic) rewards: Need for closure effects on intergroup favoritism. *Journal of Personality and Social Psychology, 75,* 383–393.

Sidanius, J., & Pratto, F. (1999). *Social dominance: An intergroup theory of social hierarchy and oppression.* Cambridge: Cambridge University Press.

Silverman, B. I. (1974). Consequences, racial discrimination, and the principle of belief congruence. *Journal of Personality and Social Psychology, 29,* 497–508.

Singh, R., Choo, W. M., & Poh, L. L. (1998). In-group bias and fair-mindedness as strategies of self-presentation in intergroup perception. *Personality and Social Psychology Bulletin, 24,* 147–162.

Smith, A. D. (2001). *Nationalism: Theory, ideology, history.* Cambridge, UK: Polity.

Smith, M. B. (1992). Nationalism, ethnocentrism, and the new world order. *Journal of Humanistic Psychology, 32,* 76–91.

Spencer, H. (1892). *The principles of ethics* (Vol. 1). London: Williams and Norgate.
Stangor, C., & Thompson, E. P. (2002). Needs for cognitive economy and self-enhancement as unique predictors of intergroup attitudes. *European Journal of Social Psychology, 32*, 563–575.
Stephan, W. G., & Stephan, C. W. (1984). The role of ignorance in intergroup relations. In N. Miller & M. B. Brewer (Eds.), *Groups in contact: The psychology of desegregation* (pp. 229–255). Orlando: Academic.
Sumner, W. G. (1906). *Folkways*. Boston: Ginn and Company.
Sumner, W. G. (1911). *War and other essays*. Freeport: Yale University Press.
Sumner, W. G., Keller, A. G., & Davie, M. R. (1928). *The science of society*. New Haven: Yale University Press.
Tajfel, H. (1981). *Human groups and social categories: Studies in social psychology*. Cambridge: Cambridge University Press.
Tajfel, H. (1982). Social psychology of intergroup relations. *Annual Review of Psychology, 33*, 1–39.
Tajfel, H., & Turner, J. C. (1979). An integrative theory of intergroup conflict. In S. Worchel & W. G. Austin (Eds.), *The social psychology of intergroup relations* (pp. 33–47). Monterey, CA: Brooks-Cole.
Turner, J. C. (1981). The experimental social psychology of intergroup behaviour. In J. C. Turner & H. Giles (Eds.), *Intergroup behaviour*. Oxford: Basil Blackwell.
Turner, J. C. (1999). Some current issues in research on social identity and self-categorization theories. In N. Ellemers, R. Spears, & B. Doosje (Eds.), *Social identity context, commitment, content* (pp. 6–34). Oxford: Blackwell.
Turner, J. C., Hogg, M. A., Oakes, P. J., Reicher, S. D., & Wetherell, M. S. (1987). *Rediscovering the social group: A self-categorization theory*. Oxford: Basil Blackwell.
Van den Berghe, P. L. (1978). Race and ethnicity: A sociobiological perspective. *Ethnic and Racial Studies, 1*, 401–411.
Van den Berghe, P. L. (1995). Does race matter? *Nations and Nationalism, 1*, 357–368.
Van Dijk, T. A. (1993). *Elite discourse and racism*. Newbury Park, CA: Sage.

Chapter 4
Transforming Violent Masculinities in Serbia and Beyond

Ivana Milojević

Abstract This chapter examines the gendered nature of physical acts of violence. The argument is made that physical violence is predominantly linked with a particular construction of masculinity in Serbia and beyond. These violent masculinities are in turn supported by cognitive templates that stem from patriarchy and are thus linked with structural, cultural and epistemological violence commonly practised even during times of negative peace. The chapter first defines the problem of violent masculinities and investigates their many and varied manifestations. Several theoretical frameworks are used to analyse these manifestations, such as feminist critique of a patriarchal cognitive framework and peace educators' critique of pedagogical practices that prepare for and help justify violence. Furthermore, the Freudian concept of narcissistic injury, the Jungian concept of the shadow and the Stones' concept of disowned selves are used to point out the psychological factors that may contribute to some men's conscious or subconscious desire or decision to engage in acts of violence. Analysis of predominantly Serbian masculinities in the context of Yugoslav wars is offered as a case study; an example of (1) the interconnection between various forms of violence and (2) how broad theoretical frameworks could be used to analyse concrete manifestations of violence within a particular geo-historical context. The chapter concludes with a discussion on strategies and cognitive templates needed as a prerequisite in order to enhance and/or construct alternative non-violent oriented masculinities.

Keywords Gender • Performativity • Psychology • Masculinities • Violence • Peace

I. Milojević (✉)
Faculty of Arts and Social Sciences, University of the Sunshine Coast,
Maroochydore, DC QLD 4558, Australia
e-mail: imilojev@usc.edu.au

O. Simić et al. (eds.), *Peace Psychology in the Balkans: Dealing with a Violent Past while Building Peace*, Peace Psychology Book Series, DOI 10.1007/978-1-4614-1948-8_4,

Introduction: The Problem, Definitions and Issues

> Rado ide Srbin u vojnike, dva ga vuku a trojica tuku!
> [Gladly a Serb enlists (to be a soldier), two (men) are dragging him and three are beating him!]

To meaningfully analyse multiple manifestations of violence, it is crucial to investigate the gender power structure and the social psychology of gender. This is because the vast majority of acts of direct violence are committed by male members of the human species. Galtung (2009) estimates that 'above 90% of criminal and war violence is committed by men,' confirming the theory that 'violence and being a man seem to go hand in hand'.

> Compared with women, men, especially young men, are overwhelmingly involved in all types of violence. It is mostly men who commit acts of personal violence – against women and girls, as well as towards other men and boys. Men are also most often implicated in other types of organized or institutional violence as victims and perpetrators of violence. Around the world ... militaries consist of only men or mostly men. Men fight more than women – in wars, in the home, schoolyard, and on the street. It is primarily men who are drafted into jihadi, nationalist or separatist movements or who perpetrate acts of terrorism. In general, men use weapons more than women, and are imprisoned and murdered more than women. It is also a fact that, in general, men control more resources and wield more power than women (UNESCAP, 2003, quoted in Warters, 2010, pp. 659–660).

To further tackle the issue of masculinities and violence, discussion on crucial theoretical concepts is first required. This is done in the next two sections that deal with issues of gender, masculinity and femininity. The chapter will then more specifically discuss the ways in which the different psychologies of gender were utilised during the 'masculinity wars' that took place in the former Yugoslavia in the 1990s. The final section of the chapter investigates alternative peace-oriented masculinities and their potential to sever the link between masculinity and violence.

The main argument in this chapter is that a crucial link between a particularly imagined, socially constructed masculinity and physical violence exists in Serbia, the former Yugoslavia and beyond. The main focus of the chapter is an examination of mechanisms – psychological, educational and symbolic – behind the creation of gendered group identities, specifically the ways in which hegemonic masculinities are linked with violence. The primary research questions posited here are: what must be activated, in the cognitive sphere, to enable previously benevolent men (relatively speaking) to engage in acts of collective violence? What are some of the psychological and pedagogical processes that transform nonviolent males into perpetrators of violence? More concretely, what role does their perceived maleness play in that process? Furthermore, how are masculinities imagined as part of the overall personal and social identities so as to enable and justify violence? Data for the analysis is drawn from various research projects conducted by this author and others, relevant literature, as well as from the author's own personal experiences and memories while living in former Yugoslavia and Serbia.

Performativity and Psychology of Gender and the Concept of Hegemonic Masculinity

Similar to the assertion within peace studies that peace is not merely a state (i.e. absence of direct violence) but also a process (i.e. a presence of social actions that promote positive peace and structural justice); gender in gender studies now also denotes a process (of enacting femininities and masculinities) rather than a state (of being a woman/man). That is, gender is now understood as something we *do* rather than who we *are*, a role that we perform and which is socially constructed. This focus on the performativity of gender (Butler, 1990) is critical to our understanding of how hegemonic femininities and masculinities are created.

Of particular interest here is the concept of hegemonic masculinity, developed in the 1990s, which refers to the 'pattern of practice (i.e., things done, not just a set of role expectations or an identity) that allowed male 'dominance over women' (Connell, 2005, p. 832) as well as the predominance of hegemonic masculinity over other alternative masculinities. Hegemonic masculinity requires both compliant masculinities as well as women (real and symbolic femininity) to exist as its opposites. It also requires discourses on 'real men' and desirable manhood, which are in the context of patriarchal societies most commonly defined by stereotypical psychological traits of machismo. As explicitly stated by a Serbian war volunteer:

> All my life I dreamt about being in a war, because, I guess, the crucial test of manhood is when a man goes to war. Screw the man who did not serve the army and was never in a war . . . that is a real job for a man. There is nothing for women to do there. We know what their duty is: to heal, to cure, and to lie down in bed so that the warrior can relax and so on. There is nothing else for them. Even as to the cooking and the washing while at war, the men have to do that. The war is a real manly mission (quoted in Milićević, 2006, p. 278).

Or, as confirmed by a couple of participants in a study by Milojević and Markov:

> *A real man* has to know how to use weapons, and if needed, to protect his family and country, and not to wait for somebody else to do so.
>
> To me, being a soldier means honour. That also means that you are a mature, capable person and not asocial.
>
> Through the army *men become stronger*, more *disciplined* and *serious*...if our fathers could [serve the army] today's young men can do the same also (Milojević & Markov, 2008, p. 183, italics added).

Even though hegemonic masculinity is not 'normal in the statistical sense' (Connell, 2005) given that only a minority of men might enact it, it certainly is normative within the context of a dominator (Eisler, 2000), patriarchal society. Such a society is characterized by the existence of highly asymmetrical gender roles and the consequent 'differential social psychology of men and women' (Gilligan, 2001, p. 58). Men are requested to possess psychological traits such as mental endurance, bravery, the valuing of high social achievement, respect of authority, self-control, and being low in empathy and sensitivity to other people (Brock-Utne, 2010, p. 210). Women, on the other hand, are requested to exhibit 'feminine' qualities such as 'tenderness, intimacy, nurturance, passivity, dependency, forgiveness, and the capacity to feel anything, psychical or emotional, including pain, fear, depression, love, compassion, vulnerability, sadness' (Gilligan, p. 63). Sadly, the range of emotions allowed for men to exhibit and feel is minimal, and mostly limited to anger and its variants such as rage and hate. In the Serbian and Yugoslav contexts, hegemonic masculinities have also been those that are allowed expression of certain feelings (such as feeling confident, annoyed, aggravated, frustrated, cranky, impatient, irritated, angry, detached) whilst suppressing others (such as feeling affectionate, compassionate, loving, afraid, worried, sad, vulnerable, helpless). In such a context men are psychologically prepared to enact violence; as for example when a 'narcissistic injury' and 'narcissistic rage' are evoked. As described by Barash and Webel, these two concepts are connected to the psychological condition of narcissism:

> Narcissism involves infatuation with one's self, and in moderation it is considered a normal stage in personality development. But when the individual associates himself or herself with a larger group, especially with the nation-state, slights or injuries to the group are easy to perceive as injuries to one's self. The resulting 'narcissistic rage' may involve an unrelenting compulsion to undo the hurt; in the pursuit of this vengeful 'justice', great violence may be self-righteously employed (2002, p. 125).

This great violence is then 'self-righteously' employed, but not by either himself or herself; it is almost exclusively enacted by men. Together with the 'narcissism of minor difference' (Freud, 1913) narcissistic injury/rage became the psychological mechanism behind the practical use of homicide and genocide during the wars in the former Yugoslavia. In the early 1990s, the unifying and multicultural Yugoslav identity further disintegrated and separate categories of 'us' and 'them' were accentuated. In accordance with the 'collective violence pedagogy' (Milojević, 2006) separation between 'us' and 'them' also meant the invention of the category of 'the other,' even if that other was up until very recently part of 'us'. The attribute of the lesser (wrong, deficient in some ways) was then attached to that other and finally a sense of threat – them coming after us – was created. War was made psychologically possible by either or both sides wanting to heal and avenge previous trauma or by justifications of why engagement in pre-emptive actions had to take place.

It is no accident that such vengeful justice is enacted almost exclusively by men. Within 'the culture of violence called patriarchy' (Gilligan, p. 62) the notion of hegemonic masculinity is 'literally defined as involving the expectation, even the requirement, of violence' (Gilligan, p. 62). Within the context of a warrior, bellicose or 'dominator' (Eisler, 2000) societies masculine cultures that are imagined and promoted as the ideal are always connected with violence:

> From this world comes a hegemonic masculinity that requires subservient masculinities and women exist as its counterpart. Violence then becomes a way for men to accomplish masculinity and to maintain positions of privilege within the hierarchy. Masculine identity is often so closely linked to violence that violence may be the glue that holds communities of young males together. Acts of violence serve to both create the male self and to valorize the masculine ideal (Cook-Huffman, 2010, p. 214).

The notion of hegemonic masculinity recognises the plurality of masculinities as well as the hierarchy of masculinities, which is often asserted and maintained via direct and structural violence (Connell, 2005, p. 832). And while violence may be exercised 'against young men [themselves] during rites of passage into manhood

… the mark of male maturity… is most often a demonstration of one's capacity to exercise violence against others' (McInturff, 2010, p. 223).

Prior to the 1990s wars, all 'capable' Yugoslav men were already initiated into such a militaristic mindset. They had already received a military training whose principal task has always been to 'overcome the average individual's [men's] deep-seated-resistance to killing' (Paige, 2002, p. 26). Compulsory drafting in former Yugoslavia provided this training as well as an avenue for 'boys to be made into men':

> …in the military men could learn how to do basic things: fold their clothes, iron, wash, make the bed … I believe that military term should last between 12 and 18 months, so all men would become stronger and tougher and not stay mama's babies.
>
> …it is important for a man to separate from his folk for a certain time, so he could in fact 'grow up' … The army is good for the man to get himself together, to consider what he wants to do further in life, to get stronger and physically better prepared for the future. (Participants in a study, quoted in Milojević & Markov, 2008, pp. 180–181).

The rite of passage, of turning boys into men and men into soldiers was a compulsory rite of passage in the former Yugoslavia during the period 1945–1991. This explains certain difficulties in distinguishing between soldiers and civilians during wars in former Yugoslavia and sheds some light into the horrendous crime that took place in Srebrenica. The patriarchal mindset considers each capable male over a certain age a soldier, a potential warrior, irrespective of a particular man's inclinations, level of military training or even inability to use weaponry effectively or access it. Patriarchal societies assign all men the role of 'violence-objects,' argues James Gilligan (2001, p. 59). They are assigned the role of fighting in wars and most commonly 'not given any choice about the matter':

> …if they refuse to treat other men as objects of violence, and thereby simultaneously become objects of those men's violence, they will be shamed and insulted (called cowards) and then turned into objects of their own army's violence. 'Deserters' have traditionally been shot. And just as men are shamed for refusing to treat other men and themselves as violence-objects, they are honored for being willing to do so. (James Gilligan, 2001, p. 59).

Hegemonic masculinities via past war heroes are utilised in order to glorify and reward men's willingness to turn themselves and other men into violence objects. Within this discourse on hegemonic masculinity, a good Serbian man, for example, is a hero who fights for his people, refuses to negotiate and does not settle for less than total victory. Two prerequisites are needed to become a Serbian hero: maleness and the skilled use of weapons. When it comes down to conflicts with 'others,' all else is cowardly, naive, inefficient or counterproductive. This message has been reinforced in the collective consciousness of the Serbian and Yugoslav people. Indeed like most other nation-states, these two nations were also symbolically born on killing fields; the former during the mythical 1389 Kosovo battle against the Ottomans and the latter during the WWII when partisans fought and defeated Nazi occupiers as well as domestic 'enemies of the people' (Croatian Ustache and Serbian Chetniks). From these killing fields women were largely absent, except in their roles of mothers of warriors, such as mythical Mother Jugovići, or supporters of men and their war efforts, such as the second key female figure in Serbian mythology, *Kosovka Devojka*/Kosovo Girl. Socialist partisans argued for flattened class hierarchies as well as, up to a point, flattened gender hierarchies. A woman warrior/resistance fighter – *partizanka* – gained prominence both during the reality of WWII as well as later symbolically during the existence of former Yugoslavia. Nevertheless, this new archetype for women did very little to challenge the overall warrior culture. Her biggest achievement was to fight and die like a man. The pedagogy of warrior culture further teaches: '*Bolje grob nego rob!*' [Better grave than slave!] and '*Bolje rat nego pakt!*' [Better war than pact!] – slogans used to mobilise against foreign occupation and immortalised in Yugoslav/Serbian history textbooks. Other messages that glorify heroic death and male bravery were also easily found in Serbian and Yugoslav textbooks. The following are examples from the fifth and sixth grade readers used in Serbia in the early 1990s, at the height of the wars taking place in Croatia and Bosnia:

> A coward dies several times in his life, a hero only once.
> He who dies honorably is remembered for one hundred years, and he who dies without honor is forgotten by his own children.
> A proper hero does not die at home.
> An honorable death celebrates your life.
> These tombs are not graves, but the cradles of new forces (Pešić, 1994, p. 69).

The overall message is this: new life comes from death, from sacrificing oneself in the wars of one's people, which is both a 'mission impossible' and a 'masculinist birth par excellence' (Lake, 1992). Deserving males – those exhibiting hegemonic masculinity that turns themselves and other men into objects of violence – are reborn into the eternal life, forever remembered by their thankful compatriots. In sum, patriarchal societies ascribe very strict and asymmetrical roles for genders and different expectations of how these gendered roles are to be fulfilled. Particular psychological mechanisms are used, such as engendering ideal hegemonic masculinity that can feel or exhibit only emotions such as anger and rage and the honouring of men who engage in 'righteous' violence. These mechanisms are then employed to motivate men to engage in violent acts as well as to provide the overall rationale for violence.

Shadow

> What can a man say about woman, his own opposite? I mean of course something sensible, that is outside the sexual program, free of resentment, illusion, and theory. Where is the man to be found capable of such superiority? Woman always stands just where the man's shadow falls ... (Jung, 1927).

A novice, such as a primary school student, engaged with educational materials produced in Serbia and former Yugoslavia during the twentieth century (i.e. school textbooks) could easily conclude the following:

- Our people are perfect: they 'only wage just wars and therefore always win' eventually (Pešić, 1994, p. 78).

- Our current freedoms and rights are paid for in blood, by 'graves and bones of ancestors and contemporaries' (Pešić, 1994, p. 61).
- Very few women existed in history or did anything of significance.

Prior to and during wars on the former Yugoslav territory in the 1990s, such narratives were re-activated and re-interpreted. All nationalist ideologies in former Yugoslavia became intrinsically linked and 'grounded on a purposefully constructed aggressive and violent masculinity' (Papić, 1994). They helped enhance the desire for a leader who could play the 'father of the nation' role. Examples include Slobodan Milošević in Serbia, Franjo Tuđman in Croatia and A. Izetbegović in Bosnia. Women, for their part, became part of the territory to be conquered (Seifert, 1993). Rape and abuse of women followed as part of male communication in wars and a symbolic articulation of male victory or defeat (Seifert). This violence in wars was supported by certain aspects of patriarchal culture that ranged from 'mild degradation' of women, i.e. women's nonexistence as human beings, subjects of knowledge or decision makers, to extreme misogyny (Blagojević, 2000). The latter extreme misogyny in Serbian culture manifested via narratives on the 'good Serbian woman' who is either alive but silent and invisible or famous but no longer in existence/dead (Blagojević).

Once again, none of this is by accident. Patriarchal society relegates women to a private sphere and honours them not by their engagement with violence, which is reserved for men, but by their 'chastity outside marriage, and fidelity (and fertility) within marriage' (Gilligan, 2001, p. 60). While it assigns the role of 'violence-objects' to men, the role assigned to women is that of a 'sex-object,' argues James Gilligan. To this we could add a variant, the role of a beauty-object as well (Wolf, 1991). The stronger the patriarchy, the more resilient this template is. Consequently, the patriarchal mindset that is internalised by both sexes sees it as 'more 'appropriate' to kill a man than to kill a woman' (Gilligan), which is another reason why Gilligan uses the term 'violence objects' for men. It also sees as more 'logical' the demand that women renounce their 'own sexual subjectivity' (Wolf) by not having sexual wishes and activities of their own choosing except in being their husbands' sex-objects. To renounce the protection women's assigned gender role supposedly gives her from violence, a woman must either assert some sexual subjectivity of her own or enter a public sphere. It thus also comes as no surprise that occasional women who dared to speak and challenge war-making efforts during wars in former Yugoslavia – such as Belgrade's *Žene u crnom* (Women in Black) – were accused of being 'whores' (Žene u crnom, 1994, p. 16) and thus deserving of vicious threats to 'be controlled' and silenced via violence. More sinister were the destinies of many individual Bosnian women, daughters, wives and mothers of 'other men', who were turned into 'whores' by collective rapes by men from the 'other side' so that their chastity could be removed, protection from violence assigned to their gender taken away and they themselves killed. Tens of thousands of women were raped in this manner during the Yugoslav wars of the 1990s. Many of them were killed after their ordeal. Those that survived became 'damaged goods', not only psychologically but also sometimes seen as such in the eyes of their community and 'their' men.

Men, on the other hand, have most commonly been shamed for chastity, encouraged to be sexually virulent and promiscuous, to thereby further 'prove' their hegemonic masculinity. Collective rape of women during wars became a ritual of male bonding, a way to prove to other men that they indeed are sex-subjects, capable of using their sexual organ as a weapon via which their hegemonic masculinity is confirmed. Here lies the key differentiation argues James Gilligan between the social psychology of men and women within the context of a patriarchal society:

> Women are insulted not by having their courage or their capacity for sexual activity called into question, but rather, by accusations that they are too active sexually, or active outside the bounds their gender role prescribes for them (meaning exclusively in marriage): 'slut', 'whore', 'bitch', 'tramp'. ... But what is most relevant here is that women are shamed not for being too submissive, dependent, unaggressive, and sexually inactive or impotent, as men are, but rather, for exactly the opposite traits: being too rebellious, independent, aggressive, and sexually active. Thus, if a woman responds to being shamed by becoming aggressive or violent, that may only lead to more shame rather than, as for men, to less (Gilligan, 2001, p. 58).

Men thus use violence to undo the shame, while women are going to be shamed even more if they act violently. In 'extreme times', when wars and collective violence take place, a group may decide that, due to the group's overall much lower access to various mechanisms of power, it is acceptable for women to also actively participate in the execution of direct violence. Yet even then, women's access to violence is usually secondary to those of men, who remain the leaders, decision makers as well as the predominant 'meat' on the frontlines. This exception during extreme times notwithstanding, violence is a masculine prerogative in the same way that chastity is feminine (Gilligan, 2001). Being the prerogative of primarily hegemonic masculinities, violence is then 'appropriately' utilised only by 'top dogs' (Galtung, 1971). They are the men who wield political and economic power, which allows them access to decision-making, i.e., national leaders. This logic and structure does not change if an occasional woman becomes a nation-state leader; she too must demonstrate willingness to use violence to control others, to control the 'underdogs' or the 'threatening other'. Once in positions of power, both men and women are expected to exhibit the psychological qualities of hegemonic masculinity, such as mental endurance, self control, high achievement and low empathy. This phenomenon sheds some light into the behaviour of male 'fathers and leaders of the nation' as well as into the behaviour of many female influential political figures. During the Yugoslav wars, examples include political figures such as Mirjana Marković and Biljana Plavšić and their USA counterpart, Madeline Albright, a proponent of NATO military intervention. This resilience of patriarchal logic and structure also validates connections feminist theorists (i.e. Damousi & Lake, 1995; Enloe, 1993, 2000; Grant & Newland, 1991; Peterson, 1993; Pettman, 1996; Reardon, 1993) made between the gender power order and its influence on the shape, meaning and prosecution of wars and other acts of collective violence. No war has taken place without being influenced by society's gender politics. Each war has in turn influenced gender relationships. As summarised by Cook-Huffman:

> As the public sphere became a male sphere, the state also became a bearer of gender. Direct violence (rape, battery, incest), structural violence (denial of health care and education, sex segregated work and pay), and cultural violence (the ideology of the nuclear family and motherhood, notions of women's work) become the tools the state uses to keep hierarchies of dominance in place. ... The conflation of manhood, battle, militarism, and nationalism reproduces violence and exalts it as a natural expression of masculinity and the nation state (Cook-Huffman, 2010, p. 214).

Global/local social movements that aimed to transform this culture of violence, such as peace, women's and ecological social movements, thus proposed alternatives to the above, with in world-views that give more freedom to construct one's own identity, including one's own sexual and gender identity. Since hegemonic masculinity is defined by the progression from male genitalia to male identity to masculine behaviour to desiring a female partner, its shadow and threatening self is anything that breaks this chain of masculine development. This explains why homophobia is such a 'closely related source of violence' (Gilligan, 2001, p. 62) and why gay pride parades were met with such hatred in Serbia as late as 2009 and 2011, forcing organisers to cancel the planed events. There are hardly any worse insults to be thrown in the 'real' man's direction for the purpose of shaming than 'poofta' or 'faggot' (*'peder', 'pederčić'*), except maybe being called a 'sissy' or 'cunt' (*'pička', 'pizda'*). This is because the psychological worldview of patriarchy considers anything and everything constructed as 'feminine' or intrinsic to women valueless by default.

Critical to the purposes of peace building in this context of a patriarchal or dominator society, negotiation and nonviolent conflict resolution have often been equated with weakness and passivity, both seen as 'feminine qualities'. 'Real men' do not negotiate; they fight. They do not mediate; they serve justice. They do not compromise; they use violence to assert righteousness. Once again, this underlying worldview and rationale for violence is exhibited in a Serbian history textbook:

> *Moderate and peace-loving* ruler Stefan Uroš III Dečanski (1321–1331) was not captivated by conquest and his goal was to maintain the state he inherited from his father. Neighbours understood his *peacefulness as weakness*, and so Bosnia, Byzantium and Bulgaria *attacked* Serbia (Kočić, 2007, p. 135, italics added).

The message here is that those who occasionally negotiate rather than fight may in fact endanger their own people. Furthermore, the text indicates that it is important to 'realise' that 'others' are rarely to be trusted, even when they pretend to provide aid:

> Looking for a solution to a difficult situation the family of Despot Đurađ was divided; one group was suggesting migration to Ugarska, the second surrender to the mercy of the Turks or their mercilessness and the third group was arguing that they should resist [Turkish invasion] at all costs. Finally a *compromise solution* was found and the daughter of Despot Lazar married Bosnian prince Stefan Tomašević. ... However, Stefan Tomašević did not even attempt to resist the Turks, but *instead gave them* Smederevo on the 20th June, 1459. This was *the end of Serbia* as a state and the *beginning of Serbian slavery* under Turkish rule which lasted 345 years (Kočić, 2007, p. 154, italics added).

Such texts do not encourage psychological qualities such as forgiveness, empathy with others, consideration of others' needs and behaviour that demonstrates these qualities, such as compromise and resolving conflicts non-violently. Instead, they teach about the dangers of such qualities and behaviours. This is because these traits are all seen as 'feminine' or characteristic of women, the shadow self of hegemonic masculinity, and as such, like women themselves, are assigned inferior status within existing patriarchal gender power order. Not only that, traditional patriarchal cultures fear women in general, considering femininity as a 'dangerous, unpredictable and disruptive element' (Trebješanin, 2006). Thus, psychologically, while within patriarchal societies women also need to deal with the male aspect present in their collective unconscious (i.e. Jungian animus), the real pressure is mostly on men, who must transcend the female aspect (i.e. Jungian anima) if they are to be awarded status and power in a community and society. As expressed by a famous Serbian writer, Jovan Dučić (1931): 'A man rules a woman only when he rules over himself, and we rule over ourselves only when we think more than we feel.' Each and every man must thus transcend the woman within himself, i.e., his own qualities of compassion, empathy, caring and reluctance to engage in violence, as well as the capacity to be in touch with his emotions. As previously argued, the most potent method by which this is done is violence, both psychological as well as direct. A 'real' man may violate himself, such as by damaging his own body whilst engaging in competitive, risk-taking and 'toughness-showing' activities or even better, the bodies of those 'subservient others'.

The pressure on men to act violently and simultaneously appear completely composed, to always be rational, strong and brave to the point of being omnipotent, exerts a significant psychological stress on them. This is because in order to project an image of hegemonic masculinity, in addition to disowning their 'inner woman' or archetypal feminine qualities, men must also disown their inner 'vulnerable child,' which embodies their sensitivity and fear (Stone & Stone, 1993). Such repression in itself represents an example of cultural, epistemological and psychological violence that dominator societies use to maintain hierarchical social arrangements. Epistemological violence or world-views that provide a rationale for direct, structural violence and psychological violence, such as shaming those who refuse to be violent, are necessary tools in this context. They are needed for the development and enactment of hegemonic masculinity, which then consequently must validate itself via the use of direct and structural violence. Direct and structural violence, for their part, create conditions within which epistemological and psychological violence is used, and the culture of violence is thus reinforced.

Certainly, the disowning of one's inner woman is not only psychologically violent for men who must meet the ideal of hegemonic masculinity; it is also violent for women and other men over which dominance is to be exercised. Whatever is disowned, argue Hal and Sidra Stone (1993), unless it is integrated, has the potential to turn into demonic energy wherein violence against the self and the others is exercised. For why else would men use violence against women, if they indeed are passive and weak, subservient and nurturing (Cook-Huffman, 2010, p. 214)? Furthermore, if men are provided opportunities for expressing their 'natural' as well as psychological and spiritual inclinations in wars and for violence, why do veterans have such high rates of suicide and Post-Traumatic Stress Disorders, including high rates of PITS, i.e., Perpetration-Induced Traumatic Stress? All these are the shadows of hegemonic masculinity, reflections of violence against the self who cannot bear killing his own positive and peace-oriented qualities or seeing the reflection of his own demonic force in the eyes of those against whom he commits violence (Beara & Miljanović, 2006). What is even harder to bear for the self that disowns is the absence of justification for why that disowning had to be done. Consequently, if war efforts are challenged, the barrage of hostility will follow. The voice of consciousness that demands no killing is to be done has to be silenced, and the best way to silence it is to verbally and physically attack those that still vocalise it. This may explain why demands for peace by peace activists are often met with aggression and even hate. By attacking the disowned peace-oriented self, and those that still carry it, justification of violence is once again provided. And the culture of violence is thus further reinforced.

Masculinity Wars

As argued in the previous section, dominator culture does not allow women's input, language of needs and emotions or a discussion on 'feminine' (read weak, unsuccessful or dangerous) means of conflict resolution, such as negotiation, mediation and conflict avoidance. At best, it relegates them to the margins of a society. Thus prior to and during Yugoslav wars – from textbooks, to mainstream media and political discourses – hardly any pacifistic messages existed and no stories of women as actors in resolving conflicts via non-violent means were reported. Once established, this cognitive template provides a fertile ground for collective violence pedagogy and narcissistic injury or rage to take place. The resulting wars then become not so much fights over territory or ideology but violent fights over that ultimate prize – the enactment of hegemonic masculinity.

The wars over the disintegration of Yugoslavia provide numerous examples of the links between masculine identity and the use of violence. This was true not only with regard to local patriarchal societies but also in relation to the international 'diplomatic' realm of global patriarchy, which for centuries has influenced the way inter-group conflicts were commonly 'resolved'. A case in point is the 1999 bombing of Serbia and Montenegro by NATO. From the start, NATO asserted its masculinity via its connection with civilization (Blagojević, 2000; Ortner, 1974), by the strength of its military weaponry, as well as by its emotional detachment from the conflict itself. 'Individuals who operate from an ideology of supremacy are more likely to hold a range of biases, such as racism' (Woolf & Hulsizer, 2010, p. 61) or orientalism, thus also the belief in 'the white man's burden' and his responsibility to 'civilise' others. Consequently, it was people of 'the Balkans' (Todorova, 1997), who in the western media were construed as irrational, primitive and emotional, never the NATO soldier. To support such a view, the western media continuously promoted the notion that NATO soldiers and pilots were merely doing their 'jobs'. The barbaric other, (i.e. irrational and hysterical female), on the other hand, was seen to be fighting due to unresolved emotional issues, such as grief and trauma. As the social attribution theory within the field of psychology asserts, 'we' are forced to act violently because of forces beyond our control with blame ascribed to other groups or to environmental circumstances, while 'they' act violently because of their innate, personal dispositions. Examples include beliefs that 'they' are evil, aggressive, barbaric, and 'naturally' violent. It was not only western nations that used such explanations to justify their own violence and render problematic the violence of others; rather, this template was used by all sides involved in Yugoslav wars in the 1990s.

Alternative Peace-Oriented Masculinities

Previous sections have analysed some of the mechanisms by which men are encouraged or goaded to engage in violence. However the more important question is: what makes men choose pacifism *even* within the context of a dominator or warrior society?

Given that Serbian war deserters, draft evaders and conscientious objectors remain hidden from public view (Aleksov, 2001), it is hard to evaluate their own personal construction of masculinity. They too exist in the shadows of hegemonic masculinity whose escapades and violent actions while 'actors in history' have been well documented. However, some research (Milićević, 2006; Žene u crnom, 1995) as well as anecdotal evidence shows that in addition to resisting feelings of guilt and shame as well as the possibility of imprisonment for 5–20 years, those men also had to resist constructing their own gender identity as inclusive of hegemonic masculinity, which asks for fulfilment via participation in direct violence and wars. Masculinity does not seem to be the only or even the main factor in resisting participation in wars. Some deserters and draft evaders resisted because they did not buy into the particular political projects of nationalism that aimed at waging wars. Others were traumatised by previous experience in an earlier war and decided to evade the next one. Finally some had ideological or religious reasons for war avoidance. Still, all of them had to come to terms with discourses on hegemonic masculinity that construct them as 'cowards and lesser men, who hide 'under their mother's skirt' or leave the homeland altogether … who are 'faggots' and 'scumbags,' people whom a real Serbian man has to cut out from his inner circle' (Milićević, p. 281).

Participants in the non-violent youth movement, *Otpor* (Resistance), aimed at overthrowing Slobodan Milošević in 2000, mostly had to deal with accusations of being traitors, spies and 'foreign payees'. Occasionally they were also accused of being *pizd*e (cunts) (Forum B92, 2009). Interestingly enough, the masculinities male participants in *Otpor* modelled, however, were in stark contrast to the hegemonic masculinities promoted by war and violence supporters. The latter, such as embodied in the originators of certain Serbian paramilitary guards (Željko Ražnjatovic Arkan,

Vojislav Šešelj, 'Kapetan Dragan' and others), founded 'Tigers', 'White Eagles', 'Scorpions', 'Yellow Wasps' and 'Wolves,' which all symbolically connect the hegemonic masculine principle with violence, of being all that is piercing, penetrating, powerful, virulent and potentially lethal. *Otporaši* [members of *Otpor*], on the other hand, used flowers, songs, parades, dress-ups, humorous skits, graffiti, street theater, music performances, mock awards and elections, to name but a few of their methods and symbols. Their main symbol, a clenched fist, indicated unity and solidarity with the oppressed rather than the dominant, hegemonic group, as well as strength and defiance (Wiki, 2010). While they also used their own 'masculinities', the crucial point here is that they did not link them with violence. Alternative masculinities therefore do exist and it is not necessary for men to 'turn into women' in order to prevent violence. All that is needed is that the teaching women receive regarding violence as the undesirable method for conflict resolution, be extended to the male gender as well. This already is the case in certain families, groups and societies who teach boys directly and indirectly to solve conflicts using non-violent strategies. Thus, despite hegemonic masculinities' totalising tendencies in our contemporary world, it is possible for each and every individual male to resist the world-view propagated within patriarchal societies and construct his masculine identity without the need to prove his manhood through violence. Most significantly, Serbian Otporaši, war resisters and non-violent protesters, unlike Serbian hyper-masculine volunteer and official army units, engaged in partnership with women during this struggle. As their acts of resistance often embraced feminine principles of support, caring and empathy with others, perhaps they even embraced the woman within themselves. Instead of 'disowning,' a psychological process of integration (Stone & Stone, 1993) took place, even though this was most likely done unconsciously.

Very recently some new initiatives, such as a club for young teenage men called *Budi Muško* [Be a Man] focused on consciously redefining what comprised the desired Serbian masculinity. Reframing the dominant discourse on masculinity away from its association with violence is crucially important for all societies, but especially for post-conflict ones. According to the *Budi Muško* club (2010), 'a real man' is: 'not violent, respects girls and is sexually responsible'. Many other positive and creative ideas on what a 'real man' is are discussed in their projects, in schools and at workshops. The club also works in close partnership with women and girls.

Alternatives to violent masculinities therefore do exist. In fact as the literature on peaceful societies shows (i.e. Bonta, 1996; Boulding, 2000; Eisler, 2000; Kelleher, 2010; Lawlor, 1991), they have always existed. Alternative world-views within peaceful societies are underpinned by spiritual, philosophical and cognitive templates that consider violence as harmful, unnecessary and detrimental, rather than as arising from 'human nature', unavoidable and even moral. These alternative world-views reject the story about 'good violence' and 'bad violence'; that violence is justifiable in 'some cases'. Most importantly, normative masculinity is not defined via the use or the right to use 'good' violence. Furthermore, in more egalitarian societies, i.e., many traditional, peaceful societies, differentiation between masculinity and femininity is not imagined in hierarchical terms. Crucially, aggression and violence are not automatically connected with maleness; on the other hand, angry persons and warring neighbours are perceived in negative terms and as negative role models (Kelleher; Boulding). Both boys and girls are raised with values of nurturance, harmony, self-restraint, cooperation, sharing and generosity, fair and mutual exchange (i.e. ceremonial gift giving); and all these values are integrated within a world-view and cosmology that focuses on the interconnectedness of all life (Bonta; Boulding).

In terms of Buddhist psychology, the hierarchies and 'othering' promoted by patriarchal societies via hegemonic masculinity are all part of a collective delusion that fails to recognise interdependence and inter-connectedness as the ultimate nature of reality. Violence is to behaviour what paranoia is to thoughts, argues Gilligan:

> Violence is the behavioral equivalent of paranoia, the acting out of the core delusion that other people are dangerous to oneself and that one can only defend oneself by attacking or even killing them. ... Homophobia, patriarchal or 'sexist' attitude (with a devaluation of everything 'female' and an over-valuation of everything 'masculine'), [are] a defensive exaggeration of the male gender role, in the form of a kind of hyper-masculinity or 'machismo', and [via] the constant threat or reality of violence... (2001, pp. 64–65).

Thus in psychological terms, hegemonic masculinities, as expressed in dominator, patriarchal, warrior cultures, are *dysfunctional* despite their representing the norm. Judging by the consequences to the physical and emotional health of all involved, dominant men as well as the men and women they dominate, they are dysfunctional in socio-psychological terms. Hegemonic masculinities are also dysfunctional in purely psychological terms, because they exhibit many elements of distorted thinking patterns, as outlined within cognitive therapy approaches:

- *All* women are inferior and everything connected with femininity is potentially dangerous to masculinity (overgeneralisation).
- Masculinities and everything they stand for are desirable and awe-inspiring while femininity is exactly the opposite (magnifying and minimising).
- All men should think and behave like 'real men' at all times (overgeneralising and 'shoulds').
- By letting go of violence and the military, we won't be able to defend ourselves because 'violent others' will attack us (catastrophising, filtering, mind-reading).
- People are either good or bad, depending on whether they are part of our group or one of 'them'; you are either a hyper masculine man or no man at all (polarized thinking).

The transformation of these hegemonic masculinities and the logic behind them, as well as the creation and enhancement of gender partnership in families and societies, seems a logical prerequisite for the prevention of direct, structural and cultural violence and for the creation of global and local peace cultures. Crucially, all cultures, including extreme dominator cultures, have had alternative stories that promote peace-oriented masculinities.

For the sake of creating peace in all its forms and at all levels, it is imperative to strengthen these alternative practices, worldviews and discourses on nonviolent masculinities, in Serbia and beyond.

Conclusion

Even though gender does not stand alone in determining one's identity but exists in 'a complex relationship with other identity markers, including age, race, religion, ethnicity, language group, caste, class and sexuality, which can exacerbate inequality and vulnerability to violence or mitigate them' (McInturff, 2010, p. 223), gender still 'profoundly affects the likelihood that an individual will participate in a violent act, or be the subject of a violent act' (McInturff, p. 222). Gender also has an impact in determining the type of violence to which a particular individual will be subjected (McInturff). At the group level, it influences the rationale and meaning behind the enactment of acts of collective violence. Much has been written about ethnic and religious identity markers that were part of the overall 'propaganda system' (Stojanović, 1994, p. 109), which has made wars on the territory of former Yugoslavia 'psychologically possible' (Stojanović). The role of gender has too often been neglected except when specifically dealing with gender-based violence, i.e., violence against women in general and during times of war in particular.

This chapter suggested a critical link between a particularly imagined, socially constructed, hegemonic masculinity and physical violence (in Serbia, former Yugoslavia and beyond, that is, within patriarchal/dominator societies). It investigated various psychological mechanisms behind creation of gendered group identities, specifically the ways by which hegemonic masculinities are linked with violence. Lastly, it described alternative masculinities that sever the link between manhood and violence, asking that they be encouraged and further enhanced. This should be done so that the detrimental and dysfunctional hegemonic masculinities, as imagined within patriarchal/dominator societies, can be further weakened and hopefully eventually transcended.

References

Aleksov, B. (2001). *Resisting the war in Yugoslavia: Thoughts on empowerment and disillusionment.* Retrieved July 22, 2010, from http://www.wri-irg.org/nonviolence/nvse09-en.htm.

Barash, D. P., & Webel, C. P. (2002). *Peace and conflict studies.* London: Sage.

Beara, V., & Miljanović, P. (2006). *Oh where have you been, my blue-eyed son? An existentialistic contribution to the understanding of war trauma and PTSD.* Novi Sad, Serbia: Association for mental health protection of war veterans and victims of wars 1991–1999.

Blagojević, M. (2000). Patriotizam i mizoginija: mit o srpskoj muškosti (Patriotismand misogyny: Myth of Serbian masculinity). In M. Blagojević (Ed.), *Mapiranje mizoginije u Srbiji: diskursi i prakse (Mapping misogyny in Serbia: Discourses and practices)* (pp. 281–310). Belgrade, Serbia: AZIN.

Bonta, B. D. (1996). Conflict resolution among peaceful societies: The culture of peacefulness. *Journal of Peace Research, 4*, 403–420.

Boulding, E. (2000). *Cultures of peace: The hidden side of history.* Syracuse, NY: Syracuse University Press.

Brock-Utne, B. (2010). Gender, socialization, and militarism. In *The Oxford international encyclopedia of peace* (1st ed., Vol. 2, pp. 207–211). Oxford: Oxford University Press.

Budi Muško Club. (2010). Retrieved July 22, 2010, from http://www.budimusko.org/.
Butler, J. (1990). *Gender trouble: Feminism and the subversion of identity (subversive bodily acts, IV bodily inscriptions, performative subversions)*. New York: Routledge.
Connell, R. W. (2005). Hegemonic masculinity: Rethinking the concept. *Gender and Society, 6*, 829–859.
Cook-Huffman, C. (2010). Gender and conflict. In *The Oxford international encyclopedia of peace* (1st ed., Vol. 2, pp. 211–215). Oxford: Oxford University Press.
Damousi, J., & Lake, M. (Eds.). (1995). *Gender and war: Australians at war in the twentieth century*. Cambridge: Cambridge University Press.
Dučić, J. (1931). Blago Cara Radovana. Beograd.
Eisler, R. (2000). *Tomorrow's children: A blueprint for partnership education in the 21st century*. Boulder, CO: Westview Press.
Enloe, C. (1993). *The morning after: Sexual politics at the end of the cold war*. Berkeley, CA: University of California Press.
Enloe, C. (2000). *Manoeuvres: The international politics of militarizing women's lives*. Berkeley, CA: University of California Press.
Forum B92. (2009). *Gay Parada 2009*. Retrieved July 20, 2010 from http://forum.b92.net/index.php?s=d295759d6a16db031cc4df2d9380e983&showtopic=50864&st=2085&p=2452190&#entry2452190.
Freud, S. (1913). *Totem and taboo: Some points of agreement between the mental lives of savages and neurotics*. London: Hogarth Press.
Galtung, J. (1971). Structural and direct violence: A note on operationalization. *Journal of Peace Research, 1*, 73–76.
Galtung, J. (2009). Women and men, peace and security. *European Commission speech – Making the difference: Strengthening the capacities to respond to crises and security threats*, Brussels, May 3, 2009. Retrieved April 7, 2010 from http://www.peaceactionme.org/blog/johan-galtung-s-view-europe-women-and-men-peace-and-security.
Gilligan, J. (2001). *Preventing violence*. New York: Thames and Hudson.
Grant, R., & Newland, K. (Eds.). (1991). *Gender and international relations*. Milton Keynes: Open University Press.
Jung, C. (1927). Woman in Europe. In S. H. Read, M. Fordham, & G. Adler (Eds.) (1964), *Civilization in transition* (pp. 113–133). London: Routledge & Kegan Paul.
Kelleher, W. F. (2010). Peaceful societies. In *The Oxford international encyclopedia of peace* (1st ed., Vol. 3, pp. 382–384). Oxford: Oxford University Press.
Kočić, D. (2007). *Istorija: za I razred srednjih stručnih škola (History: For I grade of specialist high schools)*. Beograd: Zavod za udžbenike.
Lake, M. (1992). Mission impossible: How men gave birth to the Australian nation – nationalism, gender and other seminal acts. *Gender and History, 4*, 305–332.
Lawlor, R. (1991). *Voices of the first day: Awakening in the aboriginal dreamtime*. Rochester, VT: Inner Traditions International.
McInturff, K. (2010). Gender and violence. In *The Oxford international encyclopedia of peace* (1st ed., Vol. 2, pp. 222–226). Oxford: Oxford University Press.
Milićević, A. S. (2006). Joining the war: Masculinity, nationalism and war participation in the Balkans war of secession, 1991–1995. *Nationalities Papers, 3*, 265–287.
Milojević, I. (2006). Collective violence pedagogy and the neohumanist peace-oriented response. In S. Inayatullah, M. Bussey, & I. Milojević (Eds.), *Neohumanist educational futures: Liberating the pedagogical intellect* (pp. 146–167). Taipei, Taiwan: Tamkang University Press.
Milojević, I., & Markov, S. (2008). Gender, militarism and the view of the future: Students' views on the introduction of the civilian service in Serbia. *Journal of Peace Education, 2*, 175–191.
Ortner, S. (1974). Is female to male as nature is to culture? In M. Z. Rosaldo & L. Lamphere (Eds.), *Woman, culture and society* (pp. 67–87). Stanford, CA: Stanford University Press.
Paige, G. D. (2002). *Nonkilling global political science*. Honolulu, HI: Center for Global Nonviolence.

Papić, Ž. (1994). Nationalism, patriarchy and war in ex-Yugoslavia. *Women's History Review, 1*(1994), 115–117.

Pešić, V. (1994). Bellicose virtues in elementary school readers. In V. Pešić & R. Rosandić (Eds.), *Warfare, patriotism, patriarchy: The analysis of elementary school textbooks* (pp. 59–80). Belgrade, Serbia: Centre for Anti-War Action, Association MOST.

Peterson, V. S. (Ed.). (1993). *Gendered states: Feminist (re)visions of international relations theory*. Boulder, CO: Lynne Rienner Publishers.

Pettman, J. J. (1996). *Worlding women: A feminist international politics*. London: Routledge.

Reardon, B. (1993). *Women and peace: Feminist visions of global security*. Albany, NY: State University of New York Press.

Seifert, R. (1993). Krieg and Vergewaltigung. Ansätze zu einer Analyse. In A. Stiglmayer (Ed.), *Massenvergewaltigung. Krieg gegen die frauen* (Vol. 1, pp. 37–48), Franfurt am Main. Translated to Serbo-Croatian as Rat i silovanje (War and rape), *Feminističke sveske* (Feminist notebooks), Beograd: Ženski Centar.

Stojanović, D. (1994). History text-books mirror their time. In V. Pešić & R. Rosandić (Eds.), *Warfare, patriotism, patriarchy: The analysis of elementary school textbooks* (pp. 81–110). Belgrade, Serbia: Centre for Anti-War Action, Association MOST.

Stone, H., & Stone, S. (1993). *Embracing our selves: The voice dialogue training manual*. Mill Valey, CA: Nataraj Publishing.

Todorova, M. (1997). *Imagining the Balkans*. Oxford: Oxford University Press.

Trebješanin, Ž. (2006). Stereotip o ženi u srpskoj kulturi. Centar za informativnu dekontaminaciju Banja Luka. Retrieved June 10, 2010, from http://magazin.6yka.com/print/282.

Warters, W. (2010). Male violence, unlearning of. In *The Oxford international encyclopedia of peace* (1st ed., Vol. 2, pp. 659–660). Oxford: Oxford University Press.

Wiki. (2010). Otpor. Retrieved on July 20, 2010, from http://en.wikipedia.org/wiki/Otpor!

Wolf, N. (1991). *The beauty myth: How images of beauty are used against women*. New York: Anchor Books.

Woolf, L. M., & Hulsizer, M. R. (2010). Social-psychological approaches to peace. In *The Oxford international encyclopedia of peace* (1st ed., Vol. 4, pp. 60–64). Oxford: Oxford University Press.

Žene u crnom. (1994). *Žene za mir*. Beograd: Žene u crnom.

Žene u crnom. (1995). *War deserters in the former Yugoslavia: A compilation*. Beograd: Žene u crnom.

Chapter 5
Making or Breaking the Peace: The Role of Schools in Inter-Ethnic Peace Making

W. Duffie VanBalkom and Mirjana Beara

Abstract This chapter discusses the role that schools play in mitigating inter-ethnic tensions, with special reference to the Balkan conflicts (1991–1999), and the decade of fragile re-integration that followed them. The paper explores the role education can play in creating the conditions for inter-ethnic conflict; the responsibility of schools as places of reason, comfort and stability during the conflict; and the place of curriculum and pedagogy in either reproducing or reframing the narratives and myths that can lead to inter-ethnic peace making or trans-generational reproduction of the conditions for further conflict. The paper draws on relevant peace- and social psychology concepts such as ethnic distance, segregation and discrimination, negative and positive peace, stress coping strategies, and child psychology concepts to explain the power of school -sanctioned narratives in explaining ethnicity and conflict to children of impressionable age. Multi-ethnic primary schools in the former Yugoslavia are used to provide the historical context of episodic and structural violence and peace building attempts, for this conceptual paper.

Keywords Inter-ethnic conflict • School narratives • Peace psychology • Conflict reproduction

---

W.D. VanBalkom (✉)
University of Calgary, 2500 University Drive NW, Calgary, AB, Canada
e-mail: vanbalk@ucalgary.ca

M. Beara
Rumenacka 130/22, 21000 Novi Sad, Serbia
e-mail: mirjana.beara@gmail.com

O. Simić et al. (eds.), *Peace Psychology in the Balkans: Dealing with a Violent Past while Building Peace*, Peace Psychology Book Series, DOI 10.1007/978-1-4614-1948-8_5,

Introduction

This chapter discusses the role that schools play in mitigating inter-ethnic tensions, with special reference to the conflicts (1991–1999) in the former Yugoslavia, and the decade of fragile re-integration that followed them.[1] We explore the role education can play in creating the conditions for inter-ethnic conflict; the responsibility of schools as places of reason, comfort and stability during the conflict; and, perhaps most importantly, the place of curriculum and pedagogy in either reproducing or reframing the narratives and myths that can lead to inter-ethnic peace making or trans-generational reproduction of the conditions for further conflict.

With the exception of family, children normally spend more time at school than in any other institution. Principals and teachers are respected role models, and their opinions count. In times of war or other calamities, the mere functioning of a school provides a certain stability and hope. Hence, *the way* schools and educators present different ethnic groups, and explain inter-ethnic relations, and encourage peaceful co-existence, have an important bearing on the ability of children to construct peace in their lives.

A considerable body of literature exists on children and youth after conflict, but little on the influence of the school experience on peace or inter-generational reproduction of the conditions of war. Much of the relevant peace- and social psychology literature draws, understandable and appropriately, on psychological concepts such as ethnic distance, segregation and discrimination, negative and positive peace, stress, coping strategies, and resiliency, socialization, and the broad realm of developmental psychology. We want to draw attention to the powerful potential of schools, as unique psycho-social "spaces" in fostering inter-ethnic peace making. Schools exercises this influence through curriculum, pedagogical practices, role-modelling, educational policy, interaction with parents and the larger community, and the school-sanctioned narratives in explaining ethnicity and conflict to children of impressionable age.

Schools as Socialization Space

"No institution has, by law, such complete and prolonged access to impressionable minds at a young age as public education has. Education is never value-free." (VanBalkom, 2010, p. 1). During times of war, children are particularly vulnerable and teachers can provide a nurturing and supportive "home away from home", where children can, albeit temporarily, find a semblance of peace and security. *The way* in

[1] We draw on our study of teacher narratives about conflict and other ethnic groups, and gratefully acknowledge the generous support of the Social Sciences & Humanities Research Council of Canada for this multidisciplinary research in three jurisdictions of the Former Yugoslavia: Serbia, Bosnia and Herzegovina, and Kosovo.

which schools and educators present different ethnic groups, explain inter-ethnic relations, and encourage peaceful co-existence, have an important bearing on the ability of children to construct peace in their lives, before, during and after conflict.

Schools are vulnerable to political influence, even in peaceful times. In pre-conflict Yugoslavia, for example, schools commonly "cooperated" with prescribed and formalized social and political events such as political manifestations, obligatory school visits that glorified tragic historic events, or cultural events that endorsed a communist ideology. In the years preceding the conflict, schools started to resist those formalized and imposed ways of exchange with their social environment (Radovanović, 1997). Being able to "open" and "close" these boundaries with political and social contexts, allowed schools some limited autonomy to embrace or resist political coercion through their structures, policies, curriculum and particularly their pedagogy.

While much has been written about the role of education in reproducing culture and social order, little attention has been paid to the role of schools in conflict. On the one hand, particularly in developing country contexts, education is a valued ticket to prosperity. On the other, it is viewed as an instrument of the State, used to reproduce the existing social strata and the conditions of inequality, through differentiated access, quality, curricula and pedagogy (Freire, 1972). Education can play a key role in preventing conflict and building peace, but also may be deliberately (ab)used in conflict situation (Tomlinson & Benefield, 2005). The critical tasks of education in fragile states has been recently articulated (Rose & Greeley, 2006) but we know little about the pivotal role schools play in starting conflict, and the subtle and not so subtle role they can play during conflict and after war in either reproducing the conditions for further conflict or supporting a process of healing and reconciliation (Smith & Vaux, 2002; Spink, 2005).

Schools play a key role in reproducing mainstream national culture and oppressing minority culture and aspirations. The treatment of North America's aboriginal populations in government imposed residential schools attests both to the damage schools can inflict upon children and the power of inter-generational reproduction of oppression and conflict. At the same time, schools also play a role in strengthening the resilience of people to carry on and keep a cultural spirit alive, despite attempts at forced integration. In South Africa, for example, nine parallel education systems assured the apartheid system of privilege was maintained, but much of the confidence for the anti-apartheid struggle was also born in the schools (VanBalkom & Ncgongo, 1998). Education was at times a subversive activity, with teachers planting the seeds of resistance in subtle or not so subtle ways. During the anti-apartheid conflict, teachers and particularly principals were also targeted as representatives of state oppression, and sometimes chased away from their schools by newly empowered and self-assured pupils.

During periods of inter-ethnic conflict and civil war, when neighbourhoods and families are torn apart, schools can be nurturing places of security and relative stability for children. However, education is never value-free. Schools, through their structures, policies, curriculum and pedagogy, can offer a moderated view of the conflict and "the others" or feed the fears and hatreds that habitually accompany such conflict. Research indicates that children form conceptions of war and peace at an early age (Hakvoort, 1996; Raviv, Oppenheimer & Bar-Tal, 1999). While these conceptions are generally simplistic, and ready to be further shaped by influential adults, significant findings of Cooper (1965), and subsequently of Alvik (1968) and Hakvoort (1996), indicate that children's ability to articulate issues of war precedes their verbalization of peace, and the latter is often simply seen as an absence of war, rather than a proactive cooperation of community relations. To frame this in a positive way, schools need to examine the role they play in creating the context and processes for "children [to] assimilate the concepts and acquire the attitudes and values, associated with a culture of peace." (Schwebel, 2001).

After conflict, primary attention is paid to rebuilding education infrastructure and addressing urgent gaps in teacher education, text books and other material needs. With much of the State structures in tatters, NGOs often fulfill important gaps working on various peace-building and reconciliation initiatives, including those with youth, but only recently has research been conducted on the central role of schools in the conflict cycle (Kirk, 2007; Seitz, 2004), critical for post-conflict peace building (World Bank, 2005; USAID, 2005a, 2005b). The European Commission for Education (2000) has provided a number of quality indicators to guide young people to become effective citizens, and the role of schools in building peaceful civic cultures is seen as a catalyst to this process.

National Identity and Inter-Ethnic Conflict

The former Yugoslavia is situated in an exceedingly complex part of the world. Winston Churchill is credited with the observation that the Balkans "produce more history than they can consume". It has been an intermittently violent history since human settlement in pre-Roman times. While charismatic leaders such as Tito were able to temporarily impose a "peace of sorts" on the underlying ethnic tensions, a lack of political will has perpetuated the divergence of ethnic-nationalist narratives that reproduce the conditions for repeated conflict. Druckman (2001) makes the case that nationalist feelings may well be unstable dispositions that can be aroused, and that the conditions which influence group membership "can be manipulated by groups or their leaders to produce the 'desired' behaviour" (p. 51).

In post-WW II Yugoslavia, the creation of an "*official* memory of the war was central to the formation of a trans-national Yugoslav identity" (Keene, 2001, p. 242). While individuals' could formally identify themselves as Serb, Croat, Muslim, Macedonian, etc. in education registrations and the census surveys of the Socialist Federative Republic of Yugoslavia, explicit expressions of ethnic identity were diminished and discouraged in favour of developing a common Yugoslav identity. It certainly was forbidden to speak publicly about the inter-ethnic conflicts and previously committed atrocities, especially those "committed by the partisans that had been led by Tito" (Agger, 2001, p. 11). Similarly, while religious customs and practice were not explicitly prohibited, they were for every "good communist" unacceptable.

As ethnicity and religion are closely aligned in the region, this further dampened any overt expression of ethnicity. Increasingly, patriotic citizens would *publicly* identify themselves as Yugoslavs, despite a conflicting, *private* ethno-national identity that was nourished within the family. Particularly those of mixed ethnic marriages/families, but also other "patriotic" citizens and loyal communists, found comfort in the inclusiveness of the Yugoslav identity. While embracing the Yugoslav identity was encouraged and praised in schools, as Tajfel's Social Identity Theory suggests, increased self esteem, particularly important to school age children, is supported by the ability to view one's own group as better than another (Tajfel, 1982). Certainly children continued to perceive important differences, despite the official, common Yugoslav identity: "For years, all the ethnic groups lived in peace, but you could always tell by the height of the hedges between properties how neighbours were related: No fence, if they were family, small hedges if the neighbor was also Albanian and a bit higher fence if the neighbors were Serbs." (Teacher, Kosovo; reflecting on growing up in rural Kosovo).

As the process of disintegration started, in the beginning of 1990s, republics of "constitutive nations" aimed to gain their independence as nations and consequently "actively obliterated the national memory of multiethnic Yugoslavia" (Keene, 2001, p. 242). "These developments both facilitated and necessitated a reassessment of the now independent nations' history, orientation, symbols and identity" (Kanet, 2007, p. 407), and official narratives and reassessment of what constituted (desirable) citizenship. The suppressed memories of previous tensions and atrocities were "defrosted, and began emanating" negative emotions that had been kept dormant by a policy of taboo and repression during the previous 50 years (Agger, 2001, p.11). Political leaders encouraged members of the majority ethnic group in each republic to identify stronger with their ethnic identity, playing the "two psychological needs' cards" of Kelman's (1988) "dichotomy of a need for self-protection, and a need for self-transcendence" (in Druckman, 2001, p. 50). Thus, political and military leaders were able to exploit an inner conflict between a need for personal security, afforded by one's ethnic group in harmony with others, and an appeal to one's obligations to the greater cause of defending nationhood against the forces that were trying to destroy it. As people struggled to sort out their moral obligations and dual identities (Yugoslav and ethnic), national leaders capitalized on the growing difficulties to live anywhere, except among one's ethnic majority.

Ethnic identity rose quickly in importance, as "nationality" and religion determined citizenship with all rights thereof, or a *persona non grata* status in the nascent nation states. According to Turner's theory of self-categorization, "people evaluate their own group as superior only when they can clearly see differences between members of their own and other groups." (Druckman, 2001, p. 54). These dissimilarities can be real (eg. religious differences) or distorted and fabricated. As the conflict in the former Yugoslavia progressed, stereotypical attitudes towards others became more pronounced and accepted, even encouraged by political elite, and discrimination against those who were not "of right ethnicity" found expression in job firings, being refused services, verbal and physical aggression, and isolation. This resulted in mass exodus to "motherlands" of ex-Yugoslavia. Serbs from Croatia and Bosnia fled to Serbia, Croats from Serbia and Bosnia took refuge in Croatia, Albanians from Kosovo fled to Albania, etc.

Bosnia-Herzegovina was particularly complex as the territory was not as clearly associated with an ethnic majority, and many so-called Muslims (now Bosniaks), were forced to stay in war afflicted zones, flee to North America or Western Europe, or find refuge in regions of other republics/emerging states, largely inhabited by Muslim citizens, such as the Sandzak region in Serbia and Montenegro. It became very important to recognize to "which flock one belonged" and to find a majority people of the same flock to join quickly. "Mixed marriages represented the most radical negation of the ideology of ethnic purity and ethnic cleansing" (Agger, 2001, p. 8). Therefore, they became "unacceptable" for new nationalistic states. It is estimated that large percentage of refugees that took refuge in the USA and Western Europe were from mixed marriages. Nationalism, provided not only a basic sense of belonging, but also became a source of security. Mutual fear and group polarization steadily grew in strength, and the protection of one's own ethnic group became essential for survival.

Narratives of people about their history and identities, and therefore their justifications (or attempts to explain) of what was happening, followed this trend. They shifted from transnational narratives, including partisan myths about the "attainment of the revolution" and "the brotherhood – unity of nations and nationalities" to more narrow, ethnic-national narratives. A shift took place from the official unity story, enforced by communist ideology, to the narrow and ethno-specific political, nationalistic and religious narratives, whose saplings were kept alive in secret in the discourse of families and trusted ethnic circles. National narratives started to emerge, which were supported by survivors' memories of "ethnic cleansing" and atrocities that took place in WWII, or much earlier in history, at the hands of neighbors and former "friends" of a different ethnic nationality.

Education, Curriculum and Conflict

Education always has a fundamental role to play in identity formation, but we emphasize the particular complexity of this process, in the former Yugoslavia and the subsequent formation of a number of multi-ethnic states. Collective memories, if unmitigated by sustained efforts to explore a deeper understanding about a conflict and its alternatives, will stay alive for a long time. Taylor (1998) speculates that Serbs children's memories about World War II atrocities perpetrated by the Croats, fed a desire for revenge in the conflict nearly 50 years later. Such sustained memories undoubtedly gave rise to narrative constructions that supported an ethnonational basis for inner group cohesion and a sense of victimhood. Cairns (1996) observes that family, schools and history books have an influence on the politicalization of children, in subtle ways, and that during political conflict families unite in their ideological and political fight against a common enemy. Public schooling offers the primary vehicle to influence the thinking that can support identity formation, including the development of nationalist (as opposed to patriotic) sentiments.

The shifts in Yugoslavia's national history curricula are particularly illustrative. Before the conflict they reflected a surprising consistency in articulating 'official narratives' about the justified partisan 'defensive war against the occupiers and domestic traitors', despite the relative autonomy that each Republic had in defining their curricula. The post-war rebuilding of the country, marked heavily with the personal cult of Josip Broz Tito and communist ideology, featured prominently. This ideology wasn't universally accepted, particularly by some intellectuals, and criticism wasn't without its risks, but by and large, the general population accepted as inevitable that the history taught in schools did not necessarily reflect their lived experiences.

That official history was "adjusted" on a number of occasions to accommodate the geopolitical changes, as were other curricula such as geography and language courses. In the 1990s, for example, one of the stated goals of the Serbo-Croatian language and literature in Serbia the "development and nourishment of positive attitudes towards languages and the cultural heritage of nations and national minorities of Yugoslavia, and to strengthen the conscience about their destined interconnections, need of cooperation and joint life in SFRY" (Prosvetni glasnik, 1990). In 1993, however, each jurisdiction claimed the previously common language as its own, teaching Serbian, Croatian, or Bosnian, emphasizing differences where it could and no longer focusing on mutual interdependence and collaboration.

Since the conflict, the now independent nations have all re-written their curricula, effectively "cleansing" it from cultural influences from others of the defunct Yugoslav federation. Whereas the rich literary and scientific contributions of authors from all the republics, including translated works from minority authors, were previously celebrated most of these were gradually removed in favour of "national authors". Thus, in addition to people refugees, cultural refugees have emerged, as poems, stories, novels, and songs of others have been cleansed from the curriculum. It was not easy for education authorities in any of the jurisdictions to keep up with the political correctness of the moment, and the Serbian Ministry issued more than 20 consecutive curriculum changes in the decade and a half after the start of the conflict.

Education lies at the heart of ethnic segregation (Fisher, 2006) and repeated inter-generational conflict throughout the region. The Kosovo war, for example, can be traced directly to the change in policy that made education in the Albanian mother tongue illegal. In response, the Albanian majority created a parallel system of education, financially sponsored in part from abroad and by volunteer teachers, that marked the beginning of a violent separation from Serbia (VanBalkom & Buleshkaj, 2005). What precise role educational institutions play in solving, masking or perpetuating inter-ethnic conflict has not been widely researched. While education remains a source of tension, local school authorities try to respond to the needs of children from different ethnic origins and to the shifting directives, particularly with regards to such contentious issues as history, geography curriculum and language of instruction, from Ministries of Education in their respective jurisdictions. Further consideration might be given to the development of peace "as a pattern of active cooperation, ...[with] implications for curriculum construction and for the preparation of textbooks" (Alvik, 1968, p. 189).

Zgaga (2001) point to the centre-periphery power struggles over curriculum. Bosnia and Herzegovina differs substantially from Serbia, in this respect, with the former being highly decentralized and struggling with a lack of uniformity, while the latter's highly centralized structure undermines local decision making, innovation and local relevance. All jurisdictions have recognized the importance of finding the right balance in centre-periphery decision making and are attempting to build appropriate capacities to achieve it.

Sometimes the response to inter-ethnic tensions includes purposeful segregation, perceived as a means to keep these tensions manageable, as is the case with Serbian schools in Kosovo and the common "two schools under one roof" in Bosnia and Herzegovina, in which Bosniak and Croat students "share" a school in different shifts.

Most schools in the region are, however, multi-ethnic in nature, providing education to two or more distinct ethnic communities. As a result of the conflicts, internally displaced persons and refugees, and a resettlement process that is still in progress, the ethnic composition of these schools and ethnic power hierarchy has continually shifted during the last two decades. Additional sources of friction, such as new-comers vs old timers, religion and gender have made the situation exceedingly complex (Kirk, 2007). Despite these challenges, the different ethnic backgrounds of students and their family culture, language and identity need to be positively acknowledged as a prerequisite to social and physical peace (Trnavčevič, 2007), and teachers need to cooperate across different jurisdictions to achieve a welcoming and democratic education system in South-east Europe (Zgaga, 2006). Relatively recent research in Serbia, indicates that, even after the conflict, teachers are indeed interested in horizontal (peer) learning with colleagues from the ex-Yugoslav republics of Slovenia (14.4%) and Croatia (10.3%), on the basis of a shared culture, history, and language (Beara, 2009).

Education plays a role in identity construction, impacted by school cultures of ethnic intolerance, violence and nationalism (Davies, 2004; Kirk, 2007). During the conflict, children endured unprecedented stress, including forced moves, discrimination, violence, uncertainty about family members at the front, bombings, shortages of essential goods, and loosing loved ones to the war. Schools are often a first response to these stresses and a source of explanation or meaning-making in the prevailing madness. However, teachers are themselves under similar stress, and have little professional training or experience in responding to the myriad of ways traumatic stress may manifest itself in the lives of their pupils:

> My school was located between the Army barracks and a military storage facility. The NATO bombardment started on March 24th and lasted until May 31st. During this time, children mostly stayed home, but teachers were obliged to be at school. Being in-between two main targets, we lived in daily fear. The bombings had blown out all the school windows and the roof was damaged. On the last day of the bombing campaign, the residential building across the schoolyard was hit and 13 people died. My sister was hurt, but survived. It's hard to concentrate on teaching with all that going on *(Teacher, Novi Pazar, Serbia).*

When teachers are ill prepared for addressing such complex issues in ways that comfort children, can be understood by them, and are un-biased, their best intentions may still produce negative consequences. Simplistic, unexamined responses may, inadvertently or purposefully, exacerbate inter-ethnic conflict.

Teachers are also not altogether free in the way they respond to these emerging and shifting challenges. During times of war, education systems, state-controlled media, the economic policy levers and other tools at the disposal of the State join in the support of the pervasive military and political agenda. Thus, the conflict years in the former Yugoslavia saw frequent policy changes on such potentially explosive issues as language of instruction, minority student integration and teacher compensation. Frequent curriculum changes, particularly with regards to the selective re-writing of the history, geography and citizenship curricula (Low-Beer, 2001) also marked the period of (post) conflict, with implications for inter-ethnic relations, ethnicity-based self esteem issues and the creation of new, but perhaps divisive, ethno-centric narratives.

Some of these changes merely tried to keep up with real geographical changes such as shifting borders, ethnic migrations etc. while others were of a political nature, attempting to advance a particular explanation of the causes of the conflict. For example, in 1995, the geography curriculum for eighth grade of primary schools in Serbia provided a short overview of the recent the SFRY disintegration. Teachers were instructed to explain both the "inner and external factors" that caused Yugoslavia's disintegration. (Milošević, 1995, pp. 8–9). The former included natural and artificial borders, as well as "ethnical and non-ethnical" borders. The latter, included a discussion about the appropriate aims of population politics. These might stem the skewed population growth due to a "demographical explosion" in the southern regions of Kosovo and the Raska region (which have a majority Muslim population), in contrast with the "white plague" (low birthrate) in the northern region of Vojvodina and in Central Serbia (which have Serb majorities). Children were to understand that positive population politics are "to decrease the birthrate in regions of high birthrate and to increase the same (by promoting families with at least three children) in depopulated regions" (Milosevic).

As instruments of the State, schools will continue to be ideally positioned to further the interest of the elite, to emphasize a particular historic perspective and to perpetuate a general belief system, "demonizing enemies, idealizing the self, and avoiding realistic empathy" (White, 2000, p. 52). Notwithstanding the State-initiated changes in policies and curricula, the specific and nuanced *implementation* of these at the local level is of paramount importance in mitigating inter-ethnic tensions at the school and, by extension, the local community. In particular, how do teachers and school principals *talk* about different ethnic groups and about the conflict? How are conflicts in class or on the play ground understood and resolved? How do the narratives shed light on the central role schools play in shaping children's perceptions of self, their ethnic group and the way they map out a peaceful life for themselves within the multi-ethnic community? How teachers explain "the other" and inter-ethnic conflict to children is of great importance in breaking an intergenerational conflict cycle. These personal narratives hold great promise for deeper understanding and reconciliation, despite dominant, ethno-nationalist alternative versions of truth (Dudouet, Fisher & Smelze, 2008; Franovic, 2008).

The Place of Schools in Creating a Preferred Future

More than 40 years ago, Hare and Blumberg (1977) already advocated that, if peace education is to make a difference in fostering non-violence, education should be broadly understood, beyond the limits of formal schooling, to including learning in all its dimensions. Peace education, important as it may be for both reconciliation and prevention, is primarily cast as another 'subject', often subsumed within existing curriculum structures such as 'citizenship education' or even 'religious education'.

While these efforts, generally, aren't harmful, they miss the bigger picture: by relegating peace to a defined timeslot in the curriculum, we miss the important integrative function of values. Peace is an important subject for psychologists, political scientists and other intellectuals to study, but if education is meant to make a practical difference in fostering peaceful co-existence, children must learn that peace is a way of *feeling, valuing, being and doing.* The praxis of peace education calls for the creation of purposeful lived experiences, and for the spirit of peace to be integrated into every school subject, into the culture of the school and the way in which the school relates to community.

Much of what children learn in schools is transmitted through the implicit or hidden curriculum, including teacher values, teaching methods, classroom organization, discipline, and other forms of behavior modeling, outside the explicitly state-mandated curriculum. Interpreting, internalizing and copying what they see and hear is the very foundation of a learning process embraced by babies and carried into adulthood. The authority of school, school principals and teachers, makes the hidden curriculum particularly powerful in shaping values and behaviors, an area not well captured in peace education initiatives. Hakvoort and Oppenheimer (1998) have pointed out that our understanding of the ways children comprehend peace and war is hampered because we largely ignore the impact of socialization agents such as teachers.

For example, until recently it was not uncommon in Serbian schools to have Roma children relegated to the back of the class. In Bosnia and Herzegovina, many schools have completely segregated Bosniak (Muslim) children from contact with Christian children through two distinct shifts in the same school. Teachers may well introduce a formal peace education program, used separately with each of these two groups of children, but the *theory of peace* will be overshadowed with the *practice of ethnic segregation.* In Kosovo, Serbian and Albanian children are, by and large, completely segregated in different communities and schools and little interaction takes place between them. Although some schools have started peace education programs, as 'the others' are absent, the implicit curriculum's peace-making impact is largely defined by the teacher narratives about other ethnic groups, and little is known about these.

Impacting the implicit curriculum in post-conflict contexts such as the former Yugoslavia is sufficiently complex. It often involves changes in pedagogy, the development of school leadership and culture, the creation of enabling structures that make the school a welcoming and safe place for *all* children and parents, and, perhaps above all, the professional development of teachers and other educational specialists, regardless of their subject area. Such development must be cognizant of the context and history of the conflict and sensitive to the impact that inter-ethnic conflict and war have had on all concerned. Teachers embody the implicit curriculum, and the personal psychological impact that they carry with them needs to be explored, recognized and co-opted for peace making to be meaningfully integrated into school life.

Children, too, must be ready to explore issues of ethnic diversity and peace, that may represent reminders of a recent conflict, and non-engagement with such sensitive topics is a legitimate and understandable protective mechanism. In the context of school-based peace education initiatives, children generally accept the legitimate authority of teachers and schools to decide what needs to be taught and learned. Careful thought must be given to school culture, policy, structures and processes that support a peace-making agenda. It is far from clear at the moment, for example, whether the segregation in many Bosnian schools, described above, is a much needed interim phase that avoids conflict and supports healing, or prevents meaningful inter-ethnic integration and reconciliation. We echo Christie (2006) in advocating for a "conscientization" process, aimed to transform individuals and groups by building a common consciousness of the necessity of living together in active peace. Such an effort is appropriately situated in schools where enlightened teachers, enabling leadership, an inclusive curriculum and, ironically, children of other ethnic groups are the necessary conditions for successfully breaking the inter-generational cycle of animosity.

References

Agger, I. (2001). Reducing trauma during ethno-political conflict: A personal account of psycho-social work under War conditions in Bosnia. In D. J. Christie, R. V. Wagner, & D. A. Winter (Eds.), *Peace, conflict, and violence: Peace psychology for the 21st century*. Englewood Cliffs, NJ: Prentice-Hall.

Alvik, T. (1968). The development of views on conflict, war and peace among school children: A Norwegian case study. *Journal of Peace Research, 5*, 171–195.

Beara, M. (2009). Profesionalni razvoj nastavnika u uslovima tranzicije. U N. Kapor Stanulovic (ur.). *Efekti tranzicije na porodične i profesionalne životne procese*. Novi Pazar: Državni univerzitet, str. 67–80.

Cairns, E. (1996). *Children and political violence*. Oxford, UK: Blackwell Publishers.

Christie, D. J. (2006). What is peace psychology the psychology of? *Journal of Social Issues, 62*(1), 1–17.

Cooper, P. (1965). The development of the concept of war. *Journal of Peace Research, 2*, 1–17.

Davies, L. (2004). *Education and conflict: Complexity and chaos*. London: Routledge.

Druckman, D. (2001). Nationalism and war: A social-psychological perspective. In D. J. Christie, R. V. Wagner, & D. A. Winter (Eds.), *Peace, conflict, and violence: Peace psychology for the 21st century*. Englewood Cliffs, NJ: Prentice-Hall.

Dudouet, V., Fisher, M., & Schmeltze, B. (2008). *Dealing with the past in Israel-Palestine and in the Western Balkans: Story-telling in Conflict – developing practice and research.* Berghof working paper Nr. 5. Berghof Research Center for Constructive Conflict Management, Berlin.

European Commission Directorate-General for Education and Culture. (2000). *European report on the quality of the school education; sixteen quality indicators*. Luxembourg: Office for Official Publications of the European Communities.

Fisher, A. (2006). Integration or segregation? reforming the education sector. In M. Fisher (Ed.), *Peacebuilding and civil society in Bosnia-Herzegovina: Ten years after Dayton*. Munster, Germany: Lit-verlag.

Franovic, I. (2008). *Dealing with the past in the context of ethnonationalism.* Berghof occasional paper Nr. 29. Berghof Research Center for Constructive Conflict Management, Berlin.

Freire, P. (1972). *Pedagogy of the oppressed.* Harmondsworth, UK: Penguin.

Hakvoort, I. (1996). Children's conceptions of peace and war: A longitudinal study. *Peace and Conflict: Joural of Peace Psychology, 2*(1), 1–15.

Hakvoort, I., & Oppenheimer, L. (1998). Understanding peace and war: A review of developmental psychology research. *Developmental Review, 18*, 353–389.

Hare, A. P., & Blumberg, H. H. (1977). *Liberation without violence: A third party approach.* Lanham, MD: Rowman & Littlefield.

Kanet, R. (2007). Identities, nations and politics after communism (introduction). *Nationalities Papers, 35*(3), 407–410.

Keene, J. (2001). The filmmaker as historian, above and below ground. *Rethinking History, 5*(2), 233–253.

Kelman, H.C. (1988). *Nationalism, national sentiments, and international conflict.* Paper prepared for the Workshop on Nationalism and International Conflict, National Academy of Sciences, Washington, DC.

Kirk, J. (2007). Education and fragile states. *Globalisation, Societies and Education, 5*(2), 181–200.

Low-Beer, A. (2001). Politics, school textbooks and cultural identity: The struggle in Bosnia and Herzegovina. *Paradigm 2/3.*

Milošević, M. (1995). *Orijentacioni raspored nastavnog gradiva geografije za VIII razred osnovne škole*. Beograd, Serbia: Zavod za udžbenike i nastavna sredstva.

Radovanović, S. (1997). *Škola i društvena sredina*. Beograd, Serbia: Institut za pedagogiju i andragogiju.

Raviv, A., Oppenheimer, L., & Bar-Tal, D. (Eds.). (1999). *How Children Understand War and Peace: A Call for International Peace Education.* Somerset, NJ. USA: John Wiley and Sons Inc.

Rose, P., & Greeley, M. (2006) *Education in fragile states: Capturing lessons and identifying good practice.* Paper prepared for the DAC Fragile States Working Groups, Sub-team for Education Services.

Schwebel, M. (2001). Promoting a culture of peace in children. *Peace and Conflict: Journal of Peace Psychology, 7*(1), 1–3.

Seitz, K. (2004). *Education and conflict: The role of education in the creation, prevention and resolution of societal crises—consequences for development cooperation*. Eschborn, Germany: GTZ.

Službeni glasnik – prosvetni glasnik. (1990). *Pravilnik o nastavnom planu i programu osnovnog obrazovanja i vaspitanja.*Retrieved September 06, 2010, from http://www.mp.gov.rs/propisi/propis.php?id=134.

Službeni glasnik – prosvetni glasnik. (1993). *Pravilnik o nastavnom planu i programu osnovnog obrazovanja i vaspitanja.* Retrieved September 06, 2010, from http://www.mp.gov.rs/propisi/propis.php?id=134.

Smith, A., & Vaux, T. (2002). *Education, conflict and international development*. London: DFID.

Spink, J. (2005). Education and politics in Afghanistan: The importance of an education system in peace building and reconstruction. *Journal of Peace Education., 2*(2), 195–207.

Tajfel, H. (Ed.). (1982). *Social psychology of intergroup relations*. Cambridge, UK: Cambridge University Press.

Taylor, C. E. (1998). How care for childhood psychological trauma in wartime may contribute to peace. *International Review of Psychiatry, 10*, 175–178.

Tomlinson, K., Benefield, P. (2005). *Education and conflict: Research and research possibilities.* Retrieved March 17, 2010 from http://www.eric.ed.gov/ERICDocs/data/ericdocs2sql/content_storage_01/0000019b/80/3f/66/a4.pdf.

Trnavčevič, A. (2007). School leadership and equity: Slovenian elements. *School Leadership and Management, 27*(1), 79–90.

US Agency for International Development (USAID). (2005a). *Fragile states strategy.* Washington, DC: USAID.

US Agency for International Development (USAID). (2005b). *Youth and Conflict.* Washington, DC: USAID Office of Conflict Management and Mitigation.

VanBalkom, W. D. (2010). Educational transformation with a New global urgency. *LEARNing Landscapes Journal, 3*(2).

VanBalkom, W. D., & Buleshkay, O. (2005). Parathënie. In M. Fullan (Ed.), *Forcat e Ndryshimit: Vazhdim.* Pristina, Kosovo: Ndermarrja Gazetare Botuese ADEA Publishers. (Contextual Foreword to the Albanian edition of Michael Fullan (1999) Change Forces: The Sequel).

VanBalkom, W. D., & Ncgongo, R. (1998). Education reform in South Africa: Challenges, adversaries and considerations. *International Journal of Educational Reform, 7*(1), 1–9.

White, R. K. (2000). Psychological aspects of the Kosovo crisis. *Peace and Conflict: Joural of Peace Psychology, 6*(1), 49–55.

World Bank. (2005). *Reshaping the future: Education and post conflict reconstruction.* Washington, DC: World Bank.

Zgaga, P. (2001). *The situation of education in the SEE region: Final content report on the project "support in OECD thematic review of educational policy in soputh eastern Europe".* Ljubljana, Slovenia: Centre for Educational Policy Studies.

Zgaga, P. (Ed.). (2006). *The prospects of teacher education in south-east Europe.* Ljubljana, Slovenia: Tiskarna Littera picta d.o.o.

Part II
Examining the Present

Chapter 6
Journalistic Views on Post-Violent Peacebuilding in Bosnia and Herzegovina

Karmen Erjavec, Zala Volčič, Melita Poler Kovačič, and Igor Vobič

Abstract In this chapter we focus on the media portrayal content of a specific traumatic event and journalists' discourse about it in Bosnia and Herzegovina (BIH). Despite the growing role and authority of journalists in shaping our understanding of collective pasts, the possible role of journalists as active agents in contributing to heightening tensions has been marginalized. Analyzing media texts can demonstrate how a "specific, limited truth" about the start of war in BIH is being selected, instrumentalized, and legitimized in the public awareness. Focus on journalists' perceptions of war and positive post-violence offers an understanding of different views about the start of the war, and guilt. This is why the basic research questions here deal with how journalists in BIH represent the violent past. Specifically, how do they cover a specific traumatic event and what are their perceptions about possibilities of realizing positive post-violence? Research on post-conflict processes looks at the ways in which people attempt to recreate their social fabric in ways appropriated to the changes in their social environment. Thus, the larger question that we are interested in here is whether journalists, like storytellers, frame their stories according to their ethnical belonging and the cultural environment? Furthermore, what media conditions might make possible positive post-violence after violent conflict?

Keywords Journalism • Media • Violent past • Traumatic event • Narratives

K. Erjavec (✉) • M.P. Kovačič • I. Vobič
Faculty of Social Sciences, University of Ljubljana, Kardeljeva pl. 5, 1000 Ljubljana, Slovenia
e-mail: karmen.erjavec@fdv.uni-lj.si; melita.poler-kovacic@fdv.uni-lj.si; igor.vobic@fdv.uni-lj.si

Z. Volčič
School of Journalism and Communication, Centre for Critical and Cultural Studies, The University of Queensland, Brisbane, QLD, Australia
e-mail: z.volcic@uq.edu.au

O. Simić et al. (eds.), *Peace Psychology in the Balkans: Dealing with a Violent Past while Building Peace*, Peace Psychology Book Series, DOI 10.1007/978-1-4614-1948-8_6,

There is a substantial body of literature from a variety of perspectives that suggests that the media in former Yugoslav countries contributed to the spread of national(ist) societies, providing little space for a democratic solution to the violent conflicts that followed (for example, Reljic, 2001). Currently, observers point out that in the media, ethno-national ideology remains the dominant ideology through which the media represent social reality (Jusic, 2008). Furthermore, most media coverage tends to concentrate on reporting violent incidents connected to ethno-nationalistic issues, rather than maximizing public understanding of the causes and contexts of these violent issues. Some media organizations even drive the conflicts themselves, because profit pressures remain the main reasons behind journalism performance (Džihana, 2009; Jusic, 2004).

Many local and international scholars alike argue that especially in Bosnia and Herzegovina (BIH) reporting patterns are mostly homogenized according to ethno-national lines, as well as their connection with dominant political discourses within ethnic groups. In that, BIH, as Kurspahić (2003) writes, witnesses nonviolence with conflictual perceptions of the past. Furthermore, it is argued that the BIH state is politically unstable, and its media system is not able to create a viable and democratic public sphere. From a peace psychologists's perspective (Christie, Tint, Wagner, & Winter, 2008), the situation in BIH could be described as post-violent, dominated by nonviolence, which has a strong potential to return to violent actions in order to address the traumatic past (Kurspahić, 2003; Erjavec & Volčič, 2009). Peacebuilding, the promotion of healing from direct violence and the reduction of structural violence is an important task for societies like BIH in order to prevent the eruption of violence in the future (Christie et al., 2008).

On one hand, studies about wars and post-war situations in the region of former Yugoslavia (e.g., Erjavec & Volčič, 2009; Kurspahić, 2003; Reljic, 2001; Skopljanac Brunner, 1999) show that the media have been and continue to be one of the crucial factors in re-creating conflicts and violence. On the other hand, media can play a crucial role in building peace and non-violent cultures. Media have an important role in promoting post-violent peacebuilding. This is needed especially in the former Yugoslav context, where politicians and other key social actors continue to instrumentalize the media for (re)production, legitimatization, and distribution of their exclusionary nationalistic ideology and everyday politics (Kurspahić, 2003. However, in the post-violent situation in BIH, as in other societies, the majority of members of a particular ethnic group continue to receive information about other groups through the news media which remains the crucial site for the dissemination of nationalistic ideologies.

In this chapter we focus on the media portrayal of a specific traumatic event and journalists' discourse about it in BIH. Despite the growing role and authority of journalists in shaping our understanding of collective pasts (Zelizer, 1993), the possible role of journalists as active agents in contributing to heightening tensions has been marginalized. In our work we combine the interests of media scholars and peace psychologists. Most peace psychologists deal with individuals and conflicting social groups, while not paying special attention to the role of journalists who can help to promote war and peace. Similarly, media scholars rarely analyze journalists' selective traumatic memories, their role in (co)creating peace, and their mission in post-conflict situations (see Galtung, 2007).

Analyzing media texts can demonstrate how a "specific, limited truth" about the start of war in BIH is being selected, instrumentalized, and legitimized in the public awareness. Focus on journalists' perceptions of war and post-violent peacebuilding offers an understanding of different views about the start of the war, guilt, and possibilities for realizing peace (Christie et al., 2008). This is why the basic research questions here deal with how journalists in BIH represent the violent past. Specifically, how do they cover a specific traumatic event and what are their perceptions about the possibilities of post-violent peacebuilding? Research on post-conflict processes looks at the ways in which people attempt to recreate their social fabric in ways appropriated to the changes in their social environment. Thus, the larger question that we are interested in here is whether journalists, like storytellers, frame their stories according to their ethnicity and the cultural environment? Furthermore, what media conditions might make post-violent peacebuilding possible?

The first part of this chapter deals with the media representation of the crucial case of "Dobrovoljačka" that represents the start of the war in BIH (Džihana, 2009). Specifically, the case of "Dobrovoljačka" refers to the killing of eight Yugoslav National Army (YNA) soldiers[1] on Dobrovoljačka Street in Sarajevo, on May 3rd 1992. We analyze both the Bosniak and the Serbian daily press in BIH. Critical discourse analysis was used in order to analyze the ways in which the mainstream daily press in BIH represented the case of "Dobrovoljačka" in 2009. This time frame is important, because it was in 2009 that different trials against alleged Serbian and Bosniak war criminals, such as Karadžić and Ganić, were beginning to take place. Four daily newspapers, two from the Federation of BIH and two from Republic of Srpska, have been chosen for the analysis of how the media in these two BIH entities, which were at war in the 1990s, frame the case of "Dobrovoljačka".

In the second part we focus on the journalists' perceptions of the case of "Dobrovoljačka", i.e., their arguments about the start of the war and the guilt linked to it. While analyzing their discourse, we also attempt to pay attention to their articulations on the possibilities of post-violent peacebuilding. To uncover their perceptions, we interviewed eight journalists who wrote about "Dobrovoljačka" in Bosnian newspapers in 2010.

The first section of the chapter presents a short theoretical background of peace psychology and the importance of studying media and journalists. The second section briefly describes the events on Dobrovoljačka Street on May 3rd 1992 in Sarajevo. Then, the methods and data are presented. We offer the analysis of the media coverage of the case of "Dobrovoljačka" and in-depth interviews with the journalists.

---

[1] In media reports it was stated that 42 people were killed, 73 were injured, and 215 were taken as prisoners, but they did not refer just to the attack on the Yugoslav National Army vehicles on Dobrovoljačka street. Namely, the media reports covered the connected events and armed conflicts at other locations at the same time (Džihana, 2009).

In the last section, we turn to the analysis and interpretation of materials. We argue for constructive, journalistic narratives, while suggesting that professional journalistic sources can help society in the process of *working through* the trauma, and so contribute to post-violent peacebuilding.

Theoretical Background

According to Christie et al. (2008), peace psychologists recognize that restored psychological functioning is crucial, not only to address the task of revitalizing public services and infrastructure but also in order to interrupt cycles of violence often perpetuated through the transmission of trauma across generations (Lumsden, 1997). For example, cycles of violence have been conspicuous in BIH, where collective trauma has laid the groundwork for future episodes of mass violence (Christie et al., 2008). The intergenerational transfer of nationalistic identities replete with mental representations that depict past glories and humiliation constitutes a kind of maintenance of collective traumas. When not properly mourned, feelings of victimization are passed on from generation to generation, and collective memories create psychological conditions for more violent episodes (Tint, 2010).

For our research, LaCapra's (1994) conceptualization of "acting out" in public spheres is helpful. He suggests that groups and individuals "work through" trauma in order to relate it to the cultural domain, mediated by different cultural agents, most importantly, journalists. *Working through* involves a mode of representational repetition, one that provides a critical perspective on problems, and offers space for symbolic action in a responsible manner that makes change possible. Again, here, media play a crucial role – media provide spaces for coming to terms with the past in community structures which is crucial for building peace; groups in conflict must be brought together not only to articulate their past pain but also to envision an interdependent future (Lederach, 1997). A key question for peace psychologists in post-violent contexts is how to assist war-affected people in coming to terms with their experiences while promoting reconciliation processes more widely throughout society (Christie et al., 2008). Reconciliation work is evolving from an exclusive focus on post-traumatic stress disorders to addressing a wider variety of mental health issues, including grief and depression, along with key psychosocial issues such as family separation, interpersonal and intergroup distrust and the destruction of community resources.

We are interested in how journalists in BIH understand the process of post-violent peacebuilding since it is precisely journalists who in (post-)conflict areas make a relevant contribution to the process of social perception of history, the present time, and future (Assman, 2004). We follow here peace psychology's argument that post-violent peacebuilding is not about achieving permanent peace, but that it is about an effort to depart from violence, and the "acting out" of trauma. Media play a crucial part in this process, since media can provide a means of better understanding of the other in a way that promotes understanding, appreciation, and connections between different cultures and strengthens peace communication.

Brief Political Context: The Case of "Dobrovoljačka"

The Socialist Federative Republic of Yugoslavia (SFRY) was created by six different nations or republics, and "Titoism" was founded on the assumption that economic and political homogenization would lead to the creation of a pure workers' state. After the death of its president, Josip Broz Tito in 1980, the suppressed nationalisms started to occupy the social spheres. In BIH, the combination of different ethnic groups (43.7% Muslims, 31.3% Serbs, 17.3% Croats, 7.7% "Yugoslavs" (Statistički bilten, 1991)) led to nationalistic tensions. The pressure on the Bosnian Serbs and Croats to follow the "national appeal" was increasing; Belgrade was calling for "all Serbs in one state", and Zagreb was promoting Tuđman's Croatian Democratic Union as "the main party of all Croats" (MacDonald, 2002, p. 123). During the first free multiparty elections in BIH in 1990, three nationalistic parties won, which led to permanent nationalistic disputes.

The problem of defining the beginning of the war in BIH is ideologically and politically linked to the question of identifying the group responsible for the conflicts that followed. This is connected to the question of who is responsible for the war incident on Dobrovoljačka Street in Sarajevo. Through different interpretations of the Dobrovoljačka case, war actions become differently understood, justified and legitimated – this is why this case is important for research and analysis. It is a complex case because it holds numerous different interpretations, as yet with no consensus.

The "Dobrovoljačka" case refers to the death of eight YNA soldiers on Dobrovoljačka Street in Sarajevo, on May 3rd 1992, during the Territorial Defense Forces', Patriotic League's and Green Berets' attack on the vehicles in which there were members of the Command of the Second Military District from the army base in Bistrik. A day before, on May 2nd, the president of BIH Alija Izetbegović, his daughter and the vice-president of the Bosnian government Zlatko Lagumdžija were being held by the YNA at the Sarajevo airport after returning from negotiations in Lisbon. They were later transferred to the army base in Lukavica. An agreement was reached about exchange of the president Izetbegović for the commander of the Second Military District, Milutin Kukanjac, who was at the time held in the army base in Bistrik. After the agreement, in the afternoon on May 3rd, Izetbegović, his daughter and Lagumdžija were transferred from Lukavica to Bistrik in an armed vehicle of UNPROFOR. The following questions remain a subject of an investigation: who actually arranged the exchange; at whose responsibility the following events occurred, and who issued the first shot. The attack occurred despite an agreement among representatives of the Republic BIH and the Socialist Republic of Yugoslavia on a peaceful withdrawal of the YNA from the territory of BIH. For this crime, representatives of the political and military elite of the Republic BIH are suspected (Džihana, 2009).

Historians agree that the war was largely carried out by the Serbian paramilitary units and the YNA, when they attacked Sarajevo in spring of 1992 and succeeded in conquering close to 70% of the country's territory (see for example, Kurspahić, 2003; MacDonald, 2002; Ramet, 2005; Woodward, 1995). They are also held responsible for some of the most brutal acts of violence exercised against the non-Serb populations, which involved mass killings, rape, and torture. Numerous massacres of the civilian population (97207 civilian deaths) (*Population losses in Bosnia & Herzegovina 92–95,* 2007) from all involved sides were committed and more than two million out of a total pre-war population of 4.3 million became internal or external refugees after the war. The war crimes were committed on both sides, but the international community largely agrees that Bosniaks are the main victims and Serbs the main perpetrators in this war (MacDonald, 2002).

On December 14, 1995, the Dayton Peace Agreement brought an end to the Bosnian war and divided BIH into two entities: the Federation of Bosnia-Herzegovina (with 51% of the territory) in which mostly Bosnian Muslims and Bosnian Croats live, and Republic of Srpska (with 49% of the territory) populated almost exclusively by the Bosnian Serbs. Today, this political entity is almost ethnically pure, and functions as a state within a state, having its own parallel political (including media) institutions (Repe, 2008).

Methodology

In our research, we used critical discourse analysis and in-depth interviews. Critical discourse analysis aims to analyze "the mental frameworks – the languages, the concepts, categories, imagery of thought, and the systems of representation – which different classes and social groups deploy in order to make sense of, figure out and render intelligible the way society works" (Hall, 1996, p. 26). These mental frameworks serve as an orientation to society and are essential for cognitive survival in everyday life. Three key textual analyses were performed: the analysis of macropropositions, the representation of social actors and key words. The semantic macrostructure is derived from the local meanings of words by macro-rules, such as deletion, generalization, and construction (van Dijk, 1980). Such rules combine similar meanings with higher-level abstract meanings or construct different meaning constituents in higher-level event or social concepts, which enable us to identify "the main idea unit" in the form of several sentences, a paragraph, entire news stories, etc. We found macropropositions which were published or missing in a news item about the phenomenon "Dobrovoljačka". In order to explore the media representation of the Dobrovoljačka case, we also analyzed how the key social actors were framed in this case, i.e., who was included in the domain of "us", and who was positioned as "them". Hall's "discourse of difference" is the most effective method to think through these binary positions. Hall (1989) understands "discourses of difference" (p. 913) as those that make a distinction between "us" and "them". The fact that meanings of "us" and "them", implying identification with and differentiation from, are not ontologically given, but ideologically constructed becomes even clearer through linguistic analysis. We also analyzed the selection of key words in news items, i.e., how the daily press was naming the event on Dobrovoljačka Street on May 3rd 1992. It is widely accepted that the choice of words used by journalists is by no means arbitrary. The choice is not only the journalists' own creation but is connected to their own society and cultural context (Fowler, 1991).

The sample for our analysis included nine news items, published from February 2009 until the end of June 2009 by two Bosniak's newspapers from Sarajevo *Oslobođenje* (two items), and *Dnevni Avaz* (three items), and two Bosnian Serbian newspapers from Banja Luka (Republic of Srpska) *Nezavisne novine* (two items), and *Glas Srpske* (two items). They were all dealing with the case of Dobrovoljačka from May 2nd and 3rd 1992. We were interested in how the traumatic event is presented in these newspapers. The criteria used for selecting daily newspapers were readership and regional representation (Džihana, 2009). According to Jusic (2004, pp. 74–76), these daily newspapers have the highest circulation in BIH, and the most powerful impact on political and public life.

In-depth interviews helped us to explore how Bosniak and Serbian journalists in BIH cope with the past, search for the truth, and aim to help the process of peacebuilding. In-depth interviews were appropriate because they enabled us to go deeper, to uncover new guidelines, open novel problem dimensions and provide us with a clear, accurate and inclusive argument based on a personal experience (Burgess, 1982). We conducted eight in-depth interviews (with two journalists from each analyzed newspaper), i.e., with four Serbian and four Bosniak journalists. We selected these journalists according to the authorship of the analyzed articles. All of them lived in BIH during the war. All of the interviews were conducted in the respondents' native languages by one of the Slovene authors of the project, transcribed verbatim and analyzed in terms of recurring "readings". The interviews were carried out in November 2010. To ensure the respondents' anonymity, we labeled our informants only by the newspaper they work for. Our questions referred to the following specific key topics: (a) the meaning and media representation of the case of Dobrovoljačka; (b) the definition of post-violent peacebuilding; (c) the role of media in helping post-violent peacebuilding; and (d) the perception of possibilities for post-violent peacebuilding. On the basis of these themes we structured our questions, while adjusting them for each interview.

Newspapers' Representation of Events on May 2nd and 3rd 1992

A comparison of macropropositions in news items about the case of Dobrovoljačka in Bosniak and Serbian daily newspapers unveils the main differences in covering and interpreting of what happened on May 2nd and 3rd 1992 in Sarajevo.

The analysis of social actors shows that the Bosniak daily newspaper *Oslobođenje* reported about the event primarily by citing Bosniak sources. On the basis of the analysis, we can make the following macroproposition, i.e., basic information about the events in questions: "The YNA General Kukanjac is to be blamed for the victims on Dobrovoljačka Street, because he wanted the YNA to safely return to Lukavica with the prisoner Izetbegović. When the Bosniaks defended the president, an incident occurred in which members of YNA suffered." The analysis of key words revealed that in order to describe events in which victims died, this daily newspaper primarily used the word combination "death of the YNA soldiers" already in the headline "For the death of YNA soldiers General Kukanjac is to be blamed" (27. 2. 2009), and the euphemistic word "incident" (see the example below). The newspaper blamed the YNA and specifically, YNA's General Kukanjac, for the attack, because Kukanjac wanted the YNA to return to Lukavica by using president Izetbegović, who was kidnapped a day earlier, as their guard. The newspaper constructed the meaning that the YNA did not have any intention to let Izetbegović go, which was probably just a "manipulation". The role of Bosniak forces is represented as "liberating the president" and "defending the state". For example:

> "That day, we were defending Sarajevo... We were defending the state, liberating the president! ...", says Švrakić Sr. But, the most important is, he thinks, that for the victims on Dobrovoljačka General Kukanjac is responsible... It was Kukanjac's idea that they pass the Vrbanja bridge where there were the YNA points already. This would make it impossible for us to return Izetbegović to the Presidency of BIH (For the death of YNA soldiers General Kukanjac is to be blamed/Za pogibiju vojnika JNA je kriv general Kukanjac, 27. 2. 2009, *Oslobođenje*).

Similarly, *Dnevni Avaz* published news items which cited exclusively the Bosniak sources. The statement of Ejup Ganić, a member of the Presidency of BIH, was repeated several times. The analysis of macropropositions pointed to the macroproposition that "on May 3rd 1992 on Dobrovoljačka Street in Sarajevo the state of BIH was defended and the president who had been kidnapped earlier was being liberated". This is a "concise" interpretation of events which includes a word with a powerful connotation, "a terrorist act", which is used after September 11th 2001 in a way to justify all means to defend a state, i.e., a nation (Erjavec & Volčič, 2007).

> Namely, on May 2nd 1992, a terrorist act was performed in which the president of the state was kidnapped, Alija Izetbegović. All of us who were involved in rescuing the president – the symbol of the state – are now guilty because it did not end in a way as it had been planned (Ganić: These stories from Serbia are ridiculous/Ganić: Te priče iz Srbije postale su mi smiješne, 26. 2. 2009, *Dnevni Avaz*).

In the third news item, *Dnevni Avaz* cites the statement of Avdo Hebib, the president of Patriotic League of BIH and the organizer of protests in Sarajevo against the warrant for 19 citizens of BIH issued by Serbia. Based on his statement we can make the following macroproposition: "Since the YNA captured the president Izetbegović, the Bosniak forces were forced to let the YNA leave Sarajevo. While departing, the YNA soldiers were shooting at civilians, and Bosniaks only responded to this attack". In the article, the goal of Bosniak forces is clearly stated several times, i.e., "they were liberating the president". The analysis of social actors showed that the key persons made responsible for this event were "the YNA soldiers who were the first to shoot civilians... they were armed to their teeth and in armed cars". If the reader of *Oslobođenje* does not get to know who shot first, this is clear to the reader of *Avaz*: the YNA soldiers shot first, therefore they are to be blamed for the death of their own soldiers – since the newspapers framed the initial shooting as determining the blame for the start of the war.

Nezavisne novine referred to many more sources than other newspapers. Similar to *Dnevni Avaz,* they cited Avdo Hebib when covering the demonstrations against the warrant. Based on his statement, we can establish the same macroproposition as in *Dnevni Avaz*. The newspaper used the statement of Dušan Kovačević, a former YNA Colonel, who participated in the event on May 3rd 1992. We can create a macroproposition that "the Bosniak forces, despite an agreement on peaceful withdrawal from Sarajevo and an international guarantee… attacked the YNA from an ambush and thus announced the war in BIH". Thus, the key message here is that Bosniaks started the violent campaign against the Serbs and are to be held responsible for the start of the war in BIH. They broke an agreement with the YNA. Thus, the daily newspaper clearly stated that for the event and the war in BIH the Bosniak forces are to be blamed, although they were not explicitly named. Members of the YNA were represented as innocent because they had been attacked from an ambush. The following citation is characteristic of this claim:

> Dušan Kovačević, a former YNA Colonel who was in the convoy of vehicles which was getting out of Sarajevo and which was attacked, said that with this event the attackers announced the war in BIH, and with which, as he said, the general pursuit of Serbs in Sarajevo began. "An agreement existed, under the guarantees of the international community, the United Nations and the European community, and the guarantees of the Presidency of the then Republic of BIH, that in the convoy we will leave Sarajevo as prisoners. We trusted the agreement which was violated. The soldiers were killed from an ambush," Kovačević told (For the crime, no one yet held responsible/Za zločin niko nije odgovarao, 5. 5. 2009, *Nazavisne novine*).

The event itself was described as "a war crime". The analysis of macropropositions showed that *Glas Srpske* does not present a detailed course of events, but regularly repeats the same message of the Serbian participants in the events and cites Serbian sources, i.e., that "despite an agreement on withdrawal from Sarajevo and the international guarantee, the Bosniak forces attacked the YNA from an ambush and thus announced the war in BIH". The analysis of social actors revealed that *Glas Srpske* clearly wrote that with the Bosniak forces' attack on the YNA, "the pursuit of Serbs" began as well as "the war in BIH". In this way they constructed the message that the Bosniaks began the war in BIH.

> A former YNA Colonel Dušan Kovačević, who was in the attacked convoy of vehicles, said that with this event the attackers announced the war in BIH, with which the general pursuit of Serbs in Sarajevo began. An agreement existed…. We trusted the agreement which was violated – Kovačević claimed (The additional report on Dobrovoljačka"/Dopuna prijava za "Dobrovoljačku", 17. 6. 2009, *Glas Srpske*).

One can note that the media in BIH continue to represent reality in ethnocentric way, favoring a bipolar way of seeing the world, as evidenced by the analysis of their coverage of "Dobrovoljačka" events. The above citations show how the media do not seek to represent the interests of the whole population, but rather focus on "our" side of the story. To conclude, the media were never passive observers of social reality, but active agents and the tools of (ethno-nationalistic) elites in the political developments. The media coverage of "Dobrovoljačka" reflects the interests and perspectives of the ethnic fractions represented by each media organization.

In BIH national and religious divisions continue, and a fragmented media landscape continues to encourage the divisions between "us" and "them". These strategies enable the media to place their reporting in specific ethno-national contexts. Therefore some facts are not talked about and are completely omitted, whereas other are emphasized, some questions are asked and some are unimaginable, some answers are given and some are omitted.

Without the involvement of the media the war would have been almost unthinkable, and their role in helping to create peace, through coping with the past and its different interpretations, is crucial. The media news stories have to start to provide the space for conversations that include various differing voices in the society.

Journalists on Dobrovoljačka and Post-Violent Peacebuilding in BIH

Meaning and Representation of the Case of Dobrovoljačka

In our interviews, all eight journalists stated that the case of Dobrovoljačka remains a crucial case in demonstrating sharp media divisions and social spaces in BIH. A typical statement from the interviews reads: "[The] Dobrovoljačka case is exemplary – because it shows sharp divisions in our society, especially within media spaces" (journalist, *Dnevni Avaz*). But, journalists offered different interpretations of why these divisions continue to exist in BIH. On the one hand, journalists of *Glas Srpske* accused the Bosniaks and "their" media of not admitting the Dobrovoljačka crime, supposedly committed against the Serbian soldiers on Dobrovoljačka Street, and for not admitting guilt for the start of the war in BIH: "It is clear that one of the three groups [Bosniaks] is not interested in uncovering and admitting this crime because this also means admitting the responsibility for the start of the war" (journalist, *Glas Srpske*). On the other hand, journalists of the Bosniaks' daily *Dnevni Avaz* accused Serbian journalists of creating divisions in BIH, because they represent a completely false picture of the case of Dobrovoljačka:

> They try to show completely falsely… in the Serbian media… that 43 soldiers were killed in Dobrovoljačka and that, a war crime was committed … Dnevni Avaz proved that 6 soldiers were killed … Armed YNA soldiers were a part of the convoy… and they were a legitimate target to be shot at – according to the Geneva Convention (journalist, *Dnevni Avaz*).

Journalists of *Oslobođenje* and *Nazavisne novine* did not directly accuse the other ethnic side of being "guilty" for the start of the war. Surprisingly, the journalist of the Bosnian Serbian daily *Nazavisne novine* actually accused the Serbian side of insisting on the representation of the case of Dobrovoljačka as a war crime committed by Bosniaks. He for example disagreed with the official Serbian interpretation that continues to present Bosniaks as the guilty ones for the beginning of war and the war itself. In that, the journalist thinks the purpose of Dobrovoljačka media coverage is to construct a counterweight to the Serbian war crimes and thus allows the Serbs to free themselves from guilt: "Dobrovoljačka holds a more meaningful and powerful status for the Serbian side, because… unlike Srebrenica and all other horrible scenes of war crimes, the Serbs can show and argue that this is actually a crime committed by the BIH army" (journalist, *Nezavisne novine*). This was the only statement that both journalists, Bosniak and Serb, agreed upon. We can interpret this through clearly identified Serbian strategy of insisting that this event led to the war in BIH. However, one single event cannot be solely blamed for the start of the war. The wars in the former Yugoslavia were the consequence of organized and planned nationalistic politics, especially the Serbian one from the mid 1980s on (see Kurspahić, 2003; MacDonald, 2002; Ramet, 2005; Woodward, 1995).

The Role of Media in Co-Creating Post-Violent Peacebuilding

On the one hand, Bosniak journalists of *Dnevni Avaz* and *Oslobođenje* defined post-violent peacebuilding as recognizing causes for the war, admitting guilt for the war and for the consequences of the war and insisted that Serbian politics should be largely held responsible. Furthermore, the Serbian war criminals should be put on trial: "Post-violent peacebuilding means that the Serbian side should be confronted with the causes and consequences of the war completely. There should be an insistence upon the responsibility of both Serbian individuals and the Serbian politics" (journalist, *Dnevni Avaz*).

Bosniak journalists demand and expect from Serbian counterparts that in their media coverage, a clear dichotomy of victim versus perpetrator is established, whereby Bosniaks are asserted as victims, and Serbs as perpetrators. A typical statement goes like this:

> I can honestly tell you that there will be no positive atmosphere in Bosnia until the Serbian colleagues will write the truth in their media... And the truth is: we are the victims, they have attacked us, and they have to take the responsibility for it (journalist, *Dnevni Avaz*).

On the other hand, journalists of *Glas Srpske* defined post-violent peacebuilding as willingness to forgive the other nation and continue life without searching and reasserting the causes of the war: "To me, to reconcile means to be ready to forgive someone and to continue living without returning to causes which led to the conflict over and over again" (journalist, *Glas Srpske*). So, journalists of *Glas Srpske* do not want to deal with the causes and the Serbian guilt for the war anymore. Journalists of *Nezavisne novine* have a less demanding definition of post-violent peacebuilding, as they defined it as respecting the laws and being tolerant of other social groups: "To me the most important is the respect for the laws, respecting others and the different ones regardless their ideological differences or affiliation to another religious or national group" (journalist, *Nezavisne novine*).

If the Bosniak journalists demanded that the Serbian journalists clearly identify the victims and perpetrators in this war, the Serbian journalists wanted the Bosniak journalists to stop to insist on the dichotomy of who is a victim and who is a perpetrator.

> Look, there will be no peace. After the war, we listen to only one and the same old story, all the time. Peacebuilding? No way – at least until Sarajevo journalists continue to insist that the Serbs are the perpetrators and that they are all the poor victims. This is simply not true and they have to stop with that. Simple as that (journalist, *Glas srpske*).

All interviewed journalists agreed that the media have the key role in the process of creating post-violent peacebuilding; however, journalists of *Dnevni Avaz* and *Glas Srpske* unanimously claimed that the role of the media seems to be in searching and mediating "their" truth and defending their specific ethnic interests:

> I think that we compete for who will establish the absolute truth ... Our absolute dedication to Bosniaks is necessary, as Bosniaks do not have a medium which would exclusively defend the interests of Bosniaks (journalist, *Dnevni Avaz*).

Journalists of *Nezavisne novine* and *Oslobođenje* emphasized the meditative role of the media, arguing that the role of the media is "to report professionally" (journalist, *Nezavisne novina*), but "from the wider perspective, without excluding the ethnic communities" (journalist, *Oslobođenje*). These journalists offer their responses according to professional journalistic ideology (Fishman, 1980; Tuchman, 1978), where "professionalism" establishes what are legitimate areas for journalistic inquiry and thinking, and how these themes should be covered. Tuchman conceptualized "news net" (1978), a system of values, routines and practices that journalists cast to catch news. Rather than a function of routine, or the practical application of news values, the professional discourse legitimates and prescribes certain modes of understanding. Here the journalists' discourse enunciates and articulates certain aspects of reality to be of public interest and delegitimating that which falls beyond its scope. Having defined legitimate fields of newsworthiness professionalism then shapes what can be said of a given "area". It is held that these prescriptions are the product of a journalistic conventionalism that is inherently ideological and ill-equipped for providing substantive knowledge about wars. In that, the Serbian journalists "hide" behind their arguments for "being professional only" and downplay any emotional involvement. They continue to be ethnocentrically oriented.

Journalistic Work in Covering War Crimes

There are two different opposing viewpoints regarding the relationship between journalistic work and personal feelings of the reporters. All interviewed Bosniak journalists lived through the war as soldiers or/and as victims; therefore, it is psychologically difficult for them to carry out the journalistic work, especially when they have to cover the war crimes. They understand their work as a continuation of the struggle, and a fight for the truth. They emphasize that their optimism is displayed mostly by the fact that they (still) live and work in BIH. At the same time, they all admit that "complete peace" in BIH is not to come very soon, as Serbia has not yet admitted its guilt for the war in BIH, and the courts process war crimes very slowly. Bosniak journalists believe that there will be no reconciliation among the Bosniaks and the Serbs in BIH until the crucial war criminals are convicted. Thus, journalists of *Dnevni Avaz* said that they cover war crimes in a great pain, as they witnessed war crimes during the war themselves and now they relive them while doing their job. Still, they believe that in the name of Bosniaks they must fight for the truth about the war in BIH. They claim that they know the truth very well as they were witnesses to this war. For these journalists, searching for the truth about the war from a subjective perspective is *a personal* and *professional* commitment.

> You know, I'm someone who lived through the war, the whole war in Bosnia and Herzegovina. I'm one of the witnesses. This is very painful when I write about the war. But on the other hand, I'm very proud to work in a newspaper which represents the theory that we must face the truth about the war ... As a direct witness I know what was happening, therefore I know how to write ... I'm an optimist, but I think that this is a lengthy process ... war crimes are processed slowly ... Serbia did not admit its guilt (journalist, *Dnevni Avaz*).

Journalists of *Oslobođenje* see their individual contribution to post-violent peacebuilding in sacrificing for BIH again by overcoming the ethnic division, taking the general public interest into account and writing for all the citizens of BIH:

> Personally it's very difficult for me to go back into the past and deal with war memories, considering that I was a victim of this war in Sarajevo ... But, one has to take yet another sacrifice for the whole state in which democracy will be on a higher level, where all the nations will live their life together, in peace and tolerance ... We must ignore our personal interests, interests of the nation, and look at the general interests ... write for all the citizens ... I'm an optimist (journalist, *Oslobođenje*).

On the other hand, journalists of *Glas Srpske* and *Nezavisne novine* have no real difficulties while covering war crimes. According to their arguments, history does not influence their work, as the public expects facts and not emotions: "The past has not influenced me, the public looks for facts and not emotions" (journalist, *Glas Srpske*). Although journalists can never be totally objective, the dilemma of journalistic objectivity is even more explicit in war and postwar societies. The opinion cited above can be understood as a strategy of denying one's own role in the war in BIH. Especially journalists of *Glas Srpske* emphasized that reconciliation is possible only in the framework of a divided BIH: "Personally I'm for reconciliation in the framework of BIH as established by the Dayton Agreement and in which the Federation of BIH and the Republic of Srpska normally exist, so that no one despises anybody, insults anybody, etc." (journalist, *Glas Srpske*).

The interviews explored the cultural battle over the right to shape society's stories of the past. Our informants have two contrary narratives about the coverage of Dobrovoljačka that are determined by their ethnic memberships. Bosniak journalists understand their journalistic work as a painful one, full of troublesome emotions. In general, it appears that Bosniak journalists attempted to establish their own authority as witnesses, survivors, and victims of the war. They see their work as a continuation of the war; they see their mission in helping to uncover the war crimes. Serbian journalists hold no special affect towards their work, and express no painful feelings in covering the war crimes. They see themselves strictly as observers, and professional journalists. They do not strive for the transformations within BIH, since they support the political context, where the Republic of Srpska has the status of a para-state.

We argue that journalists, like storytellers, shape their stories according to their ethnic identity and cultural environment. As we show, the journalists are members of an interpretative community that they belong to. Their own different interpretations compete for their place in BIH. In short, we suggest that on the Bosniak side, we witness a painful engagement with the past and uncovering war crimes; and on the Serbian side, we see a strategic distance from the past and war crimes.

Discussion and Conclusion

This chapter attempted to illuminate a perspective insufficiently studied in peace psychology and media studies: the role of journalists as agents of memory and co-creators of post-violent peacebuilding. Journalists have a responsibility to shape society's collective memory through newspapers, and in that, they importantly contribute to the post-violent peacebuilding. Following the discursive analysis and narrative approach, we explored the journalists who shape narratives, focusing on the media texts and the *people behind the texts*.

The analysis revealed the complex process involved in determining the authority of the storytellers to engage in telling the story of Dobrovoljačka. The discursive analysis revealed that, on the macro semantic level, two daily newspapers with their own, narrow ethnic orientation, offered two opposing interpretations of the case of Dobrovoljačka. On one hand, the Bosniak daily newspaper *Dnevni Avaz* represented the event of Dobrovoljačka Street as Bosniak forces defending the president of the Republic of BIH Izetbegović, whom the YNA captured a day earlier. The act is represented as a crucial event where BIH was being defended. On the other hand, the Serbian daily newspaper *Glas Srpske* represented the event as a Bosniaks' massacre of the Serbs, and as the beginning of the war in BIH. The kidnapping of Izetbegović did not get covered in the Bosnian Serbian media, and the reports claimed that the Bosniak side attacked the YNA soldiers who just peacefully wanted to leave Sarajevo. The less ethnically oriented Serbian *Nezavisne novine* represented a more diverse perspectives of events. Based on media representation, we can establish the key media strategy: the analyzed daily newspapers set the causes and the consequences of the event in question with different starting points. In the media and politically, the struggle for the starting point of the war is the crucial strategy for political legitimization of the war. The starting point of the war is equated with the guilt for war. In that, the media continue to be drawn into the advancement of values preferred by the ruling political elites. The war-time dichotomies continue to involve divisions between us – the victims – and them – the perpetrators.

Similarly, the in-depth interviews with journalists showed that the case of Dobrovoljačka is crucial because it uncovers the division of the social and media scene in BIH, which is interpreted in different ways. On the one hand, journalists of *Glas Srpske* accused Bosniaks and their media of not wanting to admit the crime committed against the Serbian soldiers on Dobrovoljačka Street and admit guilt for the beginning of a war in BIH. On the other hand, journalists of the Bosniaks' daily newspaper *Dnevni Avaz* accused the Serbian journalists of responsibility for the division, as they create a completely false picture of this case. Journalists of *Oslobođenje* and *Nazavisne novine* did not accuse the other side directly.

Defining post-violent peacebuilding strategies was similarly based on the ethnic key of belonging. On the one hand, the Bosniak journalists of *Dnevni Avaz* and *Oslobođenje* framed the post-violent peace situation as admitting the causes, guilt and consequences of the war on the side of the Serbian politics, and capturing and convicting the Serbian war criminals. On the other hand, journalists of *Glas Srpske* defined it as willingness to forgive the other nation and to continue with their life without searching for causes of the war, which indicates a desire for tabooization of the causes of war as well as for the war itself.

Regarding subjective feelings in connection to journalistic work, the interviewees offered two different views. All the Bosniak journalists understand their work as a continuation of the struggle for BIH and they argue that permanent peace is not to come soon, as Serbia has not yet admitted its guilt, and the courts deal with the war crimes slowly. On the other hand, journalists of *Glas Srpske* and *Nezavisne novine* see no difficulties in covering war crimes, claiming that one has to leave history behind. Particularly journalists of *Glas Srpske* emphasized that permanent peace is possible only within the framework of a divided BIH. They understand peacebuilding as a continuation of the status quo with no accusations that the Serbs are to be blamed for the war in BIH. The strategy of denying the role of Serbian journalists in the war in BIH and tabooization of this period can also be seen in their readiness to talk a lot about Bosniaks as attackers on Serbs in the case of Dobrovoljačka. However, they did not want to talk in general about the war in BIH and journalists' role in the war.

LaCapra (2001) argues that "a crucial issue with respect to traumatic historical events is whether attempts to work through problems, including rituals of mourning, can viably come to terms with . . . the divided legacies, open wounds, and unspeakable losses of a dire past" (p. 45). Our research shows, however, that journalism in BIH has essentially not changed from the 1990s, when the professional ideology of a so-called "nationalistic journalism" was dominant (Ćurgus, 1999, p. 128). The characteristic of mainstream journalism at the time was a "blood-and-soil" superiority, "my-nation-right-or-wrong" version and "us-versus-them" mentality. Journalists of *Dnevni Avaz* and *Glas Srpske* still foster the same ideology which is based exclusively on the ethnic key of covering the social happenings. These journalists have taken up a "collaborative role" (cf. Christians, Glasser, McQuail, Nordenstreng, & White, 2009, p. 196), which implies a relationship with the ethnic centers of power that clashes with the libertarian ideal of a free and autonomous press, and represents an acknowledgement of the political power. This perception is based on a "national or ethnic duty". Journalists of *Nezavisne novine* and *Oslobođenje* consider the views of other social groups in BIH some more and attempt to follow the libertarian ideal.

One of the key findings of this research is that the interviewed journalists understand the post-violent situation very diversely, while at the same time they do not believe that achieving peace and harmony will come soon. They do not hope for the realization of the process of complete peace and reconciliation in the near future.

The research also showed that among Bosniak and Serbian journalists, particularly among journalists of *Glas Srpske* and *Dnevni Avaz,* there is a strong intergroup distrust, even hatred. All journalists pointed out that the media play the key role in post-conflict context, but acknowledged that they align themselves with ethnic factions. As journalists, they see themselves doing their job, of searching for, publishing and defending their own truth, i.e., a specific "truth" about the war in BIH, which was especially emphasized by journalists of *Glas Srpske* and *Dnevni Avaz*. Thus, the key role of the media is subjected to the ethnic goal. However, all journalists advocate the possibilities for peaceful co-existence and see the role of the media and peace psychology as crucial to help building peace.

Our finding that understanding of post-violent peacebuilding and willingness to reconcile depends on the ethnic affiliation or the affiliation to the group of victims or aggressors is also crucial here. It is of the primary importance for a victim that the perpetrator publicly admits the guilt and that war criminals are captured and convicted, and that damage is repaired. Bosniak journalists insist that the Serb journalists clearly acknowledge that the Serbs were the main perpetrators during the war. Serbian journalists claim that the Serbs were not the main perpetrators and that the Bosniaks should move on – and not continue to insist on the dichotomy of victim versus perpetrator. If this does not stop, then BIH will never achieve the state of positive peace.

For those who are affiliated to the social group of aggressors, it is important that the guilt and war history are not dealt with. Even more, journalists of *Glas Srpske* said that for them post-violent peace situation means preserving "the legalized war ethnic partition" (Verdery & Burawoy, 1999, p. 188), only without accusations of Serbs as the guilty ones for the war, i.e., a kind of quiet reproduction of the status quo. Different analyses on social role of victim and perpetrator in the Balkans show that the acceptance of naming of who is a perpetrator and who is a victim remains crucial for establishing peace. For example, Kosovo Albanians in the 1980s demanded to be recognized as victims, and Serbs as perpetrators. After 2000, the roles were changed and the Kosovo Serbs demand that they be treated as victims (Andrejevich, 1997; Graczyk & Giannakos, 2006). Of course this can be dangerous, as the history of nations on the territory of the former Yugoslavia can teach us that a history not coped with can soon be repeated in a way even more bloody (Ramet, 2005).

In BIH two diametrically opposing truths about the war still exist; the guilt for the war has not yet been publicly admitted; the main war criminals have not yet been captured, and the existent court processes on war criminals have not yet been finished (Erjavec &Volčič, 2009). Until these conditions are fulfilled, mental representations based on the collective memory with an ethnic view on history and construction of identity of a specific group as victims can create psychological conditions that can result in more violent episodes. In that lies the importance of peace psychology that focuses on the importance of recognizing the perceptions of "other" ethno national communities, since this can contribute to the process of post-violent peacebuilding. Peace psychology offers interpretation and intervention tools for journalists and in that, peace psychologists' arguments are important for journalists in particular, since they should be equipped with conflict resolution skills which could enable them to become more effective professional and ethical human beings. The journalists then can mobilize involved parties in order to debate and foster communication between all sides. In a way, all sides have to agree to develop a sense to break with a past and to create a sense to move on – a departure into new type of relationship that is based on trust. However, this can only be done once the guilty come to terms with their own past behaviors.

It is crucial to recognize that private, commercial, profit oriented media in particular can undermine the ability of citizens to act as rational actors engaged in public debate, since research has proven that they generally cultivate the expected ethnocentric ideology and hate emotions. In that, one specific recommendation for the media in BIH would be to suggest that the media should start to provide special sections and programs dedicated solely to peace issues. In an effort to contribute to the absence of violence, it is media programs that can offer spaces for voicing, talking, truth-telling, active listening, and response. Media are needed that create a narrative that enables a process of working through the trauma instead of reproducing the nationalistic spaces. Namely, journalism's use of the past has consequences for how a specific community accommodates it.

References

Andrejevich, M. (1997). The sandžak: A perspective of Serb-Muslim relations. In H. Poulton & S. Taji-Farough (Eds.), *Muslim identity and the Balkan state* (pp. 180–193). London: Hurst & Company.

Assman, A. (2004). Four formats of memory: From individual to collective constructions of the past. In C. Emden & D. Midgley (Eds.), *Cultural memory and historical consciousness in the German-speaking world since 1500* (pp. 19–37). Oxford/Bern: Peter Lang.

Burgess, R. G. (1982). The unstructured interview as a conversation. In R. G. Burgess (Ed.), *Field research* (pp. 107–110). London: Routledge.

Christians, C. G., Glasser, T. L., McQuail, D., Nordenstreng, K., & White, R. A. (2009). *Normative theories of the media: Journalism in democratic societies*. Urbana, IL/Chicago: University of Illinois Press.

Christie, D. J., Tint, B. S., Wagner, R. V., & DuNann, B. (2008). Peace psychology for a peaceful world. *The American Psychologist, 63*(6), 540–552.

Ćurgus, V. K. (1999). Oblačenje novena [New Clothes]. In N. Skopljanac-Brunner, A. Hodžić, & B. Krištović (Eds.), *Mediji i rat* [Media and War]. Beograd: Mediji.

Džihana, A. (2009). *Media reporting on European integration in Bosnia-Herzegovina*. Sarajevo, Bosnia: Mediacentar Sarajevo.

Erjavec, K., & Volčič, Z. (2007). "War on terrorism" as a discursive battleground: Serbian recontextualization of G.W. Bush's discourse. *Discourse & Society, 18*(1), 123–138.

Erjavec, K., & Volčič, Z. (2009). Rehabilitating Milošević: Posthumous coverage of the Milošević regime in Serbian newspapers. *Social Semiotics, 19*(2), 125–147.

Fishman, M. (1980). *Manufacturing the news*. Austin, TX: University of Texas Press.

Fowler, R. (1991). *Language in the News*. London, New York: Routledge.

Galtung, J. (2007). *Handbook of peace and conflict studies*. London: Routledge.

Graczyk, D. A., & Giannakos, S. A. (2006). The face of Kosovo Albanian nationalism. *Mediterranean Quarterly, 17*(4), 142–159.

Hall, S. (1989). *Ideologie, kultur, medien: neue rechte, rassismus*. Hamburg, Germany: Argument.

Hall, S. (1996). *Modernity: An introduction to modern societies*. Cambridge, MA: Blackwell Publishers.
Jusic, T. (2004). Bosnia and Herzegovina. In B. Petković (Ed.), *Media ownership and its impact on media independence and pluralism*. Ljubljana, Slovenia: Peace Institute.
Jusic, T. (2008). *Media discourse and politics of ethnic conflict: Case study former Yugoslavia. Intima javnosti*. Beograd, Serbia: Institut za filozofiju i društvenu teoriju.
Kurspahić, K. (2003). *Prime time crime: Balkan media in war and peace*. Washington, DC: United States Institute of Peace Press.
LaCapra, D. (1994). *Representing the holocaust: History, theory, trauma*. Ithaca, NY: Cornell University Press.
LaCapra, D. (2001). *Writing history, writing trauma*. Baltimore: The Johns Hopkins University Press.
Lederach, J. P. (1997). *Building peace: Sustainable reconciliation in divided societies*. Washington, DC: United States Institute for Peace Press.
Lumsden, M. (1997). Breaking the cycle of violence. *Journal of Peace Research, 34*, 377–383.
MacDonald, D. (2002). *Balkan holocausts?* Manchester, UK: Manchester University Press.
Population losses in Bosnia and Herzegovina 92–95. (2007). Research and Documentation Center Sarajevo. http://www.idc.org.ba/project/populationlosses.html.
Ramet, S. (2005). *Thinking about Yugoslavia*. New York/Cambridge: Cambridge University Press.
Reljic, D. (2001). *Killing screens: Media in times of conflict, European institute for the media*. Düsseldorf/Paris: BM.
Repe, B. (2008). Primer Karadžić. *Mladina, 31*, 42–45.
Skopljanac Brunner, N. (1999). *Mediji i rat*. Beograd, Serbia: Argument.
Statistički bilten. (1991). Sarajevo: Republic's Bureau for Statistics, Media centre Sarajevo press.
Tint, B. (2010). History, memory and conflict resolution: Research and application. *Conflict Resolution Quarterly, 27*(4), 369–400.
Tuchman, G. (1978). *Making news: A study in the construction of reality*. New York: Free Press.
Van Dijk, A. T. (1980). *Macrostructures*. Hillsdale, NJ: Lawrence Erlbaum.
Verdery, K., & Burawoy, J. M. (1999). *Uncertain transition: Ethnographies of change in the post-socialist world*. Lanham, MD: Rowman & Littlefield.
Woodward, S. L. (1995). *Balkan tragedy. Chaos and dissolution after the Cold War*. Washington, DC: The Brookings Institution.
Zelizer, B. (1993). Journalists as interpretative communities. *Critical Studies in Mass Communication, 10*(3), 219–237.

Chapter 7
War Through Other Means: Examining the Role of Symbols in Bosnia and Herzegovina

Iva Pauker

Abstract Symbols make visible the abstractions of social relationships, and are therefore a useful barometer of inter-ethnic relations. In the post-war period in former Yugoslav states, ethnic conflict is often carried out through symbols which replicate and reinforce ethnic antagonism. During the wars of the 1990s physical destruction was often focused on highly symbolic (non-military) targets such as mosques, churches, museums and libraries in order to erase the symbols of the enemy group while plastering the area with symbols of the victorious group in order to claim the territory, symbolically as well as physically. The post-war situation, particularly in Bosnia–Herzegovina, is fraught with symbolic conflict. The tensions surrounding the flag of Bosnia–Herzegovina is a prominent example where complete disagreement over pre-existing arsenal of symbols resulted in a complete new design with no resonance for anyone. Minarets and churches are erected not so much in an effort to serve their respective religious communities as much as in an effort to symbolically claim contested territory. This chapter will examine how the conflict has continued to be played out in the symbolic sphere in former-Yugoslav society, while also seeking to identify potential for symbols to unite and heal.

Keywords Culture • Symbols • Violence • Remembering • Healing

While the war in Bosnia–Herzegovina officially came to an end in 1995, the roots of conflict, which resulted in the wars of 1990s, have not been adequately resolved. Peace psychologists argue that the focus on physical violence, while often rightly an immediate and urgent concern, should not mask deeper symptoms of which physical

---

I. Pauker (✉)
School of Social and Political Sciences, The University of Melbourne, Australia
e-mail: iva.pauker@gmail.com

O. Simić et al. (eds.), *Peace Psychology in the Balkans: Dealing with a Violent Past while Building Peace*, Peace Psychology Book Series, DOI 10.1007/978-1-4614-1948-8_7,

violence is but one, even if the most devastating, manifestation (Christie, Tint, Wagner, & Winter, 2008). A more nuanced understanding of violence, moving beyond the dichotomy of simple presence or absence of physical violence as a barometer of conflict is required in order to adequately address the geo–historic and systemic roots and manifestations of conflict (Christie, 2006). Post-war Bosnia–Herzegovina to date has been an example of what peace psychologists label *negative peace*, namely a context where overt violence has been addressed but structural violence, inequitable social order and ethnic apartheid persists (Christie et al.). One key feature of this negative peace in Bosnia–Herzegovina has been the inter-ethnic symbolic conflict, which played an antagonistic and divisive role in the war and has persisted after the war officially ended. Understanding how this symbolic conflict is perpetuated, and how it could potentially be ameliorated is crucial if post-war Bosnian society is to build on the achieved negative peace in order to also to attain a deeper and more sustainable positive peace.

This chapter will briefly outline some important theoretical contributions on the role of symbols in political communities before outlining the main symbols representing ethnic groups and political entities in Bosnia–Herzegovina today. The first case study, the post-Dayton effort to determine the official state flag of Bosnia–Herzegovina, is discussed in order to clearly illustrate the post-war symbolic antagonism, and highlight the lack of common, pan-Bosnian symbolic vocabulary in the post-war era. In addition to the conflict over the abstract symbols of nationhood, the very physical space has become a battleground, with ancient and new buildings enlisted in the battle to claim exclusive rights to territory. The building of religious structures in two Bosnian cities, Mostar and Banja Luka, will be the subject of the next two case studies, in order to examine how this symbolic conflict plays out at the local level in contemporary Bosnia–Herzegovina. The last two case studies, the Think BiH campaign and the Bruce Lee statue, illustrate two attempts to develop inclusive symbols which would equally represent all of Bosnia–Herzegovina's ethnic communities in an effort to create a pan-Bosnian identity. The first case study addresses the 2005/2006 Think BiH advertising campaign which aimed to encourage a sense of Bosnian–Herzegovinian identity and citizenship, while the second case study addresses the erection of the Bruce Lee statue in Mostar in 2005 as a universal symbols of justice drawn from young Bosnian people's engagement with global popular culture.

The Political Role of Symbols: A Brief Theoretical Outline

The symbolic realm is an important barometer of conflict and peacemaking, as it is often the only visible manifestation of invisible social structures and conflicts. In his seminal 1967 article on political symbolism, Michael Walzer noted that "in a sense, the union of men can only be symbolized; it has no palpable shape or substance" (Walzer, 1967, p. 194). He elaborated that "[t]he state is invisible; it must be personified before it can be seen, symbolized before it can be loved, imagined before it can be conceived" (Walzer). Zdizislaw Mach, writing some years later elaborated on the power and function of symbols by arguing that: "Social order…is expressed and above all justified symbolically by reference to supreme values" (Mach, 1993, p. 38). Because these supreme values are very abstract in nature, they are normally expressed and communicated through the use of symbols.

National symbols are not merely decorative and descriptive, they also, importantly, play a *proactive* function. Symbols have an active role in the identity-building process, and have the power to direct society towards certain behaviors and actions (Mach, 1993, p. 39). As Cohen notes, symbols enable us to "see" what is actually invisible: the nature of social relationships (Cohen, 1974).

> One of the most important of these (symbolic) functions is the objectification of relationships between individuals and groups. We can observe individuals objectively in concrete reality but the relationships between them are abstractions that can be observed only through symbols. Social relationships develop through and are maintained by symbols. We "see" groups through their symbols (Cohen, 1974, p. 30).

This power dynamic is particularly evident when examining the standard symbolic arsenal of modern nations which includes flags, crests, currencies, anthems, monuments and holidays, to name just a few common national symbols (Cerulo, 1995, p. 13). It is not therefore surprising that these symbols, the "trappings" of sovereignty and nationhood, are often the first order of priority for national elites in search of sovereignty (Cerulo). The choice and use of symbols is often conscious and deliberate on the part of the elite. Cerulo argues that:

> every national symbol – anthems and flags as well as crest, currencies, monuments, mottoes, etc. – represents a carefully constructed, carefully projected image of identity that results from a conscious decision-making process (Cerulo, 1995, p. 5).

Mach maintains that "symbols are...selected and combined so as to achieve a desired state of people's minds; to appeal to values, to refer to ideas to stir emotions and to stimulate action" (Mach, 1993, p. 37). Particularly because they appeal to people on a cognitive as well as emotional level, symbols are excellent tools for political manipulation.

> Politicians manipulate symbols...in order to induce people to make choices based on the values they are promoting (which are evoked by the chosen symbols), or to associate themselves with those values (Kaufman, 2001, p. 29).

Symbols and identity are only constructed in perceived opposition: what we *are* is only defined against what we are *not*; "contradicting good, civilized, progressive, clean, well-mannered, moral, to bad, primitive, reactionary, dirty vulgar, immoral" (Mach, 1993, pp. 42–43).

Symbols can be replaced, but importantly, cannot be eliminated from the political and social landscape. Walzer argues that "since men cannot orient themselves in the political world without unit or reference symbols, the systems are replaced even as they are called into question" (Walzer, 1967, p. 198). Which new reference symbols will replace the old symbols depends on the availability of new "reference worlds" (p. 198). In times of symbolic upheaval, ancient symbols can provide temporary intellectual and emotional comfort. Symbols of the 'nation' provide the security of a transindividual community enabling the individual to clearly recognize friends and enemies and "to solve (even in a mythological, vicarious way, through fantasy) otherwise excruciating dilemmas" (Tismaneanu, 1997, p. 108).

Social symbols invariably embody an inclusion/exclusion dichotomy. In conflict and post-conflict societies in particular, symbolic boundaries are created that divide the social world into "our" domain and "their" domain. "Social space is organized according to this division, and patterns of interaction between members of different groups are established" (Mach, 1993, p. 42). The Swastika symbol in Germany in the 1930s and 1940s, "created two independent and adversarial symbolic vocabularies in Germany", namely that dividing the German society into the Aryan people, who were represented by the Swastika; and the non-Aryan society, who were not only excluded by the symbol but were also forbidden to use it (Cerulo, 1995, p. 20).

These lessons of exclusionary politics waged through the symbolic realm enable us to better identify sites of conflict beyond simple physical violence, and the stages of conflict escalation which occur through the symbolic realm in order to address more effectively post-war conflict and reconciliation.

Nationalism Through Symbols in Post-War Bosnia–Herzegovina

The multi-ethnic Socialist Federal Republic of Yugoslavia (SFRY) disintegrated along national lines, descending into war at the beginning of the 1990s. Cigar, Magas, & Zanic (2001) argue that "the wars were conducted at two levels of reality: the actual and the imaginary, the physical and the symbolic" (Cigar et al., p. xxvii). They maintain that the destruction of sacred objects and cultural monuments was particularly painful for all communities because "they represent an attack on the symbols of their identity, on the referential framework that enables them to orient themselves in space and time" (Cigar et al., p. xxvii). The attack on symbols had a twofold purpose during the war. The first intent was to subject the targeted population to terror and thus pressure them to leave. The second intent was to create ethnically and religiously homogenous areas, which Cigar et al. maintain was a "fundamental component and objective of the war" (Cigar et al., p. xxvii).

However, the destruction also played a second key role beyond intimidation of the 'enemy' population, since it continued well beyond the deportation or killing of these target populations.

> those very monuments of their material presence were treated in principle as a weapon with which competing communities hold a given territory and which must, therefore, be destroyed with other weapons – typologically different, but essentially the same – so as to 'liberate' the territory in question and appropriate it in all its dimensions (Cigar et al., 2001, p. xxviii).

This appropriation of territory through physical building and monuments as well as publically displayed ethnic symbols has continued beyond the war, as will be discussed in greater detail in the case studies later in this chapter. Firstly, the symbolic arsenal of Bosnia's three constituent ethnic groups, the 'tools' employed in this symbolic conflict, will be outlined.

National Symbols in Post-Yugoslav Bosnia–Herzegovina

Under the Yugoslav federation, republics had reflected in their official symbolic arsenal the ethnic identity of the majority population of the republic, with the notable exception of Bosnia–Herzegovina, which had no single ethnic majority. After the dissolution of Yugoslavia until the Dayton agreement each ethnic group used its own ethnic symbols in Bosnia–Herzegovina. The ethno-national symbols in use in neighboring Croatia and Serbia have came into use in Bosnia–Herzegovina in order to symbolize the Bosnian Croat and Bosnian Serb communities. For this reason the Croatian and Serbian symbolic motifs will be discussed below, along with the symbolic representations of Bosnian Muslim (or Bosniak) community.

Representing then Nation: The Main Motifs of Croat, Serb and Muslim Nationhood

The dominant motif of Croatian nationhood is the red and white checkerboard crest, the *šahovnica*. There has been some argument over whether the contemporary use of *šahovnica* should be interpreted as appropriating and rehabilitating World War II era fascist symbolism, or whether this is an unfair tainting of an old, and legitimate symbol. Campbell certainly seems to agree with the former interpretation, arguing that:

> Invoking World War II imagery has been an integral part of Croatia's reemergent nationalism…the appropriation of Ustasa symbols – such as the name of the currency (Kuna) and the red-and-white checkerboard shield (the sahovnica) on the flag – have helped produce this interpretation (Campbell, 1998, p. 9).

While the use of the *kuna* as the currency was certainly a more direct linking to the WWII *Ustaša* state, the use of the *šahovnica* is more complicated. The *šahovnica* has been in use as a symbol for Croats from the fifteenth century, firstly representing only the Croatia proper and not Dalmatia and Slavonia which are represented by other coats of arms (now included on top of the current Republic of Croatia coat of arms). From the nineteenth century it was used to represent all Croats in official Austro–Hungarian insignia.

As (Fig. 7.2) illustrate, during the socialist Yugoslavia, the Republic of Croatia's coat of arms retained the *šahovnica* emblem, meaning that the symbol was never discarded as a symbol of Croats, making protests about its (continued) use problematic. The "U" symbol, seen on the WW II coat of arms and representing the *Ustaša* was banned during the communist years and was not used officially during the war, although it made an appearance among some paramilitary units on graffiti. The *šahovnica* was and remains the most important and extensively used Croat symbol. Bosnian Croats flew the Croatian state flag and used the *šahovnica* motif extensively during and after the war in Bosnia–Herzegovina, as will be discussed in more detail later on in the chapter in the context of the city of Mostar.

Fig. 7.1 Croatia's WWII symbols

Fig. 7.2 Republic of Croatia, SFRY(1945–1990)

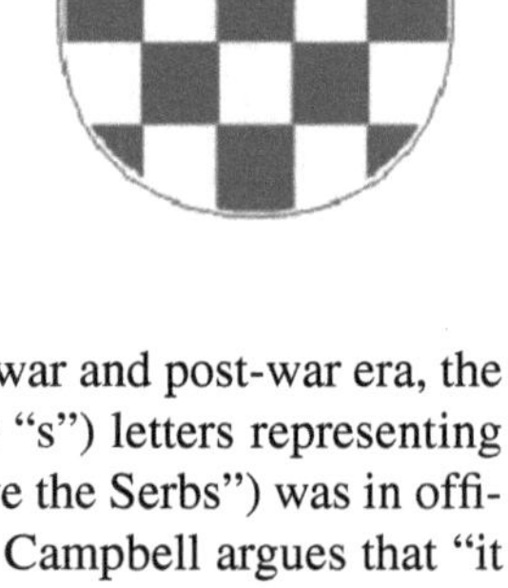

Fig. 7.3 Republic of Croatia (1990–)

Similarly, the most frequently used Serb symbol in the war and post-war era, the Serbian Orthodox cross bracketed by four cyrillic "c" (or "s") letters representing the slogan "*samo sloga spašava srbe*" ("only unity can save the Serbs") was in official use (without the actual cross) in socialist Yugoslavia. Campbell argues that "it is the Serbs who have most vigorously connected religion and nationalism, especially in their use of the Serbian Orthodox cross bracketed by the cyrillic letters for their motto" (Campbell, 1998, p. 45). Sells also notes "the three-fingered hand gestures representing the Christian trinity" which can be added into the symbolic arsenal of the Serbs (Sells, 2003, p. 15).

Fig. 7.4 The Serb cross

Fig. 7.5 Republic of Serbia coat of arms (1945–2004)

Fig. 7.6 Republic of Serbia coat of arms (2004–)

In Bosnia–Herzegovina the Serbian flag and the Serb cross became the most frequently-used markers of Serb territory, with the cross becoming the most widely used motif in pro-Serb graffiti. However, like the Croatian *šahovnica*, this symbol was in official use in the socialist Yugoslavia, as can be seen by looking at Fig. 7.5 above: the Republic of Serbia's coat of arms during this period. Notably, however, the cross itself was not present. Although the Yugoslav state tolerated religious observance and religious institutions it did not sanction them officially.

Fig. 7.7 Republic of Bosnia–Herzegovina flag (1945–1991)

Fig. 7.8 Republic of Bosnia–Herzegovina coat of arms (1946–1991)

The Yugoslav republic of Bosnia–Herzegovina, in contrast to Croatia and Serbia, did not display any overtly ethnic symbolism, containing on the flag only a small image of the Yugoslav flag on simple red background. The crest similarly avoided all historical and ethnic symbolism (Figs. 7.7 and 7.8).

At the breakout of war in Bosnia–Herzegovina, when Bosnian Serbs and Croats adopted the symbols of Serbia and Croatia, the Bosnian Muslims revived the blue and white *fleur-de-lys* coat of arms of the Medieval Bosnian kingdom. In addition, the more overtly Muslim motif, a green flag with a yellow crescent and star came into more common usage, with the color green in general becoming associated with the Bosnian Muslim nation.

The conflation of nationalism and religion evident among the symbols of Croats, Serbs and Muslims is not a new phenomenon, with national communities often defining their boundaries through their adherence to a particular religious doctrine. In a conflict where ethnic distinctions and religious distinctions were practically interchangeable, religious symbolism took on a key function. In Bosnia–Herzegovina universal religious symbols came to be utilised for nationalist purposes across the three main ethnic groups of Bosnia–Herzegovina. The cross and the red and white chequerboard represents the Croats, the cross surrounded by four "C", the Serbian (Orthodox) nation. The green colour, Arabic script and Quaranic inscriptions represent the Muslims.

Velikonja argues that these symbols "were used regularly by the warring sides, either individually or as part of broader political or military symbolism." (Velikonja,

Fig. 7.9 Medieval Bosnia coat of arms King Tvtko reign, fourteenth century

Fig. 7.10 Independent Bosnia flag, 1878

2003, p. 29). There were a number of ways these religio-national symbols were used to signal identity. Velikonja notes that these symbols:

> were worn on uniforms, as personal military decorations (e.g., badges bearing religious symbols, green bands tied around the forehead with or without Qur'anic inscriptions, rosaries), and on military equipment and weapons, flags, etc. Uniforms and appearance were sometimes inspired by religious or religionational tradition, e.g., beards and Islamic outfits on the Bosniak side, and Chetnik-like attire on the Serbian side. Some Bosniak military units assumed names that were inspired by their religion, and in which rigorous religious customs were practiced (e.g., the Green Berets, El Mujahidin, the Green Legion, Muslim Brigades). Among their number were volunteers from various Islamic states (Velikonja, 2003, p. 30).

The *fleur-de-lys* motif was an attempt to represent the Bosnia-Herzegovina as a whole. It was a standard used in King Tvrtko's fourteenth century kingdom, which in addition to Bosnia-Herzegovina encompassed areas of contemporary Croatia. While a *fleur-de-lys* flag was officially adopted as the flag of Bosnia–Herzegovina in 1992, for Bosnian Croats and Serbs, however, this flag became specifically associated with Bosnian Muslims. This seems to be particularly the case because the motif was used by the Army of Bosnia–Herzegovina's (ABiH) largely-Bosnian Muslim forces during the war (Figs. 7.9 and 7.11).

Part of the peace implementation process established by the Dayton Agreement required establishing a commission of persons representing all three groups to propose some alternatives to the existing *fleur-de-lys* flag that would be acceptable to all three ethnic groups. The established commission proposed three designs, but the parliament did not agree on any of the proposed flags. The main objection raised by

Fig. 7.11 Flag of B-H (1992–1998)

Fig. 7.12 The flag of B-H (1998–)

Croat and Serb representatives was the complete lack of ethnic symbolism in the designs (Poels, 1998). The most favoured design received 16 yes votes and 18 no votes (Poels). This was the design subsequently chosen and imposed by the High Representative (Fig. 7.12).

The Flag Institute, was consulted on the process of choosing a new flag for Bosnia–Herzegovina and published an article detailing some of the issues surrounding the potential symbolism to be present on the flag. In the Article he wrote for the institute, Jos Poels, noted:

> Green or crescent or fleur de lys would be associated with the moslems; the red and white chess board pattern with the Croats and the combination of red, white and blue or an eagle with the Serbs (Poels, 1998).

The High Representative chose a design of a yellow triangle on a blue background with a row of white stars. The triangle is vaguely reminiscent of the shape of Bosnia on a map, as well as apparently symbolically representative of the three constituent peoples of Bosnia Herzegovina. The gold colour represents the sun, the universal symbol of life, the blue, the exact shade of the EU blue stands for Europe, as do the stars (Poels, 1998). Hayden recounts that: "[a]t the press conference introducing the flag, the high representative's press officer admitted that it 'looked like a box for breakfast cereal'" (Hayden, 2002). Hayden notes that what was even more important was that "[a]t a more basic level, however, the high representative chose as a symbol of Bosnia a flag that had no emotional meaning whatsoever to the people it was meant to symbolise" (Hayden).

While inter-ethnic clash over symbols resulted in the HR-enforced neutral state flag, at the level of entity flags the ethnic symbols remained. The Federation flag signifies the Bosnian Croat nation by the use of the color red and the *šahovnica*, while the Bosnian Muslims are represented by the color green and the *fleur-de-lys*, this time on a green background. A concession to the EU was made by including the EU motif of a circle of stars on a dark blue background (Fig. 7.13).

Fig. 7.13 Federation flag (1996–2007)

Fig. 7.14 Republika Srpska flag (1992–)

At the beginning of 2007 the Constitutional Court of Bosnia–Herzegovina has proclaimed both entity coat of arms motifs unconstitutional, as they do not represent all three constituent nations of Bosnia–Herzegovina (CCB 2006). As a consequence, the Federation flag was withdrawn from usage. No significant progress has been made on this question to date as no shared symbols have been identified which would represent the Bosnian community as a whole, and that would be acceptable to the national elites overwhelmingly represented in the parliament.

Mostar: Symbolic Representations of the Croat-Muslim Divide

On the ground and across Bosnia–Herzegovina, national belonging and "ownership" of territory has constantly been reinforced, even after the war officially ended. Croatian flags and *šahovnica* symbols are in evidence throughout the Croatian-dominated areas in post offices, on telephone cards, restaurant walls and street signs, to the point that Torsti concludes "it has been hard to tell from what one sees that one is not in Croatia proper". Echoing Michael Bilig's banal nationalism thesis, Torsti argues that "the Croat nation has been 'flagged' overwhelmingly in Bosnian Croat areas" (Torsti, 2004, p. 146).

The city of Mostar in particular has exemplified warfare through symbolism in post-war Bosnia. Mostar is the largest city in the Herzegovina region, which forms the southern tip of Bosnia–Herzegovina. The last census in 1991 counted 76,000 inhabitants of which 34% expressed themselves as Muslim, 29% as Croat, 19% as Serb and 18% as Yugoslav (Bose, p. 100). During the war Mostar was divided between Croat and Muslim forces, and became the focus of Bosnian-Croat efforts to establish a separate entity, Herceg-Bosna. Although Herceg-Bosna did not eventuate, by the war's end Mostar was partitioned between Croats and Muslims, with the Croat-controlled western remaining the de facto capital of Croat Bosnia. No updated census data is available, but anecdotal evidence suggests that the city has become progressively more Croat due to migration of ethnic Croats from other parts of Bosnia–Herzegovina into the city, and the migration out of Mostar by other ethnic groups. Croats are now estimated to make up approximately 60% of the population, while the Serb proportion of the population has dwindled significantly (Gunzburger-Makas, 2006).

In Mostar, as Bose has noted, "The most striking aspect of…partition consists of visual symbols used to mark zones and boundaries of territorial control." (Bose, 2002, p. 141) The border of Muslim territory on the west bank is marked by a line of minarets belonging to mosques built since the end of the war. Croatian territory, conversely, is marked by Christian, specifically Catholic, symbols and structures. The beginning of Croatian Mostar is marked by an imposing Catholic cathedral. In order to reinforce the Croatian claim on Mostar, in June 2000 the Croat political party, Croatian Democratic Community (HDZ) and the Croatian Defence Council (HVO) installed a large, imposing cross on Mount Hum, which overlooks the entire town (Bose, p. 141). The cross was inaugurated in an elaborate ceremony which included the keynote speech in which the HVO General Stanko Sopta described Mostar as "the capital of the Croat nation" in Bosnia–Herzegovina (Bose, p. 142). The message was not lost on Mostar's Muslim inhabitants, causing tension in the Muslim part of the city that day (Bose, p. 141).

Street names in Mostar have also been co-opted into the war of symbols. In the Muslim areas of East Mostar, the street names retain their pre-war names, including the Marshall Tito street. In the Croat areas, however, street names now most closely resemble those of Croatia's capital, Zagreb (Torsti, 2004, p. 152). Therefore while Mostar technically remains a multi-ethnic town the Muslim-Croat entity, in practice through the use of symbols and physical structures as markers of ownership, it has been very effectively ethnically segregated.

Banja Luka: Undermining the Serb Republic with a Mosque

In the case of Republika Srpska, antagonistic symbolism is even more prevalent, claiming the entity exclusively for the Serb nation and rejecting Bosnia–Herzegovina as a state. Bose notes that at the end of 2001, the border crossing between Bosnia–Herzegovina and Croatia flew the Serbian flag, and border stamps only named the border town in Cyrillic, making no mention of the state of Bosnia–Herzegovina (Bose, 2002, p. 158). This rejection is further reinforced in the way Republika Srpska and Bosnia–Herzegovina are commonly represented on public maps in this entity. In the schools in Republika Srpska, the maps show:

> either the Serb Republic only, or the Serb Republic connected to Serbia with similar colours and the rest of Bosnia in a different colour so that it appears to be a different country. The same has been true for all sorts of products with maps: telephone cards, weather forecasts in newspapers and on the television of the Serb Republic (Bose, 2002, p. 159).

Schools are often named after Serb national heroes whose portraits, along with Orthodox saints, often hang on school walls. Pictures of Draža Mihajlović and the double-eagle, "a symbol of Serbdom" are on sale on everything from keyrings to T-shirts (Bose, 2002, p. 159).

As has already been noted in the case of Mostar, it is not only the symbols of nation and state which have become a battleground between Bosnia's ethnic groups. Ancient and new buildings are enlisted in the battle to claim exclusive rights to territory. One prominent example of buildings as symbols in post-war Bosnia–Herzegovina, is the case of the Ferhadija mosque in Banja Luka. Banja Luka, an important provincial town before the war, became the centre for Bosnian Serbs during the war, and the seat of the Republika Srpska government in post-Dayton Bosnia–Herzegovina (Bose, 2002, p. 154). Before the war Serbs made up just over half of Banja Luka's population. While no post-war census has taken place in Banja Luka, it is understood that the war-time expulsions and post-war migrations have resulted in a city that is now overwhelmingly ethnically Serb in composition (Stefansson, 2006).

The Ferhadija mosque, built in 1579, was a major historic feature of Banja Luka until it was demolished in May 1993 by Serb military units (Bose, 2002, p. 154). It was one of 16 mosques in Banja Luka in 1992, all of which were destroyed during the war. After a protracted effort and years of pressure from international community for the mosque to be rebuilt, the Banja Luka city authorities approved the reconstruction (Bose, p. 155). On the eighth anniversary of its destruction, 7 May 2001, a ceremony was arranged to lay the foundation-stone for the mosque's reconstruction. On the day of the ceremony, however, between 2,000 and 4,000 Serb demonstrators disrupted the event (Bose, p. 155). Rocks, stones, bottles and eggs were thrown at Bosnian and foreign dignitaries, prompting the attendees to seek shelter in the adjoining Islamic community centre. Several of the Bosnian Muslims who were attending the ceremony were "brutally beaten", "prayer rugs were set on fire", and the "green flag on the Islamic community centre, building was torn down and set ablaze" (Bose). Five of the buses which had transported some of the Bosnian Muslim civilians from Federation towns were also set on fire. In an obvious effort to offend the Muslims in attendance, a piglet was let loose in front of the building, and proceeded to dig up the ground marked for the corner stone (Bose). Thirty people were injured in the riot including one man who "had been beaten unconscious on his prayer rug" and who died in hospital 2 weeks later (Bose, p. 156). The ceremony was postponed, and when it was finally held a month later, the 1,000–2,000 strong crowd which showed up was held at bay by a "resolute and organised police operation" (Bose, p. 158).

Why did the Ferhadija ceremony cause such riots when in the first half of 2001 nearly 1,800 Bosnian Muslims returned to Banja Luka without major incident? (Bose, 2002, p. 159). Bose argues that the reason for the rioting over the mosque was the symbolic implication of its reconstruction. A reconstructed Ferhadija in the middle of Banja Luka would claim equal rights to existence for Muslim faith and heritage alongside Serb Orthodox structures in Banja Luka, thereby undoing the

Serb community's exclusive claim to the city. The prospect of the reconstruction of the mosque, therefore:

> represents a violation of and fundamental challenge to the symbolic basis of the precept of partition. It represents a negation of the principle of a space *exclusively* belonging to (or at the very least, unambiguously dominated by) one national community, and a symbolic reinstatement and re-validation in principle of the concept of an *intercommunal space* (Bose, 2002, p. 160).

However, as Bose argues, the Ferhadija riots do not mean that the situation in Banja Luka is neither completely bleak nor necessarily permanent. "Those who rioted and those who tacitly supported" Bose argues, "are acutely aware that while BiH may be deeply divided along national faultlines, it is *not* partitioned as fully and permanently as they would prefer" (Bose, 2002, p. 160). As at the end of 2010, work on the reconstruction of Ferhadija is slowly progressing without further incidents.

The Symbolism of Religious Buildings

More than 2,000 culturally-significant buildings were damaged during the war, according to the Institute for the Protection of Cultural, Historical and Natural Heritage of Bosnia. These include 1,115 mosques, 309 Catholic churches, 36 Serbian Orthodox churches and 1,079 other public buildings (Herscher, 1998). As Herscher argues "architecture was understood by those prosecuting the war as a clear sign of historical ownership of those territories" (Herscher). In order to be able to label this specific and deliberate destruction of buildings for their symbolic value two terms have come into usage: "warchitecture," as a term describing the deliberate destruction of architecture; and "urbicide," meaning the deliberate destruction of cities because of their typically multicultural environments (Herscher).

Velikonja (2003) notes that while sacred buildings which were the first to be destroyed, they were often the first to be replaced, and often through sponsorship by foreign countries or their religious communities. He notes specifically the Greek Orthodox Church, the Islamic community particularly from Saudi Arabia, and the Roman Catholic Church. It was not unusual that after the enemy's religious buildings were destroyed and a town "cleansed", that these destroyed buildings were replaced with religious buildings representing the victorious group for whom the town has been claimed. In a post-war society where much of the essential infrastructure was destroyed, the high priority given to building religious structures, which after all are symbolic rather than practical, is particularly illustrative of the central role of ethno-religious symbols in Bosnian war and post-war society.

In towns and cities across Bosnia–Herzegovina it is clear that the diversity present before the war has either been significantly reduced or completely eliminated. As no census has taken place since the war began, there are no accurate figures or statistics to clearly illustrate the post-war demographic situation, or to what extent the multiethnic diversity and coexistence prevalent before the war has been destroyed. If for example there are no Muslims currently residing in a town where a number of mosques were destroyed is there a point to rebuilding the mosques? Will those buildings then become monuments and museums of the town's relocated or murdered inhabitants instead of buildings serving living communities? Perhaps resources should be directed instead towards supporting the return of those who fled, and establishing much needed infrastructure like schools or medical facilities. It certainly appears that churches and mosques in post-Yugoslav states are less about serving the worship needs of their faith communities and more about asserting their physical presence in contested geopolitical space.

Shared Symbols, Shared Space

What is at stake in the war of symbols in Bosnia–Herzegovina is the concept of *shared space*, namely space "belonging equally to all communities which has been the key to coexistence in Bosnia for centuries" (Bose, 2002, p. 141). This concept, Bose argues has been 'grievously damaged' since the breakup of Yugoslavia and the war. This is demonstrated by the difficulty of finding symbols that represent the whole of the Bosnian community, an issue which has been a recurring feature of Bosnia's post-war social and political landscape. The most prominent example of this is the difficulties encountered in setting some basic, functional symbols for the state in Bosnia–Herzegovina, as was noted earlier in the discussion of Bosnia–Herzegovina's flag. It took almost 3 years for Bosnia's politicians to agree on the state's flag and coat of arms. Ultimately, the flag and the national anthem, notably without lyrics, were imposed by the international community, through the position of High Representative. Bosnia–Herzegovina's currency is equally devoid of any local symbolism; the Convertible Mark (KM) was named after and pegged to the German currency (until the introduction of the Euro).

While symbols that divide are easy to identify, those with a potential to unite a post-conflict society and create this desperately needed sense of shared space are more difficult to conceptualise. In post-war Bosnia–Herzegovina the task of symbolically representing and uniting a divided community appears almost insurmountable, and yet it is crucial step in reconstructing Bosnian society. In order to examine how this is being addressed in Bosnia–Herzegovina, two projects attempting to breach this symbolic division are discussed in detail, the Think BiH campaign, and the erection of the Bruce Lee statue in Mostar.

Think BIG, Think BiH

The "Think BiH", advertising campaign was rolled out across Bosnia–Herzegovina's media and public space in 2005 and 2006. With the slogan "Think BIG, Think BiH", the initiative aimed to "promoting Bosnia–Herzegovina inside its own borders" (Bosnia unveils Bruce Lee bronze, 2005). The project was organised by Nazif Hasanbegović, from Concept Metropolis Communications (CMC), a Sarajevan

Fig. 7.15 The campaign "stamp" logo

advertising agency, and supported by the Goethe Institute and the American Embassy. Hasanbegović, the campaign director, explained the motives behind the project, arguing that:

> The purpose of this project is to find a minimum of common criteria for developing a state identity (which is currently absent). The project aims to develop those factors that will promote the acceptance of a state not guided by national or party interests and egoism, nor by ideological motivation and exclusivism, but rather only by the desire to promote basic values of the state (Schroen & Hasanbegovic, 2006).

He maintained that the campaign seeks to achieve this by "motivating individuals to think about the common state as an advantage and a virtue, and not as something that denies national diversity and cultural particularities." Hasanbegović stated:

> we..wish to show the public that as long as they are motivated by positive ideas things can move on from deadlock. However, we also wanted to show the rights and responsibilities which the public has towards the state (Schroen & Hasanbegovic, 2006).

A selection of images from the campaign are reproduced below. Figure 7.16 shows the biggest 14 towns in Bosnia–Herzegovina, each represented by a clock and each showing a different time. The TV ad developed from this image shows the clocks starting all at different time, but moving rapidly towards showing the same time. The ad alludes to the existence of different thinking across Bosnia, and the need for a sense of unity, of being "on the same page". Figure 7.17 emphasizes the diversity of Bosnia with the slogan "This is reality", presumably attempting to reach those that still wish to live in homogenous communities, and who think that a homogenous life is still possible. This ad states that Bosnia–Herzegovina is a multiethnic and multi-confessional society and must be accepted as such. However, this image does not necessarily convey a positive message in this instance, the image/slogan combination almost comes across as a threat or a warning: "this is the reality of BiH, and you better get used to it'.

Noticeably, the only "symbol" of Bosnia–Herzegovina employed in the first set of ads is a simple outline of the state map utilized to form the "stamp" motif (Fig. 7.15) of the campaign which contains the words "think" in the Cyrillic (representing Serbs), Latin alphabet (representing Croats and Bosnian Muslims), as well as German and English (representing the campaign partners and/or the international

Fig. 7.16 Clocks representing Bosnian towns

Fig. 7.17 This is reality

outlook of the Bosnian society?). Figure 7.16 is the only representation of BiH symbols, showing the crest of the state of Bosnia–Herzegovina.

While the idea is commendable, it is doubtful that selling the idea of Bosnia–Herzegovina through advertising techniques used to sell washing powder or a supermarket chain will achieve the desired goal. The ads are noticeably absent of any truly 'local' content – the images are for the most part global – most of the ads would be as applicable to Australia, Britain or France as they are to Bosnia–Herzegovina. The only exception to this is Fig. 7.18, which refers to the constitution of Bosnia–Herzegovina. Even this ad, however, implicitly admits that a large proportion of BiH's citizens *do not* consider themselves BiH citizens. It is hard to imagine an ad of similar nature in Australia, reminding the citizens of Victoria, for example, that they are also citizens of Australia.

Fig. 7.18 All citizens of any entity are by that very fact, also citizens of Bosnia Herzegovina, Constitution of Bosnia–Herzegovina

Instead of surreptitiously avoiding all symbols and images of any significance to Bosnians, the campaign might be more effective, although admittedly far more difficult to conceptualize under current conditions, if it highlighted the shared and inclusive aspects of Bosnia's history and culture.

Bruce Lee and Mostar: Global Pop Culture as a Symbol of Reconciliation

In response to this divisive politics which have typically been evident in post-war Bosnia in general, and Mostar in particular, one NGO group based in Mostar came up with a novel project – they decided to erect a life-size bronze statue of Bruce Lee. The statue was inaugurated in late November 2005 in a park in the middle of the city, the only monument built in post-war Bosnia–Herzegovina that has not been accompanied with a public outcry from at least one ethnic group.

This is an initiative promoted by two founders of a local NGO, Urban Movement, Veselin Gatalo and Nino Raspudić. In an article written before the raising of the monument, Raspudić discussed the general intentions behind the monument project:

> in the city where everything is split/divided, we would like to remind that, outside of the vicious circle of national conflict, there still exist numerous things that are common to all inhabitants/citizens of Mostar (Raspudic, 2005).

Gatalo stated at the unveiling ceremony: "We will always be Muslims, Serbs or Croats...but one thing we all have in common is Bruce Lee" (Bosnia unveils Bruce Lee bronze, 2005). At the unveiling, Gatalo discussed the reasons behind the specific choice of Bruce Lee, an icon of global pop culture:

> He's far [enough] away from us that nobody can ask what he did during World War II, during World War I, or what his ancestors did under Turkey. He's ... not Catholic, not Orthodox, not Muslim...Bruce Lee is part of our idea of universal justice – that the good guys can win (Kampschror, 2005).

Raspudić elaborated on the moral lessons Bruce Lee embodies for the younger generation in a format with which they are familiar and to which they can relate:

> For generations and generations that were raised on his seventies movies, he was the embodiment of honesty, fight for justice, protection of the weak, loyalty to his friends and master. At the time when all moral values are underestimated, when kids in Bosnia and Herzegovina carry guns in school and find their role models in criminals, the monument to Bruce Lee in the center of the town would be a reminder on our childhood dreams about [a] more righteous world ... (Raspudic, 2005).

Kampschor argued that "the Bruce Lee tribute will stand as the only monument raised in postwar Bosnia without an uproar", although the direction in which the statue will face was a sensitive issue, the statue unable to entirely circumvent the politics of symbols so embedded in contemporary Mostar (Kampschror, 2005). Facing West the statue would be interpreted as defending west Mostar from east Mostar, or vice versa. The statue could also not be positioned to face south, as then it would be deemed to be defending Mostar from Croatia. Therefore, the Bruce Lee statue was carefully positioned to face north, where "he looks nowhere" (Raspudic).

One of the organizers, Raspudić, argued that the initiative was attempting to regain meaning for public spaces "and at the same time to question the significance of monuments and symbols, old ones as well as new ones" (Raspudic, 2005). He noted the importance and the power of pop culture in bringing together former enemies:

> The "low" registry [mass culture, kung fu, childhood heroes] s being revalorized, for its power to evoke little ordinary things of everyday life that do not have anything to do with politics and ideologies, and that bring people and nations together instead of separating them (everybody is fond of Bruce Lee: Bosniaks, Croats and Serbs, left and right political options...).

The monument of Bruce Lee is political precisely because of its apolitical, 'low-brow' and protest content, highlighting the distrust in and the inadequacy of current political symbols. It also situates Bosnians in a global community of values and aspirations, transcending the constraining and problematized nature of local symbolic reference points. While the statue was short-lived, vandalized within hours of installation, it nevertheless marked a promising attempt to transcend inter-ethnic symbolic divisions. The Bruce Lee statue project showed the role that (global) popular culture could potentially play in reconciling ethnic divisions in post-war Bosnian society.

Conclusion

In a post-conflict society existing ethnic symbols pose a difficult problem as they often embody and perpetuate the recent conflict. By widening the definition of conflict, and allowing for a multidisciplinary approach to the measurement and amelioration of post-war inter-ethnic conflict, peace psychology enables us to address the developments taking place in the symbolic realm of post-conflict societies. In a society where all local and historical symbols have been (mis)appropriated for nationalist purposes, and have been used to perpetuate conflict through other means, a symbolic vocabulary which transcends ethnic divisions is desperately needed. The battleground for post-Yugoslav states in general, and Bosnia–Herzegovina in particular, is whether these values continue to be based on supreme and exclusive rights of a particular ethnic group, or transform towards a more inclusive and pluralistic conception of the Bosnian political community. The changing nature of monuments and symbols in post-Yugoslav states will certainly be a salient litmus test.

References

Bose, S. (2002). *Bosnia after Dayton: Nationalist partition and international intervention*. London: C. Hurst & Co.

Bosnia unveils Bruce Lee bronze. (2005, November). *BBC News UK*.

Campbell, D. (1998). *National deconstruction: Violence, identity, and justice in Bosnia*. Minneapolis, MN: University of Minnesota Press.

Cerulo, K. A. (1995). *Identity designs: The sights and sounds of a nation*. New Brunswick, NJ: Rutgers University Press.

Christie, D. J. (2006). What is peace psychology the psychology of? *Journal of Social Issues, 62*(1), 1–17.

Christie, D. J., Tint, B. S., Wagner, R. V., & Winter, D. D. (2008). Peace psychology for a peaceful world. *American Psychologist, 63*(6), 540–552.

Cigar, N., Magas, B., & Zanic, I. (2001). Introduction. In I. Zanic & B. Magas (Eds.), *The war in Croatia and Bosnia-Herzegovina, 1991–1995*. Portland, OR: Frank Cass Publishers. pp. xxxi, 383 p.

Cohen, A. (1974). *Two-dimensional man: An essay on the anthropology of power and symbolism in complex society*. London: Routledge/Kegan Paul.

Constitutional Court of Bosnia and Herzegovina, Decision U-4/04, Sarajevo. November 18, 2006.

Hayden, R. M. (2002). Let Dayton be Dayton. In G. T. Dempsey (Ed.), *Exiting the Balkan Thicket*. Washington, DC: Cato Institute.

Herscher, A. (1998). Remembering and rebuilding in Bosnia. *Transitions, 5*(3). ww.tol.org.

Kampschror, B. (2005). Bosnians Agree: Commemorate Bruce Lee. *Christian Science Monitor*. November 23, 2005. Newspaper article available online. http://www.csmonitor.com/2005/1123/p07s02-woeu.html.

Kaufman, S. J. (2001). *Modern hatreds: The symbolic politics of ethnic war*. New York: Cornell University Press.

Mach, Z. A. (1993). *Symbols, conflict, and identity: Essays in political anthropology*. Albany, NY: State University of New York Press.

Makas, E. G. (2006). Competing visions of Postwar Mostar. In "Cultural Encounters in Urban Space" European Association for Urban History Conference. Stockholm.

Poels, J. (1998). Bosnia and Herzegovina: A new 'neutral' flag. Retrieved August 1, 2006, from Flag Institute: www.flaginstitute.org/fibosnia.htm.

Raspudic, N. (2005). Relations 2005: De/construction of Monument, Bosnia–Herzegovina. Retrieved March 15, 2006, from http://www.projekt-relations.de/en/explore/deconstruction/start.php.

Schroen, M., & Hasanbegovic, N. (2006). Think BIG! – Misli BiH!. Sarajevske Sveske (Sarajevo Notebook), No. 13.

Sells, M. (2003). Crosses of blood: Sacred space, religion, and violence in Bosnia–Herzegovina. *Sociology of Religion, 64*(3), 309–331.

Stefansson, A. H. (2006). Homes in the making: Property restitution, refugee return, and sense of belonging in a post-war Bosnian town. *International Migration, 44*(3), 115–137.

Tismaneanu, V. (1997). Fantasies of salvation: Varieties of nationalism in postcommunist Eastern Europe. In M. D. Kennedy (Ed.), *Envisioning Eastern Europe: Postcommunist cultural studies* (4th ed., p. 249). Ann Arbor, MI: University of Michigan Press.

Torsti, P. (2004). History culture and banal nationalism in post-war Bosnia. *Southeast European Politics, 5*(2–3), 142–157.

Velikonja, M. (2003). In Hoc Signo Vinces: Religious symbolism in the Balkan wars 1991–1995. *International Journal of Politics, Culture and Society, 17*(1), 25–40.

Walzer, M. (1967). On the role of symbolism in political thought. *Political Science Quarterly, 82*(2), 191–204.

Chapter 8
Imagine Being Alone: Making Sense of Life in Contemporary Bosnia and Herzegovina by Remembering the Past

Sandina Begić

Abstract The purpose of this chapter is to explore the ways in which people experience changes that are transpiring in their society and how the experience of living through these changes influences their perception of their society and their place in it. The setting that is the focus of my study is Sarajevo, the capital of post-war Bosnia and Herzegovina, 14 years after the signing of the Dayton Peace Accords, which ended the 1992–1995 war in this country. Through a single case study, I examine how a woman who has spent her entire life in the same neighborhood talks about changes that are taking place in her country, her city, and her neighborhood. The findings suggest that the experience of displacement is possible even if one had never been physically displaced, an experience that appears to be inextricably linked to the perceived loss of socio–cultural context. This finding could serve as a basis for future investigations into how loss of social context relates to peoples' experience of belonging, a research venture that is especially warranted in today's changing world, with many people losing their sense of belongingness due to either actual physical displacement or social and cultural changes that are transpiring both in their immediate environment as well as globally.

Keywords Bosnia and Herzegovina • Transition • Displacement • Belongingness • Social change

S. Begić (✉)
Frances L. Hiatt School of Psychology, Clark University,
950 Main Street, 01610 Worcester, MA, USA
e-mail: sbegic@clarku.edu

O. Simić et al. (eds.), *Peace Psychology in the Balkans: Dealing with a Violent Past while Building Peace*, Peace Psychology Book Series, DOI 10.1007/978-1-4614-1948-8_8,

It is year '69, my old man and I,
On bicycles
Riding toward Ilidža,[1] toward rivers and meadows
Where common people from Sarajevo gather
Blankets, beer, barbeque and volleyball
Colorful as a traditional rug
And from the radio tunes of a familiar song
And news from Vietnam

My old man said then
"You see everybody knows that politics is a simple thing
When you prepare coffee, you always set aside an extra fildžan[2]
In case someone stops by"
...

Spring '92, hot iron blew away
All neighborhoods and all gatherings
They said everything was a lie, a deceit...

My old man, cleaning the ruins, said then
"It is not my yellow Yugo[3] or my apartment that I mourn
But the fact that I will never again set aside an extra fildžan
In case someone stops by"

Excerpts from a No Smoking Band song "Fildžan viška[4]"

We live in a progressively complex, rapidly changing world, in which changes that are taking place both locally and globally can have multiple effects – adverse and favorable – on social ties in one's immediate environment. They can lead to feelings of estrangement and alienation, but they can also be a source of new meanings (Hermans & Dimaggion, 2007; Valsiner, 2003). Although processes of globalization and with it associated localization impact all people and societies (Stiglitz, 2002), they can be particularly intensified in societies that are marked by political and structural violence.

The present study, set in Bosnia and Herzegovina (BiH), a postwar society, in which changes associated with globalization are exacerbated by the recent war and the postwar period marked by stale processes of transitioning from war to peace, from socialism to democracy, from planned to free market economy, explores the complex interplay between the pressing demands of our changing world and the important role relationship plays in human life (e.g., Jovchelovitch, 2007; Maček, 2001; Turner, 1982). In her recent article on the relationship between trauma associated with political displacement and personal development in the context of Zimbabwe, Knight (2006) remarks that the negative emotions which were occasionally experienced by her key informant, a white displaced ex-farmer, were not

[1] A popular outing spot on the outskirts of Sarajevo.

[2] A small coffee cup from which coffee is traditionally drunk in this region.

[3] A type of car manufactured in the former Yugoslavia.

[4] A spare coffee cup.

necessarily related to the loss of his farm; instead, they were more associated with the loss of friendships of other ex-farmers. Building on this finding, the present study explores how a middle-aged woman, who has lived in the same Sarajevo neighborhood her entire life, including the time of siege and the postwar period, makes sense of her present life by remembering the past. I hope that my key informant's testimony yields insight into the complex relationship between social change and personal development more generally and can stand as an example of how people undergo changes in a particular geopolitical context, that of contemporary Bosnia and Herzegovina.

Dramaturgicality of Everyday Life

"No society is without some mode of metacommentary," or in Geetz's terms, a "story a group tells itself about itself" (Turner, 1982, p. 104). Turner applies the concept of metacommentary to theater, and asserts that every society has a play it "acts about itself – not only a reading of its experience but an interpretive enactment of its experience" (p. 104). According to Turner (1982), it is this social drama of everyday life that keeps us alive. Similarly, Karahasan (1993) conceptualizes the culture of Sarajevo (and Bosnia and Herzegovina) as a dramaturgical culture. He asserts that in a dramaturgical culture the principal relationship between the elements of the system is oppositional. They are positioned against each other and are mutually bounded precisely by this opposition in which they define each other. In other words, in a dramaturgical cultural system every member of the system needs the Other as an affirmation of one's identity.

Tensions between structure and communitas (anti-structure) that exist in any society are critical to sustaining the existence of a society, while at the same time safeguarding the feeling of community (Turner, 1974). Following Turner, liminality, a phase during which communitas emerge, can be conceptualized as a time and space of transition from one system to another – a situation or phase which is marked by ambiguity and can lead to new meanings and perspectives. In Turner's (1974) words, liminality "occurs in the middle phase of the rites of passage which marks changes in an individual's or a group's social status and/or cultural or psychological state" (p. 273). This conceptualization of liminality suggests that it is a temporary phase during which the subject "passes through a realm or dimension that has few or none of the attributes of the past or coming state" and "is betwixt and between all familiar lines of classification" (Turner & Turner, 1978, p. 2).

Countries of the former Eastern Bloc can be perceived to have gone through the three phases of the rite of passage as described by Turner and Turner (1978): preliminary phase (separation), liminal phase, and the final phase of aggregation. In the preliminary phase, societies are separated from the old system (communism), followed by the liminal phase of being "betwixt and between" the old and the new system, concluding with the final phase of integration into the new system (democratic 'European family'). This process of transition from one system to another is marked by symbolic death of the old system (communism) and birth of a new (democratic) nation.

Turner (1974) further asserts that during the liminal phase social class and roles are de-emphasized and sometimes even ignored. A somewhat paradoxical example would be wartime, when social class loses its importance and people form communitas in which all become more or less equal regardless of the social roles they occupy in peacetime. Although counterintuitive, the experience of selflessness might be amplified in the time of crisis, when people's sense of humanity is perhaps even more accentuated than during non-crisis times. Exploring how her key informant switches between different modes of thinking in contemplating his and others' participation in the Bosnian conflict, Maček (2001) points out that "the experience of war forces us to make our own individual ethical choices in every given situation" and concludes that "if we recognize this fact, it becomes very hard to escape the personal responsibility for the choices we make and the actions we take" (p. 219).

Bosnia and Herzegovina: A Society in Transition

What happens if a society enters the state of permanent liminality, when transition from one state to another cannot be completed, and an individual, a group, a society is 'stuck' in the liminal phase waiting for the objective conditions to change?

Postwar BiH seems to be 'stuck' in the liminal phase, not any longer in the old system but not yet in the new one, not any longer in war but not yet in peace. It seems to be permanently "betwixt and between" two states. Many people in BiH complain that the feeling of solidarity is almost entirely gone 14 years after the war. There is little trust, and people feel that even neighborly relationships have been strained by the omnipresent feeling of uncertainty and distrust (United Nations Development Programme [UNDP], 2008). This can be associated with what Turner (1974) describes as "reversed effect" liminality can have – the possibility of "either a Hobbesian war of all against all, or an existential anarchy of individuals, each doing his or her own thing" (p. 285). This is similar to what de Rivera (1997), following MacMurray, describes as a situation when the concern for oneself becomes dominant and conceals "the caring that is latently present." When this happens, "the person feels uncared for and is faced with a choice" and "may decide they cannot depend on the other and must take an individualistic path and look out for himself or herself. Alternatively, the person may decide that *if* they are good and do what is expected of them *then* they will be taken care of, so they take a conformist path" (p. 6).

Both Turner and MacMurray stress that there is an alternative developmental path a person or a society can take. Turner (1974) asserts that "if men operated within and according to the norms of the structure without seeking to subvert those norms to their own self-interest or factional goals" then, in his view, "the result in terms of peaceful, just, social coexistence would be similar to those produced by spontaneous, existential communitas" (p. 284). He further emphasizes that this position "implies, on the one hand, a bonding of individuals by rituals or propriety, and, on the other, a safeguarding of each individual's independence within the general interdependence" (p. 284). This is similar to what de Rivera (1997), following MacMurray, suggests as an alternative path to either individualism or conformism. In de Rivera's words:

> [P]ersons may be able to restore personal relationships by having their caring for the other resurface to dominate self-concern and direct the relationship with the other. Making this choice often requires choosing socio-emotional relations such as forgiveness, acceptance, faith, vulnerability... This does not mean that one person is submerged in the other but that a person is available to cooperate out of a genuine concern for the other knowing that the other is, likewise, concerned for the self (p. 7).

Turner's work on structure and communitas provides a conceptual foundation for how societies function and why it might be interesting to understand the role komšiluk (neighborhood) plays in the context of BiH, because it is komšiluk which functions as communitas in BiH, closer to liminoid than to liminal, for it is not governed by strict rules, but by voluntary decisions of individual persons to either participate in it or not. It should be noted that neighborhood in BiH is not limited to a shared living space; it implicates sharing one's life, worries, hopes, fears, and gossip during coffee drinking rituals, shared meals, chatting, births and deaths.

Contextualizing the Present Study

It is important to place participants in everyday life in BiH in the geohistorical political context of their changing society (e.g., Christie, 2006; Christie, Tint, Wagner, & DuNann Winter, 2008), in which not only economic and political systems are changing, but also its architecture and population structure. Old family houses are increasingly being replaced by modern buildings. The makeup of neighborhoods has changed due to wartime displacement and with it associated rapid urbanization. For example, the majority of the Sarajevo's Sephardic Jewish population has left for Israel in an organized exodus during the most recent war (Karahasan, 1993). Neighborhoods which were populated by members of different ethnic groups are now populated by displaced persons. These demographic changes may create tension between old inhabitants and newcomers, who, aside from being members of the same ethnic group, might have little in common in terms of their values and ways of life.

The coffee drinking ritual, which constitutes one of the most important social practices in BiH, is a social event in its own right as virtually everything is done over coffee – from socializing and dating to business transactions. When prepared at home, coffee is traditionally prepared in large quantities, even if only two people are drinking it. The reason behind this practice is that one never knows when a friend or a neighbor might stop by; hence, there is always an extra fildžan for the un-expected guest. This practice is very important because it signifies the openness of the Bosnian household to one's neighbors who seldom announce their visit. The changing demographic structure of many neighborhoods and towns across BiH, in addition to economic, political, and other forms of uncertainty, impact the important feeling of neighborhood. Resettled persons (new neighbors) and returnees (new old neighbors) bring their values, beliefs and practices which may be perceived to be refreshing and mixing with existing practices of the host neighborhood can lead to the emergence of new meanings and value systems. However, they can also be perceived as threatening already existing values and practices of the host neighborhood (and community) and lead to the hardening of the boundary between old and new neighbors.

Methodology

My key informant, who I will refer to as Esma in this chapter, is in many ways an average Sarajevan. In fact, she self-identifies as a Sarajevan, who "was born, has always lived and will most likely die in Sarajevo." Before the war, Esma was employed in a major factory where she had a "great income." Today, she is retired but because her pension is too small to live on, she is forced to work to make a decent living. Esma remembers life in the old system with great nostalgia and is discontent with the present situation in her country. Although she does not complain about her current personal situation, she dreads old age mainly because she fears that people have changed so much that nobody will be there to provide her company or help her if she becomes ill and unable to care for herself.

Esma and I knew each other and lived in the same neighborhood for 13 months, she as a lifelong resident and I as a researcher and a 'returnee from America'. I asked her if I could have an audio-recorded conversation with her. She agreed but was surprised that I 'chose' her to participate in my study since she felt that she was not "competent" to speak on the situation in her country, describing herself as "just another ordinary person," who did not know much about "the science" I was "doing". I assured her that she should not dread the science I was doing. After all, I was interested in her experience of living in her society and her neighborhood, and she certainly knew more about it than I.

It might be worth noting that I was accepted into the neighborhood because I was dating one of the neighborhood boys. In that respect, my position was not one of an utter outsider – I 'married into' the neighborhood. The interview, or as I prefer to call it, our conversation (see Bibace, Clegg, & Valsiner (2009) for a discussion on participant terminology), started with Esma preparing coffee for us in her modest apartment. We had a conversation like many times before, only this time our conversation was recorded, which initially created some awkwardness, but after the first cup of coffee, the recorder that was sitting among the coffee utensils became unnoticeable. Although our conversation was conducted in the culturally appropriate conversational style, my questions to Esma, modeled after Cantril's (1965) self-anchoring approach, were guided by my interest in illuminating how people make sense of life in their changing society, how they shape relationships with others in their environment and how they are being shaped by the experience of living in their changing society.

Interview data were subjected to the phenomenological psychological method of data analysis (Giorgi & Giorgi, 2003; Wertsch, 1977). Within this approach, the researcher's goal is to understand the account provided by the interviewee from the interviewee's point of view and "the way the situation appears to the subject, the meanings of the objects and events for him, and the participation in terms of which such meanings arise" (Wertz, 1977, p. 24). It needs to be noted that since this study is based on a single case, all conclusions drawn from it should be treated tentatively as it might be difficult to draw general conclusions based on a single case. On the other hand, there are certain advantages to the case study approach, as it provides depth over breath, which is gained by conducting studies with a large sample. In the social sciences there is a place for both approaches: the case study approach provides a deeper understanding of the phenomenon under study whereas the use of interviews with large groups of people yields a more general understanding (e.g., Berg, 2001; Denzin & Lincoln, 1994; Rubin & Rubin, 2005).

I would like to express my deepest gratitude to Esma, who not only genially welcomed me into her neighborhood and her home, but also shared with me her treasured memories of the shared life with her neighbors and the many dilemmas she has about her changing society. Although Esma initially felt that she was not 'competent' to speak on the situation in her country, I regard her as an expert, as she certainly has a much deeper understanding of life in her changing society which is rooted in her experience than I or any other researcher coming from abroad.

Findings and Discussion

One interesting – and unanticipated – effect of my conversation with Esma is the impact the interview, in its own right, might have on the co-converser/interviewee. In this sense, the interview method could be viewed as a form of intervention for it brings to the fore the function of speaking and – through speech – remembering the time that is perceived as *normal*. It may even motivate people to reconnect with others – old or new neighbors – to re-establish existing or build new relationships. This is nicely exemplified in the following quote:

> I talk too much, but this feels good. Imagine if two or three more people were participating in the conversation. How nice that would be! It would be nice to have people from different generations because each generation has something specific which is unique to them...I don't like to be burdened by the past, what has happened has happened. But then again, those beautiful things leave traces, and they resurface when you go back into the past in a conversation. That is nice... By god, it feels good when I return into the past.

Two hours into our conversation, Esma seemingly suddenly discovered how good it felt to talk about memories – or perhaps it would be more appropriate to write remembering and sharing the instances of remembering with others. The interpersonal, communal sharing of one's life with others represents a very important aspect of life to her. This is what is so painfully missing in her life, her neighborhood and her society more generally, in which traditional communal ways of interpersonal relating are becoming replaced by individualism.

Esma in her Changing Society

The most interesting aspect of my conversation with Esma was her use of *war,* not solely as a reference point but as a border between two lives, one that existed before the war and one that exists now. More specifically, it is not war per se that she associates with the present situation in her country as she had a great deal of hope during and immediately after the war. War, which could not go on forever, represented change and "every change brings something new." This hope that her country after the war would become a society of equal opportunities for all its people was the driving force for her during the war. In that regard, the perceived change from "good life" in the old system to "bad life today" did not happen suddenly as the result of the war; it was (is) a process. In Esma's words, as "years keep piling up and nothing is changing for the better, not even 'h' is left of that hope."

The present political situation in her country permeates my conversation with Esma. She regards the current political system as highly inefficient and a source of all tensions, instability and uncertainty. She feels betrayed because the politicians "see the common people only during the pre-election period" when they campaign for their votes. The rest of the time, they are only concerned with "staying in power" and "filling their pockets." Esma compares the present situation in her country to the old single party system from the past. Even though she lives in a democratic society today, Esma prefers the old one party system, in which there was no room for voting.

> Let me tell you, if we go back to communism. Yes, there was corruption then as well, but I had [financial security] too… I wasn't aware of corruption back then… Only now in retrospect do I realize some things, but I had a good life too. I could afford vacation on the coast… I had terrific income with which I could live comfortably the entire month. Now, I cannot do anything with my pension. I am forced to work to have some kind of existence.

Although she acknowledges that the old system was far from perfect, she stresses that in the old system, she did not have to worry about her existence. Hence, politics did not really have any impact on her. It simply did not matter who was in power and whether they were corrupt. As she puts it, "when you are financially secure, you are not interested in who governs the country." Today, she cannot make a decent living on her pension and has to work to make the ends meet. Consequently, this leads her to develop interest in politics because it has direct impact on her quality of life.

Esma in her Changing Neighborhood

In my conversation with Esma, I was particularly struck by her use of interpersonal relating as one of the most significant aspects of life. She at length speaks about deterioration of neighborhood, which she associates with simplicity, sharing, openness and insouciance. Even when she talks about herself or her country, Esma uses neighborhood as a reference.

Esma's biggest fear is solitude. She is somebody who has shared her entire life with her neighbors, and privacy is not something she desires. Although she acknowledges that neighborhood has both positive and negative aspects, one knows that one is never alone. However, today, people are becoming alienated, and this is something that troubles Esma very much as it has direct implications for her life.

> People don't live together any longer; they live next to each other. You know how it used to be before, this person steps in, that person steps in. Now, everybody is locked up. Everybody just walks by. If you are ill, even if somebody comes to see you, they are annoyed by your illness. I am terribly scared of old age. Solitude and old age are what I terribly dread. I am not afraid of death, only old age and illness. Imagine being alone and there is nobody to help you?

For Esma, neighborhood is very important. It is important for pragmatic reasons. One's neighbor is the closest person to come to help if one is in need.

> [I]f you are in pain, you will tell your neighbor that your stomach hurts and he'll make you tea. If you don't have to eat, he'll say: "Come on, I know you don't have" and he'll share with you. That relationship between neighbors. Or, if something happens in your household, he [your neighbor] will be the first person to stand by you and go through it with you.

However, there is more to neighborhood than this. Esma remembers her neighborhood before the war with great pleasure and nostalgia. She excitedly speaks about those times in the 1950s when everything was scarce, but life was pleasurable because it was simple. Esma admits that there were times when neighbors would get into arguments, then one would take sides and "pour oil into fire," but even those situations are described as the 'charms' of the old times.

> People argued more. That was interesting. The noise. You go out, throw in a few comments, get the argument more heated, but all of that was harmless. Those were the charms of that life. Now, I say, I was the happiest before the war when raja [common people] congregated on the street to socialize.

Acknowledging the effect of the war and displacement in deterioration of the feeling of neighborhood, Esma stresses that neighborly relations are not something that is given. They develop over time and have to be nurtured. To demonstrate the impact of war and displacement on the feeling of neighborhood, I offer a lengthy quote from Esma:

> The old neighbors are gone. Old neighbors left, some new people came. That old neighborhood in which you were raising your neighbor's children together with your own doesn't exist any longer. Now, you walk through your neighborhood, and you don't know anybody... That is the neighborhood you became one with... From early on you learned about and from your neighbors. Now, you don't have time to learn, you don't know what he [new neighbor] is like, how and if he will accept you. Then, the moment comes when you are going through some crisis. Is that person suitable to confide yourself in? With the old neighborhood, you already know them; you can open your heart to them. With the new ones you cannot. There is a big wall, Berlin Wall, which is not bridgeable. One has to nurture the environment in which one was born and within which one developed, spent one's childhood... And the new, especially after the war, it is not that you cannot establish contact, you don't have the nerves [patience]. You have to test the new ground. Did you succeed or not? People don't decide easily to make that step... Before, you are born with people, you go through their house, everything was open. All of that means a lot for life.

It is striking that Esma does not even use the word *neighbor* when she talks about her new neighbors thus emphasizing the dynamic nature of neighborhood. People and neighborhoods are interconnected, and it takes time for a neighborhood feeling to develop. Just as neighborhood shapes the development of each individual person who lives in it, so does each person shape the development of his/her neighborhood. Ethnic cleansing that occurred during wartime and with it associated mass displacement along ethnic lines has resulted in many ethnically 'pure' neighborhoods and even entire towns. Yet, this ethnic homogenization seems to be causing much tension among ordinary citizens who do not necessarily identify members of the same ethnic group as members of their in-group. A study conducted by Kelly (2003) is very illustrative in this regard. In her research on Bosnian refugees in a London suburb, Kelly discovered that Bosnian refugees had a difficult time forming a community around their common experience of being resettled to a new country. To them, the fact that they were from the same country did not mean much, with one woman explicitly stating that she has more in common with her lifelong neighbor of different ethnic background than with a person who is of the same ethnic background but comes from a different part of the country.

Esma Between Two Worlds: Communalism Versus Individualism

To Esma, life before, which she will "never forget," is strictly opposed to life today, which is almost not even worth discussing. She spends a significant amount of time talking about her life before, whereas only briefly does she mention her life now. In that sense, she talks about the present only to set it in opposition to life before. Esma blames the technological advances, fast-paced life, existential concerns of young people who cannot afford to have children and distancing of people from each other for the current situation. In her monologue, Esma constantly switches between before and now, which to her represent two diametrically oppositional states.

> Now, if my neighbor has a car, I will stand on my head to get that car too. How will I get it? It doesn't matter what I will eat, as long as I get that car. Before there was one standard, but people were happy. They communicated. They socialized. There was always laughter. Okay, people argued too, but argument is also a form of communication… Now, I go out and there are no children playing on the street. Before, I would go out and a neighbor would give a piece of bread to her child and then she would call all children and feed them too. And we didn't have much back then, but oil and sugar on a piece of bread were so sweet. I will never forget that! Now, if you give me the biggest cake, I would forget it. It doesn't represent anything. It has no value. Nothing has value… What is dearer to you, a villa or sharing your life with others?

Esma deploys a rhetorical question, which is not directed at me, but at some generalized other, at people in general who – in her view – have forgotten what is really important in life. She conveys a strong sense of alienation from the present system to the point where it almost seems as if she does not live in the present; instead, she draws her motivation to live from the past and her memories of the simple life she once had. Esma struggles with finding her place in her changing society, in which one system of values is becoming replaced by another. In her words:

> One can have everything, but it doesn't mean anything... My time has passed. I had a good life in the old system. What is most important, I could sleep on the street, and nobody would tell me to get up or to get lost. Not too long ago, we weren't even locking our doors.

The fact that she was not locking her door signifies the freedom that is important to her. It is not the freedom associated with accumulation of material wealth or voicing one's opinion in public life that matters to her, but the freedom of not having to worry about the future or personal safety. She even contemplates if the time of war was better than "what we have today" and concludes that even though conditions were harsh, "we were all equal, at least psychologically speaking – we all depended on humanitarian aid and were struggling to survive." For Esma, negative communication is better than no communication. As she puts it, "even though communication was at times negative, now there is none. That is the problem!"

Concluding Remarks

Through the prism of a single informant, this chapter yields a glimpse into how people experience and make sense of the multiplicity of changes that are transpiring in their immediate environment, that of contemporary BiH. Even though my key informant, Esma, was never physically displaced from her neighborhood, she still experiences strong feelings of non-belongingness associated with the loss of social context and friendships. By reminiscing about the past, it almost seems like she is seeking the restoration of relationships with others. In her narrative, Esma intentionally constructs tensions between past and present, between self and others, and out of these tensions, she constructs meanings identifying interpersonal relating as the most important aspect of life.

Although the past – the time before the war associated with communal life – is almost absent from the political discourse, it is very much present in the stories of the ordinary people. After the war, the memories of the war were still fresh in people's minds and it is understandable that they were reluctant to trust others. However, as time is passing, it is possible that the ethnic divide among ordinary people is gradually becoming replaced by longing for genuine human-to-human relating (e.g., de Rivera, 1997; Maček, 2001; Turner, 1982). Building on the existing literature (e.g. Jovchelovitch, 2007; Kelly, 2003; Knight, 2006), I propose that the sense of displacement, experienced by my key informant, does not only represent an obstacle but also potentiality. As noted by Knight (2006), even though individuals can "psychologically and socially survive for a while" without support of community and friendship, this type of support "is soon sought after, and once again becomes a valuable asset in the process of recovery and re-settlement" (Post-flight phase: 12–18 months section, para. 1). Along these lines, the experience of isolation associated with the sense of displacement, could prompt individuals to consider the position of the social Other, motivating some to restore broken relationships with old neighbors and perhaps even reach out to new neighbors.

Finally, it needs to be reiterated that since this study is based on a single case, conclusions drawn from it should be treated tentatively. Future research involving studies on entire neighborhoods could build on the findings of the present study by exploring how prior experiences, personal goals and expectations serve as mediators in making sense of changes that are taking place in many societies throughout the world, particularly those that are troubled by political or structural violence. Such studies would not only contribute to the psychological literature, but could potentially lead to crafting more comprehensive intervention strategies that are rooted in the experience of everyday life or, to borrow from Maček (2001), the "political power of socio–cultural life."

References

Berg, L. B. (2001). *Qualitative research methods for the social sciences*. Boston: Allyn and Bacon.

Bibace, R., Clegg, W. J., & Valsiner, J. (2009). What is in a name? Understanding the implications of participant terminology. *Integrative Psychological and Behavioral Science, 43*(1), 67–77.

Cantril, H. (1965). *The pattern of human concern*. New Brunswick: Rutgers University Press.

Christie, J. D. (2006). What is peace psychology the psychology of? *Journal of Social Issues, 62*(1), 1–17.

Christie, J. D., Tint, B. S., Wagner, R. V., & DuNann Winter, D. (2008). Peace psychology for a peaceful world. *American Psychologist, 63*(6), 540–552.

De Rivera, J. (1997). *Emotion and the formation of social identities*. Unpublished manuscript.

Denzin, N. K., & Lincoln, Y. S. (Eds.). (1994). *Handbook of qualitative research*. London: Sage.

Giorgi, A. P., & Giorgi, B. M. (2003). The descriptive phenomenological psychological method. In P. M. Camic, J. E. Rhodes, & L. Yardley (Eds.), *Qualitative research in psychology: Expanding perspectives in methodology and design* (pp. 243–273).

Hermans, H. J. M., & Dimaggion, G. (2007). Self, identity, and globalization in times of uncertainty: A dialogical analysis. *Review of General Psychology, 11*(1), 31–61.

Jovchelovitch, S. (2007). *Knowledge in context: Representations, community and culture*. New York: Routledge.

Karahasan, D. (1993). *Dnevnik selidbe*. Zagreb: Duriex.

Kelly, L. (2003). Bosnian refugees in Britain: Questioning community. *Sociology, 37*(1), 35–49.

Knight, Z. G. (2006). The trauma and beyond trauma of political displacement: An exploratory case study of one white Zimbabwean farmer. Retrieved from http://www.massey.ac.nz/~trauma/issues/2006-1/knight.htm.

Maček, I. (2001). Predicament of war: Sarajevo experience and ethics of war. In B. E. Schmidt & I. Schroder (Eds.), *Anthropology of violence and conflict* (pp. 197–224). London: Routledge.

Rubin, H. J., & Rubin, I. S. (2005). *Qualitative interviewing: The art of hearing data*. Thousand Oaks: Sage.

Stiglitz, J. (2002). *Globalization and its discontents*. London: Penguin.

Turner, V. (1974). *Dramas, fields, and metaphors: Symbolic action in human society*. Ithaca: Cornell University Press.

Turner, V. (1982). *From ritual to theater: The human seriousness of play*. New York: PAJ Publications.

Turner, V., & Turner, E. (1978). *Image and pilgrimage in Christian culture: Anthropological perspectives*. New York: Columbia University Press.

United Nations Development Programme Bosnia and Herzegovina (2008). *The silent majority speaks: Snapshots of today and visions of the future of Bosnia and Herzegovina.* Retrieved from http://www.undp.ba/index.aspx?PID=3&RID=43.

Valsiner, J. (2003). Beyond social representation: A theory of enablement. *Papers on social representations, 12*, 12.1–12.8. http://www.psr.jku.at/.

Wertz, F. J. (1977). *Being criminally victimized: Method and findings.* Unpublished monograph.

Chapter 9
Internalizing and Externalizing Symptoms in a Sample of Bosnian Young Adults: Ten Years After the War

Namik Kirlić and Adela Langrock

Abstract Currently, little is known about the psychological impact of the difficult post-war situation in Bosnia-Herzegovina [BH] among young adult survivors of the 1992–1995 war. While several studies have explored the immediate impact of this war on the psychological well-being of BH children and adolescents, it is also important to consider it within the context of the stress inducing political, economic, and psychosocial post-war environment. This study examined the internalizing and externalizing symptoms of 134 young adults in Bosnia-Herzegovina 10 years after the war. In addition, the presence and severity of current post-war stressors were assessed. A significant percentage of the participants presented clinical levels of internalizing and externalizing symptoms and reported moderate levels of stress regarding the post-war environment. However, comparisons of environmental contexts and adjustment indicate that stress-free personal/professional relationships and leisure activities may serve as protective factors against less controllable stressors such as the difficult post-war political environment. Overall, our findings indicate that the difficult post-war environment in Bosnia-Herzegovina continues to affect the psychological well-being of the young adults who experienced war during their youth.

Keywords Young adults • War • Stress • Bosnia-Herzegovina • Internalizing and externalizing symptoms • Psychological well-being

---

N. Kirlić (✉) • A. Langrock
Department of Psychology, Middlebury College,
Bicentennial Hall 220, Middlebury, VT 05753, USA
e-mail: nkirlic@gmail.com; alangroc@middlebury.edu

O. Simić et al. (eds.), *Peace Psychology in the Balkans: Dealing with a Violent Past while Building Peace*, Peace Psychology Book Series, DOI 10.1007/978-1-4614-1948-8_9,

Introduction

Currently, little is known about the psychological impact of the difficult post-war environment in Bosnia and Herzegovina [BH] among young adult survivors of the 1992–1995 war. In the years that followed, several studies have evaluated the immediate impact of countless traumatic war events on the psychological well-being of children and adolescents in BH (Goldstein, Wampler, & Wise, 1997; Layne et al., 2008; Powell & Durakovic-Belko, 2000; Pullis, 1998; Smith, Perin, Yule, Hacam, & Stuvland, 2002). Alarming accounts of psychological maladjustments have been reported, and some studies point to their persisting nature several years after the war, usually attributed to the presence of daily traumatic war reminders. However, little research has been done on the subject of the post-war stress-inducing political, economic, and psychosocial environment among BH children and adolescents. Given the overwhelming exposure to trauma during the war, the presence of trauma reminders in the post-war environment, and more than a decade of difficult daily circumstances, it is of utmost importance to evaluate the cumulative effect of such stressful encounters on the psychological well-being and adjustment of BH children and young adults.

By definition, psychological stress involves a relationship between an individual and his or her environment that is appraised as exhausting or exceeding his or her resources and endangering his or her well-being and healthy development (Grant et al., 2003; Lazarus & Folkman, 1984). Large scale violent conflicts, such as wars, are not only isolated and extreme traumatic stress events in the life course of an individual that expose him or her to aggression and violence, but they also portray the violent side of society and threaten the social order (Lomsky-Feder, 1996). Moreover, wars may create continuous and cumulative strains on children's immediate family and their environment, including an adverse impact on society's social resources, political stability, and economic growth. Therefore, not only do large scale armed conflicts pose a significant threat to the psychological well-being of children and adolescents, but stressful post-war environments may have an on-going adverse psychosocial and developmental impact on this population. In fact, following a war, the apparent threat of or the actual loss of both material (e.g., housing, economic viability) and/or psychosocial resources (e.g., self-efficacy, social support/connections) is considered to be among the most important predictors of the psychological impact of stress (Freedy, Shaw, Jarrell, & Masters, 1992; Galea et al., 2002; Hobfoll, 1989; Ironson et al., 1997; Schlenger et al., 2002).

Although previous psychological research has documented that current stressors are more predictive of psychopathology than prior stressors (see the review in Grant, Compas, Thurm, McMahon, & Gipson, 2004), a complicated reciprocal relationship between stressors and the development of psychopathology implies that stressors not only predict subsequent increases in symptoms of psychopathology, but also, symptoms of psychopathology predict subsequent increases in the experience of stressful events (Grant et al., 2003, 2004). In other words, prior exposure to an uncontrollable stressor (i.e., war) may lead to immediate psychopathology (e.g., anxiety disorder), which, in turn, leads to an additional increase in experience of otherwise controllable stressors (e.g., poor peer relationships, failure in achievement of tasks), which, in turn, leads to an additional increase in psychopathology (e.g., depression).

Indeed, a wide range of psychological symptoms have been associated with war trauma including sadness, anxiety, guilt, grief, insomnia, hypervigilance/startle reactions, fatigue, fear of reoccurrence, phobias, avoidance, numbing, cognitive and memory symptoms, and aggressive and delinquent behaviors (Al-Khawaha, 1997; Angel, Hjern, & Ingleby 2001; Farwell, 1999; Muldon & Cairns, 1999; Paardekooper, de Jong, & Hermanns, 1999). Interestingly, studies examining the long-term effects of war on South African, Cambodian, Gutemalan, Croatian, Somali, Oromo, Sudanese, and Ugandan children found that, for some, symptoms of psychopathology persist over time, while for others, they decrease (Adjukovic & Adjukovic, 1998; Allodi, 1989; Cairns & Dawes, 1996; Clarke, Sack, & Goff, 1993; Halcon et al., 2004; Kinzie, Sack, Angell, Clarke, & Ben, 1989; Mikasaj-Todorovic, 2004; Miller, 1996; Paardekooper et al., 1999). These researchers attribute such findings to the amount and severity of exposure to traumatic war experiences, child's age, coping abilities, family's coping and post-traumatic stress reactions, but also due to the daily circumstances and protective factors related to family and community mechanisms.

Therefore, the degree to which the daily circumstances and family and community mechanisms affect the post-war psychological well-being and adjustment of children and young adults in war torn areas must be accounted for, as it may provide an insight into potential existing mediating interventions against the harmful effects of war and post-war environments. It can be further concluded that the psychosocial health of this population, as it relates to the post-war environment, has great implications for the sustainability of peace and future re-development, therefore requiring a significant research focus.

BH's declaration of independence from Yugoslavia in 1992 led to the bloodiest armed conflict in Europe since the World War Two. Citizens of BH, including children, were subjected to several years of mass violence and ethnic cleansing, shelling and destruction of densely populated areas, detention camps, displacement, and shortages of food, water, and shelter. Roughly 100,000 BH citizens were killed in this period, 7% of which were children (Research and Documentation Center Sarajevo, 2010).

Previous research points to an overwhelming number of traumatic war events among BH children. Two large studies of children and adolescents in besieged Sarajevo (Husain, 1996; in Pullis, 1998) and displaced children in Zenica (Goldstein et al., 1997), report that the majority of children witnessed separation, exposure to combat, death or violent injury of loved ones, sniper attacks, victimization by military forces, destruction of buildings, and food, water, and shelter shortages. Most children experienced multiple traumatic events, ranging from 10 to 13 severe traumatic events (Goldstein et al., 1997; Smith et al., 2002). Measures of psychological impact in these studies found that a large majority of participants (between 80% and 100%) met criteria for PTSD, including re-experiencing of traumatic events, avoidance, and increased arousal (Husain, 1996; in Goldstein et al., 1997; Pullis, 1998). Additionally, significant depressive symptoms and high levels of anxiety were reported.

It has also been documented that such symptoms persisted several years after the war among some BH children. Researchers longitudinally examining the long-term effects of the BH war on children, reported significant clinical levels of PTSD, depressive symptoms, and the number of high stress reactions two years after the war (Smith et al., 2002), albeit with a slight decrease over time (Dapic & Stuvland, 2000). One study, conducted four years after the war, found that 55% of participants continued to have significant PTSD symptoms and 20% experienced symptoms of depression (Zotovic & Stanulovic, 2000). It has been suggested that these findings may be a result of taxing daily circumstances. In fact, one post-war study found displaced children from Srebrenica to have higher levels of depressive symptoms and delinquent/aggressive behaviors than their non-refugee peers, attributing this finding to the rather difficult current conditions, lack of resolve, and lack of support from adults (Dapo & Kolenovic-Dapo, 2000).

The present study was conducted in 2005, roughly 10 years after the Dayton Peace Agreement, which put an end to the war in BH. In 2005, BH remained a country in turmoil, with estimated 2,000 km^2 of mined areas (UNICEF, 2007), many still missing, much of the economy undeveloped and with limited job opportunities, political tensions posing a continuous problem, and with an outdated and ethnically divided educational system in place. The loss of material and psychosocial resources as a direct result of the war is persistent, and this is only further exacerbated by the difficult daily political, economic, and psychosocial circumstances in BH.

While post-war studies of BH children and adolescents exist, none, to our knowledge, examine the impact of war on the psychological well-being of BH young adults after a significant period of time since the war and within the context of the current difficult daily circumstances. Hence, first and foremost, the present study examines the internalizing and externalizing behaviors of young adults in BH ten years after the war. Secondly, we evaluate the presence and severity of current post-war stressors among BH young adults and their association with internalizing and externalizing symptoms. Finally, we make some conclusions regarding the implications of our results on the sustainability of peace in Bosnia-Herzegovina.

Method

Participants

The present study was conducted in 2005, roughly ten years after the end of the war in Bosnia-Herzegovina. One hundred and thirty-four young adults, all of whom resided in Bosnia-Herzegovina both at the time of the war and data collection, participated in the study. Participants' average age was 19.1 (SD ± 1.7), and 69% were female. At the time of the war, participants' age ranged from 7 to 12.

Participants were not asked to identify to which ethnic group they belonged, but the sample included all three ethnic groups (Bosniaks, Croats, and Serbs). This was ensured by researchers traveling to six different urban communities (Gornji Vakuf-Uskoplje, Konjic, Bijeljina, Sanski Most, Janja, and Tuzla), among which some were mono-ethnic, while others were multi-ethnic. In one community (Gornji Vakuf-Uskoplje), strong divisions existed between two of the three major ethnic groups. The degree of exposure to combat activities varied across these communities, yet all faced similar post-war difficulties.

Participants were approached either through youth organizations or local high schools. Participants approached through youth organizations (in Gornji Vakuf-Uskoplje, Konjic, Bijeljina, Sanski Most, and Janja) had most likely gone through some form of conflict resolution training, as well as participated in programs addressing issues of dealing with the past, peace building, and tolerance. However, none of these programs focused on dealing with trauma and healing in any systematic, therapeutic way, nor did they identify these young adults as psychologically impaired. Their priority is to provide educational, youth activism, and multi-ethnic dialog and cooperation opportunities.

On the other hand, participants approached through three high-schools (two in Gornji Vakuf-Uskoplje and one Tuzla) provided a sample of young adults more representative of the entire population. The current educational system in BH does not offer any form of counseling and is strongly divided along ethnic lines, where each ethnic group teaches its own version of language and literature, history, and government, in some areas under the system currently known as 'two schools under one roof.' In this system, two ethnic groups share a building, but operate separately and under the aforementioned divided school programs. This was the case with schools in Gornji Vakuf-Uskoplje.

Materials and Procedure

Participants signed Consent Forms and completed Questionnaires in Bosnian. The original versions were written in English, then translated to Bosnian by the researchers and reviewed by a professor of Bosnian Literature for clarity, and finally translated back to English by a professional interpreter for comparison with the original version. Both versions were approved by the Human Subjects Research Committee at Middlebury College, Middlebury, VT, USA. The questionnaire took 45 min to complete. Researchers were absent during questionnaire completion, but provided study information prior to taking consent, and conducted debriefing sessions discussing study objectives and issues facing young adults in BH.

The questionnaire consisted of the following three components:

War stress. In order to account for the presence of traumatic war experiences within our sample, we drew on contexts identified as potential sources of stress or trauma for children in two war situations: one on Eritrean youth using the Harvard Trauma Questionnaire (Farwell, 1999) and another on Sudanese refugee children (Paardekooper et al., 1999). Participants in the present study were asked to think back at the time of the war and describe each of the following contexts: (a) family situation (loss in the family, relationships with other members of the family), (b) living environment (living standard at home and in the community), (c) peer relationships (ability to spend time with peers, access to playgrounds), (d) direct exposure to war (exposure to armed conflicts and their direct results).

Current stress. We then evaluated potential sources and levels of current stress. Drawing from the United Nations Development Programme in BH Report (Abapahic et al., 2003), which examined issues of relevance and great concern to BH young adults, as we well as their stance on these issues, we identified the following contexts as potential sources of stress to BH young adults:

1. Political environment (items: governmental structures, youth participation and influence, European integrations, presence of the international community),
2. Economic circumstances (items: economic development, unemployment, family's and own financial situation),
3. Educational prospects (items: university entry, quality of instruction and facilities, cost, student government involvement, preparation for employment),
4. Relationships (items: family, peer, school, professional),
5. Leisure time (items: access to theaters, cinemas, art galleries, sports clubs, youth organization, access to the internet, ability to travel),
6. Outlook for future (items: employment, social services, presence of mine fields, sustainability of peace, the environment).

Participants first endorsed specific items within each context as stressful by circling YES or NO, followed by an option to identify any additional stressors. Finally, they rated, on a 5-point Likert scale (1- not stressful at all; 5- very stressful), how generally stressful they perceived each current stress context to be.

Outcome and adjustment measures. Achenbach's Young Adults Self-Report Questionnaire (YASR; Achenbach, 1997) was used as a measure of adjustment outcomes. YASR has been successful at identifying and assessing potential emotional and behavioral problems among young adults across different cultures, and thus seemed appropriate for the present study. It asks participants to respond as incorrect (0), somewhat or sometimes correct (1), or completely or often correct (2) to 126 items describing various thoughts, emotions, and behaviors. The scoring profile includes both raw and t-scores for adaptive functioning, empirically based syndromes, substance use, internalizing, externalizing, and total problems. YASR further derives the following syndromes: Anxious/Depressed, Withdrawn, Somatic Complaints, Thought Problems, and Attention Problems (internalizing), and Aggressive Behaviors, Rule-Breaking Behaviors, and Intrusive (externalizing). The Diagnostic and Statistical Manual (DSM) oriented scales are: Depressive Problems, Anxiety Problems, Somatic Problems, Avoidant Personality Problems, Attention Deficit/Hyperactivity Problems, and Antisocial Personality Problems. The present study reports Internalizing and Externalizing Problems data only.

Results

Description of War Events

BH young adults in the present study reported the following accounts of war experiences: nearby shelling; street fighting; total destruction of homes, schools, hospitals, and religious sites; own and injury of family members and peers; execution or deaths of close family members and peers; deportation to concentration camps; displacement; father fighting; alcoholism; shortages of food, water, electricity, and telephone communication; and segregation by nationality in schools; and refugee stigma.

Current Stress

Six contexts were used in the present study to evaluate levels of current stress among BH young adults in our sample: political environment, economic circumstances, education, personal and professional relationships, leisure time, and outlook for future. A Total Current Stress variable was computed by averaging means of individual current stress contexts in order to examine how generally stressful BH young adults perceived them to be [Cronbach's alpha, $\alpha = .77$]. Overall, participants in the present study endorsed moderate levels of current stress, as suggested by Total Current Stress variable mean of [M (134) = 3.25 ± .58].

Whether significant differences existed in endorsed levels of current stress across contexts among BH young adults, as well as a potential effect of gender, were examined next. A repeated measure ANOVA between the six contexts revealed significant differences in stressfulness ratings, $F\,(5, 119) = 51.19$, $p < .01$ (Fig. 9.1). Current economic circumstances had significantly higher stress scores than all other contexts; political environment, educational prospects and outlook for future had significantly higher stress scores than relationships and leisure time contexts. There were no significant differences in stress ratings between relationship and leisure time contexts. The between subject effect of gender and the interaction between contexts by gender were not significant, $F\,(1, 123) = .67$, $p > .05$ and $F\,(5, 119) = 2.12$, $p > .05$, respectively.

Internalizing and Externalizing Symptoms

Achenbach's Young Adult Self-Report (YASR; Achenbach, 1997) was used to examine the range of internalizing and externalizing symptoms among BH young adults in our sample. Participants in the present study endorsed moderate to high levels on

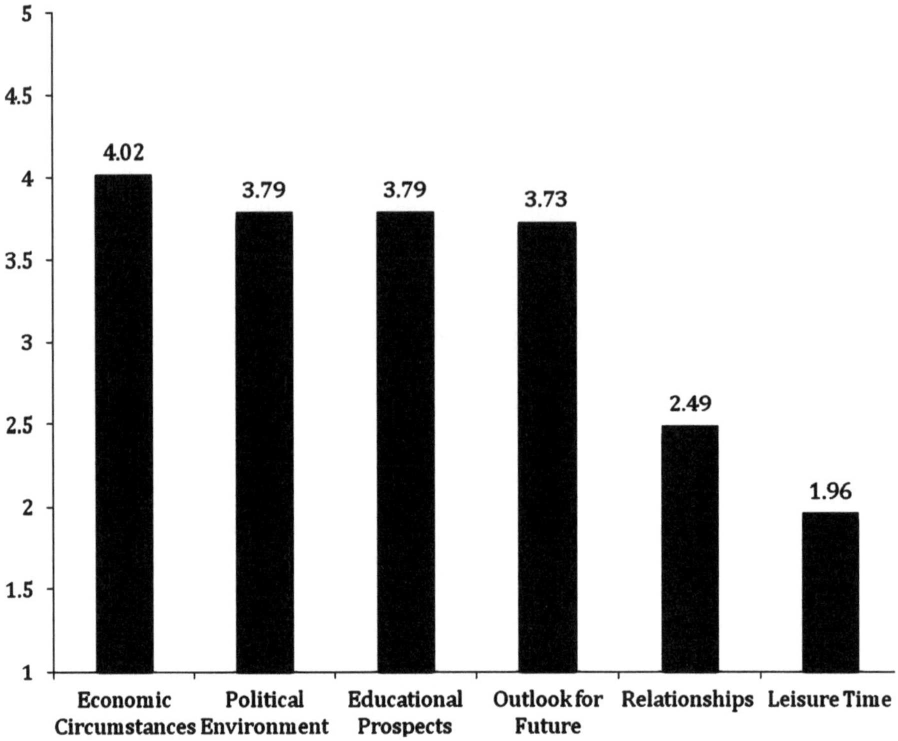

Fig. 9.1 Average rate of endorsement by current stress context for BH young adults (1- not stressful at all; 5- very stressful)

internalizing symptoms ($M=60.1$, $SD=8.8$) and moderate levels on externalizing symptoms ($M=58.6$, $SD=8.7$). More specifically, as compared to the YASR normative sample (Achenbach, 1997), 44% (17 males, 42 females) of BH young adults scored above the clinical cutoff (the 98th percentile) for internalizing symptoms. An additional 10% of the sample was experiencing these symptoms at the borderline clinical level (the 95th percentile). Such rates indicated extremely high levels of anxiety, depression, somatic complaints, social withdrawal behaviors, and thought problems. On the other hand, 35.8% (14 males, 34 females) of BH young adults scored above the clinical cutoff (the 98th percentile) for externalizing behaviors, as compared to the YASR normative sample (Achenbach, 1997). An additional 7.5% of the sample experienced these symptoms at the borderline clinical level (the 95th percentile). Rates of externalizing symptoms at this level are indicative of excessive aggressive, rule-breaking, and intrusive behaviors among participants in the present study. Independent sample t-test showed no significant differences between males and females on internalizing [t (134)=–.15, $p>.05$] and externalizing symptoms [t (134)=–.02, $p>.05$].

Associations Between Current Stress and Internalizing and Externalizing Symptoms

The final step in the analysis examined whether levels of current stress among BH young adults and their internalizing and externalizing behaviors co-varied, and whether elevated levels of current stress predicted higher internalizing and externalizing symptoms. Examination of normality assumptions within current stress contexts revealed significant skewness in the negative direction for *current economic and political environment, educational prospects, and outlook for future* contexts, while a positive direction was observed in *current relationships* and *leisure time* (Shapiro-Wilk test of normality was significant at $p < .001$ for all current stress contexts). Squared transformations did not allow for normality assumptions to be met, hence a median split was conducted to allow for examination of the association between levels of current stress and internalizing and externalizing symptoms. The median for *current economic and political environment, educational prospects, and outlook for future* contexts was 4, while *current relationships* and *leisure time* had the median score of 2. Participants scoring higher than 4 and 2, respectively, were categorized as presenting with high current stress, while those scoring lower as presenting with low current stress.

A series of one-way ANOVAs revealed a significant main effect of stressfulness on internalizing symptoms for the current stress contexts of economic circumstances [$F(1, 133) = 8.18$, $p < .01$, $d = .50$] and relationships [$F(1, 133) = 21.19$, $p < .001$, $d = .79$], while there was a trend for *leisure time* [$F(1, 133) = 3.89$, $p = .051$, $d = .39$]. For each set of analyses, the endorsement of the context as a source of high stress was associated with significantly higher levels of internalizing symptoms, as compared to the endorsement of the context as a source of low stress. Similarly, a series of one-way ANOVAs revealed significant main effects of stressfulness on externalizing symptoms for current stress contexts of relationships [$F(1, 133) = 27.76$, $p < .05$, $d = .91$] and leisure time [$F(1, 133) = 5.47$, $p = .021$, $d = .44$]. For each set of analyses, the endorsement of the context as a source of high stress was associated with significantly higher levels of externalizing symptoms, as compared to the endorsement of the context as a source of low stress. Table 9.1 displays means and

Table 9.1 Means and standard deviations for internalizing and externalizing symptoms as a function of low and high current stress within each context

	Internalizing				Externalizing			
	Low stress		High stress		Low stress		High stress	
Variable	M	SD	M	SD	M	SD	M	SD
Economic circumstances	58.35	8.72	62.65	8.33	57.90	8.86	59.64	8.51
Political environment	59.10	8.95	62.07	8.21	58.48	8.44	58.87	9.33
Educational prospects	60.01	9.16	60.32	8.15	58.69	7.96	58.47	10.07
Outlook for future	59.78	8.70	60.95	9.06	58.42	8.41	59.08	9.54
Relationships	57.10	8.17	63.63	8.21	55.25	7.43	62.52	8.53
Leisure time	59.19	9.01	62.47	7.84	57.52	8.41	61.37	8.99

standard deviations for internalizing and externalizing symptoms as a function of low and high current stress within each context.

Discussion

This study examined the present day psychological adjustment of young adults in Bosnia-Herzegovina who experienced war ten years ago, while at the same time evaluating the presence and severity of current sources of stress and their relationship with the overall psychological adjustment of this population. Our initial results are alarming in that, even ten years after the conclusion of the war, almost half of our sample were experiencing internalizing symptoms, while over a third were experiencing externalizing symptoms, at or above the clinical level (YASR; Achenbach, 1997). BH young adults in our sample falling into this category have extreme feelings of sadness, loneliness, worry, worthlessness, and lack of self confidence, in addition to not getting along well with others, enjoying solitude, complaining of various aches, lacking energy, and having intrusive thoughts. Their symptoms are accompanied by attention problems and delinquent behaviors, including excessive risk-taking, rule-breaking, and intrusive/disruptive behaviors and substance abuse, which often result in additional problems at home and in school.

It is possible that, to a certain degree, these findings reflect traumatic experiences from the war, especially because they are in line with findings from previous studies measuring the direct psychological impact of warfare on BH children (Husain, 1996, in Goldstein et al., 1997; Powell & Durakovic-Belko, 2000; Pullis, 1998; Smith et al., 2002; Zotovic & Stanulovic, 2000). However, the severity and persistence of these symptoms ten years after the exposure to war, suggests that there may be other, more current, factors contributing to the internalizing and externalizing symptoms. Studies examining the psychological well-being of BH and other children in post-war environments have partly attributed their findings to extremely difficult daily circumstances, lack of resolve, family's post-traumatic stress reactions, poor family situations, and lack of protective and supportive family and community mechanisms (Adjukovic & Adjukovic, 1998; Allodi, 1989; Cairns & Dawes, 1996; Clarke et al., 1993; Dapo & Kolenovic-Dapo, 2000; Halcon et al., 2004; Kinzie et al., 1989; Mikasaj-Todorovic, 2004; Miller, 1996; Paardekooper et al., 1999). Our findings are in line with previous research and also reveal a strong association between the presence of difficult daily circumstances and psychopathology.

More specifically, our findings suggest that the difficult post-war situation in BH is taking its toll on the psychological well-being of young adults at an alarming rate. This is evident not only in the number of current stressors identified by our participants, but also in their type, severity, and implications. Among potential present day sources of stress we studied, contexts describing the political environment, economic circumstances, outlook for future, and educational prospects generally posed as highly stressful and are significantly more stressful than participants' perceived relationships and leisure time opportunities. These highly stressful contexts were also less controllable sources of stress, thereby suggesting that they may be a larger threat to the psychological well-being of BH young adults (Grant et al., 2004). Nevertheless, emotional, cognitive, and behavioral problems in our sample did not significantly worsen with elevated ratings of less controllable sources of stress, with the exception of the economic circumstances. In fact, only those participants for whom present day economic circumstances, relationships, and leisure time opportunities contexts were acting as additional significant stressors tended to have noticeably higher levels of internalizing symptoms, while highly stressful present day relationships and leisure time were predictive of externalizing symptoms. A noteworthy observation is that larger effect sizes were reported for current relationships in both internalizing and externalizing symptoms, suggesting that, although generally a lesser source of present day stress, this context was more predictive of emotional, cognitive, and behavioral problems in our sample.

It is challenging to untangle which single context, or set thereof, is responsible for clinical levels of internalizing and externalizing symptoms among BH young adults given the complexity of experienced traumatic war events, reciprocity of exposure to stress and psychopathology, current sources of stress, and previous (war) and current losses of material and psychosocial resources (Grant et al., 2003, 2004; Hobfoll, 1989; Powell & Durakovic-Belko, 2000; Pullis, 1998). However, some conclusions and implications can be drawn. Since the majority of BH young adults in our sample endorsed the political environment, economic circumstances, outlook for future, and educational prospects as present day sources of stress, it is quite possible that they are having an additive effect on internalizing and externalizing symptoms. Moreover, economic circumstances were the most often endorsed source of stress for participants in the present study, suggesting a significant loss in material resources. This effect may only be exacerbated by the accompanying losses in psychosocial resources, such as difficult current relationships and limited leisure time opportunities. Together, they may act as a complex set of environmental and interpersonal factors contributing to symptoms of psychopathology among participants in our sample. In fact, loss of material and psychosocial resources has been implicated in predicting psychopathology in the aftermath of disasters and terrorism (Hobfoll, 1989; Hobfoll, Tracy, & Galea, 2006). On the other hand, it is also possible that participants, whose relationships are stress free and leisure time opportunities plentiful, are better equipped to cope with other less controllable present day stressors. In other words, stable, supportive, and caring family, peer, and school/professional relationships, as well as existent and healthy opportunities for leisure time, may be acting as protective family and community mechanisms, enabling BH young adults in our sample to better cope with the slew of previous and current uncontrollable sources of stress and hardships. This notion of protectiveness against stress accounted for by social support has been well documented in the literature on stress and coping (e.g., McCubbin, 1980; Prati & Pietrantoni, 2009).

Future studies should examine coping skills and strategies of BH young adults, between groups of those with and without internalizing and externalizing symptoms. Special attention should be given to the role healthy and supportive relationships play in young adults who have experienced significant trauma and on-going hardships. Finally, an examination of the psychological well-being of children born in the post-war period should be conducted in order to further evaluate the true and direct effects of the post-war situation on mental health among young adults in Bosnia-Herzegovina. One limitation to the present study is the lack of variability among predictors of current stress. It would be beneficial to further examine the direct impact of uncontrollable stressors, such as the political environment, economic circumstances, and bleak educational opportunities.

In conclusion, it may be inferred from our results that the longer the political tensions exist, the economy remains undeveloped, and the educational prospects remain bleak for BH young adults, the greater the potential for material and psychosocial resources to be further depleted, which may, in turn, diminish the protective role healthy relationships and leisure time opportunities play. This environment, where BH young adults struggle emotionally, have difficulties performing in school, and engage in risky behaviors and substance abuse, yet have fewer material and psychosocial resources to turn to for help, may have severe implications for community re-development and long-term sustainability of peace. Although "negative peace" or the absence of physical violence (Christie, Tint, Wagner, & Winter, 2008) has been achieved, the results of our study suggest that, for our participants, much work remains necessary for positive peace, or rather, the restored social order and equal access to political structures and economic and educational resources (Christie et al., 2008). Current stressors, mainly the political, economic, and educational environment, do not promote a just world and pose as potential barriers to long-lasting peace. These stressors are a subtle form of structural, systematic violence (Christie, 2006), which marginalizes BH young adults and contributes to here reported cognitive, emotional, and behavioral maladjustment. Discovered impaired psychological adjustment of BH young adults may consequently affect their preparedness for constructive conflict resolution and their ability to build a socially just and peaceful community. Hence, an elimination of political, social, and economic injustices, seen here in the form of ongoing stressors, as well as the promotion of healthy individual and collective psychological well-being, are basic rights for BH young adults, and need to be at the forefront of efforts aimed at achieving a lasting peace.

References

Abapahic et al. (2003). Youth in Bosnia and Herzegovina 2003. Are you part of the problem or part of the solution? United Nations in Bosnia and Herzegovina: United Nations Development Programme. http://www.undp.ba.

Achenbach, T. (1997). *Young adult self report*. Burlington, VT: University of Vermont, Department of Psychiatry.

Adjukovic, M., & Adjukovic, D. (1998). Impact of displacement on the psychological well-being of refugee children. *International Review of Psychiatry, 10*, 186–195.

Al-Khawaha, J. M. A. (1997). The impact of traumatic events on the psychological well-being of Kuwaitis who lived in Egypt and England during the Iraqi Invasion of Kuwait. *Dirasat Nafsiyah, 7*(4), 628–641.

Allodi, F. (1989). The children of victims of political persecution and torture: A psychological study of a Latin American refugee community. *International Journal of Mental Health, 18*, 3–15.

Angel, B., Hjern, A., & Ingleby, D. (2001). Effects of war and organized violence on children: A study of Bosnian refugees in Sweden. *The American Journal of Orthopsychiatry, 71*(1), 4–15.

Cairns, E., & Dawes, A. (1996). Children: Ethnic and political violence – a commentary. *Child Development, 67*, 120–139.

Christie, D. J. (2006). What is peace psychology the psychology of? *Journal of Social Issues, 62*(1), 1–17.

Christie, D. J., Tint, B. S., Wagner, R. V., & Winter, D. D. (2008). Peace psychology for a peaceful world. *American Psychologist, 63*(6), 540–552.

Clarke, G., Sack, W. H., & Goff, B. (1993). Three forms of stress in Cambodian adolescent refugees. *Journal of Abnormal Child Psychology, 21*, 65–77.

Dapic, R., & Stuvland, R. (2000). Longitudinal study of the war related traumatic reactions of children in Sarajevo in 1993, 1995, and 1997. In S. Powell & E. Durakovic-Belko (Eds.), *Sarajevo 2000: The psychosocial consequences of war. Results of empirical research from the territory of former Yugoslavia*. Faculty of Philosophy in Sarajevo, July 7, 2000.

Dapo, N., & Kolenovic-Dapo, J. (2000). Evaluation of the psychosocial adjustment of displaced children from Srebrenica. In S. Powell & E. Durakovic-Belko (Eds.), *Sarajevo 2000: The psychosocial consequences of war. Results of empirical research from the territory of former Yugoslavia*. Faculty of Philosophy in Sarajevo, July 7, 2000.

Farwell, N. (1999). *After liberation: Psychological well-being of Eritrean youth*. Dissertation Abstracts International Section A: Humanities and Social Sciences, 59(8-A).

Freedy, J. R., Shaw, D. L., Jarrell, M. P., & Masters, C. R. (1992). Towards an understanding of the psychological impact of natural disasters: An application of the conservation resources stress model. *Journal of Traumatic Stress, 5*, 441–454.

Galea, S., Ahern, J., Resnick, H., Kilpatrick, D., Bucuvalas, M., Gold, J., et al. (2002). Psychological sequelae of the September 11 terrorist attacks in New York City. *The New England Journal of Medicine, 346*, 982–987.

Goldstein, R. D., Wampler, N. S., & Wise, P. H. (1997). War experiences and distress symptoms of Bosnian children. *Pediatrics, 100*(5), 873–878.

Grant, K. E., Compas, B. E., Stuhlmacher, A. F., Thurm, A. E., McMahon, S. D., & Halpert, J. A. (2003). Stressors and child and adolescent psychopathology: Moving from markers to mechanisms of risk. *Psychological Bulletin, 129*(3), 447–466.

Grant, K. E., Compas, B. E., Thurm, A. E., McMahon, S. D., & Gipson, P. Y. (2004). Stressors and child and adolescent psychopathology: Measurement issues and prospective effects. *Journal of Clinical Child and Adolescent Psychology, 33*(2), 412–425.

Halcon, L., Robertson, C. L., Savik, K., Johnson, D. R., Spring, M. A., et al. (2004). Trauma and coping in Somali and Oromo refugee youth. *Journal of Adolescent Health, 35*(1), 17–25.

Hobfoll, S. E. (1989). Conservation of resources: A new attempt at conceptualizing stress. *American Psychologist, 44*(2), 513–524.

Hobfoll, S. E., Tracy, M., & Galea, S. (2006). The impact of resource loss and traumatic growth on probable PTSD and depression following terrorist attacks. *Journal of Traumatic Stress, 19*(6), 867–878.

Ironson, G., Wynings, C., Schneiderman, N., Baum, A., Rodriguez, M., Greenwood, D., et al. (1997). Posttraumatic stress symptoms, intrusive thoughts, loss, and immune function after Hurricane Andrew. *Psychosomatic Medicine, 59*, 128–141.

Kinzie, J. D., Sack, W., Angell, R., Clarke, G., & Ben, R. (1989). A three-year follow-up of Cambodian young people traumatized as children. *Journal of the American Academy of Child and Adolescent Psychiatry, 28*(4), 501.

Layne, C. M., Saltzman, W. R., Poppleton, L., Burlingame, G. M., Pasalic, A., Durakovic-Belko, E., et al. (2008). Effectiveness of a school-based group psychotherapy program for war-exposed adolescents: A randomized controlled trail. *Journal of the American Academy of Child and Adolescent Psychiatry, 47*, 1048–1062.

Lazarus, R. S., & Folkman, S. (1984). *Stress, appraisal, and coping*. New York: Springer.
Lomsky-Feder, E. (1996). Youth in the shadow of war, war in the light of youth: Life stories of Israeli Veterans. In K. Hurrelmann & S. F. Hamilton (Eds.), *Social problems and social contexts in adolescence: Perspectives across boundaries* (pp. 253–268). New York: Walter de Gruyter, Inc.
McCubbin, H. (1980). Family stress and coping: A decade review. *Journal of Marriage and the Family, 42*(4), 855–871. doi:10.2307/351829.
Mikasaj-Todorovic, L. (2004). Razlike u ponasanju maloljetnih delinkvenata prije i nakon domovinskog rata. *Kriminologija i Socijalna Integracija, 13*(1), 27–32.
Miller, K. E. (1996). The effects of state terrorism and exile on indigenous Guatemalan refugee children: A mental health assessment and an analysis of children's narratives. *Child Development, 67*(1), 89–106.
Muldon, O., & Cairns, E. (1999). Children, young people, and war: Learning to cope. In E. Frydenberg (Ed.), *Learning to cope: Developing as a person in complex societies* (pp. 322–337). Oxford: Oxford University Press.
Paardekooper, B., de Jong, J. T., & Hermanns, J. M. (1999). The psychological impact of war and the refugee situation on South Sudanese children in refugee camps in northern Uganda: An exploratory study. *Journal of Child Psychology and Psychiatry, 40*(4), 529–536.
Powell, S., & Durakovic-Belko, E. (Eds.), (2000). *Sarajevo 2000: The psychosocial consequences of war. Results of empirical research from the territory of former Yugoslavia*. Faculty of Philosophy in Sarajevo, July 7, 2000.
Prati, G., & Pietrantoni, L. (2009). Optimism, social support, and coping strategies as factors contributing to posttraumatic growth: A meta-analysis. *Journal of Loss and Trauma, 14*(5), 364–388. doi:10.1080/15325020902724271.
Pullis, M. (1998). Exposure to traumatic violence: Some lessons from Bosnia. *Education and Treatment of Children, 21*(3), 396–411.
Research and Documentation Center Sarajevo (2010). Ljudski gubici u BiH 1991–1995. Retrieved from: www.idc.org.ba.
Schlenger, W., Cadell, J., Ebert, L., Jordan, B., Rourke, K., Wilson, D., et al. (2002). Psychological reactions to terrorist attacks: Findings from the National Study of Americans' Reactions to September 11. *Journal of the American Medical Association, 288*, 581–588.
Smith, P., Perrin, S., Yule, W., Hacam, B., & Stuvland, R. (2002). War exposure among children of Bosnia-Hercegovina: Psychological adjustment in a community sample. *Journal of Traumatic Stress, 15*(2), 147–156.
UNICEF (2007, April 4). One million landmines still threatening Bosnia and Herzegovina. Retrieved from: http://www.unicef.org/bih/media_6394.html.
Zotovic, M., & Stanulovic, N. K. (2000). Time heals all sorrows? PTSD and its consequences four years after experienced trauma. In S. Powell & E. Durakovic-Belko (Eds.), *Sarajevo 2000: The psychosocial consequences of war. Results of empirical research from the territory of former Yugoslavia*. Faculty of Philosophy in Sarajevo, July 7, 2000.

Chapter 10
Family in Exile: Examining the Risk and Resilience of Refugees in Serbia

Tijana Mirović

Abstract It has been over a decade since the armed conflict in the former Yugoslavia ended. The guns went silent but for over 300,000 people who are still displaced or in exile, the positive peace is yet to come. Their basic needs are still deprived and this, coupled with previous exposure to a number of stressful and traumatic events, leaves them and their families at risk. Following the notion that risk factors refer to situations or events that increase the probability of a maladaptive state, the author analyzes some of the major risks connected with living in exile such as: poor living conditions, unemployment, isolation, trauma and loss. In addition to this, the author gives an overview of various initiatives and interventions designed to help individual and families in exile, primarily concentrating on resilience and solution focused approaches grounded in family systems theory.

Keywords Family • Exile • Risk • Resilience • Serbia

Introduction

From 1991 to 1999, Serbia was engaged in five armed conflicts: in Slovenia (1991), Croatia (1991–1995), Bosnia-Herzegovina (1992–1995), and Kosovo (1999), culminating with the NATO bombing in the spring of 1999. At the same time this was a period of significant economic downfall caused by international sanctions and the highest hyperinflation ever marked in the world (Popadic & Mihailovic, 2003). In addition, Yugoslav wars initiated the influx of a huge number of refugees. According to a refugee census conducted in 1996, there were around 538,000 refu-

T. Mirović (✉)
Counseling Center Mozaik, Maksima Gorkog 23, 11000 Belgrade, Serbia
e-mail: tijana.mirovic@gmail.com

O. Simić et al. (eds.), *Peace Psychology in the Balkans: Dealing with a Violent Past while Building Peace*, Peace Psychology Book Series, DOI 10.1007/978-1-4614-1948-8_10,

gees from Bosnia and Croatia in Serbia alone. Most of these refugees were still there when an estimated number of 250,000 Serbs and non-Albanians were forced to leave the Serbian province of Kosovo after it was put under the control of international peace forces. Because they had migrated from one part of the country to other parts of Serbia, these people were not considered refugees but Internally Displaced Persons (IDP).

With the arrival of IDPs, Serbia became the European country with most refugees and IDPs while at a same time having one of the highest poverty rates in Europe. In the year 2000, the United Nation High Committee for Refugees (UNHCR) estimated that over 60% of the Yugoslav (Serbian and Montenegrin) population lived below the poverty line. In 2003, the same agency, declared Serbia and Montenegro the European country with the most IDP and refuges (UNHCR, 2003). Today, with the same number of IDPs and 66,600 refugees, Serbia is, following Russia, the European country with second largest number of refugees (U.S. Committee for Refugees and Immigrants, 2009). When one considers the ratio of refugee population to total population, the ratio being 1:111, Serbia holds first place in Europe and eleventh in the world. Such a large ratio of IDP and refugees confirms that we really need to acknowledge the fact that refugees are still present in Serbia. Other reports (e.g. Group 484 Report, 2005) demonstrate that refugees continue to need support and assistance in dealing with traumas, losses and a variety of post displacement stressors.

The main goal of this chapter is to portray these stressors and to outline the initiatives and interventions that could be offered to refugees. First, the chapter will address some of the major post-displacement stressors such as: poor living conditions, isolation, unemployment and poverty. Second, the chapter will focus on pre-displacement stressors such as trauma and loss. Finally, we will look at various initiatives and interventions designed to help individual and families in exile, primarily concentrating on resilience and solution focused approaches grounded in family systems theory and psychotherapy.

We have chosen this systems theory because, in the existing body of literature on refugees and psychotherapy, there has been a stronger focus on individual, psychodynamic orientations rather than on family and systems orientations (Reichelt & Sveaass, 1994; Sveaass & Reichelt, 2001b). Also, while much impressive therapy and research work has been done with refugees on an individual basis, less attention has been paid to how interactions with close relatives and other supporting systems may contribute to the alleviation of suffering (Reichelt & Sveaass, 1994).

An additional reason for focusing on family systems theory is the author's professional background and trainings in psychology and family therapy. The chapter will not convey the position of a theorist or a researcher, but that of a practitioner who has worked with Yugoslav refugees for over a decade – first, as humanitarian aid worker working mainly in refugee camps and then, as a psychotherapist working within the private practice.

During my years of working with refugee families I have learned that neither the refugees not the IDPs represent a homogeneous population. Still, I've often heard people say "when you hear one refugee story, you've heard them all." Many times I found this to be true, while at the same time, realizing that nothing can melt the number of distinctive and diverse people into one homogeneous group faster than war and exile. Overnight people with different names, professions, and social status had to trade it all in for one common name -"refugees"; one mutual goal: "to survive and to stay sane" and a common faith called "the exile."

Family in Exile: Post Displacement Stressors

Exile and war are manmade disasters, often more traumatic than natural disasters (Aptekar & Boore, 1990); these disasters destroy whole communities and numerous lives. Leaving everything behind, people in exile come to a new environment where they are forced to be dependent on international aid, local institutions or relatives. As years in exile go by, some families use all the available resources and manage to move toward independence and adaptation to changes happening inside and outside of the family. Other families continue to be dependent on outside help while constantly struggling with the deprivation of basic needs that comes from unemployment, isolation and indecent living conditions.

Living Conditions

Prior to exile a vast majority of refugees had their own homes. The Association of Refugees claims that the total value of the properties that refugees left in their homelands (mainly Bosnia and Croatia) amounted to 350 billions of euros (Tanjug, 2008). The situation is similar for IDP whose homes were either burnt or inaccessible. They cannot safely get to their homes or sell them or get some reimbursement from the people who are (unlawfully) using them. Since they cannot exercise these rights, they cannot obtain credit to buy a property or receive a loan for self-employment in small businesses. Because of these circumstances, a significant number of refugees are forced to live with host families or in collective centres also known as refugee camps.

At the beginning of the 1990s, only 5% of refugees, who arrived in Serbia from Bosnia and Croatia, lived in collective centers, while others found shelter at relatives' homes. However, when a new wave of about 250,000 refugees from Croatia arrived in August 1995, the number of those living in collective centers increased to 30% (Lecic-Tasevski & Draganic-Gajic, 2005). This percentage increased even further when an additional 250,000 internally displaced persons (IDP) arrived from Kosovo after the bombardment in 1999.

Now, a decade later, a significant number of families have managed to move out of the camps and relatives' homes. Some families returned to their place of origin, some left for foreign counties, and some have managed to rent or obtain apartments in Serbia. A study conducted on 1630 IDPs from Kosovo (IAN, 2001) revealed that a majority of them live in rented apartments (64.8%), while others live at relatives' or friends' houses (21.8%). A house or a flat is owned by 8.5% of IDPs, while 4.1% still live in collective centers.

Accommodation Within Host Families

In Serbian culture, family is very important and by family one does not mean just immediate family members but all the other relatives as well. As an illustration; all people who would be called "cousins" in the USA, are called (and are considered) "brothers or sisters" in Serbia. So, when relatives in trouble come knocking at the door, families have to take them in, no matter how little space and money they have. For this reason, immediately upon arrival to Serbia, 95% of refugees found shelter not in camps, but in homes of immediate or distant family members (Mirovic, 2007).

Many refugees still live with host families, even after being in exile for over 10 years. This is why a large number of youth live in the three-generation families or together with aunts and uncles. The ties between these family members are often very strong. In most parts, they are all involved in raising children and making important family decisions. They are consulted in times of need and invited to join in at celebrations and times of joy (Mirovic, 2007). These kinds of relationships have often helped refugees feel less isolated and less out of place. Also, since living together usually meant the sharing of chores and concerns, refugees residing with relatives seemed to have a stronger sense of being both helpful and helped.

It is important to say, that in some cases, living with relatives became a stressor rather than an advantage. This was often the case when there was an ongoing conflict between members of refugee and host families. In our experiences, these conflicts were usually initiated around the issues of money, limited living space, personal boundaries, negotiation of roles, differences in values and so on. Sometimes, family solidarity and loyalty declined in time with the increase of poverty, and host families' exhaustion with their own suffering and problems (Vlajkovic, Srna, Kondic, & Popovic, 1997).

The cohabitation clearly, called for adjustments on both sides and even though it could cause tensions between host and refugee families, living with hosts proved to be an important protective factor for refugees. Research conducted by the Institute for Mental Health in Belgrade (Vlajkovic et al., 1997), showed that 27% of children and adolescent refugees placed with host families exhibited symptoms which justified classification within certain psychiatric diagnostic categories. These symptoms were even more numerous when the young people were placed in collective centres; a total of 39% met psychiatric diagnostic criteria in these conditions. By comparison, only 11.6% of the local same age population exhibited disorders which could be classified as psychiatric. Clearly there is empirical support for the thesis that living in exile can be traumatising and detrimental and, more broadly, that living conditions have an effect on mental health and wellbeing.

Accommodation in Collective Centres (Refugee Camps)

The fact that living in refugee camps seems to be more harmful than other arrangements could be explained by both poorer resources and worse living conditions commonly associated with collective centres. Even though the number of camp inhabitants can vary from 5 to over a 100 people, most of the collective centers look the same. They are overcrowded (sometimes there are up to 20 people in a room planned for 5), they are unsanitary (with common bathrooms and often no running water), and totally unfit for normal, family functioning. Most of these camps are closed factories, old schools or workers' barracks so they do not have playing areas for children or common rooms for social activities such as playing cards or watching TV. This is significant because both experience and research show that having a common room for socializing and continuation of daily routines or rituals is a very important protective factor for people in refugee camps (Vlajkovic et al., 1997). The lack of possibilities for fun and recreational activities leave refugees with a lot of free and unstructured time. This increases passiveness and activities such as drinking, fighting or arguing. Another risk factor associated with most refugee or IDP camps is their location. The majority of these camps are situated far from urban areas, which diminishes the possibility of finding work, continuing education or being integrated into society. All this contributes to various negative effects.

In their research, Non-Governmental organization (NGO) "Group 484" (Group 484 Report, 2005) found three types of negative effects associated with living in collective centres: psychological, social and economic. Psychological effects include: reduced dignity and self-respect, increased passivity and indecisiveness about what to do next, weakening of social and other competencies, increased use of alcohol and sedatives, etc. All of these problems contribute to negative economic effects such as increased poverty connected with inertness and a kind of passivity that is manifest in waiting for free meals and hand-outs. Other negative effects are connected to social problems that include: increased conflicts within and between families, violence and increased social isolation.

The Report does not mention any positive effect associated with living in collective centres. There is however, a possibility that staying within a group that shares similar customs and beliefs as well as similar experiences could be beneficial. In their work with Bosnian refugee families in Sweden, Eastmond, Ralphsson and Alinder (1994) found strong bonds between families who went through traumatizing events together. The refugees they interviewed felt that being geographically close to one another would have been a vital resource in coping with their experience and reconstituting their life in exile. Another factor they found important for the reconstruction of life in exile was rapid labour market integration.

Integration into Local Community and Its Labour Market

Exile leads to a fundamental change of social status, due to the loss of professional connections, working relationships, political involvement, judicial forms of justice, economic well-being and other losses, including the loss of civil status, which limits basic human rights (Vlajkovic et al., 1997). Exile is also connected with a loss or weakening of social networks of friends and acquaintances, which significant numbers of refugees and IDPs never completely rebuild (Pavlov, Volarevic, & Petronijevic, 2006). Still, as years go by, refugees become more and more integrated into the local community. Even though there is a tendency toward connection with members of a same social group, many refugees slowly develop social networks indicative of considerable social integration into the local community (Babovic, Cvejic, & Rakic, 2007).

The group that has integrated the most includes those who came to Serbia as children or adolescents and are now adolescents or young adults. Having gone to school with locals, they have adapted local norms and made some strong interpersonal connections. The weakest integration was observed in those who were tied down to homes or collective centres (elderly, the unemployed etc.). Many of these and other refugees continue to feel stigmatized and ghettoized.

This claim is supported by an open letter in which the Association of refugees of Serbia warned the public about "marginalization, violation of human rights and increasing poverty that refugees face" (Tanjug, 2008). Basing their claims on a survey which included 2,312 refugees, the association pointed out many other issues, one being that over 150,000 seniors stopped receiving their pensions after they emigrated from Bosnia and Croatia. They have also alerted the public that they are still unable to receive travelling documents, to exercise their right to vote or to take part in bond distribution processes. Additionally, since their only newspaper was abolished due to a lack of resources and because other media rarely address issues regarding people in exile, refugees expressed concern that the public will forget that they are still present and in need. The Association feels that refugees' voices are not being heard in the media or anywhere else where "their destiny is being deliberated."

In addition to feeling forsaken from the society, refugees often feel estranged and distanced from community services and job opportunities (Babovic et al., 2007).

Unemployment and Poverty

Babovic et al. (2007) conducted research on a sample of 500 refugees and demonstrated that 59% of refugee families could be characterized as poor or at risk of poverty. The same study found that refugees have a higher unemployment rate (30.6%) than the general population (20.8%). The situation is even worse when it comes to female refugees. Their unemployment rate is higher than that of male refugees (ratio being 33.0–28.5%) and higher than the unemployment rate for women in the general population (ratio being 33.0–24.1%).

Looking at the duration of unemployment paints an even darker picture. One third of refugees had never been employed, and 68.0% were unemployed for longer than 5 years. This has great material and psychological repercussions, because by not having (or by loosing) professional status refugees lose many social roles ("boss, favourite teacher, colleague" etc.) and all benefits or rights that come from social insurance.

If they are employed, refugees usually hold positions beneath their educational level. Only 10.6% of refugees with a university degree have jobs that require higher education. In contrast, in the general population 50.0% of people with university degrees have jobs that require higher education (Babovic et al., 2007).

Within the group of IDP, there is a somewhat higher percentage employed than in refugee populations (IAN, 2001). While there is, according to the data gathered on refugee populations from Bosnia and Herzegovina, about 10% refugees in part-time or full-time employment (Milosavljevic, 2000, as cited in IAN, 2001), in the group of IDP there are 19.9% employed persons (IAN, 2001).

These rather grim statistics on refugees' and IDPs poverty and unemployment is alarming because there seems to be strong link between unemployment and different psychological problems such as couple and family conflict (Walsh, 2002), diffused anxiety, helplessness, hopelessness, low self-esteem and lost perspectives in life (Lecic-Tasevski & Draganic-Gajic, 2005).

In addition to their link with unemployment, these and other psychological problems can also be tied to pre displacement and displacement stressors such as trauma and loss. We will consider these issues next.

Family in Exile: Pre-Displacement and Displacement Stressors

Lecic-Tasevski & Draganic-Gajic (2005) revealed that a significant number of Serbian refugees suffered from psychiatric problems such as post-traumatic stress disorder (29.2%), adjustment disorder (18.6%), mixed anxious-depressive disorder (11.3%) and depressive episodes (5%). Most of the refugees examined had multiple traumas such as combat injury, loss of a family member, forced labour, witnessing of torture, sexual abuse or imprisonment.

Studying IDP's exposure to some traumatic events, IAN team (2001) found that the majority of IDPs had been exposed to traumatic events such as: combat exposure (55.3%), sudden death of a close person (44.1%), direct assault by weapons (19.6%) and so on. Within this sample, 131 persons (8%) stated they had a family member missing in the course of war without knowing what has happened to them. These data clearly show that in addition to the above mentioned post-displacement stressors, refugees and their families need to find a way to live with experienced trauma, as well as with actual and ambiguous losses.

Many individuals and families that we have worked with often believed that in time their life would improve, though they had strong doubts that they could ever recuperate from trauma and loss. While they often would ask us questions like "how could I ever live with what has happen to me" or "how do I ever replace my father?" In many cases they grieved not only about the past but also about the future consequences of what had happened. As one refugee woman told me:

> It is hard to live knowing that you have been violated and deprived of everything you were...but, you also know that it is done...left behind...it will never happen again! You just need to learn not to think about it and to live as if it never happened...Question is how you can do that with death of your husband. Everyday that I live my life without him I am reliving the whole thing...As the children grow older, I miss him even more...Knowing that he will not be there for their weddings... see their children, it is just too much. Knowing that this will never end, kills me...Slowly and everyday....

These short sentences, give very clear testimony of how difficult it is to deal with actual and symbolic losses, such as a dream of the future. The life can certainly go on, but what is lost can never really be replaced. For some refugees it seemed as if life did not and could not go on. This belief was often held by those whose loss remained ambiguous.

Victor Frankl wrote: “If the environment remains ambiguous, uncertain and incomprehensible, cognition is blocked, emotions are frozen, and continued individual and family functioning are severely hampered” (cited in Boss, 2002, p. 15). The same could be said about the ambiguous loss that occurs when a family member is either psychologically present and physically absent (abducted or missing) or when he is physically present and psychologically absent (as in a case of Alzheimer’s disease).

According to the data of International Red Cross Committee, even though the Yugoslav wars ended long ago, 15,665 people are still considered missing (B92, 2009). On the international day of missing people, families all across the former Yugoslavia try to remind the public that their loved ones haven’t been found. Holding missing members’ photographs, they stand in a circle, symbolically showing that they are still moving in a circle of “failed promises.” Every year, they make the same appeal to the governments and international community: “Help us find our loved ones. Find the necessary resources to make the exhumation and identification process faster than it is” (cited from a television statement). They send a clear message that they will never give up hope, but that they need to know the truth whatever it might be.

Surviving an ambiguous loss is difficult for even the strongest families. Boss (2002) says that lack of clarity about the loss of a family member generates confusion and conflict about who is in and who is out of the system. She calls this “boundary ambiguity,” explaining that the higher the boundary ambiguity in the family system, the greater the helplessness and likelihood of individual and family dysfunction (depression and conflict).

The shock and pain of a traumatic loss can shatter family cohesion, leaving members isolated and unsupported in their grief (Walsh & McGoldrick, 1991). However, exposure to loss per se does not mean that all affected persons need assistance. Most people adapt and for some, the threats to bonds can lead to positive if painful adaptation (Silove, 2005). In either case, loss of a family member requires reorganization of the family system, boundary shifts and role redefinition. This needs to occur in order to compensate for the loss.

The fact that the majority of Serbian refugees are women suggests that families in exile mostly compensate for the loss of a husband and a father. If the father is gone, his role has to be reassigned to someone else. In most cases that role gets divided between a mother and an older child or in some instances, the role gets assigned to a member of an extended family (grandfathers, uncles etc.).

If the father is missing, mothers often have to start working, sometimes even for the first time. This usually means leaving children alone and unattended for long periods of time. For many children I have worked with, this was the hardest thing to bear. They had already lost their fathers, their homes and their security. Finally, as a last drop, they lost the presence of their mother as well, being left to cope with everything on their own (Mirovic, 2000).

This change is hard for younger children, but maybe especially hard for older siblings and adolescents, who often have to grow up "over night." Research shows that prior to war only 0.8% of adolescents took part in reaching important family decisions; in exile this number came up to 20% (Vlajkovic et al., 1997). For some adolescents (especially males) the loss of a father meant they had to quit school and start looking for work. If the mother was the one working, older siblings had to take care of the family and of household chores. These sudden and immense responsibilities asked for a self-sacrifice that sometimes remained their way of behaving even in later relationships. Today, 15 years later, as grown adults, many of them still take care of their family of origin and most of the people in their surroundings. They often feel tired and depressed, but a strong sense of guilt stops them from saying no or doing something for themselves (Mirovic, 2010).

Seeing how being in exile could have severe and long-lasting consequences we have to ask ourselves how can we prevent this from happening? How can we help individuals and families remain resilient in the face of all the various stressors we have mentioned? Having in mind everything that has been said about refugee families and different kinds of pre-displacement and resettlement stressors, we will now look into different interventions that could be used for ameliorating refugees' adverse living conditions and barriers to mental health.

What Can We Do in Order to Improve the Way Refuges Live?

Former traumatic incidents, losses and ongoing difficulties related to resettlement and adaptation may create reduced psychological and social functioning (Sveaass & Reichelt, 2001a). Aiming to prevent this and to improve refugees' well-being, various agencies have designed actions to either reduce the pre-displacement and resettlement stressors or to foster refugees' resilience to these adversities. In the last part of this paper we will take a closer look into some of the approaches designed to foster family resilience to displacement and trauma. In this next part we will briefly mention some of the initiatives designed to ameliorate refugees' living conditions and socio-economic status.

Christie, Tint, Wagner, and Winter (2008) explain that positive peace is being promoted if political structures become more inclusive and give voice to those who have been marginalized in matters that affect their well-being (p. 547). This means that in order to stop the structural violence, we need to provide refugees with material resources as well as political representation and voice. They need to get a right to vote, better media coverage and a voice in matters that concern them. In addition to this, there needs to be more actions and projects that would reduce poverty and improve refugees' living conditions.

Some of these actions have already started and some of the changes have already occurred. The biggest initiative happened in 2004 when the Serbian Government introduced the Poverty Reduction Strategy Paper (PRSP). Addressing the specific needs of refugees and IDP, the government designed four strategies for reducing their poverty. The first strategy aimed toward the affirmation of basic human rights and planned on giving refugees documents, citizenships and health insurance cards. The second strategy focused on providing housing while the third was aimed at strengthening of socio-cultural resources and the enhancement of human capital. The fourth strategy addressed the definition of categories which would qualify for welfare or some form of social aid (cited in Group 484 Report, 2005).

In an effort to close down the collective centres and to provide refugees with healthier living arrangements the government has joined forces with international and local agencies and NGOs. In cooperation with International relief agencies, the Serbian government is working on providing conditions for the return of refugees and IDPs to their places of origin. In addition to that, some NGOs help by buying building material so that refugees can build new houses within Serbia. The brightest example could be that of a famous basketball player, Vlade Divac, who created the Divac Humanitarian Organization (HOD) and started realization of the "You Can Too" initiative. The goal of this initiative is "to help refugees in fulfilling their rights to home, employment, financial security and psycho-social help and to start new and normal life after many years" (Foundation Ana & Vlade Divac, 2007). In association with the Republic of Serbia's Committee for Refugees and UNHCR, Divac's initiative has worked on buying and adapting rural houses for refugees and internally displaced people who still reside in collective centres. During the 6 months of work, HOD has managed to raise enough money to buy 100 rural households for those people. Unfortunately, UNHCR estimation is that another 500 houses are needed to solve this major social problem (Foundation Ana & Vlade Divac, 2007).

Other very important social problems are poverty and unemployment which are both among the highest stressors connected to life in exile. Unable to find work, a significant number of refugees and IDP still depend on humanitarian aid. One study (IAN, 2001) revealed that 97.9% of IDP considers that humanitarian aid is still needed. Things they claimed to need the most were: clothing items, food, home furnishing, house renting money and heating fuel.

In order to help refugees and IDP find employment and attain economic independence, a number of Serbian NGOs (such as IAN or Group 484) offer refugees different training courses such as: English lessons, computer skills, communication skills and so on. In addition, these organizations offer training that would qualify refugees for different professions, such as construction workers, dressmakers and such (Jovic, 2004).

These educational courses have an additional benefit, because while attending a course refugees have an opportunity to socialize and form new friendships. Seeing how important and beneficial this could be, IAN has also initiated social clubs with different kinds of activities such as playing games, watching movies, reading newspapers, etc. All of these activities are aimed at creating a "safe environment" in which refugees do not feel isolated, misunderstood or stressed. In this environment, refugees become more willing to take part in support groups and seek counselling (Jovic, 2004).

This is important because although in need of psychological help, refugees are often not used to accept and benefit from this kind of help (Vlajkovic et al., 1997).

Instead of seeking psychotherapy, they resort to using prescribed or "over the counter" medication. Research (IAN, 2001; Jovic, Opacic, Vujadinovic-Speh, Vidakovic, & Knezevic, 2004) shows that 24.4% IDP and 21.4% of refuges started to take tranquilizers in exile. The same studies also found that in comparison to the situation prior to war, mental health conditions after war were typically reported as "much worse" (by 19% of IDPs and 22% of refugees) or "somewhat worse" (by 32.8% of IDPs and 43.9% of refugees). Moreover, in light of some of the differences between IDPs and refugees, some organizations have worked on offering refugees and IDP different interventions in support of their mental health.

As in the other areas of the world (see Silove, 2005), in Serbia the range of potential treatments for displaced people is wide, ranging from crisis management and brief psychological interventions for severe trauma reactions to pharmacological treatment for psychosis and severe depression. The treatments that are most commonly used include the use of Eye Movement Desensitization and Reprocessing (EMDR) and Cognitive-Behavioural Therapy (CBT) with torture survivors experiencing PTSD and depression. In addition to this different counseling centers and organizations also use Help lines, Supportive counseling and psychoeducation, Psychoanalysis, Rogers' client centered therapy, Psychodrama, Music and art therapy, Testimonial psychotherapy or Narrative Exposure Therapy (Jovic, 2004; Vlajkovic et al., 1997). More information on these approaches and their efficiency in reducing symptoms connected with exile can be found in other chapters of this volume (see Philpot and Schweitzer) and in articles dealing with refugees' mental health (such as Murray et al., 2008). So, instead of going into details in relation to these approaches, we will present a systemic family approach, which we see as highly useful in dealing with families in exile.

A Systemic Family Approach

From a systems point of view suffering is not regarded as an individual matter, so much as a part of life experiences that are continuously influencing and influenced by interpersonal relationships (Reichelt & Sveaass, 1994). Even when only one family member is traumatized or develops acute stress reactions, all family members become affected. When more family members struggle with the consequences of cumulative stress, further distress is created by dysfunctional interactions that undermine mutual support in the family (Bala, 2005). At the same time, many families report that by weathering a crisis together their relationships are enriched and more loving that they might otherwise be (Walsh, 2003).

Having all this in mind, we wondered how we, as mental health professionals, could help families to function in a way that would contribute to family members' resilience, and not to risks. Also, how could we help families become resilient not only to trauma and crises but also to cumulative and ongoing post-displacement stresses?

In order to find answers to these questions and ways to improve our work with traumatized, displaced and grieving families, we looked at successful practices

(Bala, 2005; Eastmond et al., 1994; Ganesan, Fine, & Lin, 1989; Reichelt & Sveaass, 1994; Sveaass & Reichelt, 2001a, 2001b) and some of the theories that focus on family resilience, resources, solutions and possibilities (de Shazer, 1988; Figley, 1989; Walsh & McGoldrick, 1991; White & Epston, 1990, Worden, 2009). The focus on resilience and resources makes sense because refugee families feel overburdened by the multitude of problems they face and typically have an overwhelming sense of being in a desperate situation without power and control. However, as soon as they become aware of at least some resources and possible solutions, they become more optimistic and more responsive to therapy. Consequently, they start to set clearer goals and undertake actions that help them feel more in control and closer to whatever it is that they need.

Walsh (2003) found that affirming family strengths and potential in the midst of difficulties helps families to counter a sense of helplessness, failure and blame while reinformcing pride, confidence and a "can do" spirit. Similarly, Bala (2005) found that by starting to see problems as manageable and themselves as capable of finding solutions, refugees gradually find ways to restart their disrupted lives. In addition to this, the increasing tendency to approach the refugee experience not only in terms of traumatic experiences and losses, but also in terms of strength and potentials for growth, created possibilities for better understanding of the experience of the refugee.

If we only focus on problems, displacement stressors or trauma, we increase the tendency to see all refugee families as similar and thus become more prone to offer preset and sometimes unfitting solutions. Second order cybernetics and social constructionism positions warn us that therapists could be highly influential in shaping the image of the family that emerges in the therapeutic situation, rather than being objective observers of how the family "really is" (Reichelt & Sveaass, 1994). If the therapist thinks in terms of pathology, questions are asked which bring forth pathological aspects of family life. Thus, if the therapist is interested in dysfunctional structures, these are the most likely to appear in the conversation. It is important and necessary to explore family members' reflections regarding problems, but it is equally important to ask about possible solutions and their usual coping strategies.

Ganesan et al. (1989) also suggest several areas to focus on in detail in order to create a therapeutic alliance and facilitate good treatment outcomes. These areas include finding out about life in the refugees' home country; problems and stresses that occurred then; the escape process, why they left, who came, who stayed, and any dangerous situations or losses on the way; problems and difficulties in the host country; and their current worries and future outlook. Similarly, Bala (2005) raises the following questions: How did the migration disrupt family member's lives, how did it change relations and roles in the family, how did these events change their beliefs and expectations, mutual relations and their relatedness to the outside world. Once we have determined all this we can decide on interventions that would be most favourable to that particular family.

Depending on a problem the interventions that we use could include structural and strategic manoeuvres which put therapist in a position of an expert who explores and changes dysfunctional family structures or stuck patterns of interaction. If family members have problems in respecting each other's boundaries and individual differences (often in relation to the grieving process or acculturation to a new society) we can assist them in renegotiating their roles and responsibilities. If there are conflicts, we can support them in collaborative problem solving and conflict resolution and negotiation of differences with fairness and reciprocity. With practical problems we could help family members explore possible solutions by discussing advantages and disadvantages of each proposition. If necessary we can offer family members practical information or concrete guidelines for crisis management, problem-solving and stress reduction. All of these strategies could be very useful; we however, believe that refugee families could benefit more if the therapists (or we) chose a "not-knowing" position.

The position of "not knowing" developed by Anderson and Goolishian (1988, 1992 as cited in Reichelt & Sveaass, 1994) is a perspective where the therapist avoids the role of an expert, realizing that he or she does not know what is best for the family. It implies an exploring and curious attitude and is therefore a good starting point for empowering the families as experts on their own situation.

Another way to empower families is by focusing on their strengths and possible solutions. The solution-focused approach developed by de Shazer (1988) and White and Epston (1990), focuses on what clients want to achieve through therapy rather than on the presenting problems. The therapist invites clients to envision their preferred future and then asks for positive changes and focuses on the achievement of small goals. Even slight improvements and constructive ideas are explored and reinforced, so that the notion of the family itself as a locus of solution and good ideas is strengthened. This approach was found to be particularly helpful with families that are desperate about the way they live together, feel helpless, but have a strong urge to stay together (Reichelt & Sveaass, 1994). Solution-oriented approaches could also be helpful in working with refugee families who are traumatized and have problems adjusting to a new surrounding. While respecting the suffering that the family went through, these approaches de-emphasize pathology and elicit resources, strengths and potentialities that the family possesses, but perhaps are not able to utilize in the midst of past and present traumas.

This is in accordance with Figley's (1989) studies of family therapy with traumatized families and his "Family empowerment model." This model assists families to resolve conflicts associated with the traumatic event and enables family members to recognize their strengths and feel able to take responsibilities for their lives. According to Figley (1989) good adaptation means that the family not only copes well with current trauma but also learned some valuable lessons: their coping repertoire becomes enhanced and therefore enables that system to both prevent and successfully cope with future stressors. On the other hand, families with poor adaptation choose ineffective strategies (passivity, use of drugs or alcohol) which prolong their suffering, drain the existing resources and add new stressors to the family system.

The same could be said when it comes to families dealing with loss. We have already said that losses can shatter family cohesion, leaving family members isolated and unsupported in their grief. This is why we need to help the surviving members to cherish family bonds and to direct energy to re-establishing and fostering kinship and community ties (Silove, 2005). In some cases, it could be important to help family members realize that they are not betraying a loved one by living life to the fullest. Surviving family members need to find ways to transform the living presence of a loved one into cherished memories, stories and deeds that carry on the spirit of the deceased and of their relationships (Walsh, 2002).

In helping families deal with actual, symbolic and ambiguous losses, we have often used a family resilience approach (Walsh, 2002, 2003; Walsh & McGoldrick, 1991) which aims to strengthen family capacity to master adversity. A basic premise guiding this approach is that stressful crises and persistent challenges influence the whole family, and in turn, key family processes (family belief system, organization patterns and communication processes) mediate the recovery and resilience of vulnerable members as well as the family unit (Walsh, 2002). In this approach resilience is fostered by shared, facilitative beliefs that increase options for problem resolution, healing and growth. Communication processes foster resilience by bringing clarity to crisis situations, encouraging open emotional expression, and fostering collaborative problem-solving. In family organization, resilience is bolstered by flexible structures, connectedness (cohesion) and social and economic resources. The adaptation of immigrant families can therefore be fostered by finding ways to sustain connections with valued customs, kin and the community left behind (Walsh, 2003). Strengthening these key processes in each domain has a synergistic influence on other processes. As families become more resourceful, risk and vulnerability are reduced and they are better able to meet future challenges. Consequently, building resilience can also be a preventive measure.

Resilience-based family interventions can be adapted to a variety of formats including multi-family intervention, periodic family consultations or more intensive family therapy. Research (Weine et al., 2003 as cited in Murray, Davidson, & Schweltzer, 2008) shows that family-oriented interventions may be helpful, particularly when intergenerational issues, family conflict and difficulties in resettlement are among clients' primary presenting concerns.

Whatever the primary problems might be and regardless of the approach we decide on, the families need to be treated with respect and with clear signs of empathy, support and understanding. It is important to give them an opportunity to deal with past trauma and actual difficulties, but it is equally important to help them focus on the future by assisting them in creating new plans and setting new goals. In order to reinforce hope and optimism, we need to remind them of the things that they have already accomplished and of coping mechanisms that they already have. Furthermore, we need to motivate them to expand their skills and adaptive coping responses. These resilience-oriented services "foster family empowerment as they bring forth shared hope, develop new and renewed competencies, and build mutual support and collaborative efforts among family members" (Walsh, 2002, p. 11).

This concept should however not be misused to blame families that are unable to rise above harsh conditions by simply labelling them as not resilient.

Family resilience needs to be supported by social and institutional policies and through improvement of protective factors such as community resources, positive community norms and a sense of caring (Walsh, 2003). This is especially important for families in exile who feel alienated and for families dealing with ambiguous loss. As we have already mentioned, these families feel forsaken and left to deal with this complicated issue on their own. Walsh (2002) encourages family members to ask the community to join in and reinforce their hope with visible symbols (such as yellow ribbons used for hostages) or with annual vigils and candle light ceremonies. "Family members can symbolically gain some sense of closure about their loss, in spite of its ambiguity, as the community around them helps validate and memorize what has happened" (Boss, 1991, p. 171).

An interesting example of how community resources could be used for helping families deal with loss and trauma is "Teacher as therapist" model, designed by Husain and his associates (Husain, 2005). During the siege of Sarajevo only approximately 100 mental health professionals remained in the city to serve its 60,000 children who were exposed to trauma. This disproportion between the number of mental health professionals and the children needing psychological help, motivated Husain and his team to train other professionals. Knowing that approximately 5,000 teachers remained in Sarajevo, Husain and his associates developed a model to train teachers in diagnosing and treating children suffering from PTSD and comorbid conditions. Since February 1994, the team led by Professor Husain made 16 trips to the besieged city of Sarajevo and trained 2,000 teachers and over 200 mental health professionals who, in turn helped 20,000 children (Husain, 2005). This kind of program demonstrates the impact that a single initiative can have. While we should be satisfied with these results, it is evident that in order to decrease all the exile related stressors, we need to do more. We hope that this chapter will inspire new initiatives and broaden the possibilities for better understanding of the refugee experience.

Conclusion

We have analyzed various risks connected with living in exile such as poor living conditions, unemployment, isolation, trauma and loss, as well as initiatives and interventions designed to help individual and families in exile. We have seen what a powerful impact some of this initiatives can have. On the other hand, the fact that 15 years later, we still have many families and individuals at risk shows that time alone cannot heal all the wounds. We need to consider this and to implement strategies that can ameliorate problems and foster resilience. Assisting refugees to regain lost resources and options, through employment, social networks, activity, acceptance, and respect, are necessary and vital steps. Approaching the refugee experience not only in terms of traumatic experiences and losses, but also in terms of strength and potentials for growth, helps families to counter a sense of helplessness while it reinforces pride, confidence and a "can do" spirit.

References

Aptekar, L., & Boore, J. A. (1990). The emotional effects of disaster on children: A review of the literature. *Journal of Mental Health, 19*(2), 77–90.

B92. (2009, August). Medjunarodni dan nestalih. *B92*. Retrieved April 15, 2010, from http://www.naslovi.net/2009-08-30/b92/medjunarodni-dan-nestalih/1301061.

Babovic, M., Cvejic, S., & Rakic, D. (2007). *Polozaj izbeglica na trzistu rada i ucesce u aktivnim merama zaposljavanja*. Beograd: Grupa 484.

Bala, J. (2005). Beyond the personal pain: Integrating social and political concerns in therapy with refugees. In D. Ingleby (Ed.), *Forced migrations and mental health: Rethinking the care of refugees and displaced persons* (pp. 169–183). New York: Springer.

Boss, P. (1991). Ambiguous loss. In F. Walsh & M. McGoldrick (Eds.), *Living beyond loss: Death in the family* (pp. 164–175). New York: Norton.

Boss, P. G. (2002). Ambiguous loss: Working with families of the missing. *Family Process, 41*, 14–17.

Christie, D. J., Tint, B. S., Wagner, R. V., & Winter, D. D. (2008). Peace psychology for a peaceful world. *American Psychologist, 63*(6), 540–552.

De Shazer, S. (1988). *Clues: Investigation solutions in brief therapy*. New York: W.W. Norton.

Eastmond, M., Ralphsson, L., & Alinder, B. (1994). The psychological impact of violence and war. Bosnian refugee families and coping strategies. *Refugee Participation Network, 16*, 7–9.

Figley, C. R. (1989). *Helping traumatized families*. San Francisco: Jossey-Bass Publishers.

Foundation Ana & Vlade Divac (2007). http://divac.org.rs/eng/index.html.

Ganesan, S., Fine, S., & Lin, T. Y. (1989). Psychiatric symptoms in refugee families from South East Asia: Therapeutic challenges. *American Journal of Psychotherapy, 43*(2), 218–228.

Group 484 Report. (2005). *Ostanak izbeglica u Srbiji*. Grupa 484: Beograd.

Husain, S. A. (2005). The experience of Bosnia-Herzegovina: Psychosocial consequences of war attrocities on children. In J.J. Lopez-Ibor, G. Christodoulou, M. Maj, N. Sartorius, & A. Okasha (Eds.), *Disasters and mental health* (pp. 247–255). West Sussex: Wiley.

International Aid Network – IAN. (2001). *Internally displaced persons from the Prizren area of Kosovo: Living conditions, mental health and repatriation issues*. Retrieved April 12, 2010, from http://www.ian.org.rs/publikacije/prizren%202000/bookprizren00.htm.

Jovic, V. (2004). Psihosocijalna pomoc u okviru humanitarnih intervencija – sest godina iskustva u IAN-u (1997–2003). In Z. Spiric, G. Knezevic, V. Jovic, & G. Opacic (Eds.), *Tortura u ratu, posledice i rehabilitacija, Jugoslovensko iskustvo* (pp. 71–90). Beograd: IAN.

Jovic, V., Opacic, G., Vujadinovic-Speh, S., Vidakovic, I., & Knezevic, G. (2004). Izbeglice i mentalno zdravlje – Implikacije za process repatrijacije i integracije. In G. Opacic, I. Vidakovic, & B. Vujadinovic (Eds.), *Zivot u posleratnim zajednicama* (pp. 147–179). Beograd: IAN.

Lecic-Tasevski, D., & Draganic-Gajic, S. (2005). The Serbian experience. In J. Lopez-Ibor, G. Christodoulou, M. Maj, N. Sartorius, & A. Okasha (Eds.), *Disasters and mental health* (pp. 247–255). West Sussex: Wiley.

Mirovic, T. (2000). Mladi i izbeglicke porodice. In N. Novakovic-Anastasijevic (Ed.), *Zbornih radova sa Jugoslovenskog simpozijuma o aktuelnim problemima razdvojenih porodica* (pp. 72–83). Beograd: Strucna knjiga.

Mirović, T. (2007). Adolescents in Serbia and Montenegro. In J. Arnett (Ed.), *International encyclopedia of adolescence* (pp. 842–855). New York: Routledge.

Mirovic, T. (2010). *Rane maladaptivne sheme – sheme koje prave probleme*. Beograd: Zadužbina Andrejević.

Murray, K. E., Davidson, G. R., & Schweltzer, R. D. (2008). *Psychological wellbeing of refugees resettling in Australia*. Melbourne: The Australian Psychological Society Ltd.

Pavlov, T., Volarevic, S., & Petronijevic, V. (2006). *Studija o zenama u izbeglistvu i raseljenju*. Beograd: Grupa 484.

Popadic, D., & Mihailovic, S. (2003). *Youth in Serbia: National report*. Belgrade: Proni Institute.

Reichelt, S., & Sveaass, N. (1994). Creating meaningful conversations with families in exile. *Journal of Refugee Studies, 7*, 125–143.

Silove, D. (2005). From trauma to survival and adaptation: Toward a framework for guiding mental health initiatives in post-conflict societies. In D. Ingleby (Ed.), *Forced migrations and mental health: Rethinking the care of refugees and displaced persons* (pp. 29–53). New York: Springer.

Sveaass, N., & Reichelt, S. (2001a). Refugee families in therapy: From referrals to therapeutic conversations. *Journal of Family Therapy, 23*, 119–135.

Sveaass, N., & Reichelt, S. (2001b). Engaging refugee families in therapy: Exploring the benefits of including referring professionals in the first family interviews. *Family Process, 40*(1), 95–114.

Tanjug. (2008, June). Prava izbeglica u Srbiji i svetu. *B92*. Retrieved April 15, 2010, from http://www.b92.net/info/vesti/index.php?yyyy=2008&mm=06&dd=17&nav_id=304138.

UNHCR. (2003). *Global report – Serbia and Montenegro*. Retrieved April 15, 2010 from http://www.unhcr.org/40c6d7750.html.

U.S. Committee for Refugees and Immigrants. (2009). *World refugee survey data 2009*. Retrieved April 15, 2010, from http://www.refugees.org/article.aspx?id=2324.

Vlajkovic, J., Srna, J., Kondic, K., & Popovic, M. (1997). *Psihologija izbeglistva*. Beograd: IP Nauka.

Walsh, F. (2002). Family resilience: A framework for clinical practice. *Family Relations, 51*(2), 130–137.

Walsh, F. (2003). A family resilience framework: Innovative practice application. *Family Process, 42*(1), 2–18.

Walsh, F., & McGoldrick, M. (1991). Loss and the family: A systemic perspective. In F. Walsh & M. McGoldrick (Eds.), *Living beyond loss: Death in the family* (pp. 1–29). New York: Norton.

Weine, S. M., Raina, D., Zhubi, M., Delesi, M., Huseni, D., Feetham, S., et al. (2003). The TAFES multi-family group intervention for Kosovar refugees: A feasibility study. *Journal of Nervous Mental Disorders, 191*(2), 100–107.

White, M., & Epston, D. (1990). *Narrative means to therapeutic ends*. New York: Norton.

Worden, W. J. (2009). *Grief counseling and grief therapy – A handbook for the mental health practitioner*. New York: Springer Publishing Company.

Part III
Envisioning the Future

Chapter 11
Parallel Worlds of Divided Community: Time Does Not Make Much Difference

Dinka Čorkalo Biruški and Dean Ajduković

Abstract Violent conflict can drive a wedge between individuals and ethnic groups that once used to be highly integrated, leaving the community divided in the post-conflict era. The members of two groups stay apart for a long time if there are no systemic efforts to repair social ties that make a community stable and functional. Schooling system has such a potential. After the 1991–1995 war, Croat and Serb children in the city of Vukovar in Croatia, started to go to separate schools. Language of teaching became the major line of division and the ground for perusing demands for minority education, making the issue of schooling highly controversial for those who advocate school integration and those who oppose it. We measured attitudes towards school integration and interethnic attitudes, contacts and discriminatory tendencies of Croat and Serb children in elementary and high schools in 2001 (N=718) and in 2008 (N=703). We demonstrated that without purposeful efforts that can bring the two groups closer, their polarized interethnic attitudes and behavioral intentions towards the outgroup stay basically unchanged over time, even when controlled for children's age and gender. Implications for further post-conflict interethnic community relations are discussed with emphasis on the role a school may have in this process.

Keywords Divided community • Minority education • School integration • Majority/minority relations • Post-conflict community

An old proverb says that time heals all wounds. Time passing provides an opportunity for reflection about past events, integration of painful experiences, and deciding how to move on with life. The passage of time may be especially important when the hurts

---

D. Čorkalo Biruški (✉) • D. Ajduković
Department of Psychology, Faculty of Humanities and Social Sciences, University of Zagreb, Croatia
e-mail: dinka.corkalo@ffzg.hr; dean.ajdukovic@ffzg.hr

O. Simić et al. (eds.), *Peace Psychology in the Balkans: Dealing with a Violent Past while Building Peace*, Peace Psychology Book Series, DOI 10.1007/978-1-4614-1948-8_11,

have been inflicted in the context of massive violence among people with a history of close relations. However, time itself is not a healer; it is the processes that transpire over time that are important. Some of these processes may be subconscious (Karremans & van Lange, 2008), while others include active engagement and efforts to recover from suffering. In this chapter we will present findings on the intergroup attitudes of children and adolescents assessed 6 years apart in a post-conflict community: the city of Vukovar, Croatia. We will show that if there are no purposeful efforts to bring interethnic relations closer, intergroup attitudes and behaviors do not change much and the improvement of community intergroup relations is negligible.

Theoretical Background of the Study

People are social beings and this notion has been taken into account well by Tajfel and colleagues within the framework of Social Identity Theory – SIT (Tajfel, 1981, 1982; Tajfel & Turner, 1986). The theory states that human beings define themselves not only by their personal characteristics; they derive a part of their identity – *social identity* – from the variety of social groups they belong to. If these groups are valuable and socially recognized, their members achieve positive social identity and want to maintain group membership. If the group has a low status within a society, it becomes a source of negative social identity, and its members strive to overcome it, either by leaving the group, or by investing efforts to improve the group position through the strategy of collective action. The reality of social stratification typical for many contemporary societies is one in which there is a higher-status majority and lower-status minority (see also Sidanius & Pratto, 1999). A crucial moderating variable that determines if a member of the low-status group will engage in improving the social standing of the group is the level of his/her identification with the group (Tajfel & Turner, 1986; Doosje, Ellemers, & Spears, 1999). In the absence of social identification, there is no collective action and no willingness to sacrifice in the name of the group.

Much of our socialization process is about learning how to be "a good member" of many groups. Importance, personal meaning and social salience of a particular group change throughout the life course (Worchel, 1998). Luckily enough, in many cases our race, ethnicity or nationality is only a demographic issue. However, in social contexts that are burdened with recent intergroup conflicts and consequently with divisions, belonging to a particular group becomes an attribute of major importance. Many conflict and post-conflict communities are living examples: Northern Ireland (White, 2001), Israel (Kelman, 2001), Rwanda (Staub, 2008), and the Balkans (Ignatieff, 1995). When community splits along a particular group line – racial, ethnic, or religious – and when group belonging cuts across all spheres of social life, it can be considered a *divided community* (Čorkalo et al., 2004; Hewstone et al., 2005). This is what has happened with the community we have been studying for the past 10 years – the city of Vukovar in Croatia.

Integroup Attitudes in a Divided Community

It is a well established fact that childhood experiences with out-group members profoundly shape children's out-group attitudes and behaviors (Aboud, Mendelsohn, & Purdy, 2003; Howes & Wu, 1990; Tropp & Prenovost, 2008). Moreover, they influence intergroup attitudes and behaviors well beyond the child's early age (Aboud & Levy, 2000; Durkin, 2004; Levy & Killen, 2008; Verkuyten, 2005a). By living within the social context that is divided along the group line, be it racial, ethnic, or religious, children are less prepared to establish close relations with members of the outgroup (Ajduković & Čorkalo, 2008). They lack both the experiences and skills that are necessary for dealing with differences with others; they are not used to negotiating their identities, needs and interests with children of other ethnic or cultural backgrounds. More importantly, they do not have a role-model behavior they can retrieve, since the adults in divided communities do not provide such modeling. However, children do not literally copy the intergroup attitudes of the adults. Sometimes their attitudes are not correlated with adult's intergroup attitudes (Aboud & Doyle, 1996), or the correlations are modest (O'Bryan, Fishbein, & Ritchey, 2004) or even different in majority and minority children (Ajduković & Čorkalo Biruški, 2008). Children's intergroup attitudes are influenced by the totality of the social context they live in, including the prevalent social norms (Ojala & Nesdale, 2004), their peers (Castelli, De Amicis & Sherman, 2007; Killen, Henning, Kelly, Crystal, & Ruck, 2007), and teachers (Corenblum, Annis, & Tanaka, 1997).

Among the most influencing factors that shape intergroup attitudes and relations in children is the school. Its influence has been widely recognized as a "tool" for improving intergroup relations (Hewstone et al., 2005; Schofield & Eurich-Fulcer, 2003; Zirkel & Cantor, 2004). The underlying assumption stemming from the famous contact hypothesis (Allport, 1954; Pettigrew, 1998; Pettigrew & Tropp, 2000; Tropp & Prenovost, 2008) is simple: if children and adolescents have an opportunity to meet on an equal footing, there is an increased likelihood that they will get to know each other better and have a chance to become acquaintances and even friends. Even most divided societies recognize the potential power of joint schooling of children of different ethnic background for facilitating positive intergroup relations (Beckerman, 2004; Gallagher, 2004; Schofield & Eurich-Fulcer, 2003; Zirkel & Cantor, 2004). Although the effects are sometimes disappointingly small, with controversial short-term effects for minority and majority members (Stephan, 1999), there is no doubt that joint schooling can improve interethnic relations among peers (Stephan, 1999; Aboud & Levy, 2000; Schofield & Eurich-Fulcer, 2003; Zirkel & Cantor, 2004).

Another contextual factor in shaping children's interethnic attitudes is personal experience with ethnic diversity. A recent study highlighted the role of children's experiences with ethnically homogenous and heterogeneous social environments in shaping their intergroup attitudes (McGlothlin & Killen, 2010): American children of European descent from *ethnically homogenous* schools demonstrated more intergroup bias in evaluating ambiguous peer situations and potentials for intergroup friendship compared to children of both European American and African American descent from *ethnically heterogeneous* schools. In the present study we also explored children's intergroup attitudes in the setting of ethnically separated schooling.

Studying intergroup attitudes and behaviors of a majority group is of crucial importance since this group typically expresses negative attitudes and prejudice toward (various) ethnic minority groups (Verkuyten & Masson, 1995). However, it is not only the majority group dynamics that shape the social context within a particular community, and therefore it is necessary to study attitudes and behaviors of both majority and minorities (Ajduković & Čorkalo Biruški, 2008; Griffiths & Nesdale, 2006; Verkuyten, 2002, 2006). Their relational attitudes and behaviors reflect the mutual contact situation and membership in the majority or minority group creates "a distinct social psychological situation" (Simon, 2004, p. 101). Understanding these patterns may help structure the contact opportunities that could be beneficial for both majority and minority (Guerra et al., 2010). Taking this into account, one should keep in mind that group membership is one of key variables when studying intergroup attitudes and behaviors. In the present study, we looked at intergroup majority–minority relations in the post-conflict community as a research site.

Social Background of the Study

The city of Vukovar in Eastern Croatia was re-integrated into the Croatian national territory in 1997, after having been under control of the Serbian paramilitary for almost 6 years. The destruction that the city suffered during the 3 months siege in 1991 was tremendous: 62% of homes were destroyed, 1,700 people were killed (almost 4% of the city population), 10,000 people were wounded (near 10% of the population), and 30,000 people, mostly those of non-Serbian origin, were forced to leave the city (Zunec, 1998). Before the outbreak of the war in 1991, this city with about 45,000 inhabitants (Croatian National Census, 1991) was a socially vibrant and economically prosperous community. The Croats were a relative majority (47%), the Serbs participated with 32% in the city population and other inhabitants belonged to almost 30 other ethnic groups (Čorkalo Biruški & Ajduković, 2007). This ethnic diversity was a source of pre-war communal pride (Ajduković & Čorkalo, 2004). The dynamics of the dissolution of this highly integrated community have been described elsewhere (Ajduković & Čorkalo, 2004; Čorkalo et al., 2004; Čorkalo Biruški & Ajduković, 2009). Here we want to emphasize that social processes during the war and post-war periods created a social environment burdened with material destruction, high levels of victimization and broken communal social ties (Ajduković, 2004). Issues that prevent the community from overcoming past grievances are manifold: the number of missing persons is still over 350 persons (Office of Imprisoned and Missing Persons of the Republic of Croatia, personal communication, May, 2010), the unemployment rate is among the highest in the country, and economic recovery in only in its infancy. Trauma reminders in the form of the many ruins that are still present even 19 years after the fighting make it difficult for people to move on to a future-oriented mode of living. The impoverished living conditions prevent many pre-war inhabitants from returning and making their living in the city. The social structures of the community have profoundly changed, contributing to the social disintegration.

In our longitudinal study of a representative community sample of 404 adult Croats and Serbs living in Vukovar, conducted in 2002 and 2008, participants identified the major obstacles that prevented the two ethnic groups from improving interethnic relations (Čorkalo Biruški & Ajduković, 2009). While cultural differences between two groups appeared only marginally relevant, contrary to some contemporary accounts of ethnic polarization in East European societies (Evans & Need, 2002), the burning issues were the victimization of Croats, structural obstacles and (ineffective) local administration (Čorkalo Biruški & Ajduković, 2009). The perception of ethnic structural inequalities hindered interethnic relations, sometimes making intergroup contact more counterproductive than constructive for dealing with deteriorated intergroup relations, as identified in other conflict areas (Gallagher, 1994, 2005).

Even though past victimization and economic hardships color the everyday reality of Vukovar, there is one major issue that surfaces as soon as one gets into any serious conversation about the conditions in the city – the issue of schooling. Long before the 1991–1995 war, Croatia had a tradition of minority education. Many minorities exercised this collective right, like Italians, Hungarians, Czechs etc. When Croatia declared independence in 1991, minority schooling, together with other collective rights aiming to preserve ethnic culture and heritage, became a highly salient issue for the Serbian minority. In 1995, the minority education of Serbs was acknowledged within a general peace process that resulted in the *Erdut Agreement*, signed by the Croatian government and Serbian minority representatives, and supervised by the international community. Before the war children from both ethnic groups attended the same classes and were taught in the same language. After the war, for Serbian children the language of instruction became Serbian, and for Croatian children it became Croatian resulting in the schools divided on the basis of the language. The provisional agreement was binding for 5 years, providing the period to negotiate various minority education options. Nevertheless, even 10 years after the expiration of the provisional agreement, the situation remained the same. Until September 2006, children were separated even physically, in some cases attending classes in different buildings or at least in different half-day shifts. The decision to let the children share the same school buildings and attend the school in the same time was a step forward, and it was more or less successfully organized in high-schools. In elementary schools, however, children are still mostly in different shifts.

The issue of minority education for Serbs is highly complex. On the one hand, Serbs do not want anything more than what other ethnic minorities in Croatia have exercised for a long time. On the other hand, the recent war with Croats and Serbs being major actors, left as a legacy deeply disturbed interethnic relations. At least two conflicting interests are at stake. One is the issue of collective (minority) rights protection that should be ensured following the highest standards of human rights protection in the European Union (see Pentassuglia, 2002). The other issue is the best interest of children – their right to be raised aware of their ethnic and cultural origin, but also their right to grow up in a socially integrated community. If ethnic rights are put above freedom of choice including the opportunity to choose different forms of schooling for children, then one can seriously doubt an effective protection of a child's best interest.

Having separate schools for Croatian and Serbian language perhaps made sense immediately after the conflict, when interethnic tensions were extremely high and separation of belligerent sides was the best (or only) strategy of preventing the violence. What is troublesome is that decision makers have not used the opportunity in the following period to negotiate alternative solutions that would make school an important pillar in social reconstruction processes. In many places around the world school has been used to effectively promote interethnic coexistence and improve intergroup relations, for example in the USA, Israel, Northern Ireland etc. (Gallagher, 2004; Schofield & Eurich-Fulcer, 2003; Stephan, 1999; Stephan & Vogt, 2004; McGlynn & Bekerman, 2007). Time is of the essence here: by leaving the community as it is, with no purposeful, persisting and repeating efforts to overcome interethnic barriers, it is likely that the city will continue to develop as a divided community, where ethnic division determines overall social dynamic in the community. This process is extremely difficult to reverse – having generations grow up in parallel ethnic worlds is likely to erode social capital which is based on trust, common social norms and reciprocal relations (Fukuyama, 1995; Putnam, 2001). Social capital serves as a glue binding fractions and groups to function as a unified community. Our concerns are corroborated by the opinions of adults in the community. In the study of major obstacles that prevent improvement of intergroup relations, adult participants identified separate schooling as the major obstacle. In 2002, this opinion was endorsed by 64% of Croats and 76% of Serbs while in 2008 these percentages were even higher: 78% of Croats and 86% of Serbs (Čorkalo Biruški & Ajduković, 2009).

Studying Interethnic Relations Among Young People Living in the Post-Conflict Community

As a result of the concern about the effects of growing up in an ethnically divided community, the aim of the study described in the present chapter is to examine intergroup attitudes and behavioral tendencies of two cohorts of Vukovar adolescents.

We hypothesized more positive intergroup attitudes and behavioral tendencies among the school aged youth as the time passed. As described above, one can expect that the passing of time as a major "healer" can lead to a spontaneous convergence in socially relevant intergroup attitudes due to the general post-conflict recovery of the whole society. However, we assumed these changes not to be substantial in the absence of consistent community efforts to promote positive intergroup relations. We also expected more positive intergroup attitudes and behavioral tendencies among adolescents who were more ready to attend school together with their outgroup peers. Since schooling has been identified as one of the most obvious lines of community division, we assumed that those children who were ready for joint schooling would also have more positive out-group attitudes and behavioral tendencies. Furthermore, minority attitudes were expected to be more positive than those of the majority. This prediction is not quite in line with the vast body of experimental work done under the banner of SIT. A number of studies indicated a stronger tendency of minority members to show negative out-group evaluations and intergroup discrimination towards the majority (see Leonardelli & Brewer, 2001). However, unlike laboratory experiments, majority and minority groups in real settings are not individuals arbitrary categorized in one of the groups, with low identity salience and no group history (particularly history of conflict). There are also other real-world studies contradicting the findings obtained in laboratory settings with the minimal group paradigm (for discussion related to children see Aboud & Amato, 2003). When variables of power and status were introduced in experiments, *in-group favoritism and/or discriminatory tendencies of majority* strongly emerged (Hewstone, Rubin, & Willis, 2002; Sachdev & Bourhis, 1991; Verkuyten, 2007). Furthermore, as the asymmetry hypothesis claims (Rodin, Price, Brison, & Sanchez, 1990), discriminatory behavior directed from a dominant group towards a minority is more likely to be perceived as discriminatory than vice versa. In their meta-analytic integration of findings on in-group bias in hierarchical circumstances, Mullen and colleagues (1992) found stronger in-group bias among members of high-status than of low-status groups. Because the majority is in position to demonstrate its "dominant" identity by setting the rules and discriminate, while the minority does not have this privilege (see Sidanius & Pratto, 1999), we expected higher in-group bias, more negative out-group attitudes and less amicable behavioral tendencies in the majority group. Since there were no systemic efforts that would differentially affect the intergroup relations of the two polarized groups, no interactions were anticipated, and therefore we expected the two groups to stay equally distant at both points in time.

Method

Participants

The study was conducted at two points in time: in 2001 and 2007. In 2001 the participants included 718 students from the sixth and eighth grade of elementary school and the second grade of high school (48% from Croat classes and 52% from Serb classes). The mean age of participants was $M=14.18$ ($SD=1.72$). Gender distribution was 57% boys and 43% of girls. In 2007 there were 703 students (54% in Croat language and 46% in Serb language classes), with a mean age of $M=14.16$ ($SD=1.59$), and gender distribution of 52% of boys and 48% of girls. No significant differences in either age or gender distribution between Croat and Serb classes appeared. The probability cluster sampling model was used, with all sixth and eighth grades of elementary school and second grades of high school treated as clusters from all the schools where curriculum was provided in both Croat and Serb language. More details on the sampling procedure can be found in Čorkalo Biruški and Ajduković (2007).

Measures

Support for school integration was measured with a single item asking the subjects to declare, on a four-point scale, their agreement with the statement "I do not mind going to school with children of the other ethnic group". Those who agreed were classified as the school integration supporters, and those who disagreed were classified as the non-supporters of school integration. The language of teaching was used as a proxy for children's ethnicity. Indeed there is an overlap between the language of teaching and children's ethnic background in the respective classes: for example, in 2001, 85% of children taught in Croatian language declared themselves as the Croats and in 2007 the percentage of self-declared Croats was even higher – over 88%. In the classes taught in Serbian language the percentage of children who declared themselves as the Serbs in 2001 was 93% and in 2007 it was 98%.

A set of dependent variables describing intergroup attitudes and behavioral tendencies were measured. Attitudes towards one's own group were measured as ingroup bias and nationalism. Ingroup bias was assessed as the difference in participants' evaluation of their own and the other ethnic group, ranging from −10 (maximum out-group bias) to +10 (maximum in-group bias). The participants were asked to assess their general attitude towards their own group, and then their general attitude towards the outgroup. Nationalism was assessed with the six-item scale (Čorkalo & Kamenov, 2003) with response format from 1 (strongly disagree), to 5 (strongly agree). The result was computed as the scale average, with higher results indicating stronger nationalism. A sample item reads "Although my nation is not large, there are many more capable people in my nation than in others."

The multicultural orientation of the participants was measured by three scales. Attitudes towards minority assimilation were assessed with three items including: "All the children should go to schools in Croatian language with no exceptions for minority groups". Tolerance towards ethnic diversity was measured in a nine item scale, for example, "Every country should take care to protect minority rights". The response format for these first two scales was from 1 (strongly disagree) to 4 (strongly agree) with no neutral point. Finally the five-item Cosmopolitanism scale (Čorkalo & Kamenov, 2003) included items such as: "First and foremost, I consider myself as a citizen of the world". The response format for the Cosmopolitanism scale was a standard Likert-type scale format, ranging from 1 (strongly disagree) to 5 (strongly agree). The results were computed as the scale average, with higher results indicating stronger assimilationism, more tolerant attitudes and stronger cosmopolitan orientation. More detailed description of the scales can be found in Čorkalo Biruški and Ajduković (2007).

The proxy for behavioral tendencies towards the outgroup was the reported number of contacts with the members of the outgroup and readiness to discriminate against outgroup peers in everyday situations. The number of reported contacts were coded from 1 (no or accidental contacts), 2 (acquaintances), to 3 (friends). The result on the discrimination of peers measure ranged from 0 (no discrimination) to 3 (consistent discrimination in all three typical everyday situations). There were three items in the readiness to discriminate scale including the following example item: "If I were student-on-duty at the school entrance and one of students was late, I would let him/her into the school only if s/he was a Croat/Serb"(for more information see Ajduković & Čorkalo Biruški, 2008).

Procedure

All questionnaires were administered in groups, during regular classes and completed anonymously. The researcher was a female of Croatian ethnic background. All students from both ethnic backgrounds had high proficiency in the Croatian language, so the oral instructions were given in Croatian. However, all written instructions and questionnaires were in the children's mother language.

Results

The distribution of majority and minority children, supporters and non-supporters of joint schooling at the two time points is presented in Fig. 11.1. While there was no difference between majority and minority students in 2001, ($\chi^2(1)=2.30$, $p=.075$), the difference appeared as marginally significant in 2007, when minority students supported the idea of joint schooling in higher proportion than the majority students did ($\chi^2(1)=4.47$, $p=.034$). However, the proportion of supporters was higher in 2007 than in 2001 in the both samples: for majority $z(713)=-4.99$, $p<0.001$ and for minority $z(688)=-5.55$, $p<0.001$.

In order to determine whether intergroup attitudes and behavioral tendencies differed as a function of support for school integration, minority/majority group status and time, a series of $2\times2\times2$ analyses of covariance (ANCOVA) were performed. Support for interethnic school integration (supporters/non-supporters), minority/majority group status and time of measurement (years 2001 and 2007) were treated as between-subjects factors. In our previous studies (Ajduković & Čorkalo Biruški, 2008; Čorkalo Biruški & Ajduković, 2008, 2009) differences in intergroup attitudes and behavioral tendencies amongst boys and girls and in some cases different age groups were observed. Although correlations between gender and age with dependent variables were rather small and rarely exceeded value above 0.1 (the highest correlation observed was between gender and the tendency to discriminate members of the out-group, $r(1381)=-.22$, $p<0.001$), in the present analysis we controlled for these variables.

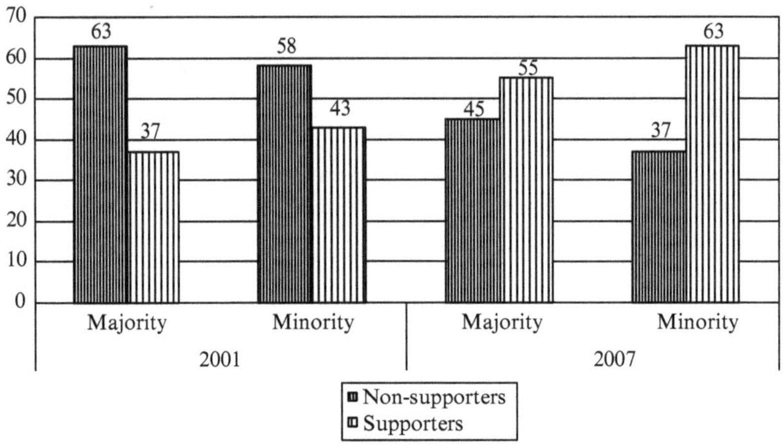

Fig. 11.1 The percentage of students from each ethnic group who support and do not support joint schooling at two time points

The results of the analyses are presented by each dependent variable (attitudes and behavioral tendencies), and summarized at the end of this section by emphasizing the most important effects of the independent variables we looked at.

As a measure of the *attitudes towards one's own group* we measured in-group bias and nationalism. Regarding the *in-group bias* while controlling for the effects of age and gender, all three main effects were significant (see Table 11.1). Children who did not favor joint schooling showed more ingroup bias ($M_{adj}=4.91$)[1] compared with their integration-inclined peers ($M_{adj}=2.67$). In 2001 children showed more in-group bias ($M_{adj}=4.52$) compared with their peers in 2007 ($M_{adj}=3.06$), indicating, as predicted, a *small* decrease in in-group bias over time. Majority children showed more in-group bias ($M_{adj}=5.38$) than their minority peers ($M_{adj}=2.19$). As shown in Table 11.1, student's initial attitudes towards school integration interacted significantly with their group status. Although inspection of mean differences suggests larger difference in in-group bias between school integration supporters and non-supporters in majority ($M_{adj}=3.67$ vs. $M_{adj}=6.85$) than in minority sample ($M_{adj}=1.28$ vs. $M_{adj}=3.33$), an analysis of simple main effects revealed both effects to be significant ($p<.001$), but with difference in majority sample being of a larger effect size ($\eta^2=.10$) while being negligible in the minority sample ($\eta^2=.05$). Here it is important to emphasize that the size of our sample caused even minor differences to be significant, which makes the interpretation of the results more complicated. No other interactions were significant.

[1] Estimated marginal means.

Table 11.1 Significant F-ratios and effect sizes of main effects and interactions in time × group status × initial schooling integration attitude ANCOVA of intergroup attitudes

	Independent variables: main effects						Two-way interactions						Three-way interactions	
	Time		Group status		Schooling integration		Group status × schooling integration		Group status × time		Schooling integration × time		Group status × time × schooling integration	
	F	η^2	F	η^2	F	η^2	F	η^2	F	η^2	F	η^2	F	η^2
In-bias	52.15***	.038	245.49***	.158	119.35***	.083	6.50*	.005						
Nation.	39.72***	.032	16.18***	.013	111.23***	.085								
Assim.			627.02***	.318			16.34***	.012						
Toler.			103.16***	.071	116.79***	.080	12.56***	.009						
Cosmo.			8.37**	.007	82.53***	.066	3.90*	.003	4.20*	.004	7.81**	.007	10.50**	.009
Contact	13.37***	.010	33.17***	.025	125.79***	.088	14.17***	.011						
Discr.	23.19***	.017	62.15***	.045	150.54***	.103	14.27***	.011	9.97***	.007				

In-bias in-group bias, *Nation.* nationalism, *Assim.* assimilationism, *Toler.* tolerance towards ethnic diversity, *Cosmo.* cosmopolitanism, *Discr.* discrimination
*p<0.05; **p<0.01; ***p<0.001

As regards to *nationalism*, three main effects were found (Table 11.1), while controlling for age and gender. Integration supporters held less nationalistic attitudes ($M_{adj}=3.14$) than non-supporters ($M_{adj}=3.63$). Similarly, the students in 2007, reported less nationalistic attitudes ($M_{adj}=3.24$) than 6 years before ($M_{adj}=3.53$), as did the minority children ($M_{adj}=3.29$) compared to majority children ($M_{adj}=3.48$). No interaction of independent variables was significant for nationalism.

The *multicultural orientation* of children was measured by three attitudinal measures: assimilation of minorities, interethnic tolerance and cosmopolitan attitudes. The hypothesized main effects of integration supporters versus non-supporters, time of measurement, and participants' group status were corroborated only partially. For the *attitudes towards assimilation* the only significant main effect was minority/majority status (Table 11.1), with the majority favoring more assimilationist attitudes ($M_{adj}=2.88$) than the minority ($M_{adj}=1.79$). A significant interaction of group status and initial attitudes towards school integration showed a larger difference in how integration supporters and non-supporters felt about assimilation in the minority sample ($M_{adj}=1.90$ vs. $M_{adj}=1.67$) than in the majority sample ($M_{adj}=2.80$ vs. $M_{adj}=2.94$). Here again the simple main effects analysis revealed both differences to be significant ($p<.001$), but indicating with more strength a difference between majority and minority non-supporters as being more prominent ($\eta^2=.25$) than the difference between majority and minority integration supporters ($\eta^2=.14$). Basically the results indicated a tendency for majority non-supporters to have attitudes more in favor of assimilation, but in the minority sample this is integration supporters who were more inclined to hold pro-assimilation attitudes. No other interactions were significant.

Regarding the *interethnic tolerance* two main effects were found (Table 11.1): integration supporters were more tolerant ($M_{adj}=3.35$) than non-supporters ($M_{adj}=3.04$) and minority students showed more tolerance ($M_{adj}=3.34$) than their majority peers ($M_{adj}=3.05$). A significant two-way interaction of integration attitudes and group status showed a similar pattern of differences as for in-group bias: mean differences suggested a larger difference in tolerance between integration supporters and non-supporters in the majority ($M_{adj}=3.29$ vs. $M_{adj}=2.84$), than in the minority sample ($M_{adj}=3.44$ vs. $M_{adj}=3.22$). However, here again both pair of differences were significant ($p<.001$), but the effect size was bigger for majority differences ($\eta^2=.09$) than for those in minority sample ($\eta^2=.02$). No other interactions were significant.

The only interaction of all three factors appeared for *cosmopolitan attitudes* (see Table 11.1 and Fig. 11.2). As indicated by a non-significant main effect of time, there were no differences in overall cosmopolitan attitudes in two point of time: children hold highly cosmopolitan attitudes. However, the significant three-way interaction revealed a more complex pattern of data and showed similar differences in cosmopolitan attitudes in minority ($p=.841$; $\eta^2=.00$) and majority ($p=.343$; $\eta^2=.00$) integration supporters and non-supporters in 2001. However, in 2007 while integration supporters held similarly cosmopolitan attitudes regardless of their minority or majority status ($p=.901$; $\eta^2=.00$), majority non-supporters were clearly less cosmopolitan then minority non-supporters ($p<.001$; $\eta^2=.02$). Nevertheless, very small effect sizes indicate that caution is warranted in not to overemphasize observed differences, although they are highly significant due to large sample.

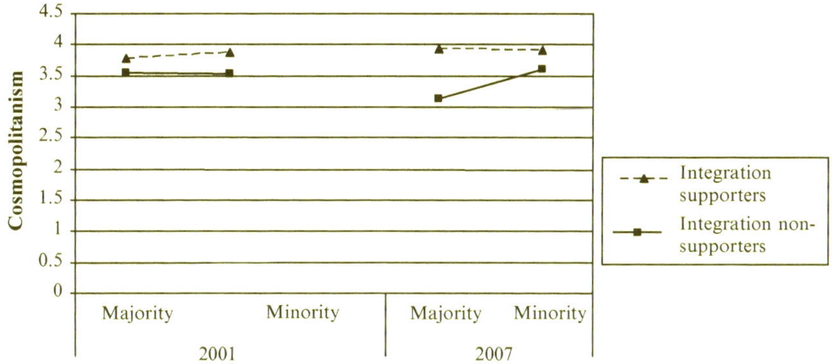

Fig. 11.2 The cosmopolitanism attitude of school integration supporters and non-supporters as a function of time of measurement and group status of participants

Behavioral tendencies towards the outgroup were assessed by the type of contact children had with their out-group peers and by their tendency to discriminate against them in everyday situations. Regarding the *contact with out-group peers* there was a difference between integration supporters ($M_{adj}=2.41$) and non-supporters ($M_{adj}=1.92$). The main effect of time showed that children had more contact in 2007 ($M_{adj}=2.24$) than in 2001 ($M_{adj}=2.09$). The main effect of group status showed more meaningful contact in the minority ($M_{adj}=2.29$) than in the majority group ($M_{adj}=2.04$). A significant interaction between initial integration attitude and group status showed that the interaction is determined by significant differences in contacts ($p<.001$; $\eta^2=.03$) between integration non-supporters in the majority and minority sample ($M_{adj}=1.70$ vs. $M_{adj}=2.10$), while such difference was not evident ($p=.331$; $\eta^2=.01$) among supporters based on their majority and minority status ($M_{adj}=2.40$ vs. $M_{adj}=2.46$). No other interactions were significant.

As for *discrimination towards the outgroup*, all three main effects were significant (Table 11.1), and two of them were qualified by significant interactions. The interaction of initial attitude towards school integration and participants' minority/majority status showed similar tendencies as the effects of these variables on the measure of contacts: while majority non-supporters of school integration tended to discriminate more ($M_{adj}=1.68$) compared to their non-supporter peers in the minority sample ($M_{adj}=1.06$) with this difference being significant ($p<.001$; $\eta^2=.05$), there was no such difference ($p=.11$, $\eta^2=.00$) among school integration supporters based on their majority ($M_{adj}=0.67$) or minority status ($M_{adj}=0.54$). The interaction of the group status and time of measurement suggested greater difference in discriminatory tendencies between majority ($M_{adj}=1.54$) and minority group members ($M_{adj}=0.89$) in 2001 than in 2007 ($M_{adj}=0.92$ vs. $M_{adj}=0.69$); however, both differences were significant although with different effect size ($p<.001$; $\eta^2=.05$ and $p<.01$; $\eta^2=.00$ respectively). It seems that for this tendency to occur a more profound change in the majority sample is responsible, indicating a sort of convergence in discriminatory tendencies between majority and minority groups. No other interactions were significant.

In sum, our analyses did not provide clear cut support for our initial hypothesis; however we do believe the results corroborated quite convincingly the main prediction: time itself did not make much difference in improving interethnic attitudes. It seems that the passing of time influenced more in-group attitudes (such as decreasing in-group bias and mitigating nationalism) than it changed overall relations towards the out-group (multicultural orientation and behavioral tendencies towards the out-group). The only exception from this obvious trend is a small temporal increase in number of contacts with the out-group. The effect of time was modified by two other independent variables (group status and initial attitude towards the integrated schooling) in a single case of cosmopolitan attitudes, where both two-way and three-way interactions indicated that the majority members who did not support school integration held the least cosmopolitan attitudes.

The effects of two other independent variables – group status and initial attitude towards the integrated schooling – are unambiguous: not only do they influence the attitudes independently, but their interaction gives an additional insight in explaining intergroup attitudes in this particular divided community. In all cases, with the exception of attitudes towards assimilation, minority members and those who initially endorsed integrated schooling also held more positive intergroup attitudes. Once more it should be stressed that strength of the effects of independent variables as shown by eta squared is usually very small and in most cases below the critical point of .09 (Gamst, Meyer, & Guarino, 2008) while even small differences were highly significant due to the sample size. This is why an additional caution in interpreting the significant results as substantial differences is warranted.

Discussion

In the present study we explored the interethnic attitudes and behavioral tendencies of young people as a function of their willingness to go to school with their out-group peers, their status as a member of the majority or minority group, and time of measurement (2001 or 2007), while controlling for children's gender and age. We examined three sets of attitudes: in-group attitudes expressed as in-group bias and nationalism; the multicultural orientation of children articulated as attitudes toward minority assimilation, attitudes regarding tolerance of ethnic diversity and cosmopolitan attitudes; and behavioral tendencies towards the outgroup, measured by contact type with outgroup peers and tendency to discriminate against the outgroup members in everyday situations. All main effects of the independent variables were evident: more favorable intergroup attitudes and behavioral tendencies were found in the minority sample, among supporters of joint schooling and in the year 2007. Interactions among all three factors were not hypothesized since there was no plausible reason, neither theoretical nor contextually applicable, to assume different effects of time depending on whether students belonged to minority or majority group and/or if they were supporters or non-supporters of the joint schooling of Croats and Serbs. Because there were no planned efforts to bring together community groups polarized around ethnicity, no substantial effects of time were expected. Since the community is tantalized by two seemingly conflicting goals: how to organize schooling to make it a tool of community integration *and* a gatekeeper of minority ethnocultural rights, it was reasonable to assume that changes over time might equally but not profoundly affect both minority and majority and supporters and non-supporter of joint schooling.

Indeed, the results mostly corroborate the initial assumptions. There was less in-group bias and nationalism in the minority sample, in supporters of integrated schools and in the second measurement. Minority group members and supporters of joint schooling had more meaningful outgroup contact and were less inclined to discriminate against the outgroup peers. However, the finding about the minority being also inclined to discriminate against the majority group is of special importance for intergroup relations. The asymmetry hypothesis by Rodin and colleagues (1990) suggests that discriminatory behavior targeted from the dominant group towards the minority is more likely to be perceived as discriminatory than the other way around. Here we found that the minority group also showed a tendency to discriminate against the majority group. A tendency of minority children to discriminate contradicts other findings obtained with children, for example Griffiths and Nesdale (2006). With a younger sample they showed clear in-group preference in the majority but not in the minority group. Moreover, in our study with adults we obtained negligible discriminatory tendencies in the minority sample (Ajduković & Čorkalo Biruški, 2008) but both minority and majority young people discriminated more than their parents and teachers (Ajduković & Čorkalo Biruški, 2008).

It seems that in ethnically divided communities where children's social life is mostly limited to their own group, they feel comfortable expressing tendencies that are otherwise not affordable, such as to being able to discriminate against the majority group (see Simon, 2004).

In all cases the interaction of the initial attitude towards joint schooling and the participant's group status indicate more profound differences in intergroup attitudes between supporters and non-supporters of joint schooling in the majority than in minority sample, as judged by the effect sizes obtained. This suggests that there is more divergent and heterogeneous attitudes among the majority sample of students when it comes to the issue of schooling. Majority students who do not support joint schooling also show more extreme intergroup attitudes than their majority peers who are supportive of the joint schooling. This issue differentiates the minority student sample as well, although to a lesser degree. What these results suggest is that the position towards joint schooling differentiates those who hold more conciliatory intergroup attitudes and report more intergroup social transactions from those who do not.

This point is exactly why school could be used as a vehicle for improving intergroup relations. The idea is not a new one and there is a vast body of research suggesting that integrated schooling is helpful in shaping more amicable intergroup relations and is especially useful for minority populations (Gallagher, 2004; Schofield & Eurich-Fulcer, 2003; Stephan, 1999; Stephan & Vogt, 2004). Although supporters and non-supporters of joint schooling differ in their relevant intergroup attitudes in both minority and majority samples, it is reasonable to assume that their opposite intergroup attitudes could converge if they had more opportunity to meet and learn about each other. Since the community does not provide this opportunity in other settings, schools could be used as a safe zone to provide socially relevant opportunities for mutual interdependence, cooperation and common goals achievement (Coleman & Deutsch, 2008).

Recent findings show that there are more benefits of intergroup contact for majority group members than for minority group members (Tropp & Pettigrew, 2005). Our study suggests that schooling can provide an important opening for improving intergroup relations. If support for school integration better distinguishes those with more tolerant intergroup attitudes in the majority group and if contact is more beneficial for majority members, then working on (school) integration could lead to softening more extreme (majority) attitudes. The reverse influence is, however, also possible: softened intergroup attitudes could lead to greater support for school integration. Nevertheless, a former mode of influence is easier to accomplish: if children of different ethnic background could meet in schools as in safe environment and on equal footing, if they have enough possibilities to get to know their peers as individuals through common learning and other joint activities, then the school can serve as a setting of the genuine "optimal contact" as suggested in the vast body of research (Schofield & Eurich-Fulcer, 2003; Gallagher, 2004; Zirkel & Cantor, 2004; McGlothlin & Killen, 2010). This type of contact influences not only children's interethnic friendships but their political attitudes as well, as shown by Stringer et al. (2010) in another highly divided society: Northern Ireland. Their results also showed less polarized views on a set of social attitudes in children who attended mixed and integrated schools compared to their peers from segregated schools. Though, a word of caution is necessary: integration efforts may be perceived as identity-threatening by both the majority and the minority. For the minority it could be perceived as an attempt to prevent them to exercise their collective rights. On the other hand, for the majority integration may be seen as an opportunity for assimilation and when faced with minority resistance and reluctance, it may become a source of majority identity threat. Here the role of teachers could be of crucial importance. Teachers that serve as role models for crossing intergroup boundaries (Aboud & Levy, 2000) would enable children to have an identity anchor and a guideline for establishing more cooperative intergroup relations.

The important role of attitudes towards school integration is highlighted by its relation to multicultural attitudes. While interacting with the minority or majority status of the participants, attitudes toward school integration also predicted attitudes towards minority assimilation and ethnic tolerance (see Verkuyten, 2005b for related findings). Regarding assimilation, the majority is more homogenous in favoring assimilation, while the minority supporters of joint schooling favor assimilation more than non-supporters (although it is important to note that none of these minority subgroups supported assimilation). As for tolerance, supporters and non-supporters of integrated schooling differed again more in the majority than in the minority, with majority supporters of joint schooling holding more tolerant attitudes than non-supporters. In general, our results on majority/minority differences in multicultural attitudes confirm what has been found in other multiethnic settings. Minority groups endorse multiculturalism, while majority group members more eagerly support the assimilation of minorities (Arends-Toth & van de Vijver, 2003; Verkuyten & Brug, 2004). As some scholars pointed out, multiculturalism could be more important for the minority than for majority (Verkuyten, 2005b, 2008), since it allows minority groups to maintain their ethnic and cultural boundaries with limited interest and acceptance of the majority culture. Just the opposite is true for the majority. This means that as long as minorities accept the dominant culture as the social mainstream they may even be welcomed; otherwise they may be perceived as a threat to the identity of the majority (Coenders et al., 2008; Verkuyten, 2005b; Zick et al., 2001). In the context of the present study, with the recent history of conflict these contesting strategies of intergroup arrangement are even more challenging.

Results on the cosmopolitanism scale corroborate what has been said about minority and majority groups being differently devoted to multiculturalism. While in 2001 attitudes towards joint schooling basically did not differentiate majority and minority, 6 years later this pattern changed and attitudes towards joint schooling differentiated better the majority: the non-supporters from the majority hold less cosmopolitan attitudes than the supporters of joint schooling. Moreover, non-supporters from the ethnic majority endorsed cosmopolitanism even less in 2007 than in 2001. Here the passing of time did make a difference for minority and majority, making the majority supporters of joint school and non-supporters even more polarized. Although both samples endorsed cosmopolitanism, majority children who opposed school integration were the least cosmopolitan. The same trend of results did not appear in other interethnic attitudes so this particular result remains unclear. It may be that cosmopolitan attitudes are of special importance, at least for the majority sample and it is for further research to disentangle specific relationship between cosmopolitanism and school integration attitudes.

There are some limitations of the study that should be mentioned. Our results would be more convincing should we have used a longitudinal instead of cross-sectional research design. Although the effects of time presented here were negligible, only longitudinal data would allow unequivocal conclusions about the effect of passing of time on intergroup attitudes and behavioral tendencies. While different cohorts could point to important trends in community interethnic relations (see Abramson & Inglehart, 1986), a follow up of the same cohort could give a more thorough insight into the potential for social change. On the other hand, a follow up study of the same cohort would result in the participants being 6 years older and entering into a whole different age group of young adults with very different social roles and responsibilities. This would yield insight into the long-term effects of separated schooling, but not on the changes in the inter-ethnic relations among the target group of young people in school. As other authors pointed out (Verkuyten & Zaremba, 2005) the issue of essence is to study interethnic relations across and over time, taking into account the societal specifics and attitudes of relevant social groups that shape the social realities of both majority and minority groups.

Furthermore, the attitude towards school integration was measured by a single item that served as one of the three independent variables. However, the sensitivity of this issue in the post-conflict community we studied and the need to use a simple indicator of support for integrated schooling lead to deciding to have a single item variable.

Another point that should be mentioned is the possible influence of the majority (Croat) ethnicity of the researchers during data collection. Although this issue was not declared, the participants could have made assumptions and reacted accordingly, especially the minority children. However, although the ethnic background of teachers in the schools predominantly depends on the language of teaching, students have been exposed to both Croat and Serb teachers. Therefore, encounter with the same or different ethnicity of the researchers was not a novel experience for the students and may be less likely to influence results. The confidential nature of the written survey also has helped assure participants that their identity was protected from scrutiny. In addition, very thorough preparatory work included a number of encounters with relevant community stakeholders (school principals, parents, community leaders etc.) before the study was conducted. This helped ensure that ethnicity would have limited effects on data collection and aided cooperative relations with study participants (for more details see Ajduković & Čorkalo Biruški, 2008; Čorkalo Biruški & Ajduković, 2007).

Conclusions

So what can be said about the effects of passing time on intergroup attitudes and behavioral tendencies of ethnic majority and minority in the polarized post-conflict community of Vukovar? As a main effect, the time produced some changes. But this finding does not warrant optimism because the effect sizes are small, in most cases bellow the critical point of 0.09 (Gamst et al., 2008). This is not surprising since there are no consistent efforts to promote positive inter-ethnic relations in this post-conflict community. The fact that schooling remains separated for the children from the two ethnic groups does not correspond to the high level of public concern with the non-integrated schooling. In the present study, time did not act differently on majority and minority young people nor did it differently affect supporters and non-supporters of integrated schooling. The only exception is the case of discriminatory tendencies, where the majority demonstrated a larger improvement in cosmopolitan attitudes. In order to bring the polarized groups closer, more needs to be done than just letting the time go by. Without active effort to transform and integrate the community, the probable long-term outcome may be more polarized groups. Fewer and fewer people will remember what it was like when socializing across ethnic borders was natural, with no anxiety or perceived threat. As the current social norm does not encourage children to socialize with their peers from the ethnic outgroup, it is not feasible to expect them to build their social world differently. The adults have the responsibility to model intergroup behaviors that are conducive to amicable inter-ethnic norms. Only adults have the power to improve intergroup relations, by various means, such as the promotion of school integration, emphasizing the value of diversity, healing the traumas of war, and ensuring the exercise of full minority rights. Making these changes is the responsibility of adults and community leaders, not children.

References

Aboud, F. E., & Amato, M. (2003). Developmental and socialization influences on intergroup bias. In R. Brown & S. Gaertner (Eds.), *Blackwell handbook of social psychology: Intergroup processes* (pp. 65–85). Malden: Blackwell Publishers.

Aboud, F., & Doyle, A. (1996). Parental and peer influences on children's racial attitudes. *International Journal of Intercultural Relations, 20*, 371–383.

Aboud, F. E., & Levy, S. R. (2000). Interventions to reduce prejudice and discrimination in children and adolescents. In S. Oskamp (Ed.), *Reducing prejudice and discrimination* (pp. 269–293). Mahwah: Lawrence Erlbaum.

Aboud, F. E., Mendelsohn, M. J., & Purdy, P. (2003). Cross race peer relationships and friendship quality. *International Journal of Behavioral Development, 27*, 165–173.

Abramson, P. R., & Inglehart, R. (1986). Generational replacement and value change in six West European societies. *American Journal of Political Science, 30*, 1–25.

Ajduković, D. (2004). Social contexts of traumatization and healing. *Medicine, Conflict and Survival, 20*, 120–135.

Ajduković, D., & Čorkalo, D. (2004). Trust and betrayal in war. In E. Stover & H. Weinstein (Eds.), *My neighbor, my enemy: Justice and community in the aftermath of mass atrocity* (pp. 287–302). Cambridge: Cambridge University Press.

Ajduković, D., & Čorkalo Biruški, D. (2008). Caught between the ethnic sides: Inter-ethnic relations of children and parents in the post-war community. *International Journal of Behavioral Development, 32*, 337–347.

Allport, G. (1954). *The nature of prejudice*. New York: Addison-Wesley.

Arends-Toth, J., & van de Vijver, F. J. R. (2003). Multiculturalism and acculturation: Views of Dutch and Turkish Dutch. *European Journal of Social Psychology, 33*, 249–266.

Beckerman, Z. (2004). Potential and limitations of multicultural education in conflict-ridden areas: Bilingual Palestinian-Jewish schools in Israel. *Teachers College Record, 106*, 574–610.

Castelli, L., De Amicis, L., & Sherman, S. J. (2007). The loyal member effect: On the preference for ingroup members who engage in exclusive relations with the ingroup. *Developmental Psychology, 43*, 1347–1359.

Coenders, M., Lubbers, M., Scheepers, P., & Verkuyten, M. (2008). More than two decades of changing ethnic attitudes in the Netherlands. *Journal of Social Issues, 64*, 269–285.

Coleman, P., & Deutsch, M. (2008). Introducing cooperation and conflict resolution into schools: A system approach. In D. J. Christie, R. V. Wagner, & D. Du Nann Winter (Eds.), *Peace, conflict and violence: Peace psychology for the 21st century* (pp. 223–239). Delhi: Indo American Books.

Corenblum, B., Annis, R. C., & Tanaka, J. S. (1997). Influence of cognitive development, self-competency, and teachers evaluations on the development of children's racial identity. *International Journal of Behavioral Development, 20*, 269–286.

Čorkalo Biruški, D., & Ajduković, D. (2007). Separate schools – A divided community: The role of school in post-war social reconstruction. *Review of Psychology, 14*, 93–108.

Čorkalo Biruški, D., & Ajduković, D. (2008). Stavovi učenika, roditelja i nastavnika prema školovanju: Što se promijenilo tijekom šest godina u Vukovaru? [Attitudes towards schooling among pupils, parents and teachers: What has changes over the six years in Vukovar?] *Migracijske i etničke teme, 24*, 159–294.

Čorkalo Biruški, D., & Ajduković, D. (2009). Od dekonstrukcije do rekonstrukcije traumatizirane zajednice: primjer Vukovara. [From deconstruction to reconstruction of a traumatize community: The example of Vukovar]. *Revija za socijalnu politiku, 16*, 1–24.

Čorkalo, D., Ajduković, D., Weinstein, H., Stover, E., Djipa, D., & Biro, M. (2004). Neighbors again? Inter-community relations after ethnic violence. In E. Stover & H. Weinstein (Eds.), *My neighbor, my enemy: Justice and community in the aftermath of mass atrocity* (pp. 143–161). Cambridge: Cambridge University Press.

Čorkalo, D., & Kamenov, Ž. (2003). National identity and social distance: Does in-group loyalty lead to outgroup hostility. *Review of Psychology, 10*, 85–94.

Doosje, B., Ellemers, N., & Spears, R. (1999). Commitment and intergroup behavior. In N. Ellemers, R. Spears, & B. Doosje (Eds.), *Social identity: Context, commitment, content* (pp. 84–106). Oxford: Blackwell Publishing.

Durkin, K. (2004). *Developmental social psychology: From infancy to old age*. Malden: Blackwell.

Evans, G., & Need, A. (2002). Explaning ethnic polarization over attitudes towards minority rights in Eastern Europe: A multilevel analysis. *Social Science Research, 31*, 653–680.

Fukuyama, F. (1995). *Trust. The social virtues and the creation of prosperity*. New York: Free Press Paperback.

Gallagher, A. M. (1994). Dealing with conflict: Schools in Northern Ireland. *Multicultural Teaching, 13*, 10–13.

Gallagher, T. (2004). *Education in divided society*. Houndmills/Basingstoke: Palgrave Macmillan.

Gallagher, T. (2005). Balancing difference and the common good: Lessons for a post-conflict society. *Compare, 35*, 429–442.

Gamst, G., Meyers, L., & Guarino, A. (2008). *Analysis of variance designs: A conceptual and computational approach with SPSS and SAS*. Cambridge: Cambridge University Press.

Griffiths, J. A., & Nesdale, D. (2006). Ingroup and outgroup attitudes of ethnic majority and minority children. *International Journal for Intercultural Relations, 30*, 735–749.

Guerra, R., Rebelo, M., Monteiro, M. B., Riek, B. M., Mania, E. W., Gaertner, S., & Dovidio, J. F. (2010). How should intergroup contact be structured to reduce bias among majority and minority group children. *Group Processes & Intergroup Relations, 13*, 445–460.

Hewstone, M., Cairnes, D., Voci, A., Paolini, S., McLernon, F., Crisp, R. J., Niens, U., & Craig, J. (2005). Intergroup contact in a divided society: Challenging segregation in Northern Ireland. In D. Abrams, M. A. Hogg, & J. M. Marques (Eds.), *Social psychology of inclusion and exclusion* (pp. 265–292). New York: Psychology Press.

Hewstone, M., Rubin, M., & Willis, H. (2002). Intergroup bias. *Annual Review of Psychology, 53*, 575–604.

Howes, C., & Wu, F. (1990). Peer interactions and friendships in an ethnically diverse school settings. *Child Development, 61*, 537–541.

Ignatieff, M. (1995). *Blood and belonging: Journey into the new nationalism*. New York: Ferrar, Straus and Giroux.

Karremans, J. C., & Van Lange, P. A. M. (2008). Forgiveness in personal relationships: Its malleability and powerful consequences. *European Review of Social Psychology, 19*, 202–241.

Kelman, H. C. (2001). The role of national identity in conflict resolution: Experiences from Israeli-Palestinian problem-solving workshop. In R. D. Ashmore, L. Jussim, & D. Wilder (Eds.), *Social identity, intergroup conflict and conflict resolution* (pp. 187–212). Oxford: Oxford University Press.

Killen, M., Henning, A., Kelly, M. C., Crystal, D., & Ruck, M. (2007). Evaluations of interracial peer encounters by majority and minority US children and adolescents. *International Journal of Behavioral Development, 31*, 491–500.

Leonardelli, G. J., & Brewer, M. B. (2001). Minority and majority discrimination: When and why. *Journal of Experimental Social Psychology, 37*, 468–485.

Levy, S. R., & Killen, M. (Eds.). (2008). *Intergroup attitudes and relations in childhood through adulthood*. Oxford: Oxford University Press.

McGlothlin, H., & Killen, M. (2010). How social experience is related to children's intergroup attitudes. *European Journal of Social Psychology, 40*, 625–634.

McGlynn, C., & Bekerman, Z. (2007). The management of pupil difference in Catholic-Protestant and Palestinian-Jewish integrated education in Northern Ireland and Israel. *Compare, 37*, 689–705.

Mullen, B., Brown, R., & Smith, C. (1992). Ingroup bias as a function of salience, relevance, and status: An integration. *European Journal of Social Psychology, 22*, 103–122.

O'Bryan, M., Fishbein, H. D., & Ritchey, N. P. (2004). Intergenerational transmission of prejudice, sex role stereotyping, and intolerance. *Adolescence, 39*, 407–426.

Ojala, K., & Nesdale, D. (2004). Bullying and social identity: The effects of group norms and distinctiveness threat on attitudes towards bullying. *British Journal of Developmental Psychology, 22*, 19–35.

Pentassuglia, G. (2002). *Minorities in international law*. Strasbourg: Council of Europe Publishing.

Pettigrew, T. (1998). Reactions towards the new minorities of Western Europe. *Annual Review of Sociology, 24*, 77–103.

Pettigrew, T., & Tropp, L. (2000). Does intergroup contact reduce prejudice? Recent meta-analytic findings. In S. Oskamp (Ed.), *Reducing prejudice and discrimination* (pp. 93–114). Mahwah: Lawrence Erlbaum.

Putnam, R. (2001). *Bowling alone: The collapse and revival of American community*. New York: Simon & Shuster.

Rodin, M. J., Price, J. M., Brison, J. B., & Sanchez, F. J. (1990). Asymmetry in prejudice attribution. *Journal of Experimental Social Psychology, 26*, 481–504.

Sachdev, I., & Bourhis, R. Y. (1991). Power and status differentials in minority and majority group relations. *European Journal of Social Psychology, 21*, 1–24.

Schofield, J. W., & Eurich-Fulcer, R. (2003). When and how school desegregation improves intergroup relations. In R. Brown & S. Gaertner (Eds.), *Blackwell handbook of social psychology: Intergroup processes* (pp. 475–494). Malden: Blackwell Publishers.

Sidanius, J., & Pratto, F. (1999). *Social dominance. An intergoup theory of social hierarchy and oppression*. Cambridge: Cambridge University Press.

Simon, B. (2004). *Identity in modern society: A social psychological perspective*. Malden: Blackwell Publishers.

Staub, E. (2008). The origins of genocide and mass killing, prevention, reconciliation and their application to Rwanda. In V. M. Esses & R. A. Vernon (Eds.), *Explaining the breakdown of ethnic relations: Why neighbors kill* (pp. 245–268). Malden: Blackwell Publishing.

Stephan, W. (1999). *Reducing prejudice and stereotypes in schools*. New York: Teachers Colleague Press.

Stephan, W., & Vogt, W. P. (2004). *Education programs for improving intergroup relations. Theory, research and practice*. New York: Teachers Colleague Press.

Stringer, M., Irwing, P., Giles, M., McClenahan, C., Wilson, R., & Hunter, J. (2010). Parental and school effects on children's political attitudes in Northern Ireland. *British Journal of Educational Psychology, 80*, 223–240.

Tajfel, H. (Ed.). (1981). *Differentiation between social groups*. London: Academic.

Tajfel, H. (1982). *The social psychology of minorities*. London: Minority Rights Group.

Tajfel, H., & Turner, J. C. (1986). Theory of intergroup behavior. In S. Worchel & W. G. Austin (Eds.), *Psychology of intergroup relations* (pp. 7–24). Chicago: Nelson-Hall Publishers.

Tropp, L. P., & Pettigrew, T. F. (2005). Relationship between intergroup contact and prejudice among minority and majority group status. *Psychological Science, 16*, 951–957.

Tropp, L. R., & Prenovost, M. A. (2008). The role of intergroup contact in predicting children's interethnic attitudes: Evidence from meta-analytic and field studies. In S. Levy & M. Killen (Eds.), *Intergroup attitudes and relations in childhood through adulthood* (pp. 236–248). Oxford: Oxford University Press.

Verkuyten, M. (2002). Ethnic attitudes among minority and majority children: The role of ethnic identification, peer group victimization and parents. *Social Development, 11*, 558–570.

Verkuyten, M. (2005a). *The social psychology of ethnic identity*. Hove: Psychology Press.

Verkuyten, M. (2005b). Ethnic group identification and group evaluation among minority and majority groups: Testing the multiculturalism hypothesis. *Journal of Personality and Social Psychology, 88*, 121–138.
Verkuyten, M. (2006). Multicultural recognition and ethnic minority rights: A social identity perspective. *European Review of Social Psychology, 17*, 148–184.
Verkuyten, M. (2007). Ethnic in-group favoritism among minority and majority groups: Testing the self-esteem hypothesis among preadolescents. *Journal of Applied Social Psychology, 37*, 486–500.
Verkuyten, M. (2008). Multiculturalism and group evaluations among minority and majority groups. In S. Levy & M. Killen (Eds.), *Intergroup attitudes and relations in childhood through adulthood* (pp. 157–172). Oxford: Oxford University Press.
Verkuyten, M., & Brug, P. (2004). Multiculturalism and group status: The role of ethnic identification, group essentialism, and protestant ethics. *European Journal of Social Psychology, 34*, 647–661.
Verkuyten, M., & Masson, K. (1995). "New racism", self esteem, and ethnic relations among minority and majority youth in the Netherlands. *Social Behavior and Personality, 23*, 137–154.
Verkuyten, M., & Zaremba, K. (2005). Interethnic relations in a changing political context. *Social Psychology Quarterly, 68*, 375–386.
White, R. W. (2001). Social and role identities and political violence: Identity as a window on violence in Northern Ireland. In R. D. Ashmore, L. Jussim, & D. Wilder (Eds.), *Social identity, intergroup conflict and conflict resolution* (pp. 133–158). Oxford: Oxford University Press.
Worchel, S. (1998). A developmental view of the search for group identity. In S. Worchel, J. F. Morales, D. Paez, & J. Deschamps (Eds.), *Social identity: International perspective* (pp. 53–74). London: Sage.
Zick, A., Wagner, U., van Dick, R., & Petzel, T. (2001). Acculturation and prejudice in Germany: Majority and minority perspectives. *Journal of Social Issues, 57*, 541–557.
Zirkel, S., & Cantor, N. (2004). 50 years after Brown v. Board of education: The promise and challenge of multicultural education. *Journal of Social Issues, 60*, 1–15.
Zunec, O. (1998). Rat u Hrvatskoj 1991–1995. 1. dio: Uzroci rata i operacije do sarajevskog primirja [The war in Croatia 1991–1995, 1. Part: The causes of war and military operations till the Sarajevo Peace Accord]. *Polemos, 1*, 57–89.

Chapter 12
OpenOption: Roma, Discrimination, and Peace Building in Macedonian Šuto Orizari

Despina Angelovska

Abstract Despite the adoption of a national strategy for social inclusion of Roma, they remain one of the most discriminated communities in Macedonia. This chapter describes an artistic project that resists the structural and cultural violence against Roma. It traces the creation of the show *OpenOption* (2009), a result of cooperation between Bologna's theater company Teatrino Clandestino and the members of Theater Roma from the municipality Šuto Orizari in Skopje. Pursuing social justice and promoting the inter-subjective exchange, this artistic cooperation will be addressed as a peacebuilding strategy that profoundly questions established cultural narratives that normalize violence towards Roma. *OpenOption* reflects upon the essential concepts of political philosophy challenging perpetuation of Roma's social exclusion, while it honors Roma's traditional contribution to a culture of peace. Finally, this chapter emphasizes the essential contribution of this committed artistic project to the mission of Peace Psychology as, reinforcing human well-being and dignity of its Roma participants, it also empowers them.

Keywords Peace Psychology • Peacebuilding • Roma • Discrimination • Theater

D. Angelovska (✉)
University of audiovisual arts ESRA, Nikola Rusinski street, n. 1,
1000 Skopje, Republic of Macedonia
e-mail: adespa@yahoo.com; despina.angelovska@gmail.com

O. Simić et al. (eds.), *Peace Psychology in the Balkans: Dealing with a Violent Past while Building Peace*, Peace Psychology Book Series, DOI 10.1007/978-1-4614-1948-8_12,

Introduction

Macedonia has adopted its national strategy for social inclusion of Roma within the frame of the international initiative: Decade of Roma Inclusion 2005–2015.[1] Despite this institutional attempt, Roma remain one of the most discriminated and marginalized communities in the country and throughout Europe. This chapter describes an artistic project that resists the mechanisms perpetrating social and cultural marginalization of Roma. It traces the creation of the show *OpenOption* (2009),[2] a result of cooperation between Bologna's theater company Teatrino Clandestino and the members of Theater Roma from the municipality Šuto Orizari in Skopje. Striving for more just social structures and enacting the intergroup contact and exchange, this artistic cooperation will be addressed as a peacebuilding strategy that profoundly questions established cultural narratives that normalize violence towards Roma. *OpenOption* reflects upon the essential concepts of political philosophy such as liberty and equality, human dignity, as well as the problem of state violence and coercion, all in relation to the Roma's social exclusion, while it honors Roma's tradition and wisdom, its culture of peace, solidarity and anti-militarism.

In the first part of this chapter we present the background of *OpenOption*, considering the larger social and political context of its creation in which Roma still suffer from constant economic and social disadvantages and violation of human rights. In the second part, we describe the genesis of the project and the political philosophy laboratory held in Šuto Orizari as it aims to dismantle mechanisms of structural and cultural violence against Roma. In the last part, we analyze the final show *OpenOption,* emphasizing its performative proposition of a new, more inclusive image, challenging stereotypes and prejudices against Roma. Finally, we stress the contribution of this common artistic project to the mission of Peace Psychology as reinforcing human well-being and dignity of its Roma participants; in addition, the project empowers Roma in the sense of (re)gaining control over their own destiny, which, as argued by peace psychologists, is central to the peacebuilding process (Christie, Wagner, & Winter, 2001, Sect. 4, Introduction).

By focusing on the analysis of *OpenOption* as it promotes creative structural and cultural changes that strive to end violence against Roma, in this chapter we aim to develop an original contribution to the field of Peace Psychology, raising our awareness of meaningful ways of fostering a culture of peace. Embracing peace psychologists' argument that changing cultures of violence into cultures of peace and reinforcing human security will require our best creativity, commitment, compassion and idealism (Christie et al., 2001, Conclusion, p. 14), we address *OpenOption* as such committed artistic initiative which we reveal as central to the peacebuilding process.

---

[1] www.romadecade.org.

[2] *OpenOption* by: Fiorenza Menni.With: Faat Abedin, Hadži Asan, Matteo Garattoni, Eva Geatti, Amet Iasar, Alice Keller, Andrea Alessandro La Bozzetta, Monica Manca, Fiorenza Menni, Mauro Milone, Paola Stella Minni, Andrea Mochi Sismondi, Laura Pizzirani, Šaban Uzeir. In collaboration with: Roma Theatre – Macedonia, Jean Michel Bruyère, Luigi de Angelis, Matthias Kaufmann, Chiara Lagani, Andrea Mochi Sismondi, Loredana Vitale Wilbi.

The Background of the Project *OpenOption*

Šuto Orizari, the First Roma Municipality in Europe

The project of artistic cooperation, *OpenOption*, was introduced in the municipality of Šuto Orizari in Macedonia. This is the first self-governed municipality in Europe with a Roma mayor and it was created when Roma began settling in the area after the catastrophic earthquake that struck the city of Skopje in 1963. The agglomeration grew spatially and demographically and Šuto Orizari became an urban part of the city of Skopje in 1966. According to the official data (State Statistical Office, 2002), the Roma minority represents 2.6% of the overall population in the country: there are 58,879 Roma living all over Macedonia, 13,311 of which live in Šuto Orizari.

Roma are also mentioned in the preamble of the Macedonian Constitution, among the other national minorities, and are guaranteed complete civil equality with the ethnic Macedonian majority (Assembly of The Republic of Macedonia, 2006). Yet, this institutional frame, which was created in the period of Socialist Federal Republic of Yugoslavia, and which promoted certain preconditions for national and political affirmation of Roma, does not guarantee them today equal participation and status inside Macedonian society. At present, the Roma community in Macedonia, even if officially recognized and protected more than in other European countries still remains one of the most vulnerable ones.

The marginalized social and political condition of Macedonian Roma has been the subject of numerous reports and analyses done by local and external experts, most often published under the umbrella of international organizations (European Roma Rights Center, 1998, 2009; Gaber Damjanovska, Skenderi, Redzepi, Bojadzieva, & Cekregi, 2006; Lakinska-Popovska, 2000; Najchevska, Aloui, & Petroska-Beshka, 1999), as well as of various academic research works (Baranya, 1995, 1994; Staniševski, 2008). Also, recently, in its *Third Report on R. of Macedonia*, the European Commission against Racism and Intolerance (ECRI) expressed deep concerns over the deplorable living conditions of many Roma in the country. In its report it stated that Macedonian Roma continue to suffer from an accumulation of economic and social disadvantages, worsened by changing economic conditions, discrimination, and insufficient attention by the authorities (ECRI, 2005, pp. 23–24).

The Decade for Roma Inclusion 2005–2015 and the National Strategy for Roma

The Macedonian Strategy for Roma was adopted in 2005. It follows ECRI' s recommendations, urging the Macedonian authorities to develop appropriate measures to address direct and indirect discrimination of Roma by developing a national strategy for Roma social integration (ECRI, 2005, p. 24). A Roma minister without portfolio, Nezdet Mustafa, was appointed as national coordinator both for the

Decade of Roma Inclusion 2005–2015, and for the National Strategy, with the aim of improving the socio-economic status and social inclusion of Roma by focusing on the priority areas of education, employment, health, and housing (Ministry of Labor and Social Policy of the Republic of Macedonia, 2004). In spite of those institutional efforts and the partially implemented national action plan, the European Commission, in its *2009 Progress Report* on R. of Macedonia (European Commission, 2009), still points out that so far these measures have had limited results, and the political commitment for the Roma strategy continues to be insufficient. Furthermore, the report argues that Roma continue to be the most disadvantaged ethnic group in the country. Similar conclusions have also been presented in the latest ECRI's report from April 2010 (ECRI, p. 30).

The same assessments could also be used to qualify the situation of Roma people all over Europe, where they live predominantly on the margins of society and are among the most deprived and discriminated communities, facing considerable obstacles to full enjoyment of their fundamental rights (Council of Europe, 2006; European Union Agency for Fundamental Rights, 2009). As Amnesty International testifies in its recent report, in some European countries Roma are prevented from obtaining citizenship and personal documents required for social insurance, health care and other benefits. Additionally, Romani children are frequently unjustifiably placed in "special schools" where curtailed curricula limit their possibilities for fulfilling their potential (Amnesty International, 2010). As stated by the Commissioner for human rights, this segregation of Roma children excludes them from mainstream society "increasing the risk of their being caught in the vicious circle of marginalization" (Council of Europe, p. 25). Furthermore, Roma in Western as in Eastern Europe, and particularly in the Balkans, have been a privileged target of hate speech and crime (Brearley, 2001; Erjavec, Hrvatin, & Kelbl, 2000; Lenkova, 1998; Mudde, 2005; Petrova, 2003). Finally, recent controversial anti-Roma policies in Italy and collective expulsions of Roma in France alert us to the extremely vulnerable position of one of the largest European minorities.

Within the realm of Peace Psychology, structural violence is defined as a "chronic affront to human well-being, harming or killing people slowly through relatively permanent social arrangements that are normalized and that deprive some people of basic need satisfaction" (Christie, Tint, Wagner, & DuNann, 2008, pp. 542–543). Structural violence is sustained by "social, psychological, economic, and political conditions that privilege some but exclude others" (Christie et al., 2001, ch. 8, p. 15). Consequently, and following all the parameters indicated before, it could be argued that the Roma community, in Macedonia as in the rest of Europe, is subjected to persistent structural violence as defined by peace psychologists.

It is within this institutionalized context of "deprivation of human needs satisfaction" (Christie, 2006, p. 5) that a constructive cooperation between the members of Theater Roma and Teatrino Clandestino was born, resisting social and cultural exclusion. Embracing a conception of art as being capable of transcending differences between people, of theater as socially and ethically responsible, *OpenOption* is a politically engaged artistic project that combines and intertwines with the mission of Peace Psychology: it endorses values associated with non violence, human rights, and social justice (Christie et al., 2001, ch. 28, p. 3).

Presentation of Teatrino Clandestino and Theatre Roma: The Encounter

Teatrino Clandestino[3] is based in Bologna, Italy. It was founded in the early 1990s by the Italian artists Fiorenza Menni and Pietro Babina who are also the artistic directors of the company and responsible for conceiving, writing, and creating all the plays and projects. Today Teatrino Clandestino is internationally recognized and prized as one of the most original and influential European companies for contemporary theater. The company's polyvalent name "Clandestino",[4] echoing the very accurately located global problem of dehumanized treatment and status of the "clandestini", illegal immigrants, reflects the political and social engagement of this theater company whose logo is an expressive red cross. The Theater Roma, based in Šuto Orizari in Skopje, started its activity in 1998 and was officially registered as an NGO in 2000. It consists of professional and amateur Roma actors whose main objective is the preservation, cultivation and presentation of Roma culture. From 2000 to 2005, Theater Roma has been financially supported by the Macedonian Government, and has obtained many prizes for its work. But since 2006, because of amendments to the policies on financing cultural activities of national interest, Theater Roma lost all state support and its activities stagnated. Today, in Macedonia, diverse theaters are supported by the state as national institutions, among which are, for example, the Albanian and Turkish theaters, but there is no national initiative nor aid for a theater of the Roma minority.

It was within such an institutionalized context that in February 2007, the members of Teatrino Clandestino visited, for the first time, Šuto Orizari and met the members of Theater Roma. This was the beginning of an ongoing collaboration which resulted in the productions of *Common Problematic Space*, first presented in June 2008 at the Festival Metamorfosi in Cascina, Italy, and *OpenOption*, whose premiere was at the international Festival VIE for Contemporary Scene in Modena, Italy, in October 2009.

The Genesis of *OpenOption: Common Problematic Space*

Resisting Structural Violence Against Roma: A Political Philosophy Laboratory in Šuto Orizari

Preparing the ground for the project *OpenOption*, the members of Teatrino Clandestino visited Šuto Orizari three times between February 2008 and May 2009, and lived there for several months as guests in Roma homes. During their first stay, the "actors-ethnographers of the post-ideological contemporary" (Teatrino Clandestino, 2009a) attempted to immerse in the everyday life of the Roma

[3] For more informations visit the Teatrino Clandestino's web site: www.teatrinoclandestino.org.

[4] "Clandestino, a": illicit, secret, underground; "immigrato clandestino": illegal immigrant; – "passeggero clandestino": stowaway.

municipality, living and behaving like community inhabitants, while trying to understand their specificities, and their vision of the world. Following the main concepts of the German philosopher Matthias Kaufmann (2007), the members of Teatrino Clandestino also organized a laboratory (a specific kind of workshop) for reflection and discussion with the members of Theater Roma as well as other artists and intellectuals of Šuto Orizari. The political philosophy laboratory provoked a very strong interest within the Roma community and an intense exchange of points of view between the participants, enlarging mutual comprehension. There, they discussed fundamental themes of political philosophy and humanity such as: freedom and equality, aspiration for a better and happier life, the possibility to pursue a personal and independent project of life, the right to move throughout the territory and across the borders, human natural capabilities, the state of nature, the relation with constraint in general, and even the legitimacy of the state (Teatrino Clandestino).

This reflective laboratory, held in Šuto Orizari, resulted in the *Common Problematic Space* project, constituting the dramaturgical basis for the show *OpenOption*. It was seeking to invert traditional roles and transform the dominant political and cultural narratives that support social dominance and discrimination, while giving the stage to those who historically have been deprived of adequate political representation. In this regard, it could be also analyzed as an initiative embracing the realm of structural peacebuilding, as defined by Peace Psychology (Mayton, 2001; Montiel, 2001; Steger, 2001).

Moreover, in this project, the Roma municipality became a valorized essential common space, a place described by the participants as "full of possibilities, a space of hospitality and reception, celebrating the visions of our register and evaporating them through the pores". At the same time, the excentred Šuto Orizari incarnated the furious and fundamental problematic space "where collisions occur" (Teatrino Clandestino, 2008). Within the frame of this laboratory, the space became a common scene of shared reflexion, discussion and confrontation on crucial social and political subjects, a place where an encounter between the subjective and political is generated.

Searching for the best possible political community. One of the main focuses of the political philosophy laboratory was a reflection on the constraints posed by the state followed by the generation of an outline of an institutional frame in which the best possible political community could develop. The discussion focused on the question of how to create an institutional framework that encourages a civil political community and provides the least possible number of constraints on the way to happiness to the citizens. Furthermore, the question raised was how the political space could offer as much help as possible (Teatrino Clandestino, 2009b).

Within this scope, the dialogue began with the Roma community of Šuto Orizari who live both inside and outside of the Macedonian State's institutional frame. The focus was on the experience of constraints and limitations, but also the means of transgressing constraints while pursuing liberty and happiness. The dialogue proved to be essential in this questioning of the necessity and the justification of every form of power, constraint, and violence, which, being an essential preoccupation of contemporary Political Philosophy (Agamben, 1998; Kaufmann, 2007), also connects to the fundamental preoccupations of Peace Psychology. In that respect, this philosophical and theatrical workshop, while aimed at the promotion of social justice, embraced the goals of psychology of peace (Christie et al., 2001, Introduction, p. 20); namely, the search for the sustainable satisfaction of human needs, and the creation of positive social conditions which minimize destructiveness and promote human well-being (Society for Peace, Conflict, and Violence, 2006, para. 3 as cited in Christie et al., 2008, p. 540). Furthermore, this workshop also challenged mechanisms that perpetuate cultural discrimination of Roma.

Why Are Roma the Last in Society?: Roma and Cultural Violence

During the second phase of the workshop for political philosophy, one of the main questions discussed was why Roma are last in society and an identification of mechanisms that support that marginalization and violence against them? Due to a vicious circle of deprivation, poverty, exclusion, and, also, dehumanization of Roma people in Europe (Amnesty International, 2009, April 8; Amnesty International, 2010, April 8; European Union Agency for Fundamental Rights, 2009) this was a crucial question to be addressed.

Roma's exclusion from society has historical and cultural roots, and peace psychologists often speak of "cultural violence" (Galtung, 1996 as cited in Christie et al., 2001, Sect. 4, Introduction) while they analyze the subjective and cultural mechanisms that sustain inequitable power relations in political and economic structures. As such, cultural violence refers to the symbolic sphere of our existence that reinforces episodes or structures of violences (Christie et al., 2008, p. 543). Freire argues that culturally violent narratives justifying cultural violence, can be transformed when there is an awakening of a critical consciousness, and a shared subjective state in which the powerless begin to critically analyze and challenge the oppressive narratives of the powerful (Freire, 1970 as cited in Christie et al., 2001, ch. 23, p. 14). In that sense, one of the main focuses of the philosophical laboratory was the articulation and re-articulation of the normalized exclusionary mechanisms of cultural violence against Roma by the inhabitants of Šuto Orizari themselves. Different examples of Roma's stereotyped representations in cinema, literature, painting, etc. were discussed and challenged, and racism and prejudices against Roma were dismantled as cultural narratives supporting and justifying ongoing power imbalances and structural violence. The members of Teatrino Clandestino have, within the framework of their project, and in consultation with the hosts of Theater Roma, made the decision to not make any video or audio recordings that reproduce stereotypes of Roma. The unique records of the process of "awakening a critical consciousness" were handwritten by Andrea Mochi Sismondi and later published in a book entitled: *Confini di amanti* (Mochi Sismondi, 2010).

With its challenge of culturally violent narratives and representations supporting and legitimizing structural violence, *Common Problematic Space* is an introduction to the project *OpenOption*. *OpenOption* embraces peacebuilding as it stages a radical transformation of the cultural and political narratives that justify domination of Roma people (Christie et al., 2001).

In Pursuit of Social Justice: *OpenOption* as a Peacebuilding Project

Towards a New Imaginary

The theatrical production *OpenOption* resulted from ideas developed during the 2 year intense encounters between the artists and residents in Šuto Orizari. Prolonging the artistic and conceptual research initiated in the project *Common Problematic Space,* it puts its spectators in front of a representation and in the heart of a debate that attempts to dismantle stereotypes, discrimination and prejudices against Roma, while proposing a new – more inclusive – imaginary, as analyzed by the authors themselves.

> Since we managed to be in the place where people speak, we are convinced it is necessary to stimulate an audience which is part of a community, the Italian one, that we believe has been seriously damaged as far as imagination is concerned. We are not talking about a cure nor a redemption, but about the attempt to raise the level of the debate by proposing a topic instead of reassuring people about the imaginative opportunities they have lost. The proposal of a topic is actually a proposal of imaginary, that is the creation of something we have never seen in the world: a conference where all philosophers are Roma people (Teatrino Clandestino, 2009c).

Taking the floor: the four Roma philosophers. The show *OpenOption* starts with a huge table occupying the stage and four Roma philosophers sitting at it: from a place of entertainment, the scene has been transformed into an essential place of reflection, where the beauty is that of thoughts being born. Against the spirit of the "bourgeois theater", in *OpenOption* the lights in the auditorium are turned on, and, instead of the traditional illusionist curtain, it is the immense EU flag covering the table and the actors-speakers that is raised, so that the spectators can see and hear what it has been masking.

OpenOption operates as a critique and an inversion of traditional political and cultural segregative roles and discourses. In the play, the members of Theater Roma take the floor: they are the four Roma philosophers reflecting on crucial questions of political philosophy. The proposal of a new imaginary of this play puts in the center of the stage those who have been excluded and silenced from the public sphere for centuries, and engages in a dialogue those who have not had the possibility to speak up and speak out. Furthermore, the performance also operates a different occupation and conception of theater itself. The traditional theater in Italian style, that was originally built in order to reproduce the very strong vertical hierarchical division of society, is here transformed into an open horizontal platform on the essential issues of political philosophy and human rights: the stage has become a space of "enlightened anarchy" (Kaufmann, 2007) meaningfully occupied by those whose entrance in the building was traditionally forbidden.

In that respect, by giving voice and listening to those who have been marginalized in matters that affect their own well-being, we argue that *OpenOption* stands as a powerful artistic initiative that reinforces positive peace in the sense in which this later has been defined by Peace Psychology (Christie et al., 2001, ch. 23, p. 14).

Moreover, as we are going to analyze it bellow, by transgressing language barriers and reinforcing the permeability to the Other, *OpenOption* promotes the essential ethical principle of social inter-subjectivity which is a precondition for the existence of a culture of peace (Butler & Stauffer, 2003).

Tradutori traditori. The four Roma thinkers speak in their Romani language on the theater scene of *OpenOption* while the Italian actors translate it for the audience. Consequently, the discussion between the actors from Teatrino Clandestino and their Roma colleagues is translated into an experimental and invented language, created during the working process, while pretending – for the Italian spectators – to be Romani language.

On one hand, this theatrically political choice of Teatrino Clandestino imposes itself as meaningful and engaged gesture of (auto-)critique. While "incarnating" as EU representatives and mediators, the actors appear on stage as "smooth talkers, fake, false, hypocrites in the invention of a language with acrid and dissonant sounds" (Leonardo, 2008, June 19). They act as a powerful critique of the EU's deceiving human rights discourses and failing strategies of social inclusion. The actors, those "politicians-impostors", those "betraying translators", while buttering up the public, at the same time, critically point out the falsity, hypocrisy, and failure of social politics that has not dismantled the massive discrimination of Roma (Leonardo).

On the other hand, making the spectators listen to the incomprehensible radically Other's story, narrated in "a strange" Romani language, whose purely functional translation indicates the inevitable loss of meaning in language, *OpenOption* critically points out the unintelligibility and the fundamental intranslatability of Roma's story. As Agamben puts it, this is a condition of "bare life" (Agamben, 1998) – of those left in no-man's land, those whose humanity stays unacknowledged (Butler & Stauffer, 2003) – for the comfortably seated EU spectators.

Still, in a magical theatrical way, this multilingual structure of *OpenOption*, in which the Romani language, incomprehensible for the majority of the non-Roma spectators, is translated into Italian, reinforces the capacity of hearing/listening and responsiveness to the Other, to the stranger and to his/her thought, transgressing language barriers. This multi-layered effect is analyzed by the creators of the project as follows:

> When a stranger speaks, you listen to the music of his language, a music which does not lack emotional power. The meaning is not conveyed by words, but it passes through other ways. Only after comes – as a support – the translation, but first you have been able to sense the emotional quality of another animal that has expressed itself. When then words come to the spectator's ears, with his eyes he can recreate the link with the person who has spoken, he's freer to perceive the signs which originated the meanings that come to him through the translation (Teatrino Clandestino, 2009a).

Finally, the project *OpenOption* acknowledges the listening, the permeability, and even the vulnerability to the Other. This is an essential ethical principle of social inter-subjectivity and a precondition for the existence of a culture of peace (Butler & Stauffer, 2003). In that respect, this rich linguistic and conceptual structure, detouring predefined and single meanings, by which the listeners become more responsive to Alterity and their perception is enlarged, has allowed the creation of a theatrical show that provides a kind hospitality in response to the warm reception that the Italian theater company has been given by the Roma community (Teatrino Clandestino, 2009a). Let us now look at how *OpenOption* questions traditional conception of contemporariness offering a positive reinterpretation of the traditionally negatively connoted "anachronism" carried by Roma.

"What Is the Contemporary?": Roma Enlightening Contemporariness

In one of his essays, inspired by a reflection from the *Untimely Meditations* by Friedrich Nietzsche (Nietzsche, 1997), Giorgio Agamben asks the important philosophical question of "What does it mean to be contemporary?" (Agamben, 2009, p. 39). Prolonging Nietzsche's untimely thought, Agamben argues that those who are truly contemporary are those who neither perfectly coincide with their time nor adjust themselves to its demands: those who are, in that sense, outdated and irrelevant. He further argues that it is precisely through this disconnection and this anachronism that they are more capable than others of perceiving and grasping their own time (Agamben, p. 40). Furthermore, he states that the contemporary is the one who firmly holds his/her gaze on his/her own time as to perceive not its light, but rather its darkness, the one who knows how to see the obscurity of the present. Contemporaries, thus, are those who do not let themselves be blinded by the lights of the century, and so manage to get a glimpse of the shadow in those lights, of their intimate obscurity (Agamben, pp. 44–45). Agamben's essay and its reflection on contemporariness is one of the crucial aspects of the project *OpenOption.*

Effectively, the script of *OpenOption* starts with the chokingly anachronistic true life story of Irina, a Romanian Roma, an EU citizen in her early twenties, who has been living in Italy for 4 years, and has been sleeping where ever she could; she has two daughters who live in Romania with her mother; every month she manages to send home 30 or 40 euros earned by begging; she did not go to school, nobody has ever gone to school in her village, there are no schools there; she is desperate (Teatrino Clandestino, 2009b). This despairing testimony is a transcript of the real conversation that F. Menni has had with Irina in the streets of Bologna. It unveils the anachronistic and dehumanized position of Roma population around Europe and acts as a critique of EU social policies (Teatrino Clandestino, 2010).

Already *Common Problematic Space* was formulating the striking question – based on the true testimony of an old Roma women, Kadmene – of "what is the use of donating a children playground if it is dismantled only two days later for selling its iron peaces in order to give children [something] to eat, the same children that were supposed to play in it?" (Teatrino Clandestino, 2008). In that respect, continuing Agamben's reflection of what is the contemporary, Irina's declaration of despair and the unbearable anachronism of her life both lead to the essential ethical and philosophical question: "What does living a decent life mean?" (Teatrino Clandestino, 2009b). And, it is with the same distancing "v-effect", that is, with the "embarrassing" life story of Irina, that *OpenOption* critically points to the lights of our time that hide its shadows and darkness, the unacceptable violence of the position of bare life and the poverty by which some people are kept on the margins of the contemporary liberalist society, and for whom some people's obviousness stays inaccessible.

> Irina: Being happy means being in good health, having money, a beautiful house and a job. It means that your children can go to school so that one day they might become influential and highly respected people: journalists, businessmen, or members of parliament. However, in the actual form of radical capitalism, the human being is always in lack of something, it is hungry for a future hunger. And this is why we are cut out, because of our actual and real hunger and poverty (Teatrino Clandestino, 2009b).

Moreover, narrating strikingly outdated Irina's story, *OpenOption,* asks what living in the contemporary society really means? As argued by F. Menni, Irina's story represents a "gap highlighting an evil, a disadvantage, a fault of what this time is proud of, that of its historical culture and its constant pursuit of progress, of a civil and political quality" (Teatrino Clandestino, 2009b). In that sense, it is, paradoxically, the "disconnected" position of Irina, the young Roma European citizen who does not reflect her time and does not conform to its requirements – as she is not granted a loan, does not follow fashion dictates, does not cross the borders as a tourist, that she contains the necessary distance needed for really seeing the present, not being blinded by its lights. It is precisely the gap, writes Menni, the anachronism that she carries – surely not a nostalgic one – that Irina, more than anyone else, can show us our time and make us grasp its meaning (Teatrino Clandestino).

Just as Agamben in his essay on contemporariness redefines the traditional notion of darkness as a particular and active form of vision (Agamben, 2009, p. 45), *OpenOption* offers also a positive reinterpretation of the traditionally negatively connoted "anachronism" carried by Roma: in the show Irina belongs to the present, but, at the same time, she keeps her distance from it, and, thanks to her ability to create this distance, she leads us to focus on contemporary society in order to understand it better (Teatrino Clandestino, 2009b). And this better and critical understanding of our time is also a precondition for the pursuit of a more just society. Rejoining "the contemporary" of Agamben's essay, Irina becomes precisely the person that perceives the darkness of her time as something that concerns her, as something that never ceases to engage her (Agamben).

Finally, Irina raises the crucial question of our time in which she has been rejected and excluded also because she has been resisting the established order of normalization and assimilation, and thus, she confronts us with the ongoing annihilation of divergent identities. Unveiling structural violence in our society, *OpenOption*, at the end, offers a new imaginary representation of Irina as an "authentic revolutionary power, because she radically questions the functioning of society

(Teatrino Clandestino, 2009b). This important critical distance from the blinding lights of our time is also conveyed in the title of *OpenOption* reflecting Roma's culture of openness that challenges normalized and rooted identities.

OpenOption – The Title and Its Meaning

The title of the project *OpenOption* resulted from a broader discussion with the actors of *Theater Roma*, during one of the last encounters of the philosophical workshop in Šuto Orizari, on the concept of living in mobile homes, caravans, camping cars, house trailers, representing places of auto sufficiency, as they served as hospitals, banks, shelters (Menni, 2010). In that respect, one of the Roma actors, Faat Abedin, was explaining to the members of Teatrino Clandestino that nobody from the Šuto Orizari community lived in a camping car, but, that, from his point of view, that possibility is not absolutely excluded. What he was referring to is a general, traditional attitude of openness regarding eventuality, necessity and possibility in the life of a Roma. Explaining how Roma relate to the events, and, trying to resume their attitude towards home and homeland, at one point, he used the term "open option" (Fiorenza Menni, personal communication).

It is following this spirit that the project *OpenOption* was conceived, in the open space of Šuto Orizari, reflecting and acknowledging Roma's culture of openness and adaptability and respect for the fundamental principle of voyage and liberty, deconstructing the violence of territorial occupations, dismantling fixed and exclusive identities, a spirit that could be an important contribution for the development of a culture of peace.

Roma, A Nation Without a State and War

Another dimension of the Roma traditional heritage acknowledged in *OpenOption*, is the culture of peace and tolerance, historically a nation without state and, thus, without war. The play also points out the violence of a homogenized and militarized society in which being a (Roma) nation without a nation-state, without a Constitution, a bank or an army to protect it, means to be consigned to deprivation and discrimination (Teatrino Clandestino, 2009b).

In an interview for the Macedonian weekly-magazine, *Forum*, Fiorenza Menny claimed that "In Šuto Orizari the parents teach their children that they should never ever participate in war. And that is extraordinary and beautiful to me. I have not heard it anywhere" (Menni & Angelovska, 2009, p. 53). Effectively, it is in front of the Italian spectators, brought up with the discourse celebrating the historical meaning of war and the myth of World War II, that the Roma pacifist, non-violent, and anti-militarist argument was put on the table as another option. Moreover, by placing in the center of the public debate Roma community's enlightened pacifist anarchy and its stateless condition, *OpenOption* seems to question the model and the concept of nation-state itself, as its acquisition and creation are historically legated to war, which is not an option for Roma, and, by critically pointing out to the Roma community's social exclusion in European nation-states, the play enacts a critique of nation-state as – by definition – supporting structural violence against minorities (Butler & Spivak, 2007).

Breaking the cycle of the prevalent masculine militarist ideology (Butler & Stauffer, 2003), Roma traditional culture of peace and tolerance, and their ethic of non-violence, that was given credit in *OpenOption*, today represents a much-needed perspective, valorized by Peace Psychology, a perspective that questions "contemporary dominant modes of representing power primarily in terms of violence" (Steger in Christie, et al., 2001, p. 592). And maybe it is precisely the position of vulnerability of the Roma community, which has been profoundly affected and injured by others throughout centuries, that creates peaceful dispositions. Such a view is consistent with the American feminist philosopher Judith Butler's definition (Butler & Stauffer) of peace as a commitment to living with a certain kind of vulnerability to others and susceptibility to being wounded. Peace as a Roma community ethos makes it possible to resist the terrible temptation of war and exhibit tolerance and recognition of the Other.

Conclusion: A Theater with Open Doors

Supporting Open Dialogue and Critique. *OpenOption* was born in order to develop a reflection on the crucial philosophical, social and political problems of our time. While resisting the perpetuation of structural violence against Roma in contemporary European society, it embraces values of solidarity and peace as they are emphasized by Fiorenza Menni in her interview.

> The European Union, historically, has resulted from the desire for solidarity. People have strived for it, they have gone out to the streets, and they have even died for it. This is what political philosophy speaks about, but, unfortunately, latter this initial desire has been displaced, and people have been excluded from this project.
>
> On the other hand, when I look at my young son, I say to myself that it is amazing to see how great a constructive energy one child has. It is extraordinary how much we are all capable of creating, putting in practice our constructive capacities. In that sense, I am not sure that our nature is violent. I tend to agree more with anarchist philosophers who say that the feeling of solidarity is stronger than violence (Menni & Angelovska, 2009).

OpenOption supports open dialogue and pluralistic perspectives and operates as an essential critique of an institutionalized system in which the well-being of some is obtained by depriving others. Moreover, *OpenOption* gives voice to those who have always been treated like second-class citizens. In this regard, it links together an essential goal of Peace Psychology, which is the reduction of structural violence (Christie et al., 2008, p. 542). It is in this respect that the peace psychologist Suzan Opotow promotes tolerance for and encouragement of discussion and critique as a first step in recognizing structural violence and identifying its causes and cures

(Christie et al., 2001, ch. 8, p. 14). Furthermore, *OpenOption* raises public awareness of the structural violence experienced by the Roma population, putting on stage the testimonies of those whose right to circulate freely is limited -- those whose search for better life is prevented. Meeting Peace Psychology goals, *OpenOption* clearly rejects this unacceptable form of violence and performs an appeal for a renewed political commitment of the European states to combat poverty and social exclusion by ensuring protection of human rights of Roma citizens.

Reinforcing dignity and empowerment of the Roma theater actors. After a few years of status quo in the activity of Theater Roma, lack of recognition and subvention by the Macedonian institutions, and a deficiency of public acknowledgment, it was thanks to their vibrant theater activity promoted by *OpenOption*, that the Roma actors have received offers for future shows and projects that allowed them to regain professional confidence and reinforcement of social position. As F. Menni argues in her interview, what could be the most important thing regarding the creation of *OpenOption* is "maybe that cooperation will help the actors of Theater Roma bring back dignity to their theater and will help them make it live again in Macedonia. And that has crucial meaning. That is a question that, for us, touches the essential political-philosophical subjects of human dignity, possibility, and freedom" (Menni & Angelovska, 2009, p. 53).[5]

It is in this sense that, finally, this common theatrical project could also be considered a means of empowering its Roma participants, in the sense of (re)gaining control over their own destiny, which, as argued by Peace Psychology, is central to the peacebuilding process (Christie et al., 2001, Sect. 4 Introduction). In that respect, by its active promotion of the well-being of the Theater Roma actors, which is here profoundly interlaced with the well being of the members of Teatrino Clandestino, the constructive and solidary energy of *OpenOption* accomplishes the essential mission of Peace Psychology (Christie et al., Introduction, p. 2).

References

Agamben, G. (1998). *Homo sacer: Sovereign power and bare life* (D. Heller-Roazen, Trans.). Stanford: Stanford University Press. (Original work published 1995).

Agamben, G. (2009). What is the contemporary. *"What is apparatus?" and other essays* (pp. 39–56) (D. Kishik & S. Pedatella, Trans.). Stanford, CA: Stanford University Press. (Original work published 2008).

Amnesty International. (2009, April). Europe's Roma community still facing massive discrimination. *Amnesty International News*. Retrieved from www.amnesty.org.

Amnesty International. (2010, April 8). Europe: Stop forced evictions of Roma in Europe. *Amnesty International Report*. Retrieved from www.amnesty.org.

[5] Still, at the moment we are writing this text, *OpenOption* has not yet been presented in R. of Macedonia.

Assembly of The Republic of Macedonia. (2006). Constitution of The Republic of Macedonia. Retrieved from www.sobranie.mk/en/.

Baranya, Z. (Summer 1994). Living on the edge: The East European Roma in postcommunist politics and societies. *Slavic Review, 53*(2), 321–344. Retrieved from http://homepages.wmich.edu/~n2senic/barany.roma.pdf.

Baranya, Z. (1995). The Roma in Macedonia: Ethnic politics and the marginal condition in a Balkan state. *Ethnic and Racial Studies, 18*, 515–531.

Brearley, M. (2001). The persecution of gypsies in Europe. *American Behavioral Scientist, 45*, 588–599.

Butler, J., & Spivak, G. C. (2007). *Who sings the nation-state?: Language, politics, belonging.* London: Seagull Books.

Butler, J., & Stauffer, J. (2003). Peace is a resistance to the terrible satisfactions of war. Interview with Judith Butler. *The Believer Magazine.* Retrieved May 2003, from www.believermag.com.

Christie, D. J., Wagner, R. V., & Winter, D. D. (Eds.). (2001). *Peace, conflict, and violence: Peace psychology for the 21st century.* Englewood Cliffs, NJ: Prentice-Hall. Retrieved from academic.marion.ohio-state.edu/dchristie/Peace%20Psychology%20Book.html.

Christie, D. J. (2006). What is peace psychology the psychology of? *Journal of Social Issues, 62*(1), 1–17.

Christie, D. J., Tint, B., Wagner, R. V., & DuNann, D. (2008). Peace psychology for a peaceful world. *American Psychologist, 63*(6), 540–552.

Council of Europe. (2006). *Final report by Mr Alvaro Gil-Robles, Commissioner for Human Rights, on the human rights situation of the Roma, Sinti and Travellers in Europe.* Strasbourg: Council of Europe. Retrieved from https://wcd.coe.int/ViewDoc.jsp?id=962605&Site=COE.

Erjavec, K., Hrvatin, S. B., & Kelbl, B. (2000). *We about the Roma. Discriminatory discourse in the media in Slovenia.* Ljubljana: Open Society Institute – Slovenia.

European Commission. (2009). *The former Yugoslav Republic of Macedonia 2009 Progress report.* Brussels: European Commission. Retrieved from ec.europa.eu/enlargement/press_corner/key-documents/reports_oct_2009_en.htm.

European Commission Against Racism and Intolerance. (2005). *Third report on "the Former Yugoslav Republic of Macedonia".* Strasbourg: Council of Europe. Retrieved from www.coe.int..

European Commission Against Racism and Intolerance. (2010). *Fourth report on "the Former Yugoslav Republic of Macedonia".* Strasbourg: Council of Europe. Retrieved from www.coe.int.

European Roma Rights Center. (2009). Multiple discrimination. *Roma Rights Journal, 2.* Retrieved from www.errc.org/cms/upload/file/roma-rights-2-2009-multiple-discrimination.pdf.

European Roma Rights Center. (1998). A pleasant fiction: The human rights situation of Roma in Macedonia. *European Roma rights center country reports series.* (Tech. Rep. No. 7: 001-054). Retrieved from: http://www.errc.org/cms/upload/media/00/11/m00000011.pdf.

European Union Agency for Fundamental Rights. (2009). Data in Focus Report: The Roma. *EU-MIDIS European Union Minorities and Discrimination Survey.* Retrieved from www.fra.europa.eu/fraWebsite/eu-midis/eumidis_roma_en.htm.

Freire, P. (1970). *Pedagogy of the oppressed.* New York: SeaburyPress.

Gaber Damjanovska, N., Skenderi, S., Redzepi, N., Bojadzieva, A., & Cekregi. L. (2006). *National vulnerability report for Macedonia – Focus on Roma.* Skopje: UNDP. Retrieved from http://europeandcis.undp.org/uploads/public/file/Report2006-angl-web2.pdf.

Galtung, J. (1996). *Peace by peaceful means: Peace and conflict, development and civilization.* London: Sage.

Kaufmann, M. (2007). *Anarchia illuminata. Una introduzione alla filosofia politica.* Napoli: Liguori.

Lakinska-Popovska, D. (2000). *Vulnerability of Roma children in the dispersed Roma communities in municipality Shuto Orizari.* Skopje: UNICEF, World Bank.

Lenkova, M. (Ed.). (1998). *"Hate speech" in the Balkans.* Athens: ETEPE.

Leonardo, E. (2008, June). Commune spazio problematico [Common Problematic Space]. *Teatro San Leonardo.* Retrieved from brainstormingartproject.blogspot.com/2008/07teatrino-clandestino-comune-spazio.html.

Menni, F., & Angelovska, D. (2009, June). Театар со отворени порти. Интервју со Фиоренца Мени [Theater with open doors. Interview with Fiorenza Menni]. *Forum Magazine, 196*, 51–54. Retrieved from www.forum.com.mk/4776.

Menni, F. (2010, June 5). Personal communication.

Mayton, D. M. (2001). Gandhi as peacebuilder: The social psychology of satyagraha. In D. J. Christie, R. V. Wagner, & D. D. Winter (Eds.), *Peace, conflict, and violence: Peace psychology for the 21st century* (pp. 307–113). Upper Saddle River: Prentice-Hall.

Ministry of Labor and Social Policy of the Republic of Macedonia. (2004, December). *Strategy for Roma in the Republic of Macedonia*. Retrieved from www.mtsp.gov.mk/WBStorage/Files/roma_strategy%20english.doc.

Mochi Sismondi, A. (2010). *Confini di amanti*. Manuscript submitted for publication.

Montiel, C. J. (2001). Toward a psychology of structural peacebuilding. In D. J. Christie, R. V. Wagner, & D. D. Winter (Eds.), *Peace, conflict, and violence: Peace psychology for the 21st century* (pp. 282–294). Upper Saddle River: Prentice-Hall.

Mudde, C. (2005). Racist extremism in central and eastern Europe. *East European Politics & Societies., 19*(2), 161–184.

Najchevska, M., Aloui, L., & Petroska-Beshka, V. (1999). *Situation analysis of Roma women and children*. Skopje: UNICEF.

Nietzsche, F. (1997). *Untimely meditations*. Cambridge: Cambridge University Press.

Petrova, D. (Spring 2003). The Roma:Between a myth and the future. *Social Research: An International Quarterly, 70*(1), 111–161. Retrieved from http://www.errc.org/cikk.php?cikk=1844.

Society for the Study of Peace, Conflict, and Violence. (2006). *About the division of peace psychology.* Retrieved from http://www.clarku.edu/peacepsychology/.

Staniševski, D. M. (2008). In the shadows of nationalisms: Social inclusion and public recognition of Roma and Egyptian identities in Macedonia. *Administrative Theory & Praxis, 30*(4), 476–495.

State Statistical Office of The Republic of Macedonia. (2002). *Edition of publications of the census of population, households and dwellings, 2002.* Retrieved from www.stat.gov.mk/english/glavna_eng.asp?br=18.

Steger, M. B. (2001). Peacebuilding and nonviolence: Gandhi's perspective on power. In D. J. Christie, R. V. Wagner, & D. D. Winter (Eds.), *Peace, conflict, and violence: Peace psychology for the 21st century* (pp. 314–323). Upper Saddle River, NJ: Prentice-Hall.

Teatrino Clandestino. (2008). *Play script of the project common problematic space*, Manuscript.

Teatrino Clandestino. (2009a). *Prologue OpenOption: The genesis of the project,* Manuscript.

Teatrino Clandestino. (2009b). *Play script of the project OpenOption*, Manuscript.

Teatrino Clandestino. (2009c). *Presentation of the show OpenOption*, Manuscript.

Teatrino Clandestino. (2010). *OpenOption*. Retrieved from http://www.youtube.com/watch?v=6fHfTtGmsy4.

Chapter 13
Overcoming Ethnic Hatred: Peacebuilding and Violent Conflict Prevention in Divided Societies

Scott Nicholas Romaniuk

Romanian nationalism is unmitigated by civic notions of national identity. It is rooted in ethnicity rather than in a concept of citizenship and rights.

Martyn Rady (1995, p. 138)

Abstract This chapter examines dynamics of Romanian nationalism, and the marginalization of the Roma and Hungarian minorities while dealing with issues of integration and assimilation. It addresses the relationship between the facilitation of peace between Hungarians and Romanians as well as episodic ethno-national intolerance and violence that has beset the Roma minority in Romania contemporaneously. The Hungarian minority's experience of the 1990s is employed to create a model of ethnic conflict dynamics as a contribution to the theory and practice of peace as part of the field of *peace psychology*. The mitigation of conflict in this case involved processes of peacemaking and peacebuilding that were used *ad seriatim* to avoid what was seen as inevitable violence between Romanians and Romania's Hungarian minority. Subsequently, the model may be employed to facilitate a peaceful relationship between Romania and its Roma minority in a similar manner.

Keywords Conflict management • Ethnic war • Hatred • Hungarians • Minority • Mutual hostility • Nationalism • Peacebuilding • Political élite • Roma • Violence

---

S.N. Romaniuk (✉)
Department of Politics and International Relations, University of Aberdeen,
687 Doehle Avenue, V9P 2V4 Parksville, BC, Canada
e-mail: scott.n.romaniuk@gmail.com; scottromaniuk@hotmail.com

O. Simić et al. (eds.), *Peace Psychology in the Balkans: Dealing with a Violent Past while Building Peace*, Peace Psychology Book Series, DOI 10.1007/978-1-4614-1948-8_13,

Introduction

The scope of external and internal threats to national and human security in the modern world-system has changed considerably in the contemporary era. While strategic interactions and causes of ethnic conflict and war have remained relatively constant throughout human history, certain events engendered by the constellation of history have provided crucibles for the emergence of stridently violent neo-traditional ideological movements and methods.

With the cessation of the Cold War, the so-called "Long Peace", and a bipolar competitive world, many observers increasingly acknowledge that a wave of ethnic conflict, violence, and fear has subsumed vast spaces of Europe not entirely comparable to that of previous periods of time (Gilley, 2004). Many of the wrongs and atrocities of the past have served as the match that touched-off some of the most violent national and ethnic conflagrations hitherto known. East-Central Europe's twentieth century history provides the perfect laboratory through which one may observe how genuine or apparent narratives of an ethno-national nature may aggravate current conflicts.

One such region of Europe that has acquired the unfair soubriquet of being backward and plagued by ethnic tension is South-East Europe, particularly Romania. Across the political spectrum within Europe, the conventional assumption persists that socio-economic and political turbulence is inextricably tied to the state's Roma minority: those who do not have enough or are disadvantaged blame others. While proposed solutions to ethnic tension and socio-economic disparity differ, many Romanians, as well as Romania's political élite, blame the Roma, especially rural migrants to urban locales. This link leads directly to the stigmatization of immigrants and minority peoples. Research illustrates that inequality rather than ethnic roots exhorts greater influence on socio-economic issues; in Romania, various types of inequality, such as inequalities in land tenure, education, and employment, are relevant to the incidence of intolerance, hatred, and even ethnic violence and conflict (Iacoboaea, 2009). In the case of Romania, the government is often accused of stoking the violence.

This chapter examines the basis of the ethnic conflict in Romania between the Romanian population and the Roma minority. It assesses the conflict spiral and current situation of systemic violence in the Romanian ethno-national state and places it soundly within the context of the burgeoning field of peace psychology. An assessment is made whether a conceptual strategy for peacebuilding and conflict prevention regarding Romanians and the Roma minority can be developed and applied to the case. It is therefore argued that peace can be achieved in much the same way that peace was achieved between Romanian's and Romania's Hungarian minority two decades ago.

The first section explores some of the ethno-national tension and violence that has gripped contemporary Romanian society since the end of the Cold War, as well as some theoretical links between ethnicity, tension, and violence. By addressing the relationship between the facilitation of peace between Hungarians and

Romanians as well as episodic ethno-national intolerance and violence that has beset the Roma minority in Romania contemporaneously, the human ability to manufacture both peace and violence as described by Deutsch (1999) is illustrated. Subsequently, the Hungarian minority's experience is employed to create a model of ethnic conflict dynamics based on the field of *peace psychology*.

Marginalization in the Ethnic Nation: The Roma and Hungarian Minorities in Romania

Obtaining an accurate picture of why some ethnic conflicts result in violent conflict between ethnic groups while other are successfully settled though non-violent means is a pernicious challenge. Since the cessation of the ideological stand-off between the Communist and democratic worlds during the Cold War, scholars and peace practitioners alike agree that the match stick that touches-off violent ethnic-conflict is largely the concept of ethno-nationalist identity (Gilley, 2004). That which may otherwise be considered a social movement, is represented through the "branding" of indigenous peoples on the basis of their political, economic, and social relationship with the host state or states. The nature of their identity is further influenced by peoples' duration and intensity of claims for self-determination and vice versa (Corntassel, 2003). Studies of such conflicts also confirms that the lack of, delayed, or derisory response by the international community to participate in the amelioration of violence in inter-ethnic conflict has also played a key role in determining the intensity and result of those very conflicts (Williams & Waller, 2004). In many ways, the cessation of the Cold War served as the catalyst for new levels of ethnic conflict potential. The collapse of communism in East-Central Europe ushered in a new era of social, political, and ethnic discord. To a great extent, however, social enmity in the region existed even before the Cold War thaw, but eventually traversed the transitional period between Cold War world and the New World Order.

While the Communist idea failed to unify as it had promised, Soviet withdrawal from East-Central Europe served as an expedient to the increasing fragility of already fragmented societies. In Romania, as elsewhere in East-Central Europe, authorities sought to replace its power with the nationalist idea. This was expected to achieve the unifying power that the Communist ideology did not. In the aftermath of the Cold War, scholars argued that the collapse of Soviet power enabled long-standing ethnic dissonance to reactivate and virulently enough to bring conflict back to the region (Dick, Dunn, & Lough, 1993). The end of the Cold War was seen as the event to "expose the central, southeastern and eastern regions to hot wars" (Dick et al.).

In spite of scholarly predictions that were made about the coming violence after the Cold War, the Communist thaw failed to produce any such envisaged violence or conflict on the scale hypothesized. As Kaufman (2002) notes, tying the altercations in Yugoslavia directly with the collapse of communism presents a somewhat fallacious reasoning for several reasons: (1) a confluence of factors contributed to the disintegration of Yugoslavia and the conflicts that resulted; (2) the conflicts that erupted were inevitable and predictable; (3) violence and war that took place in several former-Communist countries were the products of period of complacency that immediately followed the disintegration of the Soviet Union; (4) crises that engulfed other regions of the world, such as Iraq's 1990 invasion of Kuwait were deemed much more important than those occurring in Eastern Europe; (5) Western Europe was challenged with its own internal problems, which included economic recession and considerable integration processes. Despite the fact that the regions of East-Central Europe failed to live up to the hollow predictions about open warfare, there were obvious indications of turbulence and tension that could potentially lead to stridently violent events in the region.

The Roma Minority

In 1990 an organization of Romanian national extremists called Vatra Românească (Romanian Hearth) and steered by the axiom "Romanians were in Transylvania first" stirred national sentiments in the region. The group evoked emotional bonding over the territorial rights of ethnic Romanians through carefully orchestrated propaganda campaigns. Depicting minorities as a collective threat to Romanian stability and security, the organization aroused and channeled national discontents by propagating messages of hatred that even endorsed indiscriminate killing Roma (O'Loughlin & Van der Wusten, 1993, p. 152).

No ethnic issue in East-Central Europe engenders a more homogeneously negative and hostile core than that of Roma (Erjavec, Hrvatin, & Kelbl, 2000). Throughout Europe live an estimated five million Roma, with the majority residing in the east. In most places Roma minorities already living in squalid surroundings face uniformly injurious stereotypes and marginalization that often leads to violence against them (Council of Europe). This minority represents one of Romania's largest ethnic groups. Because of interest in the romantic aspects of Roma, the West has consistently demonstrated a tendency to overstate the number and role of the Roma in East-Central Europe, especially in contemporary Romania. The Roma's arrival in Romania is, historically speaking, a fairly recent event in the broader context of their migration to Europe.

By the beginning of the second-quarter of the twentieth-century, an estimated 243,000 Roma were living in Romania, or roughly 1.7% of the Romanian population during that time. During the Second major conflagration of the twentieth-century, from 1939 to 1945, the Gypsy population of Romania was subjected to pogroms and ghettoization, persecution, and outright systematic extermination in both concentration camps and labour camps under the aegis of the Nazis. By the mid-1900s, roughly 104,000 Roma remained in Romania, with just over half of this number claiming the Roma language as their native tongue (Matley, 1970).

The number of Roma living within contemporary Romania remains highly contentious. For example, according to the 1992 census, the number of recorded Roma living in Romania was 409,723 (1.8%) (Centre for Documentation and Information on Minorities in Europe—Southeast Europe [hereafter, CEDIME-SE], 2001). The Research Institute for Quality of Life estimates a number between 1,452,700 and 1,588,552 approximately 6.8% of the total Romanian population (CEDIME-SE, 2001). Other estimates report between 1.4 million and 2.5 million Roma are currently living in Romania, making this group the largest Roma population, not only in Europe, but likely in the entire world (United Nations Development Programme [hereafter, UNDP], 2002).

Just as it is difficult to find consensus on when Roma first entered the regions of Wallachia and Moldavia, there has been great difficulty in estimating and establishing agreement on the estimations of Roma populations in Romania today. Incidences of violence against Roma increasing at an alarming rate in the aftermath of the Ceauşescu régime may help explain the discrepancies between the numbers of Roma as stated in the 1992 census and the numbers that have been claimed by other organizations, including organizations that represent Roma directly.

Notwithstanding their overlooked contributions and modest integration, a new wave of anti-Roma violence was sparked in Romania as a result of structural change of the 1990s and the resurgence of nationalism. With the collapse of Communism, the National Salvation Front led by Ion Iliescu established a parliamentary democracy, which was largely democratic in name only (Tanasoiu, 2007, p. 61). The weakness of the transitioning state "provided a welcome opportunity for the representatives of the old régime to exploit public support for nationalism and used it as a powerful label for their own political ends" (Dumitriu-Seuleanu, 1997, p. 187). During the embryonic stages of Romania's political transition, Romanians engaged in numerous acts of violence towards Roma in the form of excessive violence including murder and the destruction of Roma communities. In many ways the shift, "from state-socialism to the nascent democracies was accompanied by profoundly negative effects for the Roma" (Verdery, 1993).

There are two recurring trends of the anti-Roma violence throughout the 1990s, following the collapse of the Communist state. Both trends are indicative of the incendiary role of élites in exacerbating the animosity and tension, which characterized majority sentiment. First, political, cultural, and social mobilization by the Roma is perceived as a threat by ethnic Romanian political élites and the general population, who still retain a strong sense of nationalism. The refusal of Roma to assimilate and their attempts to mobilize are considered forms of "political disloyalty" (Rady, 1995, p. 132) that threaten to create a heterogeneous society, which has already begun to occur as other minority groups, such as the Hungarians, have gained more freedoms in Romania. Second, stalled economic progress has created increased competition for jobs. Declines in the trade and industry sectors also present a threat to the job security of ethnic Romanians. The second trend transcends the new millennium and finds breeding ground in the global economic recession that grew toward the end of the first decade.

The perceived threats posed by Roma are exacerbated by the Roma's demographic structure, which makes a radical departure from the rest of the aging population in East-Central Europe. Approximately 280,000 male and female Roma were between 0 and 9 years of age, roughly 240,000 male and female Roma were between

10 and 19 years of age, and an estimated 175,000 male and female Roma were between 20 and 34 years of age. These statistics were compiled by the Council of Europe, and estimates are based on Roma populations living in Central Europe (Kalibová, 2000). By comparison, the total of Romani peoples in Romania is quite smaller than the number of non-Romani Romanian in the country. According to the CIA World Factbook, approximately 1,772,583 males and 1,681,539 females comprise those within the 0–14 age category, while 7,711,062 males and 7,784,041 females constitute the15–64 age category (CIA World Factbook, 2010). Even in spite of the noticeable disparity in population composition, the majority of the population in Romania views this demographic reality as a potentially overwhelming threat in the future (Jenne, 2000, p. 200).

In theory, the Roma have been given the opportunity to assimilate by way of government policies aimed at homogenizing Romania. The earliest assimilation policies "usually meant settling the Roma, who had reverted to nomadic lifestyle due to the persecution and exclusion they faced from majority population" (Jenne, 2000, p. 195). Later attempts adopted a "strategy of aggressive *Romanianization*" by way of forced internal migration policies and other forms of repression (Shafir, 2000, p. 101). The top-down attempts at assimilation appear to have failed for two reasons, although determining their causal relationship represents a Gordian knot. In the first place, the Roma have demonstrated their refusal to assimilate in order to preserve their distinct ethnic and cultural identity and, consequently, remain on the periphery of Romanian society (Barany, 2002). Moreover, the majority population, in terms of ethnic Romanians, has prevented assimilation on the basis of "deeply ingrained anti-Romani prejudice in the more rural societies of Romania" (Jenne, 2000, p. 195). Thus, a contestation of interests ultimately emerged whereupon the Romanian population rejected government initiatives to assimilate Roma peoples, although neither was genuinely receptive of the Roma presence in from the beginning, the initiative deteriorated at the microlevel.

Assimilationist policies in Romania not only failed, they exemplified a reverse effect of what was intended by political leaders. They were even successful in driving the minority and majority groups further apart as well as sharpening social cleavages. In general, assimilation is most successful when the focal point is "groups that are culturally similar, like Russians and Ukrainians, or for minority cultures that are assimilated before they achieve a literary consciousness or political organization beyond the kinship level" (Snyder, 2000, p. 274). Although scholars have invested a great deal of attention in studying the sources of intergroup conflict, there exists a considerable deficit in the study of forces that are able to bring groups together harmoniously rather than those which tear apart intergroup relations. The gap between persons who are ethnically and racially divergent can also be improved through emphasis on attachments to shared superordinate identities (Transue, 2007). As Kessler and Mummendey (2001) explain:

> Consistent with the common ingroup identity model, East Germans who recategorized West Germans and East Germans within the subordinate nationalist of "Germans," relative to those who continued to use the East-West German categorization scheme, displayed reduced bias toward West Germans. However, they also became more biased over time toward members of other countries (Dovidio & Gaertner, 1998, p. 1100).

The Romani Nationalist Movement exemplifies the need for increased study of the forces that are necessary for bringing together conflicting ethnic groups in any given society. This national movement not only undermines assimilation attempts and Romanian nationalist objectives, it further reveals Roma interests in preserving a distinct Roma cultural identity. Romani nationalism might be seen as a mosaic of models of national development of other groups. By linking a long-recognized identity based upon shared ethnic traits such as common language, community, and histories, with others of the same ethnic group(s), to claims for political association and self-determination [...] Romani culture has contrasted too sharply with that of ethnic majorities (Jenne, 2000, p. 197).

For East European governments, tackling the problem of the Roma, who have been viewed as less-civilized, has meant settling them and forcing them to adopt a more "culturally advanced lifestyle before they could be granted rights that had been accorded to other, better integrated minority ethnic groups" (Jenne, 2000, p. 197). Resistance to assimilation is predictable, based on Barany's argument, when one considers that "the larger the differences between the ethnic minority and the majority group, the higher the costs of assimilation, the more likely a group is going to preserve and promote its separate identity" (2002, p. 57).

The Romanian government still relies upon, to a much greater extent than in other corridors of Europe, other mechanisms with which Romanian authorities can exert even greater control over their state and populations. Accordingly, the media becomes a tool for depicting and dispersing negative images of the Roma, as is still the case. The failures of democratic reforms in the country, as well as the lack of economic welfare systems are indications that Romania has not yet completed the transition to democracy. The veneer of democracy, thus results in: (1) political élites being able to continue their policies of repression against emerging Roma mobilization; (2) the perpetuation of a cycle of fearful repression in response to Roma attempts to gain rights and strengthen their collective solidarity.

The régime's repression of Roma in these tremendously despotic fashions has resulted in several occurrences of violent acts carried out by mob-like groups of ethnic Romanians. A notable example of this violence occurred in Turulung in 1990 when 1,000 ethnic-Romanians beat and killed Roma, and thence burned their houses. Concerning this episode of violence, nine Romanians were sentenced to terms of 1–3 years in prison while a further 30 were fined for their violent actions against Roma. However, the terms were reportedly "short" and the courts decisions were issued based on the disturbance of public order and destruction of private property, not crimes committed against other persons. The judiciary failed to bring these offenders to justice by charging them with anti-Romani crimes, and the exact number of Roma victims was never explicitly noted (European Roma Rights Centre [ERRC], 2004).

Government-sponsored violence came to the forefront in the Jiu Valley Miner's attack in 1990 when the Romanian government sent 5,000 miners to Bucharest from the Jiu Valley to deal with protestors. The miners explained that their move was in response to unrest as a result of unemployed Roma (Crowe, 1999). When considered in tandem with the Turulung incident in which the judiciary response failed to charge offenders with anti-Romani acts, the type of violence that was and continues to be incited and encouraged by Romanian élites against the Roma is apparent. It also illustrates that anti-Roma sentiments are powerful enough that small incidents between ethnic groups can result in violent and fatal retaliation against the Roma.

Another example stems from a 1993 incident in which 500 ethnic Romanians rioted against Roma in Transylvania and burned 13 Roma houses. Violence reportedly occurred as an escalation of a skirmish over the death of a Romanian for which the Roma were blamed (István, 2005). Since 2008, East-Central Europe has seen at least nine arson attacks, eight shootings as well as several excessively violent assaults involving explosives against Roma communities. In Romania, hate violence against Roma reveal several particularly pernicious and disturbing trends. Roma are the routine victims of direct assaults on the streets as they travel from homes, workplaces, and markets. However, in other cases, as those having taken place during 2008, assailants are seeking-out entire Roma families and undertaking systematic assaults while they are in their homes. Most disturbing is the indication that little to no distinction is being made between, adults, seniors, or children. Violent offenses have been largely indiscriminate. The rise in violence can be attributed to what the Human Rights First group regards as the persistence of anti-Roma violence and discrimination by ordinary citizens in the context of abusive patterns of treatment of Roma by police and public authorities.

These incidents of brutality perpetrated by both Romanian political élites and the Romanian population demonstrate deep hatred and threat to the culture of peace. It derives not only from the threat that Roma mobilization allegedly poses to national homogenization; but also, because of resentment concerning Roma economic burdens on the Romanian state, which is introduced as a second trend of recent Roma violence. Subsequently, it is clear that violence is instrumental for the Romanians to discourage Roma ethnopolitical movements because Romanian political élites fear that the Roma minority will inevitably become a source of job competition if they are able to gain rights and overcome current exclusionary institutionalized obstacles. Presently, Roma marginality is perpetuated by the dismal "prospect of working in an increasingly privatized economy, in which employers could freely discriminate against them" (Jenne, 2000, p. 200).

Resentment concerning Roma economic dependency on state welfare systems, presents a second significant factor, which many cite as a central cause of continuing violence and exclusionary policies against the Roma. As the UNDP (United Nations Development Program) Report states:

> Roma participation in social protection systems is asymmetrical, specifically as a group they receive more than they pay. The asymmetry is an important cause of social tensions and ultimately exclusion (Ivanov et al., 2002, p. 6).

Some sources reiterate the pervasiveness of stereotypes of the Roma continuing to act as a source of deprivation on Romania's social services. On one hand, there is a strong indication that Romanians are exasperated by what many unemployed members of Romanian society have in spite of the fact that they are jobless. On the other hand, there are signs that the Roma are blamed for the nation's economic problems, especially given that images of Roma as indolent criminals are easily aroused in Romanian public sentiment.

Another facet of the contradictory implications of democratization on the Roma is the emergence of extreme Romanian nationalist parties, which still exist and retain enough political power to be influential—supporting policies of national homogenization, which inevitably opposes Roma goals. Further causes of violence become byproducts of the electoral process as well as the various advocate groups that operate competitively within it. In Romania these include some extreme nationalist organizations, such as the Party of Romania National Unity and the Greater Romania Party (Verdery, 1993, p. 186). These two groups, in particular, do not hesitate to use xenophobic, anti-Semitic, anti-Gypsy and anti-Hungarian rhetoric in an attempt to inflame public opinion against other nationalities and ethnic minorities within Romania.

Overall, while the Roma may have succeeded in mobilizing and sustaining some political organizations through somewhat recent democratization processes, they are still excluded from positions of power in a broader picture. Roma politicians have been unable to become elected into parliament, occupying just a single seat, the minimum that is allotted to each minority group by the government; and face newly legitimized and strengthened oppositional parties based on strong Roma hatred (European Roma Rights Center).

The Hungarian Minority

The globe is such an overlapping and inter-mixing of different cultural nations, argues Alfred Stepan, that less than 20 of the almost 200 states in the world are homogeneous nation-states. While the existence of the Roma population in Romania contributes to the sentiment, the Hungarian minority represents still another of many ethnic clusters throughout the country. For seven decades the Hungarians of Transylvania have been Romanian citizens, and participating in a social, political, cultural, and linguistic environment *as* Romanians. Approximately 1.7–2 million ethnic-Hungarians live predominantly in Romania's Transylvania region. Increasingly, there is little room in Romania for Hungarians, Germans, or anyone considered "outsiders". Romania's official stance on the issue of minorities is to assimilate, making room only for Hungarian-speaking, or German-speaking Romanians, who are considered Romanian first. Thus, Romania's policy has sought significantly to accommodate only what may be perceived of as "insiders". Anyone else is immediately branded as "nationalists" whose existence ultimately runs headlong into Romania's nationalist interests and hegemonic policies.

Considerable emphasis has been placed on the role of the Hungarian minority in the Romanian revolution. According to the 1992 census, approximately 1,624,959—7.12% of the total Romanian population—persons identified themselves as Hungarian, while estimated data accumulated by the Romanian government indicates that the number of persons whose native-tongue is Hungarian exceeds 1.8 million.

Romanian-Hungarian relations have often been one of the most critical in East-Central Europe. When the modern nation-building process took place in the nineteenth century, Hungarians in Transylvania considered themselves belonging to the Hungarian nation, while Romanians in Transylvania identified themselves as the modern Romanian national movement. Other interests and orientations that defined Hungarians politically, socially, and culturally, were tools for the development of a mythological historical narrative. In some cases, this narrative was based on conflict. The product of these fabrications was decades of political and military confrontations between Hungary and Romania.

Conflict Prevention in Romania

Long-standing enmity between Romanians and ethnic minorities in Romania is a permanent part of the Romanian historical narrative. Indeed, there has been a stable abhorrence toward both the Roma and Romania's ethnic Hungarians, but in the case of the latter, ethnic conflict did not evolve into arrant violence or war. In the case of the former, ethnic conflict has not only been a discontinuous feature of Romania's history, excessive violence and the use of brutal force have come to be common elements in the relationship as well. Romanians have dominated both minorities, and have enjoyed the benefits of their domination over them as well as the resultant social, political, and economic stratification.

Romanians, in both cases, may be viewed as a privileged group of landlords holding power over weak tenants. Their exploitation and unequal treatment of the Roma and Hungarians has not rested on power and coercion alone, rather it has involved a much more complex relationship of social, political, and economic transition amid a backdrop of Communist repression and stagnation. The Romanian ideology of domination over both groups has been routinely diffused officially by Romania's political elites, as well as by less formal sources of ideological domination. Romanians have demonstrated their belief in remaining the privileged group, deserving of good fortune, inclusion, and socio-economic dispensation while the country's ethnic minorities are deserving of marginalization and socio-economic deprivation.

The preservation of peace, or at the very least, the continuation of Romanian relations with the Hungarian-minority on a non-violent level is the result of three main factors. The first is political reform and democratic transition that occurred as a result of the Romanian government's initiative to become a part of NATO (North Atlantic Treaty Organization) and the EU (European Union). In this regard, the Romanian government changed the manner in which it addressed its Hungarian-minority. As a result of this shift in Romanian political conduct, the Hungarian government also adopted a reformed approach to its relations with Romania as part of Hungary's efforts to support Romania's bid for membership with the two organizations and subsequent entrance into their affiliated institutions and structures. The Romanian government's interest in becoming closer with NATO and the EU produced a counter-intervention against the ethnic-minority within Romania. As a result, Romania's ethnic policy improved.

The second factor that enabled the preservation of peace between Romanians and the Hungarian-minority was the carrot-and-stick approach that that EU took to initiate desired reforms within Romania. The EU has yet to admit a country to the institutions of the EU so long does not meet democratic practices criteria as set by the EU. At the time, Romania was still embroiled in ethnic-conflict and domestic disputes with its Hungarian-minority. In turn, this coerced Romanian institutions to adopt a more transparent and cooperative approach with ethnic-groups within its own borders as well as those operating external to the Romanian state. Teodor Meleşcanu, former Romanian Minister of Foreign Affairs, explains the motivating factor behind integration as, "a means and a catalyst to speed up the transition [of accession to the European Union]" (1996, p. 27).

The realization of the main objectives and priorities Romania to achieve integration with NATO and the EU, and to enjoy the full benefits offered by their respective institutions, was a prime factor in mitigating the domestic issues within Romania. Both NATO and the EU realized new sources of power and influence on Romania's interethnic relations since the mid-1990s.

Romania's miserable rating at the turn of the 1990s over its conditions for the consolidation of democracy—lack of democratic values, the government's strangle hold on civil society, poor level of economic performance and development, transitional agenda including modes through which transition was to be achieved—were all part-and-parcel to the label that was applied to Romania as having the worst chances for democratic consolidation. Romania strongly directed itself toward the establishment of a fundamental approach whereupon basic human rights, democratic rights and freedoms, economic transition, and respect for the development of a civil society would be key operatives.

The third factor that kept tension between Romania and the Hungarian-minority at bay included initiatives that took place within the minority itself. Whereas the Roma were given the opportunity to assimilate by way of government policies aimed at homogenizing Romania but have opted for segregation, the story is different for the Hungarian-minority. Hungarian reformers undertook a cooperative approach with Romanian representatives in favour of democratic reform in order to achieve their aims.

With Romania's sizeable Hungarian minority population, improving relations with Hungary was one of the most important aims of Romania in order to procure membership to the EU. Romania, with its direct interest in the EU, signed a European Stability Pact in March 1995 in an attempt to "[...] foster good neighbourly relations between the countries of central and eastern Europe" as well as to "[...] encourage the post-Communist countries to resolve mutual historical grievances regarding ethnic minorities and frontiers" (Cook, 1995). Romania also signed the framework FCNM (Convention for the Protection of National Minorities) as well as the ECRML (European Charter for Regional Minority Languages) on 17 July 1995. International law takes precedence over Romania's domestic law in the area of human rights and international treaties, as well as various EU conventions that have been ratified by Romania. Accordingly, all international law is thence applicable in Romanian law (Constitution of Romania, 1991).

Both the Romanian government and the Hungarian-minority operated in a symbiotic relationship during these processes, resulting in their mutual benefit. For example, Ethnic-Hungarians living within Romania greatly gained a considerable advantage in their cause for recognition by Romanian authorities as a result of the international human rights documentation as well as the "carrot" of EU-membership being offered to Romania. A direct benefit emerged in the form of political representation for Hungarians in the Romanian government. The Hungarian minority party, UDMR (Democratic Union of Hungarians in Romania) was included in the government coalition. Its inclusion afforded the minority considerable political leverage as the Romanian government received a significant boost in its international reputation.

Overcoming Ethnic Hatred: Lessons for Ethnic Conflict Management

While the previous sections of this chapter have addressed theories of ethnic violence and hatred, the experience of the Roma and of the Hungarian-minorities in contemporary Romanian society, this section establishes a model of ethnic conflict prevention based on the Hungarian experience as a contribution to the theory and practice of peace as part of the field of *peace psychology*. Three factors essential for peacebuilding include: (1) the inclusion of international institutions; (2) the promotion of social organizations, and the fostering of a collective civil society; (3) social reconciliation initiatives. They should be regarded and understood as *conditio sine qua non* of any well-formulated peacebuilding program.

The most significant implication that follows from recognition of interactive and cooperative strategies for conflict prevention and peacebuilding is that collective strength can severely temper chaos and violence during periods of régime change, especially in post-Soviet successor states, such as Romania. Not only does the following model address current violence or conflict in the majority-minority context, it also seeks to check *opportunities* for violence that accompany transitional periods in *weaker* states. Each element within the triadic model for peacebuilding are united by the same goals and guided by the same principles (Fig. 13.1).

Together, they create a vector of activities that converge and flow in the same direction. It should be noted that there is no leader or explicit hierarchy among the elements. However, a unique blend of organic and synthetic labours exist that work closely together. Subsequently, they can provide social, political, and legal solutions to mediate ethnic tension and conflict.

Although domestic politics and transitional waves taking place in Romania should be seen as cardinal factors in the majority-minority outcomes, emphasis should also be placed on international influence. The implication of external actors on the interethnic dynamic in relation to the Romanian government cultivated grassroots activity, empowered civil society, and brought about a change in the ethnic disposition of many political élites and their policies. To be sure, there was an

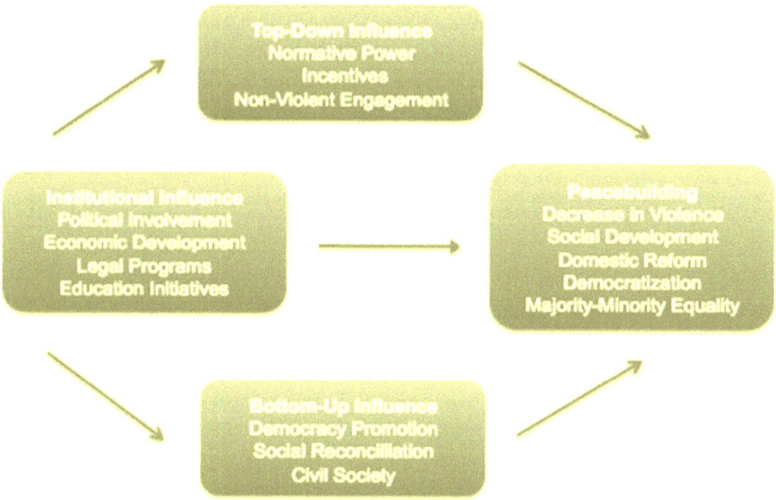

Fig. 13.1 Triadic model for peacebuilding

immediate and marked change in tolerance levels on the political stage during the mid-1990s. However, the diffusion of tolerance in interethnic relations to the bases of Romanian public society was both a sluggish and protracted process. Romanians and ethnic Hungarians were simply distrustful of one another; in much the same way Romanians and Roma share that same distrust. Nonetheless, Romania should be seen as solid an example of interethnic understanding and progress given the path the country has experienced. The reconciliation and rapprochement witnessed between Romanians and ethnic Hungarians sets the stage for strategy development that can address the same patterns of enmity observed between Romanians and the Roma minority.

Inclusion of greater numbers of international institutions during the Hungarian-minority crisis was a seminal component of achieving peace and avoiding the exhibition of extreme violence. The international human rights order has demonstrated a capacity to restrain ethnic conflict, and establishes a new standard of tolerance on all levels of societal interaction, from top to bottom. The most important aspect of the inclusion of an international human rights order is the fact that is usually diffuses from the top of the societal pyramid. In this regard, the government then retains responsibility for the proliferation of a new openness and inclusion while simultaneously benefiting from increased security within the state. During the 1990s, the Romanian government proved itself the driving force of shaping its own domestic political agenda and undertaking initiatives to alter the majority-minority dynamic. The added benefit was that the Romanian government built a more positive international reputation in a number of ways.

The second component necessary for peacebuilding is the promotion of a civil society with a specific focus on the Roma-minority. Trans-national networks seek the augmentation and strength of independent rights-based groups that would retain the specific task of monitoring the government. An increase in social organizations would also advocate for inter-ethnic cooperation in the same manner as in the ethnic-Hungarian case, and engender a greater depth of social tolerance. Since the Romanian government manufactured much of the ethnic-intolerance toward the Roma, NGO activity is a critical adjunct to the domestic-policy reform required to take place in the primary strategy.

Romania's 1996 election exemplifies the prominent role played by civil society. The events of that year demonstrate the commitment of the domestic constituency to both democratic processes as well as sustainable peace (Gallagher, 2001, p. 388). Though only a handful of NGOs were recorded to have been operating in Romania by the 1990s, the USAID (United States Agency for International Development) estimated that approximately 23,000 NGOs were registered in the country by the turn of the millennium (Andreescu, 2000). Patrice C. McMahon explains that a number of NGOs have been credited with improving the plight of the Hungarian minority by improving Romanian-Hungarian relations in some of the country's multiethnic cities during the 1990s. NGOs do not necessarily have to maintain a focus on conflict prevention or on specific issues that plague minorities to improve their situation, given that, "by association and reputation, there is a reason to believe that even the presence of NGOs—regardless of their specific focus—indirectly promotes and sustains inter-ethnic cooperation" (McMahon, 2007, p. 135).

Peacebuilding in the context of the Roma requires the presence of Romania's active social organizations, which depend significantly on foreign funding. But this is not enough. Additionally, the primary agents of change will be a result of the creation of new advocacy and social groups that concentrate on issues that affect the Roma minority indirectly as well. Romania is now tightly linked with the international community of actors and social movements committed to the prevention of ethnic conflict and peacebuilding. The country has been very successful at attracting local, regional, and international social organization attention in early every corridor of collective social action.

The third element, upon which peacebuilding between Romanians and the Roma rests, is the establishment of social reconciliation programs. The incentive of this type of initiative is to replace conflict and confrontation with a pattern of dialogue. Historical and longstanding enmity between rivaling ethnic groups can be moderated successfully by discussing issues of nationalist rhetoric, historical claims on territory, and abuses in the arena of human rights. Such an initiative has yet to be introduced within the framework of Romanian-Roma hostilities but its potential for success is illustrated through the 2000 electoral campaign in Romania known as the PER (Project on Ethnic Relations). The PER proposed to legislate nationalist rhetoric during the 2000 campaign, and represented the first instance in Romanian history whereby politicians in Romania signed and openly pledged the elimination of propaganda during the electoral campaign.

Social reconciliation initiatives possess the potential for manufacturing peace in two distinct ways. First, they publicly illustrate the commitment and promise by all parties involved to maintain open-minded attitudes and ethnic tolerance toward each other. Second, the concept makes possible the opportunity for parties to act on their declared tolerance and understanding. Although it is the first step in a more significant social reconciliation process, it enables the majority-minority to demonstrate commitment to peacebuilding as well as a source of stimulation for the respect of ethnic diversity.

Social reconciliation should be regarded as a fundamental element in the amelioration of ethnic tensions between Hungarian minorities and Romanian in Romanian society. Not only does the reconciliation process build a foundation of healing through signs of *forgiveness*, *tolerance*, and *understanding*, entering into a process of social reconciliation represents a much more profound change taking place in the societal structures of a state. As is the case with Romania, the process took place "[...] in society that provoked, promoted and sustained violence" (Schreiter, 1997, pp. 111–112). Miroslav Volf (1998) articulates the notion of social reconciliation through his "theology of embrace," in which the distinction is stressed between the "will to embrace" and the "embrace itself".

Since social reconciliation cannot be seen as a process limited to the role of any single agent, group, or belief, in mitigating or solving ethnic conflict, it should then be understood as a critical component in the formulation of a comprehensive strategy for rapprochement on the social, political, and cultural levels of a society. The peacebuilding model is reliant upon the idea of social reconstruction processes. It played a positive role in alleviating the victimization of both Hungarians and Romanians throughout the ethnic conflict that took place during the 1990s. As the promotion of peaceful attitudes and understanding between conflicting or rivaling ethnic groups grows and the hate-gap begins to close, we realize an incremental change in the democratic status of the society in question. The process of social reconciliation, in bringing groups closer together and creating an atmosphere of inclusion whereupon a greater portion of the country's peoples may participate in state operations, leads directly to democratization. Thus, our understanding of "embracing" and the "will to embrace" contributes, not just to the social reconciliation work taking place, but to all three components of the triadic model.

The three coterminous mechanisms presented herein represent the general basis of a model for peacebuilding and conflict prevention in Romania. The model seeks to approximate influence for social functioning while including members of both the Romanian side of the ledger as well as members of the Roma minority. In this sense, it may be characterized as a combination of material and normative controls. As McMahon explains about prior peacebuilding achievements in Romania, "[...] there is little evidence to suggest that normative strategies alone would have led to the important changes of the second half of the 1990s" (2007, p. 183). Thus, the model does not intend to be fuelled by normative strategies alone. It takes as its operating assumption collaboration and mutual aid.

In the case of the Hungarian minority in Romania, the increased presence of NGOs and international attention were marked factors that brought about a reduction of the tension and overt conflict between Hungarian minorities and Romanians. The same is certainly not the case in the Roma context. The impact of the strategies used by Western NGOs in relationship-development was executed through a sector-specific focus. In many cases, the NGOs operated under tight financial constraints and limited institutional support. Thus, when considered in whole, efforts toward ameliorating conflict between Hungarians and Romanians were successful because these relations received considerable attention, whereas relations between Roma and Romanians were not part of the design.

Ethnic Hungarians and Roma were treated as separate cases. Strategies and efforts employed were simply geared toward the reduction of ethnic conflict in one cultural sector of Romanian society. Moreover, a stable constitutional environment in Romania as it may pertain to the Hungarian minority has also contributed to the ongoing development of peaceful relations between the two ethnic groups while Roma people have found little vacancy in the realm of constitutional rights and freedoms, this stood as and continues to remain a sharp impetus for ongoing tension in the Roma-Romanian case.

The Hungarian-Romanian tension that was prevalent throughout the 1990s has not been extinguished, but rather reduced to a simmering tensity and should be considered latent in general terms. Throughout Romania so-called "hate-speech incubators" (Crawford, 2009) that increase the possibility of violence and collective violent action remain prevalent. An active scene of online-violence in Romania channels nationalistic discontents toward Roma, Hungarians, Muslims, and Homosexuals, to name a few minority groups within the country. The Hungarian case may have experienced a stroke of luck by decreasing in enmity prior to the new millennium. Romania experienced an incredible surge of social and political change throughout all societal levels during this time. These trends merged with uncertain and negative economic prospects for the country, yielding a rapidly deteriorating image of the Roma population, who attracted considerable attention in the form of hatred and physical violence. The combination of negative feelings and increasing frustration over social, political, and economic uncertainty within Romania had been characterized by national slogans, campaign, and hateful messages.

Taming activities that seek to directly injure and destroy, as well as those socially, politically, or economically supported—albeit indirectly—is the intended result of the model presented in this chapter. Where lies the essential connection between peacebuilding and conflict prevention, and peace psychology? As peace psychology addresses *structural* violence that deprives people of basic human need satisfaction (Christie, 1997; Pilisuk, 1998; Schwebel, 1997), this work should be considered a component of the peacebuilding efforts associated with such distinct areas of research and practice.

Even as the ethnic strife, prevalent in contemporary Romanian society, centers heavily on ethnic hatred and multi-factorial bases of interpersonal aggression and violence, it possesses nascent potential. Ethnic hatred against the Roma is a form of structural violence. When systematic and endemic factors of collective violence and hatred are moderated in one region of the world, the potential for repeating the process elsewhere increases. The result is an increased culture of peace, with each region serving as a model with which to promote peace in another region.

Conclusion

Many of the issues that surfaced between Romanians and the Hungarian minority were holdovers from decades past, but still represented the potential for further confrontation on the domestic level. Romania is now charged with managing the Roma question in its domestic political domain. More broadly, the narrative of Romanian interaction with the Roma and ethnic Hungarian minority delivers a corpus of ideas on how to learn from previous decades of violence and ethnic conflict. It is also filled with what lessons could and ultimately should be applied to the management of peace and conflict prevention in South-East Europe as well as in other parts of Europe and throughout our intricately connected global village.

As one of the central factors on overcoming ethnic conflict in Romania's domestic relations, the government's reforms were developed and implemented with the European Union and membership to European institutions at its core. Romanian officials have stated that the "carrot" incentive of EU-membership was a critical feature of the reformation that took place on Romania's interethnic domestic front. As membership into the EU and access to many of its institutions was Romania's primary goal, this imperative defined, directed, and fortified the direction of Romanian domestic policy, particularly as it pertained to the government's approach to the management of the issues centering on the Hungarian minority. Yet, the establishment of a robust civil society was also of paramount importance in the realization of a new mode of standards when dealing with ethnic strife. NGOs that sprouted throughout the country by the thousands brought about a significantly crucial transparency for Romanian politics with respect to minority rights. Social reconciliation was no less important in the establishment of a cooperative and communicative relationship between Romanian authorities and the Hungarian minority.

Ultimately, the 1990s provides key insights for addressing the Roma case. A model developed on the lessons related to that period should therefore be expected to successfully transform the current majority-minority dynamic in the Roma case. Since conflict prevention is about early detection, the Hungarian case should thus be understood and interpreted as such. Military intervention is not necessary to end ethnic violence, confrontation or hatred. Rather, as this chapter has presented, collaborative, communicative and committed governments, institutions and peoples are the seminal components to managing ethnic conflict and for building sustainable peace. Perhaps the most important lesson is that government initiatives alone are insufficient as conflict prevention strategies in and of themselves. A range of instruments from top-down to bottom-up strategies are critical for cementing ethnic cooperation and regional stability.

Every conflict requires a fresh and shared critical reflection. Since each conflict and violent scenario successfully managed provides us with a perspective with which to successfully manage the next, our efforts should focus on positive peace, and on what we can *collectively* achieve. Although there is no single model or strategy for the prevention of ethnic conflict in every corridor of the contemporary international system, there are always solutions to overcoming ethnic hatred and peacebuilding in divided societies.

Acknowledgments The author would like to express his sincere appreciation to all those who read through drafts of this chapter and provided insightful feedback.

References

Andreescu, G. (2000). Pages from the Romanian-Hungarian reconciliation, 1989–1999: The role of civic organizations. In L. Nastase & L. Salat (Eds.), Interethnic Relations in Post-Communist Romania: Proceedings of the Conference the Romanian Model of Ethnic Relations, The Last Ten Years, The Next Ten Years (pp. 89–122). Cluj: Ethnocultural Diversity in Romania Series.

Barany, Z. (2002). *The east European gypsies: Regime change, marginality and ethnopolitics*. Cambridge: Cambridge University Press.

Bernáth, G., & Messing, V. (2004). Seen from afar: Roma in the Hungarian media. *European Roma Rights Centre (ERRC)*. Retrieved February 6, 2011, from http://www.errc.org/cikk.php?cikk=1168.

Boswell, T., & Dixon, W. J. (1993). Marx's theory of rebellion: A cross-national analysis of class exploitation, economic development, class exploitation, and violent revolt. *American Sociological Review, 58*, 681–702.

Centre for Documentation and Information on Minorities in Europe—Southeast Europe (CEDIME-SE). Minorities in Southeast Europe: Roma of Romania, 2001, from http://www.greekhelsinki.gr/english/reports/CEDIME-Reports-Minorities-in-Romania.html.

Christie, D. J. (1997). Reducing direct and structural violence: The human needs theory. *Peace and Conflict: Journal of Peace Psychology, 3*, 315–332.

CIA World Factbook. (2010). Romania Demographics Profile 2010. *Index Mundi*. Retrieved February 24, 2011, from http://www.indexmundi.com/romania/demographics_profile.html.

Constitution of Romania. (1991). Art. 11, 20, In *Monitorul Oficial* (Official Gazette of Romania), Part I, No. 233.

Cook, J. (1995). Stability pact tries hard to encourage good behaviour between neighbours. *European Dialogue, 1*. Retrieved January 12, 2010, from http://europa.eu.int/en/comm/dg10/infcom/eur_dial/index.html.

Corntassel, J. J. (2003). Who is indigenous? 'Peoplehood' and ethnonationalist approaches to rearticulating indigenous identities. *Nationalism and Ethnic Politics, 9*(1), 75–100.

Council of Europe: Commissioner for Human Rights. (2009). Many Roma in Europe are stateless and live outside social protection. Retrieved November 3, 2010, from http://www.unhcr.org/refword/docid/4a7023c72.html.

Crawford, B. (2009). Speaker highlights internet sites as 'hate speech incubators'. *The University Star, 22*. Retrieved August 25, 2010, from http://star.txtstate.edu/content/speaker-highlights-internet-sites-'hate-speech-incubator'.

Crowe, D. M. (1999). The gypsies of eastern Europe since 1990. *Nationalities Papers, 27*(1), 57–67.

Deutsch, M. (1999). Hope with optimism: A commentary on Brewster Smith's article. *Peace and Conflict: Journal of Peace Psychology, 5*, 17–21.

Dick, C. J., Dunn, J. F., & Lough, B. K. (1993). Potential sources of conflict in post-c communist Europe. *European Security, 2*(3), 386–406.

Dovidio, J. F., & Gaertner, S. L. (1998). Intergroup bias. In D. T. Gilbert, S. T. Fiske, & G. Lindzey (Eds.), *The handbook of social psychology* (5th ed., Vol. 2, pp. 1184–1121). Hoboken, NJ: John Wiley & Sons, Inc.

Dumitriu-Seuleanu, C. (1997). The media: Social construction in inter-ethnic communication in Romania. In A. Klinke, O. Renn, & J. P. Lehners (Eds.), *Ethnic conflict in civil society: Proposals for a new era in eastern Europe* (pp. 177–203). Aldershot, UK: Ashgate.

Erjavec, K., Hrvaten, S. B., & Kelbl, B. (2000). *We about the Roma: Discriminatory discourse in Slovenia*. Ljubljana, Slovenia: Open Society Institute-Slovenia.

European Roma Rights Centre (ERRC). Retrieved January 10, 2010 from http://www.cidm.umd.edu/inscr/mar/data/rumromachro.htm.

Gallagher, T. (2001). Building democracy in Romania: Internal shortcomings and external neglect. In J. Zielonka & A. Pravda (Eds.), *Democratic consolidation in eastern Europe* (pp. 383–413). Oxford: Oxford University Press.

Gilley, B. (2004). Against the concept of ethnic conflict. *Third World Quarterly, 25*(6), 1155–1166.

Gurr, T. R. (2000). Ethnic warfare on the wane. *Foreign Affairs, 79*(3), 52–65.

Iacoboaea, C. (2009). Slums in Romania. *Theoretical and Empirical Researches in Urban Management, 1*(10), 101–113.

István, H. (2005). Case Study No. 151: the case of Hădăreni, fighting against discrimination and equal opportunities for Roma in court. *Local government and public service reform initiative: Managing multi-ethnic communities project.* Budapest: Open Society Institute.

Ivanov, A., et al. (2002). *The Roma in central and eastern Europe: Avoiding the dependency trap.* Bratislava: UNDP, Regional Bureau for Europe and the Commonwealth of Independent States.

Jenne, E. K. (2000). The Roma of central and eastern Europe: Constructing a stateless nation. In J. Stein (Ed.), *The politics of national minority participation in post-communist Europe: State-building, democracy, and ethnic mobilization* (pp. 269–285). Armonk, NY: M. E. Sharpe.

Kalibová, K. (2000). Caractéristique démographiques de la population rom/tsigane dans certain pays d'Europe centrale et orientale. In H. Werner (Ed.), *Les caractéristique démographiques des minoritiés nationals dans certains Etats européens* (Vol. 2). Strasbourg: Council of Europe.

Kaufman, J. P. (2002). *NATO and the former Yugoslavia: Crisis, conflict, and the Atlantic alliance.* Oxford: Rowman & Littlefield Publishers.

Kessler, T., & Mummendey, A. (2001). Is there any scapegoat around? Determinants of intergroup conflict at different categorization levels. *Journal of Personality and Social Psychology, 81*, 1090–1102.

Laitan, D., & Fearon, J. (1996). Explaining interethnic cooperation. *American Political Science Review, 90*(4), 715–735.

Matley, I. M. (1970). *Romania: A profile.* New York: Praeger Publishers.

McMahon, P. (2007). *Taming ethnic hatred: Ethnic cooperation and transnational networks in eastern Europe.* Syracuse, NY: Syracuse University Press.

Melescanu, T. (1996). The accession to the European Union: The fundamental opinion of Romania's foreign policy. *Romanian Journal of International Affairs, 2*(4), 1–10.

O'Loughlin, J. V., & Van der Wusten, H. (Eds.). (1993). *The new political geography of eastern Europe.* London: Belhaven Press.

O'Neill, D. C., & Black, R. C. (2007). A modernization theory: Economic growth, income equality and democratization. *Paper presented at the annual meeting of the midwest political science association*, Palmer House Hotel, Chicago, IL. Retrieved December 16, 2009, from http://www.allacademic.com/meta/p196991_index.html.

Oberschall, A. (1989). Opportunities and framing in the east European revolutions in 1989. In D. McAdam, M. Zald, & J. McCarty (Eds.), *Comparative perspectives in social movements.* New York: Cambridge University Press.

Pilisuk, M. (1998). The hidden structure of contemporary violence. *Peace and Conflict: Journal of Peace Psychology, 4*, 197–216.

Rady, M. (1995). *Nationalism and nationality in Romania: Contemporary nationalism in east central Europe.* Houndmills: MacMillan Press Ltd.

Sarkees, M. R., Wayman, F., & Singer, J. D. (2003). Inter-state, intra-state, and extra-state wars: A comprehensive look at their distribution over time, 1816–1997. *International Studies Quarterly, 43*, 49–70.

Schreiter, R. J. (1997). *Reconciliation: Mission and ministry in a changing social order.* Maryknoll, NY: Orbis Books.

Schwebel, M. (1997). Job insecurity as structural violence: Implications for destructive intergroup conflict. *Peace and Conflict: Journal of Peace Psychology, 3*, 333–251.
Shafir, M. (2000). The political party as national holding company: The Hungarian democratic federation of Romania. In J. Stein (Ed.), *The politics of national minority participation in post-communist Europe: State-building, democracy, and ethnic mobilization* (pp. 101–128). Armonk, NY: M. E. Sharpe.
Snyder, J. L. (2000). *From voting to violence: Democratization and nationalist conflict*. New York: Norton.
Susan, O., & Nagel, J. (1986). A competition model of ethnic collective action in American cities, 1877–1889. In S. Olzak & J. Nagel (Eds.), *Competitive ethnic relations* (pp. 17–46). New York: Academic Press.
Tanasoiu, C. (2007). The Tismaneanu report: Romania revisits its past. *Problems of Post-Communism, 54*(4), 60–69.
Transue, J. E. (2007). Identity salience, identity acceptance, and racial policy attitudes: American national identity as a uniting force. *American Journal of Political Science, 51*(1), 78–91.
United Nations Development Programme (UNDP). (2002). Roma: Human development challenges and opportunities. Retrieved August 21, 2010, from http://www.roma.undp.sk.
Van Evera, S. (1994). Hypotheses on nationalism and war. *International Studies Quarterly, 18*(4), 5–39.
Verdery, K. (1993). Nationalism and national sentiment in post-socialist Romania. *Slavic Review, 52*(2), 179–203.
Volf, M. (1998). The clumsy embrace. *Christianity Today, 42*(12).
Williams, R. M. (1994). The sociology of ethnic conflicts: Comparative international perspectives. *Annual Review of Sociology, 20*, 49–79.
Williams, P. R., & Waller, K. M. (2004). Coercive appeasement: The flawed international response to the Serbian rogue regime. *New England Law Review, 36*(4), 825–889.

Chapter 14
Coming to Terms with the Past Marked by Collective Crimes: Collective Moral Responsibility and Reconciliation

Sabina Čehajić-Clancy

Abstract This chapter addressed a question pertinent for all post-conflict societies but particularly for those characterized by commission of massive and collective violence. The question as to how people should deal with massive human rights violations committed by their group was analyzed. It was argued that acceptance of collective (moral) responsibility is the key process for sustainable, peaceful, and democratic future. This theoretical and practical argument was followed by empirical evidence from different studies (set in the context of post-conflict Bosnia and Herzegovina) illustrating possible socio-psychological predictors and consequences of acknowledgment and acceptance of collective (moral) responsibility. The findings of two empirical studies demonstrated the importance of intergroup contact for the process of public acknowledgment of one's group responsibility for committed atrocities. The findings of a third study showed that affirming a positive aspect of the self can increase one's willingness to acknowledge ingroup responsibility for wrongdoings against others, express feelings of group-based guilt, and consequently provide greater support for reparation policies.

Keywords Acknowledgment • Collective responsibility • Intergroup reconciliation • Intergroup contact • Self-affirmation

S. Čehajić-Clancy (✉)
Political Science and International Relations Department, Sarajevo School of Science and Technology, Bistrik 7, 71000, Sarajevo, Bosnia and Herzegovina
e-mail: sabina.cehajic@ssst.edu.ba

O. Simić et al. (eds.), *Peace Psychology in the Balkans: Dealing with a Violent Past while Building Peace*, Peace Psychology Book Series, DOI 10.1007/978-1-4614-1948-8_14,

Introduction

The twentieth century seems to be blighted by mass crimes and collective atrocities. From the slaughter of Armenians in 1915, Jews in the Second World War, to the genocide in Rwanda and Bosnia in the 1990s, the capacity for groups to inflict suffering and death on each other seems tragically not to have diminished. After commission of grave mass atrocities, the task of any post-conflict society is to reconstruct a just and inclusive social and political environment. A key strategy to this is to confront a past by (re)establishing justice and reconciliation. The question is how.

Despite all this appalling bloodshed, one encouraging feature of some of these conflicts has been the emergence of political debate over the question of how perpetrator groups should react or respond to what they have done (Barkan, 2000; Minow, 1998). Unfortunately, people are apt to be reluctant to admit that their own group might be responsible for the pain and suffering inflicted on members of other groups (Cohen, 2001). To put it simply, a common reaction seems to be denial. People seem to be able to find ways to deny the facts of what has been done in their group's name. In these denials – be they expressed as deliberate lies or sincere beliefs – any reconciliatory process is obstructed. Indeed, arguably it is these very same attitudes that allowed the atrocities to be committed in the first place (Cohen, 2001). Denials do not only serve the purpose of protection (and preservation) of social and personal identity but also may reinforce the commission of further atrocities. In this chapter, I will argue that acceptance of collective moral responsibility is crucial for restoration of broken and damaged intergroup relations and ultimately sustainable reconciliation. I will also present some recent empirical findings demonstrating which socio-psychological processes might facilitate willingness to personally accept collective responsibility even if one has not personally been involved in the commission of atrocities. And finally, I will finish this chapter by concluding that taking responsibility for the past is a moral prerequisite for a peaceful future.

Dealing with the Past

Before I talk about acceptance of collective moral responsibility being a crucial predictor of sustainable intergroup reconciliation, the question that needs to be asked is whether members of a post-conflict society need to deal with their past at all. Do people living in any post-conflict context need to face the past marked by various human rights violations or should they rather ignore it? There are at least two answers to this question. On one hand, one can endorse politics of forgetting for the sake of moving on, as it is often said and believed. On the other hand, one can insist on making the past (with all its consequences) a subject matter of public discourse and political actions. I believe that in order to move on as a society from a conflictual, broken and damaged intergroup relations towards reconciled and peaceful future, all members of post-conflict communities need to deal with their burden of heritage. The entire society with all its members should embark on a systematic and reflective adoption of knowledge, acknowledgment, and acceptance of truth which, preferably, should be relatively independent from other interests as posed by post-conflict transitional processes.

Forgetting or endorsing politics of forgetting is neither sensible nor logical as our present is marked and defined by the past. Our today is inevitable marked by the heritage of yesterday. The very same word heritage implies the presence of the past in the here and now. One cannot ignore the fact that our present is surrounded or burdened with economical, political, moral and cultural consequences of the past. Consequently, forgetting is not psychologically or politically possible. However, one can still choose to ignore it even if forgetting might not be feasible. But is such ignorance going to bring us forward?

I believe that coming to terms with the past is a political and psychological imperative for any post-conflict society which strives towards a democratic future, based on the rule of law and respect for human rights. Dealing with a past marked by collective atrocities and human rights violations through acceptance of collective moral responsibility is, in my view, a precondition for re-establishing a just and inclusive society based on truth, justice and reconciliation. This, however, should not imply that other social and political processes such as establishment of truth and justice are not as important as acceptance of collective moral responsibility for establishment of reconciled and just society. I, however, will focus primarily on the phenomena of collective responsibility, as the moral response to commission of atrocities.

After arguing that members of any post-conflict society need to deal with their past in order to move towards a better future, the question that arises is what kind of moral attitudes should people have towards injustices committed by members of their group and/or in one's name? In other words, all members of a political community need to ask the question "what attitude should we have or take towards the past marked by collective crimes committed in our name?" My answer to this question is: acceptance of collective moral responsibility.

Why Collective Moral Responsibility Matters?

Before trying to define the concept of collective responsibility, one should ask whether acceptance of collective responsibility is important and needed for restoration of post-conflict societies at all.

Intergroup reconciliation may be difficult to achieve without acceptance of collective responsibility (Gilbert, 2001; Lederach, 1997; Minow, 1998; Tutu, 1999). Until there is a recognition both by group leaders, direct perpetrators and also by all the other group members of what has been done (very often in their own name) and what their group's past behaviour has cost another people, there can be no real dialogue, and hence reconciliation will be impeded (Cohen, 2001).

Collective and public truth telling is one important process which can contribute to intergroup reconciliation (Staub, 2006): First, this is because victims desire and need recognition by those who hurt them in any way (Tutu, 1999). Offering acknowledgment to the victim group provides an opportunity for restoration of intergroup trust and ultimately relationships (Dimitrijevic, 2006).

Second, there is some agreement that perpetrators and their group won't be able to psychologically move forward and heal the wounds created by their actions as long as they choose to deny or justify their behaviour (Ignatieff, 1994; Staub, 2006; Tutu, 1999). Justifications, despite serving some concrete purpose (e.g., identity protection), only reinforce cycles of retaliation and a rhetoric of blame. Through sincere acknowledgment, perpetrators and all other group members can get rid of the burden or, as Hannah Arendt (1987) put it, liberate themselves from their collective heritage.

Third, acknowledgement and acceptance of responsibility by collectives entails a notion of 'never again' – the hope that exposure of the past should prevent its future repetition. Through acknowledgment of collective responsibility and provision of punishment, the occurrence of future atrocities can be discouraged (Cohen, 2001; Staub, 2006).

Finally, I would suggest that acknowledgment and acceptance of collective responsibility forms the initial psychological basis for emotions that can be felt in relation to one's group actions such as guilt, shame, or empathy (e.g., Branscombe & Doosje, 2004). For example, feelings of guilt, arising from acknowledgment and acceptance of collective responsibility, have been found to increase motivation to repair the damage caused by the behaviour of one's ingroup (e.g., Branscombe & Doosje, 2004; Brown, Gonzalez, Zagefka, Manzi, & Cehajic, 2008; Cehajic & Brown, 2008). In addition, we have also found that acknowledgment of group responsibility led to higher feelings of guilt in part because of its association with participants' willingness to take on personal responsibility for the group's actions (Cehajic, Effron, Halperin, Liberman, & Ross, in press). In other words, personal acceptance of collective responsibility acted as a significant predictor of guilt feelings felt on behalf of one's group behaviour.

After commission of grave and mass atrocities particularly those entailing killings of innocent people, the question that arise is whether one can hold all members collectively and morally responsible for crimes committed in their name. Are those who haven't done anything wrong or those who haven't been even born yet automatically responsible for crimes committed by other members of *their* group? Are they responsible even if they haven't supported nor tolerated the commission of those crimes?

Although there is some consensus regarding the necessity of acknowledgment of collective responsibility for restoration of post-conflict relations (e.g., Minow, 1998; Tutu, 1999), the question as to whether it is right to highlight the responsibility of all individuals who belong to the perpetrator group can still be debated. On the one hand, it could be argued that the concept of collective responsibility makes no sense if 'responsibility' refers exclusively to specific individual conduct. In this view, it would be inappropriate to blame people for something they neither did nor intended to do (Lewis, 1948). Unlike with personal or individual responsibility, it is not possible to prove or show the causation link between each and every group member and committed crimes in the case of collective responsibility.

On the other hand, others have regarded collective responsibility as a moral duty to respond to crimes committed in one's name and as a practical category which is a prerequisite for lasting reconciliation (Dimitrijevic, 2006). Even though I agree that acceptance of responsibility for the group's *past* behaviour might indeed be an inappropriate expectation, acceptance of responsibility for the consequences and implications of group's behaviour could be is a plausible ethical demand. The logical definition of this notion depends primarily on the nature of the crimes committed and on the character of group identity. Collective moral responsibility arises out of the fact that people share group membership in various groups that shape who these people are and that each person is at least somewhat implicated in what any member of the group does (May, 1992). In particular, in situations where collective crimes have been committed, speaking about collective responsibility becomes even more plausible.

Collective crimes need to be differentiated from individually committed wrongs. Collective crimes are crimes which have been committed by a significantly large number of people against other social groups and in the name of one's own group. According to Radzik (2001), collective crimes imply collective intent to commit specific acts, collective awareness of the nature of intended crimes, organized effort to realize the intention, and collective awareness of atrocities' consequences. Taking all this into the equation, acceptance of collective responsibility becomes a more plausible and logical concept.

In order to be more specific, we could take Serbia under the Milosevic regime during 1990s as an example. The type of atrocities committed by Serbian government at that time include mass killings, torture, execution, elimination, annihilation, property destruction, destruction of cultural, religious and other societal symbols which all would qualify as collective mass crimes (Wachtel & Bennett, 2009). Second and besides the commission of collective atrocities, normalization across the nation of the same atrocities took place including the ideological, legal, and political institutionalization of mass violence. Such an institutionalized normalization created a value system where commission of atrocities against the 'enemy' was not only accepted but also morally acceptable. Third and as a final step, it could be argued that such twisted institutionalized values and norms were internalized by majority of group members (Dimitrijevic, 2006).

In conclusion to the above, speaking and demanding acceptance of collective responsibility in terms of a moral response to atrocities committed by one's group becomes a plausible response. However, before one can speak about acceptance, one needs to demand *acknowledgment* of collective responsibility for committed crimes which is more than simply knowing the facts. It implies acknowledgment of the meaning of actions committed by one's group such as human rights violations. It implies conscious and public acceptance that the actions of one's ingroup have violated important moral precepts (Cehajic & Brown, 2010). In other words, acknowledgment of collective responsibility entails conscious and public acceptance of the meaning of one's group behaviour. However, such a conscious acceptance or acknowledgment of the character, meaning and nature of group behavior can be impeded by ideological, political or legal institutionalization of atrocities which made commission of those atrocities appear as morally acceptable in the first place. Therefore and in order to tackle the roots of the problem, acknowledgment of collective responsibility needs to extend itself to the above mentioned forms and processes of institutionalization of atrocities.

Finally and for the sake of clarity, I need to stress that acceptance of collective moral responsibility should not imply that all group members are responsible for the actions of other group members but rather express a moral duty to respond to crimes committed in one's name. Acceptance of collective responsibility does inherently imply that a whole group is held responsible but it does not and should not mean that all group members are individually or personally responsible. In the context of post-conflict reconciliation attempts, acceptance of collective responsibility should be regarded as a practical category oriented towards the future and should not be equated with collective guilt or shame. On a more specific and practical level, acceptance of collective responsibility implies psychological willingness to share in the collective blame for the misdeeds of one's group – even if one did not personally took part in those misdeeds (May, 1992). In my view, acceptance of collective moral responsibility should and cannot only refer to those who committed, supported and tolerated atrocities but also to all members of a present political community. I believe that if all post-conflict community members don't respond to their past marked by gross human rights violations through acceptance of collective moral responsibility, then democratic and peaceful future could be at stake. Simply claiming that society members with its current political system truly want a better, peaceful, peace-oriented future with democratic values is not enough. I believe that mere claims won't create such a future without effective, systematic, reflective and finally moral dealing with the past.

Acknowledgment of Collective Responsibility

And yet, despite all these arguments as to why acceptance of collective responsibility for group crimes is an important feature of intergroup reconciliation, little work has yet attempted to address the question of socio-psychological processes that might underlie this process. So far, the only clues that we have are findings provided by a recent qualitative study which seem to suggest that direct engagement with members from the other group might create a psychological readiness to acknowledge ingroup responsibility for harm inflicted on others (Cehajic & Brown, 2008). More specifically, Cehajic and Brown (2008) have interviewed eighteen people from ten different places in BIH who declared themselves as Serbs. The study had two main goals: to explore and understand socio-emotional processes of how people deal with their group's atrocities, and to identify factors that might facilitate or hinder the process of acknowledging collective misdeeds.

Overall, our findings show that people in general are not ready or willing to come to terms with collective atrocities. Such an avoidance seems to be reinforced with various negative emotional states (e.g., anger, shame, guilt, and sadness) that can arise after realizing that the ingroup has harmed others or by the use of different justification means. Besides avoiding the past, people in general reported intergroup anxiety and cautiousness during contact encounter to be a defining feature of intergroup relations which in turn led not only to higher outgroup avoidance and potentially to lack of establishment of any common ground, but also to an exclusive ingroup orientation. People tended to talk mainly about their own group's loss and suffering (victimization and victimhood orientation).

It seems that a not uncommon reaction of members of a perpetrator group is to perceive that they, and not the victim group, have suffered the most (Nadler & Liviatan, 2004). In intergroup conflict situations – as in Bosnia and Herzegovina – members of conflicting groups tend to generate various beliefs which facilitate coping with the situation. Such beliefs are usually biased, because strong motivations – such as preservation of positive social identity – often underlie information processing in conflict situations (Bar-Tal, 2000). And indeed, one such societal belief is that of one's own victimization, the idea that 'we' have suffered more. Such claims about ingroup victimhood may be regarded as a psychological coping strategy and serve the purpose of minimizing the ingroup's role in the conflict whilst simultaneously undermining processes which might contribute to reconciliation.

Although avoiding the past seems to be associated with avoidance of negative emotions as well as with lack of intergroup contact, the findings suggest positive effects of approach-oriented tendencies towards the past in a form of communication and information seeking; intergroup contact; and perspective-taking ability. The results of this study suggest that members from the perpetrator group who do have some contact with members from the victim group might express higher willingness to acknowledge ingroup crimes. Recent quantitative (Pettigrew & Tropp, 2006) and narrative (Brown & Hewstone, 2005) reviews have provided support for the 'Contact Hypothesis' (Allport, 1954), re-affirming favourable intergroup contact as a key variable in improving intergroup attitudes.

The underlying assumption of the beneficial effects of contact on acknowledgment is that being exposed to victim stories, hence to the 'other perspective of the conflict', will increase empathic feelings and at the same time decrease both intergroup anxiety and the perception of ingroup victimhood.

Another study also conducted in the context of post-conflict intergroup relations of BIH found that good quality contact with members from the victim group predicted acknowledgment of collective responsibility through an increase in perspective-taking and a decrease in perceived victimhood. Ordinary Serbian adolescents who engaged in contact with Bosnian Muslims were more ready to acknowledge that their own group was responsible for atrocities committed during the 1992–1995 war (Cehajic & Brown, 2010).

More specifically, good quality (and frequent) contact with members from the victim group seemed to assist the process of acknowledgment through promoting an other-oriented social orientation (hence perspective-taking ability) and decreasing the biased belief (however functional it might be) that the ingroup has suffered more than the outgroup (perceived victimhood).

Qualitative engagement with members from the victim group implies a certain amount of time and trust invested in that relationship. These conditions, characterizing high quality contact situations, seem to be systematically correlated with one's own *beliefs* and *perspectives* on the past war events. By being exposed to victim stories, experiences and perspectives through having meaningful cross-group relationships with members of the victim group, one might become more willing to look at 'things' from the other side and be less inclined to interpret the situation exclusively from one's own point of view.

Self-affirmation Effects

As I have already stressed out in the introduction, people, when faced with the threatening information of their group moral violations, are more likely to defend themselves from the threat at hand through denial or justifications and less likely to acknowledge and personally accept collective responsibility. My colleagues and I (Cehajic et al., in press) have recently tested the effectiveness of self-affirmation for overcoming this defensiveness and thereby enabling group members to acknowledge their group's responsibility in two different contexts (Israel and BIH). The idea behind our self-affirmation hypothesis was that acknowledgment of group responsibility for commission of atrocities may present a threat to one's own feelings of self-worth and integrity and hence be less likely to occur (particularly for those who identify highly with their group). Therefore, we wanted to test the power of self-affirmation. As expected, affirming the importance of a personal value to the self increased Israeli participants' willingness to agree with statements about Palestenians' victimization and Israeli culpability for that victimization in particular. In another study conducted in the post-conflict context of BIH, we found that Serbian participants who affirmed themselves by writing about a personal success showed a greater willingness to acknowledge their group's responsibility for the genocide committed in Srebrenica in 1995 against Bosnian Muslims. Writing about a meaningful event that made them feel personally successful increased participants' acknowledgment of ingroup responsibility for those harmed by their group aggressive actions, which increased their feelings of group-based guilt for that harm, which in turn increased their support for various forms of compensatory reparations. Our studies add to the evidence that bolstering an individual's feelings of global self-integrity can reduce his or her inclination and need to respond defensively to threatening information. Self-affirmation seems to have a capacity to foster and facilitate processes that serve the goal of intergroup reconciliation after a history of conflict and victimization.

Conclusion

Even when there is seemingly nothing that one can do to prevent an evil in the world, one has a responsibility to distance oneself from that evil, at the very least by not condoning it. Being morally or politically responsible is something that takes a lot of work; it is not merely a matter of confronting to a list of minimal rules. Moral responsibility is a heavy burden on all of us, one from which the members of a highly self-indulgent age would flee. This tendency towards thoughtlessness and comfort seems to get worse when people are in groups or organizations such as in the context of intergroup conflict.

I began this chapter with a brief discussion of how we should deal with the burden of atrocities such as the Holocaust during WWII and the Srebrenica genocide during the recent war in Bosnia which has left succeeding generations to shoulder. Although many social scientists (e.g., Hanna Arendt) are not highly enthusiastic about the notion of 'collective' responsibility, research by my colleagues and I indicates that, at least at a psychological level, such a concept can indeed have prosocial consequences. In this way, then, I believe that the burden that we all are left with should be re-construed as something conveying the moral responsibility of succeeding generations to avoid repeating the tragedies of their group's history even though political climates are not always and necessarily receptive to such demands. Consequently, political compromise shapes the extent to which both justice and reconciliation can and will be achieved. Nevertheless, I believe that all society members should take on some responsibility (if not for the past horrors) then for the moral, social, and political renewal.

> "This taking upon ourselves the consequences for things we are entirely innocent of, is the price we pay for the fact that we live our lives not by ourselves but … (within) a human community." Hanna Arendt, "Collective Responsibility" (quote taken from May, 1992).

References

Allport, G. W. (1954). *The nature of prejudice*. Cambridge, MA: Perseus Publishing.

Arendt, H. (1987). Collective responsibility. In J. Bernauer (Ed.), *Amor mundi: Explorations in the faith and thought of Hannah Arendt* (pp. 43–50). Dodrecht: Martinus Nijhoff.

Barkan, E. (2000). *The guilt of nations: Restitutions and negotiations historical injustices*. New York: W. W. Norton.

Bar-Tal, D. (2000). *Shared beliefs in a society: Social psychological analysis*. Thousand Oaks, CA: Sage.

Branscombe, N. R., & Doosje, B. (2004). *Collective guilt: International perspectives*. New York: Cambridge University Press.

Brown, R., Gonzalez, R., Zagefka, H., Manzi, J., & Cehajic, S. (2008). Nuestra culpa: Collective guilt as a predictor for reparation for historical wrong-doing. *Journal of Personality and Social Psychology, 94*, 75–90.

Brown, R., & Hewstone, M. (2005). An integrative theory of intergroup contact. In M. P. Zanna (Ed.), *Advances in experimental social psychology* (pp. 255–343). London: Elsevier Academic Press.

Cehajic, S., & Brown, R. (2008). Not in my name: A social psychological study of antecedents and consequences of acknowledgment of ingroup atrocities. *Genocide Studies and Prevention (a special issue on the Aftermath of Genocide), 3*, 195–212.

Cehajic, S., & Brown, R. (2010). Silencing the past: Contact effect on acknowledgment of ingroup responsibility. *Social Psychological and Personality Science, 1*(2), 190–196.

Cehajic-Clancy, S., Effron, D., Halperin, E., Liberman, V., & Ross, L. D. (2011). Affirmation, acknowledgment of ingroup responsibility, group-based guilt, and support for reparative measures. *Journal of Personality and Social Psychology, 101(2)*, 256–270.

Cohen, S. (2001). *States of denial: Knowing about atrocities and suffering*. Cambridge, UK: Polity Press.
Dimitrijevic, N. (2006). Moral responsibility for collective crime. *Belgrade Circle Journal (special issue Community of Memory), 1–4*, 25–44.
Gilbert, M. (2001). Collective remorse. In A. Jokic (Ed.), *War crimes and collective wrongdoings* (pp. 216–235). Oxford: Blackwell.
Ignatieff, M. (1994). *Blood and belonging: Journeys into the new nationalism*. London: Vintage.
Lederach, J. P. (1997). *Building peace: Sustainable reconciliation in divided societies*. Washington, DC: United States Institute of Peace Press.
Lewis, H. D. (1948). Collective responsibility. *Philosophy, 24*, 3–18.
May, L. (1992). *Sharing responsibility*. Chicago: The University of Chicago Press.
Minow, M. (1998). *Between vengeance and forgiveness: Facing history after genocide and mass violence*. Boston: Beacon.
Nadler, A., & Liviatan, I. (2004). Intergroup reconciliation process in Israel: Theoretical analysis and empirical findings. In N. R. Branscombe & B. Doosje (Eds.), *Collective guilt: International perspectives* (pp. 216–235). Cambridge, UK: University Press.
Pettigrew, T. F., & Tropp, L. R. (2006). A meta-analytic test of intergroup contact theory. *Journal of Personality and Social Psychology, 90*, 751–783.
Radzik, L. (2001). Collective responsibility and duties to respond. *Social Theory and Practice, 27*, 455–471.
Staub, E. (2006). Reconciliation after genocide, mass killing, or intractable conflict: Understanding the roots of violence, psychological recovery, and steps toward a general theory. *Political Psychology*, *27*, 867–894.
Tutu, D. (1999). *No future without forgiveness*. London: Rider.
Wachtel, A., & Bennett, C. (2009). The dissolution of Yugoslavia. In C. Ingrao & T. A. Emmert (Eds.), *Confronting the Yugoslav controversies* (pp. 13–47). Lafayette, IN: Purdue University Press.

Index

O. Simić et al. (eds.), *Peace Psychology in the Balkans: Dealing with a Violent Past while Building Peace*, Peace Psychology Book Series, DOI 10.1007/978-1-4614-1948-8,

MIX
Papier aus verantwortungsvollen Quellen
Paper from responsible sources
FSC® C105338

FSC
www.fsc.org

If you have any concerns about our products,
you can contact us on
ProductSafety@springernature.com

In case Publisher is established outside the EU,
the EU authorized representative is:
Springer Nature Customer Service Center GmbH
Europaplatz 3, 69115 Heidelberg, Germany

Printed by Libri Plureos GmbH
in Hamburg, Germany